LITERATURE AND MEDICINE
The Nineteenth Century

EDITED BY
CLARK LAWLOR
University of Northumbria
ANDREW MANGHAM
University of Reading

CAMBRIDGE
UNIVERSITY PRESS

University Printing House, Cambridge CB2 8BS, United Kingdom

One Liberty Plaza, 20th Floor, New York, NY 10006, USA

477 Williamstown Road, Port Melbourne, VIC 3207, Australia

314–321, 3rd Floor, Plot 3, Splendor Forum, Jasola District Centre, New Delhi – 110025, India

79 Anson Road, #06–04/06, Singapore 079906

Cambridge University Press is part of the University of Cambridge.

It furthers the University's mission by disseminating knowledge in the pursuit of education, learning, and research at the highest international levels of excellence.

www.cambridge.org
Information on this title: www.cambridge.org/9781108420747
DOI: 10.1017/9781108355148

© Cambridge University Press 2021

This publication is in copyright. Subject to statutory exception and to the provisions of relevant collective licensing agreements, no reproduction of any part may take place without the written permission of Cambridge University Press.

First published 2021

A catalogue record for this publication is available from the British Library.

ISBN 978-1-108-42074-7 Hardback

Cambridge University Press has no responsibility for the persistence or accuracy of URLs for external or third-party internet websites referred to in this publication and does not guarantee that any content on such websites is, or will remain, accurate or appropriate.

Contents

List of Contributors *page* vii
Acknowledgements xii

Introduction: Literature and Medicine in the Nineteenth Century 1
Andrew Mangham

PART I EPISTEMOLOGIES

1 Writing Realism in Nineteenth-Century British Literature and Medicine 19
 Meegan Kennedy

2 'Dissecting Piece by Piece': Experimentalism in Late-Victorian Fiction 38
 Anne Stiles

3 Exhibiting Bodies: Museums, Collecting, and Knowledge in Nineteenth-Century Literature 56
 Verity Burke

4 Anatomical Culture, Body-Snatching, and Nineteenth-Century Gothic 74
 Laurence Talairach

PART II PROFESSIONALISATION

5 Physic and Metaphysics: Poetry and the Unsteady Ascent of Professional Medicine 97
 Daniel Brown

6	Heroics, Devotion, and Erotics: Class, Sexuality, and the Victorian Nurse *Arlene Young*	119
7	Pharmacology, Controversy, and the Everyday in *Fin-de-Siècle* Medicine and Fiction *Keir Waddington and Martin Willis*	135

PART III RESPONSES

8	Disorders of the Age: Nervous Climates *Sally Shuttleworth and Melissa Dickson*	157
9	Medicine, Sanitary Reform, and Literature of Urban Poverty *Andrew Mangham*	174
10	Flexible Bodies, Astral Minds: Gendered Mind–Body Practices and Colonial Medicine *Narin Hassan*	193
11	The Other 'Other Victorians': Normative Sexualities in Victorian Literature *Pamela K. Gilbert*	211
12	Physical 'Wholeness' and 'Incompleteness' in Victorian Prosthesis Narratives *Ryan Sweet*	230

Index   247

Contributors

DANIEL BROWN is a professor of English at the University of Southampton, UK. His research is focused on the relations between literature, science, and philosophy in the long nineteenth century. Publications include *Hopkins' Idealism* (Oxford University Press, 1997) and *The Poetry of Victorian Scientists: Style, Science and Nonsense* (Cambridge University Press, 2013). He is currently completing a monograph on poetry and the place of women in Victorian science.

VERITY BURKE is Postdoctoral Research Associate on 'Beyond Dodos and Dinosaurs: Displaying Extinction and Recovery in Museums', an interdisciplinary project based at the University of Stavanger, Norway. Her work on this project examines narratives of near-extinction prevented by human intervention, and their presentation in UK natural history museums. Her wider research interests include the history of medicine, nineteenth-century jurisprudence, taxidermy, and all things museum.

MELISSA DICKSON is a lecturer in Victorian Literature at the University of Birmingham. She has a PhD from King's College, London, and an MPhil, BA, and University Medal from the University of Queensland, Australia. She is the author of *Cultural Encounters with the Arabian Nights in Nineteenth-Century Britain* (Edinburgh University Press, 2019) and co-author of *Anxious Times: Medicine and Modernity in the Nineteenth Century* (Pittsburgh University Press, 2019).

PAMELA K. GILBERT is Albert Brick Professor of English at the University of Florida. She has published widely in the areas of Victorian literature, cultural studies, and the history of medicine. Her most recent book is *Victorian Skin: Surface, Self, History* (Cornell University Press 2019). Her other books are *Disease, Desire and the Body in Victorian Women's Popular Novels* (Cambridge University Press, 1997), *Mapping the*

Victorian Social Body (State University of New York Press, 2004), *The Citizen's Body* (Ohio State University Press, 2007), and *Cholera and Nation* (State University of New York Press, 2008). She edited *Imagined Londons* (State University of New York Press, 2002), a teaching and scholarly edition of Rhoda Broughton's novel *Cometh up as a Flower* (Broadview Press, 2010), and the *Companion to Sensation Fiction* (Blackwell, 2011). She co-edited *Beyond Sensation: Mary Elizabeth Braddon in Context* (State University of New York Press, 1999) and was a co-associate editor of the *Blackwell Encyclopedia of Victorian Literature* (2015).

NARIN HASSAN is Associate Professor in the School of Literature, Media, and Communication at Georgia Tech. Her research and teaching interests include Victorian literature and culture, postcolonial and gender studies, women writers, and the history of medicine. Her book *Diagnosing Empire: Women, Medical Knowledge, and Colonial Mobility* (Ashgate, 2011) focuses upon Victorian women travellers and their engagement with colonial medicine. Her current research examines the yoga, health, and shifting conceptions of the mind, body, and spirituality in relation to British colonialism. She has published essays in *Nineteenth-Century Contexts, WSQ, Nineteenth-Century Gender Studies, Mosaic,* and a number of book collections.

MEEGAN KENNEDY is Associate Professor of English/History and Philosophy of Science at Florida State University. Her research interests include Victorian literature and culture, the British novel, Victorian science and medicine, periodical studies, and the history of technology. Her book *Revising the Clinic: Vision and Representation in Victorian Medicine and the Novel* (Ohio State University Press, 2010) examines nineteenth-century strategies for observing and recording the body. She is currently working on an NEH-funded project about Victorians' fearful romance with the microscope.

ANDREW MANGHAM is Professor of Victorian Literature and Medical Humanities at the University of Reading. He is a director of the Centre for Health Humanities at Reading. His research concentrates on the intersections between medicine and literature in the nineteenth century. He is the author of *Violent Women and Sensation Fiction* (Palgrave, 2007), *Dickens's Forensic Realism* (Ohio State University Press, 2016), and *The Science of Starving* (Oxford University Press, 2020). He has also edited *The Female Body in Medicine and Literature*

(Liverpool University Press, 2011), *The Male Body in Medicine and Literature* (Liverpool University Press, 2018), and *The Cambridge Companion to Sensation Fiction* (Cambridge University Press, 2013).

SALLY SHUTTLEWORTH is Professor of English Literature at the University of Oxford. Her research has been largely in the field of Victorian Studies, with a particular emphasis on the inter-relations between literature, science, and medicine. Her books in this area include *The Mind of the Child: Child Development in Literature, Science and Medicine, 1840–1900* (Oxford University Press, 2010), *Charlotte Brontë and Victorian Psychology* (Cambridge University Press, 1996), and *George Eliot and Nineteenth-Century Science* (Cambridge University Press, 1984). Most recently she has published *Anxious Times: Medicine and Modernity in Nineteenth-Century Britain* (Pittsburgh University Press, 2019), co-authored with Amelia Bonea, Melissa Dickson, and Jennifer Wallis. The book is based on work from the European Research Council project 'Diseases of Modern Life: Nineteenth-Century Perspectives', which she ran (www.diseasesofmodernlife.org). She was also Principal Investigator for the AHRC project, 'Constructing Scientific Communities: Citizen Science in the 19th and 21st Centuries' (www.conscicom.org).

ANNE STILES is Associate Professor of English and Coordinator of Medical Humanities at Saint Louis University. Her research explores intersections between literature, science, and religion. She is the author of *Popular Fiction and Brain Science in the Late Nineteenth Century* (Cambridge University Press, 2012) and editor of *Neurology and Literature, 1866–1920* (Palgrave, 2007). She also co-edited two volumes published by Elsevier in 2013 as part of their *Progress in Brain Research* series. Her latest work focuses on literary responses to Christian Science and New Thought on both sides of the Atlantic.

RYAN SWEET is Lecturer in English and Humanities Foundation Stage Lead at the University of Plymouth. His research is focused on disability, prostheses, and nonhuman animals in Victorian literature and culture. His first book, *Prosthetic Body Parts in Nineteenth-Century Literature and Culture*, is under contract with Palgrave Macmillan and will be appearing (thanks to Wellcome Trust funding) in open-access format.

LAURENCE TALAIRACH is Professor of English Literature at the University of Toulouse Jean Jaurès and Associate Researcher at the Alexandre Koyré Center for the History of Science and Technology. Her research interests cover medicine, life sciences, and English literature in the long nineteenth century. Her most recent book is *Gothic Remains: Corpses, Terror and Anatomical Culture, 1764–1897* (University of Wales Press, 2019). She is also the author of *Fairy Tales, Natural History and Victorian Culture* (Palgrave, 2014), *Wilkie Collins, Medicine and the Gothic* (University of Wales Press, 2009), and *Moulding the Female Body in Victorian Fairy Tales and Sensation Fiction* (Ashgate, 2007).

KEIR WADDINGTON is Professor of History at Cardiff University and a specialist in the social history of medicine. His research interests focus on nineteenth-century Britain, the environment, and the ScienceHumanities. He has published books and articles on: pollution, drought, rural public health, diseased meat, medicine and charity, nursing, and Bedlam. He is the author of *An Introduction to the Social History of Medicine: Europe since 1500* (Palgrave, 2011), *The Bovine Scourge: Meat, Tuberculosis and Public Health, 1850–1914* (Boydell, 2006), *Medical Education at St. Bartholomew's Hospital, 1123–1995* (Boydell, 2003), and *Charity and the London Hospitals, 1850–1898* (Boydell & Brewer, 2000).

MARTIN WILLIS is Head of the School of English and Professor of English Literature at Cardiff University. His research focuses on literature, science, and medicine, from 1800 to the present, and on the historic and contemporary relationship of the humanities to the sciences. His most recent publications are *Staging Science* (Palgrave, 2016), *Literature and Science* (Palgrave, 2015), and *Vision, Science and Literature, 1870–1920: Ocular Horizons* (Pickering & Chatto, 2011). His present research is focused on conditions of sleep in the nineteenth century and the relations between historical and contemporary sleep studies. He is a former chair of the British Society for Literature and Science, the present editor of the *Journal of Literature and Science*, and one of the co-directors of the ScienceHumanities Initiative, based at Cardiff University.

ARLENE YOUNG is Professor Emeritus in the Department of English, Theatre, Film, and Media at the University of Manitoba. Her most recent book is *From Spinster to Career Woman: Middle-Class Women and Work in Victorian England* (McGill–Queen's University Press, 2019). Her previous publications include *Culture, Class and Gender in the*

Victorian Novel: Gentlemen, Gents and Working Women (Macmillan/St. Martin's, 1999), and Broadview Press editions of George Gissing's *The Odd Women* and Tom Gallon's *The Girl Behind the Keys*. She has published articles on nineteenth-century literature and culture in numerous journals, including *Victorian Studies*, *Victorian Periodicals Review*, and the *Journal of Victorian Culture*.

Acknowledgements

This volume is part of a two-volume project comprising *Literature and Medicine: The Eighteenth Century* and *Literature and Medicine: The Nineteenth Century*. The editors would like to thank the team at Cambridge University Press for helping bring this ambitious project to fruition. To Linda Bree we send thanks for suggesting the project a number of years ago; her original recommendations helped us shape and organize a body of work whose remit, at first glance, appeared daunting. We are grateful to Bethany Thomas for proficiently guiding this project following Linda's retirement and for making wise suggestions when the editors were in need of advice. Thanks must also go to Tim Mason, Natasha Burton, Neena S. Maheen, and Cara Chamberlain at the Press. We are also grateful to James Green for assisting us in the final stages of the project and for casting his expert eye over both manuscripts. The Leverhulme Trust, as ever, has been wonderfully supportive of literary-medical studies: in this instance via the *Writing Doctors: Representation and Medical Personality ca. 1660-1832* Major Project that funded, in part, Clark's research time and the indexes for both volumes, which have become a marvellous aspect of the project. We would like to thank our contributors for their forbearance and inspiring ideas; we learned a great deal from their contributions and were humbled by their ability to meet deadlines.

Clark would like to thank Andrew Mangham for being such a fantastic person to work with: aside from his excellent critical acumen and editing skills, Andrew's bonhomie has made working on these volumes great fun. Clark would also like to express his deep gratitude to Allan Ingram for his long-standing support in all ways, Ashleigh Blackwood for reading this work with fresh eyes and sharp critical insight, and his lovely colleagues at Northumbria, who have always been willing to lend an ear (or hand!). As usual, Clark's family has sacrificed a great deal at the altar of academe, so he owes them much thanks and love.

Andrew would like to thank Clark Lawlor for being a brilliant co-editor. Clark's hard work and good humour have made the project an absolute pleasure to work on. Andrew would also like to thank his wonderful colleagues in the Centre for Health Humanities at the University of Reading. His students and colleagues in the Department of English Literature have continued to be a mine of support and inspiration. Last but not least, he would like to thank his family and friends for what appears to be a superhuman capacity for patience.

Introduction
Literature and Medicine in the Nineteenth Century
Andrew Mangham

The nineteenth century saw a vital reassessment of the relationship between medicine and storytelling. By 1800 healing and narrative had shared a long and complicated history; according to Stephen Rachman, 'the interdisciplinary merging of literature *and* medicine derives [...] from a cultural recognition that literature has always resided *in* medicine'. The latter, he adds, 'concerns itself with biological events, to be sure, but those events, once named, enter into language and, as such, are framed by culture and mediated by literature'.[1] Arthur W. Frank's *The Wounded Storyteller* (1995) argues that the tendency to think of health, pathology, and treatment through stories is essentially 'premodern', and that more contemporary approaches to medicine have lost the original 'feel for stories' which once allowed a 'heuristic framework' for listening to the sick.[2] This is a loss we experienced, he clarifies, around the early modern period, which is also when we first developed a pharmacopoeia of medical terms for the experiences of being unwell. The growing field of 'narrative medicine' – a field to which both Rachman's and Frank's studies belong – assumes that, with the sovereignties of technology, systems of classification, and scientific approaches to health, medicine lost the art of telling and listening to vital narratives. Rita Charon's *Narrative Medicine: Honoring the Stories of Illness* (2006) observes that today

---

[1] Stephen Rachman, 'Literature in Medicine', in *Narrative Based Medicine: Dialogue and Discourse in Clinical Practice*, ed. Trisha Greenhalgh and Brian Hurwitz (London: BMJ Books, 1998), 123–7 (124, 123). Italics in original. See also Greenhalgh and Hurwitz's contribution 'Why Study Narrative', to the same volume, 3–16.

[2] Arthur W. Frank, *The Wounded Storyteller: Body, Illness, and Ethics* (Chicago: Chicago University Press, 1995), 24. An inverted view is developed by Armand Marie Leroi in his book *Mutants: On Genetic Variety and the Human Body* (2003; London: Penguin, 2005). 'The fragments of myth, folklore and tradition that remain to us from a pre-scientific age are like the marks left in sand by retreating waves: void of power and meaning, yet still possessed of some order' (109).

patients lament that their doctors don't listen to them or that they seem indifferent to their suffering. [...] Instead of being accompanied through the uncertainties and indignities of illness by a trusted guide who knows them, patients find that they are referred from one specialist and one procedure to another, perhaps receiving technically adequate care but being abandoned with the consequences and the dread of illness.

A scientifically competent medicine alone cannot help a patient grapple with the loss of health and find meaning in illness and dying. Along with their growing expertise, doctors need the expertise to listen to their patients, to understand as best they can the ordeals of illness, to honor the meanings of their patients' narratives of illness, and to be moved by what they behold so that they can act on their patients' behalf.[3]

Narrative medicine, Charon adds, 'can help answer many of the urgent charges against medical practice and training – its impersonality, its fragmentation, its coldness, its self-disinterestedness, its lack of social conscience'.[4] In suggesting that the science and practice of modern medicine fail to cohabit the same space as the narrative of patient experience, Charon neglects to see how medicine has always been laden with stories, even at its most scientific and technological. Kathryn Montgomery Hunter is closer to the mark when she states, in *Doctors' Stories: The Narrative Structure of Medical Knowledge* (1991), that 'medicine is fundamentally narrative [...] and its daily practice is filled with stories. [...] Medicine already has something in common with literature and literary study through its figurative language and its narrative organization of the facts of illness.'[5] Like Charon's ahistorical readings of Henry James, however, Hunter's comparisons of medical diagnosis with detective plots suggest that the recognition of any intersection between literature and medicine is essentially modern and that the loaded question of how one discipline relates to the other never troubled the doctors and literary authors of a more distant past. Charon argues that 'the reading practices of the New Critics of the 1950s and the analytic thinking of the structuralists of the 1960s becomes useful again' in the field.[6] New Criticism allows us to consider the nature (form) and development (prognosis) of illness; it privileges the practice of close reading and specialist interpretation. What such an approach fails to achieve, however, is any recognition of how the

---

[3] Rita Charon, *Narrative Medicine: Honoring the Stories of Illness* (Oxford and New York: Oxford University Press, 2006), 3.
[4] Ibid., 10.
[5] Kathryn Montgomery Hunter, *Doctors' Stories: The Narrative Structure of Medical Knowledge* (Princeton: Princeton University Press, 1991), 5, 21.
[6] Charon, *Narrative Medicine*, 109.

intricate threads between narrative and health were meticulously unpicked, examined carefully, and rewoven into a range of new forms – literary, medical, and experimental – long before the heyday of the New Critics. In fact, we are not the first generation to recognise the power of plot and close analysis, nor are we the first to worry whether the advances of science will overshadow the aspects of empathy, care, and healing that are foregrounded, in large part, in an understanding of patients' stories. Part of what this volume seeks to illustrate is that, throughout a period in which the ideals of objective science came to pre-eminence in medicine, stories were not replaced but instead made even more vital to the methodological and philosophical discussions that underpin the development of modern practice. It is not enough simply to study narrative and its formal workings: we must also consider medico-literary stories in relation to the richness of their original contexts.

While it is the aim of each of the chapters in this volume to discuss forms of literature alongside, through, and against various medical contexts, this introduction will lay some groundwork by focusing on the foundations of a necessary and critical reassessment of the way language and narrative behaved within shifting clinical settings. At the beginning of the nineteenth century, Thomas Young, the indefatigable polymath and author of a number of important works on medicine, stressed the importance of reading: 'In no department of human knowledge', he urged, 'is the work of literary discrimination more necessary than in physic.'[7] For Young, 'literary discrimination' meant the consultation of textbooks and treatises in search for histories of pathology and patient testimonies which could act as guides in future prognoses and treatments. Meegan Kennedy has demonstrated the literary nature of such case histories and has suggested that they exerted considerable influence throughout the nineteenth century. This was a period in which, according to new values and praxis in the fields of hospital and scientific medicine, experts' eyes were assumed to be able to read 'at a glance the visible lesions of the organism and the coherence of pathological forms'.[8] The century thus saw, in the words of Kennedy, the valorisation of

---

[7] Thomas Young, *An Introduction to Medical Literature* (London: Underwood and Blacks, 1813), 3.
[8] Michel Foucault, *Naissance de la Clinique* (1963), trans. as *The Birth of the Clinic: An Archaeology of Medical Perception* by A. M. Sheridan (London and New York: Routledge, 2003), 2. See Meegan Kennedy, *Revising the Clinic: Vision and Representation in Victorian Medical Narrative and the Novel* (Columbus: Ohio State University Press, 2010), 6–7.

accuracy and precision to the extent that the human observer should resist not only bias but judgement or any kind of mediation, so that natural phenomena might be (nearly) mechanically recorded through the incessant, selfless labor and attention to detail of the scientist. It specifically excludes any form of imagination, intuition, or insight – modes associated with literary writing instead.[9]

Significantly, these modes of 'accuracy and precision' were linked to patient stories. Descriptions of the development and progression of illness often turned to 'narrative strategies' and 'affective narrative' in order to offer empiricist value.[10] In the first volume of this collection, Michelle Faubert's 'Physician-Authors, Predisciplinarity, and Predatory Writing: John Polidori' (Vol. 1, Chapter 8) discusses the ethical questions surrounding the use of patient case studies as the basis for creative writing. As is shown in both Kennedy's and Anne Stiles's contributions to this second volume, it was no coincidence that the period's interest in medical meticulousness was synonymous with the development of a self-reflexive form of realism in the literary world. The wish to be truthful and accurate in fictional style indicates a parallel view that 'narrative strategies' did not automatically jeopardise the perceived objectivity of any given study. New specialist medical journals such as *The Lancet* and the *British Medical Journal* set about providing, as is noted in Thomas Wakley's preface to the first issue of the former, 'a correct description of all the important Cases that may occur'.[11] Far from disappearing from modern medicine, stories continued to be regarded as uniquely important, even in the new age of the clinic.

It is also the case that the long-standing, premodern relationship between narrative and physic got caught up in the sweeping change and intense intellectual scrutiny that characterised medicine's 'scientification'. It is a fact established in all the essays in this volume, and a fact worth recapitulating, that the nineteenth century was a time of rapid evolution in the history of medicine. In addition to advances in medical research and clinical methods, the period witnessed the introduction and definition of several of the field's subdivisions, including anaesthesiology, antisepsis,

---

[9] Kennedy, *Revising*, 4. Although in slightly varying contexts, similar points about the rise of objectivity are made by Lorraine Daston and Peter Galison, George Levine, and Amanda Anderson. See Lorraine Daston and Peter Galison, *Objectivity* (2007; New York: Zone, 2010); George Levine, *Dying to Know: Scientific Epistemology and Narrative in Victorian England* (Chicago and London: Chicago University Press, 2002); Amanda Anderson, *The Powers of Distance: Cosmopolitanism and the Cultivation of Detachment* (Princeton: Princeton University Press, 2001).
[10] Kennedy, *Revising*, 32.   [11] [Thomas Wakley], 'Preface', *The Lancet*, 5 October 1823, 1–2 (1).

gynaecology, psychology, dentistry, neurology, pharmacology, and professional nursing. This was the era which saw the invention of the stethoscope, the opthalmoscope, the laryngoscope, the syringe, and the x-ray. Both blood transfusions and surgeries under anaesthesia were performed for the first time. French microbiologist Louis Pasteur identified germs as the cause of infection, and British surgeon Joseph Lister pioneered the use of antisepsis in surgery. Vaccines were developed for cholera, rabies, tetanus, diphtheria, typhoid, and the bubonic plague. Elizabeth Garrett became Britain's first female recipient of a medical degree. And the German chemist Felix Hoffmann undertook vital research into pain relief, developing aspirin and acetylated morphine just in time for the painful traumas of the early twentieth century. In this brave new world of astonishing change and advancement – in a discipline still reliant, to a large extent, on patient testimony and case history – there occurred, sometimes through accident but more often through design, a crucial reassessment of the intersection between medicine and storytelling. In-depth examinations of the ways health and its treatment were articulated and understood through the tales people told formed part of the age's review of how science, progress, and wellbeing were connected.

A major threshold in the century's exploration of these connections came about through the career and reputation of the Scottish surgeon John Hunter, a man who famously boasted that he read few case notes and preferred instead to read the 'book of nature' through the art of dissection. As one early biographer commented in 1835:

> Nature is [...] made to be her own expositor, and the treasures she has poured forth come fresh to the mind from the fountains of knowledge, unimpaired by passing through the imperfect medium of language, and unimpeachably proclaiming the genius of him by whose labours they were brought to light.[12]

Even though Hunter would actually feature many case histories in his own writings, such accounts of his methodology reveal the assumptions that underpinned his apparent preference for empiricist observation and induction. In a famous letter to his disciple Edward Jenner, some years before the latter's groundbreaking work on smallpox, Hunter chided the young man for asking his opinion on the topic of body heat:

---

[12] Drewry Ottley, *The Life of John Hunter, F. R. S.*, *The Works of John Hunter, F. R. S.*, vol. 1, ed. James F. Palmer, 4 vols. (London: Longman, 1835), 1–198 (186).

> Why do you ask me a question by the way of solving it? I think your solution is just; but why think? Why not try the experiment? Repeat all the experiments upon a hedgehog as soon as you receive this, and they will give you the solution. Try the heat: cut off a leg at the same place; cut off the head, and expose the heart, and let me know the result of the whole.[13]

It is worth reminding ourselves of this exchange because, in enquiring 'Why do you ask me?', Hunter could offer no more concrete example of the change that he himself came to symbolise in the philosophy of medical knowledge. Since the days of Hippocrates, it had been one of the gospels of the healing art that experience and bedside practice were the best means of learning medicine and of furthering the field's knowledge. Thomas Sydenham, the seventeenth-century physician often styled the 'English Hippocrates', once told a young student, 'Anatomy – Botany – Nonsense! Sir, I know an old woman in Covent Garden who understands botany better, and as for anatomy, my butcher can dissect a joint full and well; now, young man, all that is stuff; you must go to the bedside, it is there alone that you can learn disease.'[14] This prioritisation of bedside labour, which came to be known, incidentally, as the 'Sydenham method', was as distrustful as Hunter was of pure book learning. In both philosophies there was a wariness concerning language and text. Once committed to the imperfect abstractions of the written word, the book of nature was vulnerable to misinterpretation and mistranslation. Yet there is one significant difference between Sydenham's method and Hunter's: whereas the former saw experience as the counterweight to book learning, the latter's inductive approach preferred speculation and experiment as *itself* a form of reading. According to Sydenham, any person (such as his butcher) can be a specialist. However, for Hunter, 'the inductive method laid down by the great father of modern philosophy [Francis Bacon]' was 'the only sure though arduous road to knowledge'.[15] The physiological approach required strict rules of scientific induction, and this required a certain level of expertise.

Hunter inspired what A. J. Youngston called the Scientific Revolution in nineteenth-century medicine, an event which appeared to have, on the surface at least, less to do with experience and narrative accounts of actual patients, and more to do with laboratory tests and detailed

---

[13] John Hunter, letter to Edward Jenner, 2 August 1775, quoted in Ottley, *Life*, 56.
[14] Quoted in Roy Porter, *The Greatest Benefit to Mankind: A Medical History of Humanity from Antiquity to the Present* (1997; London: Fontana, 1999), 229.
[15] Ottley, *Life*, 31.

anatomizations.[16] Xavier Bichat, the French anatomist and pathologist whose labours George Eliot famously described as having 'acted necessarily on medical questions as the turning of a gas-light would act on a dim, oil-lit street, showing new connections and hitherto hidden facts of structure',[17] was, indeed, a leading light in this new scientific culture. His *General Anatomy Applied to Physiology and Medicine* (1800), was based on over 600 human dissections in which careful inductions were motivated by a sense that 'the vital forces and the excitants which set them in play, since they are incessantly changing in the stomach, kidneys, liver, lungs, heart, etc., result in perpetual instability'.[18] One can expect no regularities or patterns in medicine because to do so would be 'to build on shifting sand an edifice solid itself but which soon falls for lack of an assured base'.[19] There was need, then, for a meticulous approach to biological phenomena, an approach that was not weighed down by 'some principle *à priori*', or 'the facts related by others', but was given flight, instead, 'by the evidence of [one's] own senses'.[20] At no point did he say that patient testimonies are not to be trusted; instead, like Hunter, Bichat followed a system of empiricist scepticism that was growing within medicine and which transformed and explored, rather than jettisoned, traditional storytelling practices.

Much more theoretical in his approach to the same subject was Bichat's compatriot, physiologist Claude Bernard, a man whose 1865 *Introduction to the Study of Experimental Medicine* exerted a powerful influence on both medicine and literature of the late nineteenth century.[21] Bernard dismissed followers of the Sydenham method as mere 'systemizers', and he viewed their naïve belief in the wisdom of case studies as a kind of 'scientific superstition'. He added: 'we must trust our observations or our theories only after experimental verification'.[22] Similarly to Hunter and Bichat, he argued:

---

[16] A. J. Youngston, *The Scientific Revolution in Victorian Medicine* (London: Croom Helm, 1979). On Magendie see J. M. D. Olmsted, *Francois Magendie: Pioneer in Experimental Physiology and Scientific Medicine in Nineteenth-Century France* (New York: Schuman's, 1944).
[17] George Eliot, *Middlemarch*, ed. Rosemary Ashton (1871; London: Penguin, 2003), 148.
[18] Xavier Bichat, *Recherches Physiologiques sur la Vie et la Mort* (1800), quoted in J. M. D. Olmsted, *François Magendie*, 27.
[19] Ibid.   [20] Ottley, *Life*, 31–2.
[21] See Lawrence Rothfield, *Vital Signs: Medical Realism in Nineteenth-Century Fiction* (Princeton: Princeton University Press, 1992), 14; Andrew Mangham, 'Medical Research', in *The Routledge Research Companion to Nineteenth-Century British Literature and Science*, ed. John Holmes and Sharon Ruston (London: Routledge, 2017), 372–85.
[22] Claude Bernard, *Introduction à L'étude de la Médecine Expérimentale*, trans. by Henry Copley Greene as *An Introduction to the Study of Experimental Medicine* (New York: Dover, 1957), 37.

> We must observe without any preconceived idea; the observer's mind must be passive, that is, must hold its peace; it listens to nature and writes at nature's dictation. [...] In a word, the man of science wishing to find truth must keep his mind free and calm, and if it be possible, never have his eye bedewed, as Bacon says, by human passions.[23]

As with Hunter and Bichat, there is some distrust of human variables here, and this has significant implications for the perceived link between medicine ('truthful') and narrative ('invented'). Bernard's deductive method did, however, develop a more complex understanding of the role for intellection than Hunter's induction; whereas the latter saw experiment as a reason *not* to think, Bernard saw it as the starting point of a much longer theoretical process which he represented in teleological terms. In the quotation I provided above, he sees research as the idea of listening to nature's story; he continues:

> Our experimenter puts questions to nature; [...] as soon as she speaks, he must hold his peace; he must note her answer, hear her out and in every case accept her decision. [...] An experimenter must not hold to his [favourite] idea, except as a means of inviting an answer from nature. But he must submit his idea to nature and be ready to abandon, to alter or to supplant it, in accordance with what he learns from observing the phenomena which he has induced.[24]

Contrary to the divisions he established between the Sydenham method and experimentation, this section of Bernard's text appears to see no conflict between the artificial parameters of the laboratory and the kinds of observations that take place in non-experimental environments like the hospital ward. His descriptions of the research process importantly belie the idea of a plain fact – a 'truth', that is, which says everything it needs to say in the moment. Instead, the experimental process is made up of stories, spoken by nature, and noted down by the scientist. What this suggests, then, is that, in the new climate of scientific medicine, stories were not being taken leave of but were rather being reintegrated or reorganised in self-reflexive discussions of the modern tools and methodologies of medicine.

In his 1841 treatise *The Means of Preserving Health and Prolonging Life*, the British surgeon Anthony Carlisle, once a student of John Hunter's, quoted Sydenham as having said that 'that which is called medicine is, indeed, rather the art of prating and telling stories'.[25] Charles Lamb once

---

[23] Ibid., 22, 39.   [24] Ibid., 22–3.
[25] Anthony Carlisle, *The Means of Preserving Health and Prolonging Life* (London: John Churchill, 1841), xlvi.

described Carlisle himself as 'the best story teller I ever heard', while, to Robert William Elliston, he 'mends a lame narrative almost as well as he sets a fracture'.[26] Carlisle's success with stories occurred within the new scientific climate of mid-century. Like Bichat, he appreciated the fact that nothing stands still in the pursuit of medical knowledge. On the significance of knowing the chemistry of the blood, for instance, he writes:

> Before the constituent materials of the blood were known, it was impossible even to conjecture the nature of diseases arising from unnatural deviations in the composition of the blood. A remarkable instance of which occurs in chlorosis, producing a pallid whiteness of the countenance, accompanied by debility and irregular action of the heart, now ascertained to arise from a deficiency of the red particles of the blood, whose colour depends on iron, and for this apparently complicated malady any preparation of iron is a specific remedy.[27]

We have two stories here: one that concerns the experience of chlorosis (how do its symptoms begin, develop, and terminate? What is the process of treatment? The answer to both these questions seems to require narrative) and one that concerns the story of medicine itself, from its benighted days before the constituent elements of the blood were known to the 'present' day, in which it is possible to explain the cause of chlorosis as a deficiency in iron. The second of these stories reminds us that medicine is a textbook whose facts are almost always provisional – individual chapters, in other words, in a story whose later events are unwritten. Carlisle shares something of Bichat's scepticism, but his recommendation is not that we undertake meticulous dissections of hundreds of cadavers (he called this kind of research 'a pedantic display of diseased anatomy'[28]), but rather that we understand the most human of sciences, even at its most empiricist, as made up of developing tales. Symptoms and their treatments are narratives, to be sure, but so too is the growth of medicine through its wide range of discoveries and theories that must always sit on the intersection between one historical moment and another and must inevitably, therefore, constitute part of a much longer saga. In this impermanent world of change and incomplete knowledge, science becomes narrative. Technology, systems of classification, and clinical approaches do not silence the 'feel for stories' but constitute part of a process through which medicine operates *as* stories.

---

[26] Quoted in Don Shelton, 'Anthony Carlisle and Mary Shelley: Finding Form in a Frankenstein Fog' (2015), 3, accessed June 2019, www.researchgate.net/publication/277324488.
[27] Ibid., xxxv.   [28] Carlisle, *Preserving Health*, xxx.

* * *

Lawrence Rothfield's important study *Vital Signs: Medical Realism in Nineteenth-Century Fiction* (1992) argues that 'there would seem ample reason to examine medicine – [...] as involving the quasi-poetic elaboration of something like a style, point of view, or mode of representation that conveys truth-value – as a constitutive element of the realistic novel and its allied genres'.[29] This volume suggests that the constitutive influence works both ways. While it is clear that medicine had an impact on the aims and ambitions of nineteenth-century fiction – and we are interested in exploring such connections – contributors are also motivated by the concept of literature's teleological elaborations, points of view, and modes of representation, as providing a theoretical basis and framework for reading medical knowledge. Medicine and literature of the nineteenth century shared an interest in the way in which knowledge is constituted – how stories are developed and also what happens when 'narrative' and 'evidence' fail to get along. The age of the clinic pioneered a capacity for studying the links between patient testimonies, nature's narratives, and the vision of scientific medicine in ways that typified, and learned from, the literary.

This volume begins with four chapters whose discussions delve deeper into the connections between genre and medical knowledge. Meegan Kennedy, to begin with, explores how literary realism developed alongside, but was not identical to, medical realism in 'Writing Realism in Nineteenth-Century British Literature and Medicine' (Chapter 1). Charting how recent scholarly work has focused on the overlap between literary and medical realisms, Kennedy argues that it is useful to consider the key differences between the two methodologies as well. Ironically, the term that scholarship has often associated with realist fiction – *mimesis* – appeared in nineteenth-century medical contexts as a form of *false* representation. This divergence in meaning signals, for Kennedy, key formal and linguistic differences between literature and medicine – differences that are shown to be as important as the similarities, not least because physicians did not always deny their aesthetic sensibilities but drew parallels between their work and that of novelists. Medical and literary attempts to negotiate, overcome, or uphold the differences and similarities between their work was part of the crucial discussion of what it means to tell the

---

[29] Rothfield, *Vital Signs*, 14.

truth: the Victorians understood that all realism was representation, and that representation could only ever approximate the real.

Next, '"Dissecting Piece by Piece": Experimentalism in Late-Victorian Fiction' by Anne Stiles (Chapter 2) describes how Victorian novelists responded to the development of medical experimentalism. During the 1870s, for example, British neurologist David Ferrier performed a series of revolutionary cerebral localisation experiments, linking specific parts of the brain with distinct movements, emotions, and behaviours. In the following decade, German microbiologist Robert Koch discovered the bacteria responsible for tuberculosis and cholera, placing the emergent germ theory of disease on a firmer scientific footing. Stiles shows how literature became a means of responding to advances in such medical research in both the form and content of its narratives. The naturalistic mode, she demonstrates, was modelled on the experimental techniques of physiologists like Bernard. Works we now think of as genre fiction, however, including Gothic novels and scientific romances, also responded to experimental physiology by gravitating towards forms that tested imaginary hypotheses against a series of controls.

In 'Exhibiting Bodies: Museums, Collecting, and Knowledge in Nineteenth-Century Literature' (Chapter 3), Verity Burke draws our attention to the under-studied emergence of display and exhibition cultures in nineteenth-century medicine. She illustrates how conflicts between direct observation of material specimens and what can be learned from textual representation became the foundation of a century-long discussion of the tensions between the value of the body as material specimen and the representation of the same in textual and narrative form. Museum catalogues and visitor letters provide crucial insight into the conflicts that emerged between what is displayed and what is described. This is a vital context for understanding the representation of the body in fiction. Offering a new reading of Wilkie Collins's detective novel *The Law and the Lady* (1875), Burke's chapter outlines how, in the impressions left by material specimens on nineteenth-century literary culture, we find a rich exploration of what constitutes materialist and specialist knowledge of the human body.

The final essay in this 'Epistemologies' section (Part I) is Laurence Talairach's 'Anatomical Culture, Body Snatching, and Nineteenth-Century Gothic' (Chapter 4). Expanding on Kennedy's and Stiles's illustrations of how medical realism provides a means of examining and testing the reaches and limits of literary realism, Talairach discovers in medicine the inspiration for Gothic fiction. Studies of literature and medicine in the nineteenth century have followed Rothfield's understanding that 'medicine enjoys by far the closest and most long-standing association with the issue of mimesis and knowledge so crucial to critical conceptions of realism'.[30] Yet, as Burke's focus on sensation fiction and Talairach's focus on the Gothic demonstrate, the stories and developments of medicine inspired a wide range of genres – not least because literature took influence from medicine's sensational failures and controversies as well as its successes in developing a sort of epistemological precision. In Talairach's essay, we turn to the outrage caused by the body-snatching scandals of early- to mid-century. The Apothecaries Act (1815) introduced formal qualifications for the practice of medicine.[31] This led to an increase in the number of dead bodies needed in anatomical demonstrations and dissections. It is exactly around this time, Talairach illustrates, that literature provided a unique insight into the debates around medical practice and education. By looking at examples from John Galt, Mary Shelley, Samuel Warren, Wilkie Collins, and Robert Louis Stevenson, she illustrates both how literary texts drew on the Gothic paraphernalia inherent to attempted regulation of the practice of anatomy and how the Gothic enabled literature to record and examine cultural responses to medical practice, good and bad.

The next three essays (Part II) are concerned with how differing literary modes responded to the professionalisation of medicine – to the emergence of the trained medical professional and to his or her role in inspiring a new dialogue between our two disciplines. In 'Physic and Metaphysics: Poetry and the Unsteady Ascent of Professional Medicine' (Chapter 5), Daniel Brown examines the roles that poetry played in observing, commenting upon, and supplementing the uneven progress of nineteenth-century professionalisation. Lyric poetry offered consolation to such medical students and practitioners as John Keats, and tensions between the scientific interests of medicine and the need for spiritual or intellectual enrichment are also traced in Alfred, Lord Tennyson's 'In the Children's Hospital' (1880). As the century progresses, however, the scientific

---

[30] Ibid., 12. The alternative view explored by Janis McLarren Caldwell is that, 'although we have come to regard "clinical" and "Romantic" as oppositional terms, clinical medicine emerged from the same culture that nourished Romantic literature. [...] Romantic medicine was remarkable [...] for its efforts to balance the patient's story and the body's evidence, and this balancing act was a breakthrough for medical diagnostics'. *Literature and Medicine in Nineteenth-Century Britain: From Mary Shelley to George Eliot* (Cambridge: Cambridge University Press, 2004), 1, 8.
[31] Roy Porter, *The Greatest Benefit to Mankind: A Medical History of Humanity from Antiquity to the Present* (New York: Norton, 1997), 316–17.

respectability and professionalism that medicine acquires becomes more of an inspiration for poetry like Oscar Wilde's and that of the pioneer of malaria treatment Ronald Ross. In Brown's survey of the relationship between medicine and poetry, we see a gradual breaking down of the division between verse's lyricism and science's hard scepticism; in its place there emerges a shared interest in human health and viability.

Next, in 'Heroics, Devotion, and Erotics: Class, Sexuality, and the Victorian Nurse' (Chapter 6), Arlene Young discusses the rise of professional nursing. Coupled with reforms in nursing education were advances in medical and sanitary science, which demanded more professionalised nursing practices and procedures. Notwithstanding, there was considerable resistance to the introduction of better-off women into any workforce, and especially into a form of employment that required women to have intimate contact with the bodies and the bodily fluids of patients, half of whom were men. What Young discovers in textual responses to, and representations of, new nursing practices is a curious and very Victorian fixation on sexuality. In journalism and works like 'The Story of a Nurse', published in *The Graphic* and in a later collection entitled *Tales of the Children's Ward* (1894), Young discovers investigations of a tension between the sexualised 'gamp' figure and the new Nightingalean professional, as well as the signs of a new beginning for the reputation for the professional nurse.

The last professional field we look at in this section is that of pharmacology. Keir Waddington and Martin Willis's chapter 'Pharmacology, Controversy, and the Everyday in *Fin-de-Siècle* Medicine and Fiction' (Chapter 7) focuses on one broad category of Victorian medicine: the manufacture of pharmacological products and the advance of physic. By addressing a more commonplace set of controversies and a greater naturalism in literary representation, they point the way to a different association between sensationalism (or the lack of the same) and routine medical practice. Focusing on L. T. Meade's *Stories from the Diary of a Doctor* (1893–1895) and Arthur Conan Doyle's *Round the Red Lamp* (1894), Waddington and Willis explore how the study of genre at the *fin de siècle* allowed the exploration of the relationship between medical theories and advances, on the one hand, and the daily demands of common practice, on the other. Their chapter concludes Part II with an important reminder of the need to balance the controversial with the everyday in order to gauge a truer nature of the intersections between literature and medicine.

Part III, the final section of the volume, is concerned with literary responses to specific and important developments in nineteenth-century medicine. Firstly, 'Disorders of the Age: Nervous Climates' (Chapter 8), by Sally Shuttleworth and Melissa Dickson, draws on a wide range of literary and medical texts to analyse the interwoven strands of mental, social, and economic health in the last decades of the century. The arresting opening scene of *Daniel Deronda* (1876), set in a fictional German spa town, is used to bring into focus many late-Victorian concerns with the diseases of modernity. Gwendolen Harleth becomes a key figure, according to Shuttleworth and Dickson, in late-Victorian representations of the over-stimulated, nervous, and disoriented experience of the age's pressures. *Daniel Deronda* and George Gissing's *The Whirlpool* (1897) trace close, mutually confirming, interactions and connections between literary and medical discourses. What emerges is a more complex understanding of constructions of neurosis in the decades before Freud. Theories and treatments of the diseases of modern life and hereditary degeneration are not only, in their words, 'deeply embedded in social and cultural operations; [but] the category of modernity itself [is] actively constructed and deployed within medical and literary discourse'.

We then turn to my chapter, 'Medicine, Sanitary Reform, and Literature of Urban Poverty' (Chapter 9). Focusing on the figure of William Gaskell, husband of the famous author, dissenting minister, reformist, and poet, I discuss how the literature of 'social problems' interacted with the emerging field of sanitary science. The city of Manchester and the working-class family periodical are examples of ferments where ideas on what constitutes knowledge of questions relating to poverty and poor sanitation are channelled through an intricate relationship shared by medicine, reportage, and fiction. I read the poems of William Gaskell alongside the sanitary work of Thomas Southwood Smith. Both men contributed to the radical *Howitt's Magazine* and both sought to reframe the social project in such a way that an analysis of the very means of knowing underpinned the representation of urban health problems. This was an epistemological strategy, and insight, that came about through the intersections of medicine and literature – through their shared spaces, vocabularies, and means of representation.

From sanitary medicine we move on to colonial medicine in Narin Hassan's 'Flexible Bodies, Astral Minds: Gendered Mind–Body Practices and Colonial Medicine' (Chapter 10), where the influence of health practices imported from the nineteenth-century colonies is brought into focus alongside key literary texts. Continuing a discussion begun in Volume 1 with Hisao Ishizuka's essay in Chapter 5 on the rise of biliousness in the long eighteenth century, Hassan explores the ways in which the late-Victorian period saw a burgeoning interest in Eastern philosophies and traditions – an interest that reflected new ideals in Western health and wellbeing. Through the non-fictional writings of Genevieve Stebbins and Annie Besant, in particular, yogic and meditation techniques are observed as having provided a powerful 'antidote to the evolving theories of Western allopathic medicine, which focused largely upon a divide between minds and body and categorised female bodies and minds as weaker and susceptible to disorder'. In the Eastern-inspired writings of Victorian women we find a new language in which female health and spirituality are allowed to transcend the categories of pathology created for them by male-dominated medicine.

In 'The Other "Other Victorians": Normative Sexualities in Victorian Literature' (Chapter 11), Pamela K. Gilbert reassesses the links between literature and the developing fields of sexology and sexuo-psychopathy. Like Waddington and Willis, who show an interest in the reaches and limits of 'everyday' medicine, Gilbert turns to the now-neglected question of the normative – and therefore largely invisible – sexualities that existed outside of the direct purview of heterosexual experience. It is demonstrated how the specific constraints of audiences and forms of literature have done much to militate against our awareness of sexualities that are neither specifically endorsed nor proscribed by the pervasive courtship plot of the novel. Gilbert examines the function of instances of extra- and pre-marital, same-sex, 'unusual' or multiple-partner 'sexuality' in fiction from William Harrison Ainsworth's Newgate novel *Jack Sheppard* (1840) to Anthony Trollope's 'Mrs General Talboys' (1863). In doing so, she illustrates a growing awareness of 'other' sexualities in nineteenth-century medicine, as well as a determination in literature of varying forms to represent and explore modes of non-normative experience.

In the final essay (Chapter 12), 'Physical "Wholeness" and "Incompleteness" in Victorian Prosthesis Narratives', Ryan Sweet picks up a topic explored in Volume 1 by D. Christopher Gabbard (Chapter 9), by showing how the nineteenth century saw significant advances in both the development of prosthetic technologies and the wider, specialist interest in forms of disability. He shows how a 'trade' in artificial limbs took off due to the fact that, following the implementation of Listerian principles of antisepsis, more patients were surviving surgical amputation. Advances in prosthesis design and manufacture responded by providing safer, more practical, and more 'aesthetically pleasing' options. In the period's popular literature Sweet discovers evidence of how there emerged a social privileging of physical wholeness – a 'wholeness' that encouraged the effacing of physical loss from public view. The concept of the 'normal' body had long been championed by government-sponsored statistics and the New Poor Law, and so it appeared more important than ever for individuals to conceal bodily losses and avoid the stigma attached to physical difference or 'incompleteness'. Sweet's chapter explores these contexts in literature, such as the short stories 'Lady Letitia's Lilliput Hand' (1862) by Robert Williams Buchanan and 'Prince Rupert's Emerald Ring' (1895) by T. Lockhart. Such works, it is argued, provide insight to the dominance of bodily integrity. In fiction we see the demand for wholeness simultaneously endorsed and failed in its maintenance of the conceptual biases and imbalances that define its dominance.

This volume suggests, then, that medical developments had a significant impact on the shape and texture of the period's literature, from novels and poems, to short stories and journalism. On the other hand, we see the art of telling stories underpinning wider philosophical and pragmatic debates running through the medical field. In the words of Trisha Greenhalgh and Brian Hurwitz, 'we fall ill, get better, get worse, stay the same and finally die by narrative'.[32] But we also grow healthier, in our development of the medical field, by narrative, too: the history of medicine is a history of story, just as literature is tied to the changes and developments in the enterprises relating to health and sickness. The task in hand, then, is not simply the rescuing, or appreciation, of patient stories through the appropriation of literary techniques, but the understanding of the way the tools and benefits of medicine have emerged through, and continue to be characterised by, a complex appropriation and analysis of literary modes.

---

[32] Greenhalgh and Hurwitz, 'Why Study Narrative?', 5.

PART I

Epistemologies

CHAPTER I

Writing Realism in Nineteenth-Century British Literature and Medicine

Meegan Kennedy

Clinical Medical Realism and Literary Realism

What does it mean to write realism? Nineteenth-century medical and literary authors helped develop the genre as we know it, but they rarely used the term themselves and did not entirely agree on the method. Nineteenth-century medical realism embraces distinctive contradictions: authors relentlessly link routine to life-and-death matters; their version of 'plain speech' is obscure to the lay reader; and their path to plain speech is often, paradoxically, mediated through instruments. Further, the historical trajectories of literary and medical realism diverge, and literary and medical authors work in relation to different plots and truths.

Scholars have focused on what literature and medicine share, something of a rejoinder to C. P. Snow's influential 'two cultures' narrative of the twentieth century.[1] Peter Logan, responding to G. S. Rousseau's 1981 plaint about the scarcity of work on literature and medicine, notes that the linguistic and cultural turns in literary criticism offered productive methodologies for cross-disciplinary work.[2] Logan elsewhere argues that the 'nervous narratives' of eighteenth- and early nineteenth-century medicine both enable and undercut narrative authority in the British novel.[3] Lawrence Rothfield argues that nineteenth-century medicine offered the novel an especially productive set of discourses, and he demonstrates how clinical realism, pathology, physiology, experimental medicine, and the like provided models of representation.[4] Likewise, Janis McLaren Caldwell explores the effects of 'Romantic materialism', demonstrating

---

[1] C. P. Snow, *The Two Cultures and a Second Look* (Cambridge: Cambridge University Press, 1969).
[2] Peter Logan, 'Literature and Medicine: 25 Years Later', *Literature Compass* 5:5 (1980), 964–80.
[3] Peter Logan, *Nerves and Narratives: A Cultural History of Hysteria in Nineteenth-Century British Prose* (Berkeley: University of California Press, 1997).
[4] Lawrence Rothfield, *Vital Signs:* Medical Realism in Nineteenth-Century Fiction (Princeton: Princeton University Press, 1992).

how literary authors used both empirical methods and 'transcendental' ones, and showing the centrality of sympathy and openness in both literature and medicine.[5] While most scholars have emphasized the effect of medicine on literature, some also trace the effect of literature on medicine.[6] Athena Vrettos argues that both medical and literary cultures contributed to the 'fictions' that Victorians constructed to understand illness.[7] I survey the 'commons' of medical and literary writing from eighteenth-century curious cases, through nineteenth-century clinical cases, to Freud's psychoanalytic cases.[8] Recent work also examines the interplay between empirical medicine and romantic genres.[9]

Clinical medical realism developed alongside but is distinct from nineteenth-century literary realism. It shares the core commitments of literary realism, especially the general ideal of recording specific, everyday content using a clear, direct style. However, significant differences between these genres developed through the decades. Clinical realist authors, writing for a professional medical audience, established distinct writing strategies to meet ideological and practical requirements. Both clinical and literary writers worked within (and sometimes against) an evolving realist code of writing committed to specificity of context; ordinary setting, character, and events; 'plain speech'; skepticism and detachment; attention to detail, which supports verisimilitude and empiricism; and psychological depth of character. Clinical medical writing became a distinct genre as medical authors came to agree on those aspects of the realist code that best supported the newly professionalizing field.

Specific Historical Context

Both literary and medical realists demonstrate a strong commitment to a specific historical context for their narrative. Nineteenth-century medical practitioners who adopted clinical realism (mostly physicians and surgeons)

---

[5] Janis McLarren Caldwell, *Literature and Medicine in Nineteenth-Century Britain: From Mary Shelley to George Eliot* (Cambridge: Cambridge University Press, 2004).

[6] Athena Vrettos, *Somatic Fictions: Imagining Illness in Victorian Culture* (Stanford: Stanford University Press, 1995); Caldwell, *Literature and Medicine*; and Meegan Kennedy, *Revising the Clinic: Vision and Representation in Victorian Medicine and the Novel* (Columbus: Ohio State University Press, 2010), for example.

[7] Vrettos, *Somatic Fictions*.   [8] Kennedy, *Revising*.

[9] Tabitha Sparks, *The Doctor in the Victorian Novel: Family Practices* (London and New York: Routledge, 2016); Laurence Talairach-Vielmas, *Wilkie Collins, Medicine and the Gothic* (Cardiff: University of Wales Press, 2009); Louise Penner, *Victorian Medicine and Social Reform: Florence Nightingale among the Novelists* (New York: Palgrave Macmillan, 2010).

kept records of their own practice: the case records of their patients and sometimes other observations and experiments (post mortems, laboratory work). These histories were set in a specific time and place – especially early in the century, when climatic medical theories encouraged doctors to note the wind and weather during disease onset and progress. Individual case records, if kept in narrative form, were usually written as an aid to memory and for a private audience (a larger audience for hospital patients). John Hughes Bennett, for example, told medical students, 'I cannot too strongly impress upon you the importance of noting these down in a book at the time, rather than trusting to the memory. [...] [T]he reports of cases, dictated aloud by the professor, and written down at the bed-side by the clerk, [...] constitutes the only trustworthy method of drawing up cases with accuracy.'[10] Case histories were published in print journals or medical textbooks with the aim of sharing medical knowledge about a particular disorder or training the medical community, forming part of the canon of knowledge in the field.[11] Some physicians published articles in lay periodicals, expanding general knowledge about medicine and its practices. Others built on lectures and parliamentary proceedings to argue for public health practices; these authors connect individual health to a specific historical context. The uncertainty about disease etiology and transmission – for example, debates between miasmatic and contagionist practitioners – meant that practitioners asked about many quotidian details of patients' lives to garner much potentially relevant information. Bennett trained students to ask patients about their 'age; constitution; hereditary disposition; trade or profession; place of residence; mode of living as regards food; epidemics and endemics; contagion and infection; exposure to heat, cold, or moisture; irregularities in diet; commencement of the disease; rigors'.[12] Other case-taking outlines were even more specific.

Ordinary Character, Setting, Events

Eighteenth- and nineteenth-century English literary realism has a long history representing the 'middle way': the striving middle classes (including the edges of the working and upper classes) rather than the aristocrats of romance or those working people struggling in sordid or grim

---

[10] John Hughes Bennett, *An Introduction to Clinical Medicine* (Edinburgh: Sutherland and Knox, 1853), 8.
[11] For histories of the case history, see Julia Epstein, *Altered Conditions: Disease, Medicine, and Storytelling* (New York: Routledge, 1995), and Kennedy, *Revising*.
[12] Bennett, *Introduction*, 5.

conditions as portrayed by social realists or, later, naturalists. We see this from early in the history of the novel, with *Robinson Crusoe* (1719) and *Pamela* (1740), and it remained a foundational element.

In contrast, the nineteenth-century British practitioners who were most likely to adopt realist techniques were those who had been hospital trained (especially abroad) and worked in an urban, clinical setting with working-class patients. These medical communities regularized record keeping and valued publication. High mortality rates kept middle- and upper-class patients out of these contexts for much of the century. Although practitioners treating private patients might subscribe to clinical norms – we see in *Middlemarch* (1871) a provincial British surgeon treating respectable householders, straining to maintain metropolitan, continental clinical standards – the archive for mid-century medical realism generally concerns the bodies and lives of the poor and desperate.

Both literary and medical realist texts proclaimed their dedication to chronicling quotidian events rather than extraordinary ones. In practice, however, both recorded a range of events from trifling to grand. Few novels present a strictly romantic or realist approach, instead demonstrating some hybridity in plot, character, or style. In medicine, even with the turn to comprehensive, routine tracking of patient records, a tradition of collecting extraordinary ('curious' or 'singular') cases persists from eighteenth-century practice. In a period before clinical realism, the autopsy, and experimental medicine, practitioners ruminating upon a curious case probed the edges and the categories of the known world. During the turn to clinical realism, authors shied away from curious talk and extraordinary language, shifting instead toward the detached tone and data collection that enabled the 'numerical method' (statistics) and the advances of public health. Violent treatments like bleeding and purging fell out of favor, and even the drama of the operating theater could become more 'routine' with the introduction of ether and antisepsis. Influenced by hospital medicine, the practice of daily record keeping encouraged the accumulation of a mass of routine notes on each case (day-to-day sleep, diet, patient temperature, climate), interspersed with written descriptions of landmark events and interactions. While curious cases persisted, they were renamed 'interesting' and were integrated within a spectrum of what Georges Canguilhem terms the normal and the pathological.[13]

---

[13] Georges Canguilhem, *Le Normal et le Pathologique, Augmenté de Nouvelles Réflexions Concernant le Normal et le Pathologique*, trans. as *The Normal and the Pathological* by Carolyn R. Fawcett with Robert S. Cohen (1966; London: D. Reidel, 1978). See Kennedy, *Revising*, 50–3, 93–100.

Tell It Straight

While medical and literary realisms share a commitment to the portrayal of everyday people and subjects, medical and literary authors very differently interpret the realist preference for 'plain speech'. Literary writers from Wordsworth to Gaskell to Hardy crafted their art from the spoken vernacular of working people. Doctors, on the other hand, developed a written rhetoric characterized by a complex, specialized professional language. Their code of written conduct, while it reached its modern form toward the end of the nineteenth century, has its roots in the 'plain speech' recommended by the Royal Society from its origins in 1663. Because medical writing relies on specialized, Latinate terms, doctors' 'plain speech' is evident not in the immediate texture of their language but in its detached style and logical structure. For example, John Harley's 1871 survey of 'The Pathology of Scarlatina' summarizes 'Case 25' in formal narrative:

> Charlotte B—, aet. 5, was admitted on the second day of a severe attack of scarlatina. The rash was vivid on the fourth day, and there was glandular swelling of both sides of the neck. Pulse 120. [...] On the fourteenth day the bowels were very loose, and the abdomen distended; the angles of the mouth excoriated [...] the respirations being 64 and the pulse 130 to 140 on the twenty-seventh day [...]. Death was preceded by a fluttering pulse and great orthopnoea.

This records a sad event for the family – her four-year-old brother is 'Case 21' and had died some days earlier – but the physician was not surprised at the outcome, and the record maintains a detached and forthright tone: 'The heart contained the usual firm entangled clots'.[14]

Nineteenth-century realists value a transparent narrative. Literary and medical texts both desire transparency and suspect mediation, but they demonstrate this differently. While novelists like George Eliot and Anthony Trollope avoid a heavily mediated plot, they permit their narrators the occasional intrusive aside. Victorian medical case histories instead often have a single omniscient narrator, writing in first person, as a prime actor in the drama. The plot is not simply the patient's experience of illness but details the narrator's intervention in that illness. Later in the century and in public health reports, patient cases may form a collation of offerings from multiple narrators and are supplemented by additional reports, figures, tables, and graphs, providing alternate or parallel narratives.

---

[14] John Harley, 'The Pathology of Scarlatina, and the Relation between Enteric and Scarlet Fevers', *Medico-Chirurgical Transactions* 55 (1872), 103–38 (118–19).

Skepticism, Detachment (and Sympathy)

Many critics see a strong moral imperative underlying Victorian realism.[15] Both medicine and literature balance detachment and sympathy as moral values, but they resolve this tension differently. Novelists are more likely than doctors to emphasize sympathy as a final aim;[16] G. H. Lewes writes that realist art is distinguished by the artist's 'emotional sympathy' or 'sensibility' for those he portrays. Some critics focus on the importance of sympathy to the realist project, while others emphasize novelists' attempts to provide an objective record of human experience. Andrew Mangham, for example, reads Charles Dickens's work as realist in its debt to forensic medicine and skeptical detachment.[17] However, objectivity and sympathy are not necessarily opposed. George Eliot, famously, hoped that her novels' experiments in objective observation might prompt readers to feel greater sympathy for others.[18] And Rae Greiner claims that 'sympathy produces realism', although her definition of 'sympathy' is more like intellectual 'fellow-feeling' than sentimental emotion.[19]

The aspirant nineteenth-century practitioner was taught that detachment underwrote medical progress. This was evident in the regularization and quantification of case histories, in the advice on how to approach skittish patients, and in the advance of the numerical method (accumulating medical knowledge by collating cases statistically) and of new observational instruments. All these elements of clinical 'case-taking' threatened to alienate the practitioner from his patient. But physicians insisted that sympathy and insight could coexist with a mechanical observation. They tussled over the correct balance of 'art' versus 'science' in medical practice – the medical art requiring a more subjective or intuitive understanding of the patient. Bennett echoed common advice when he reminded his students, 'It should never be forgotten that you are examining a fellow-creature, who possesses the same sensitiveness to pain and the same feelings as you do, and that everything that can increase the one or wound

---

[15] Amanda Claybaugh, for example, sees a sense of purpose in the realist novel, derived from reformist literature. Amanda Claybaugh, *The Novel of Purpose: Literature and Social Reform in the Anglo-American World* (Ithaca: Cornell University Press, 2007).

[16] G. H. Lewes, "Realism in Art: Recent German Fiction," Westminster Review n.s. v. 14, no. 2 (Oct 1858), pp. 488–518.

[17] Andrew Mangham, *Dickens's Forensic Realism: Truth, Bodies, Evidence* (Columbus: Ohio State University Press, 2016).

[18] George Eliot, *Adam Bede*, ed. Carol A. Martin (1859; Oxford: Oxford University Press, 2008), 159–67.

[19] Rae Greiner, *Sympathetic Realism in Nineteenth-Century British Fiction* (Baltimore: Johns Hopkins University Press, 2012), 9.

the other should be most carefully avoided. Prudence, kindness, and delicacy, are especially enjoined upon those who treat the sick.'[20]

This is not to say that nineteenth-century doctors consistently held to clinical realist principles in their work and in their writing; they strategically turned to literary realist and romantic techniques. In some case histories, the narrative shows the traces of human connection and points to links with literature. In cases with romantic elements such as a suspenseful or tragic conclusion or an exotic patient or disease, medical authors are more likely to turn to literary techniques like figurative language, analogy, or a narrative persona. Narrative approach accounts for the realist effect of clinical case histories, which record spectacular, sensational, or tragic events (stroke, accident, hemorrhage, amputation, death) in dispassionate, distancing prose.

Verisimilitude and Empiricism: Attention to Detail in Description

Instead of 'mimesis', nineteenth-century writers often strove for verisimilitude: lifelike or realistic description of a meticulously realized visual textscape, achieved through scrupulous attention to the detail of human experience. Verisimilitude is not, of course, the same as realism. Thus Lewes's memorable critique of Charles Dickens – that the actions of his characters were like the twitches of vivisected frogs, that his visions had a hallucinatory vividness and universal power but no depth – was that Dickens's characters had verisimilitude but no realism: they were assemblages of brilliantly realized characteristics that became lifelike rather than alive.[21]

Some interpret verisimilitude not as 'lifelike' but as 'true to life' or 'taken from life'. Even this does not guarantee realism. Indeed, a fascination with verisimilitude characterizes certain types of nineteenth-century romance. Both Charles Reade and Wilkie Collins structured sensation novels around famous cases. Reade drew on his library of newspaper cuttings for 'real-life' detail. But George Orwell notes that 'most of [Reade's heroes]' are 'a kind of superman', that 'he had no sense whatever of character or of probability', and that his novels 'offer as complete a detachment from real life as a game of chess or a jigsaw puzzle'.[22] Appropriately, Reade's 1856 novel *It is Never Too Late to Mend* is subtitled *A Matter-of-Fact Romance*.

---

[20] Bennett, *Introduction*, 5.
[21] George Henry Lewes, 'Dickens in Relation to Criticism', *Fortnightly Review* 11 (1872), 141–54; see especially 144, 146, 148–9.
[22] George Orwell, 'Charles Reade', *New Statesman and Nation*, 14 August 1940, in The Collected Essays, Journalism and Letters of George Orwell, 4 vols. (London: Secker and Warburg, 1968), vol. 2, 34–7 (37).

While novelists may offer useless details as metonymic signifiers related to the plot (as Jakobson suggests) or as descriptive debris indicating historicity (as Roland Barthes suggests), medical authors curate a different practice regarding detail.[23] Over the century, physicians and surgeons move away from or reimagine the rhetorical strategy of lengthy passages of description, while literary authors continue to embrace this strategy. Medical practitioners still include detailed verbal descriptions of patients, but they begin to rely more heavily on quantifiable data and on figures (tables, charts, and images). By the twentieth century, medical cases have adopted the markedly detached, prescriptively structured format familiar to readers of the modern scientific report, which dampens narrative force and buries the shock of verisimilitude.[24]

The record-keeping practices of the clinic imposed new discipline upon case making. The empirical base of clinical medicine encouraged (eventually required) laborious record keeping. Clinical-realist practitioners diverged from old-fashioned peers and predecessors who worked from system and theory. The new clinical 'empiricists', trained in empirical methods, represented the next wave of medicine. They should not be confused with 'empirics' (quacks), named for their seat-of-the-pants experiential education, but both reacted against the book learning of the systematists. Catherine Gallagher argues that verisimilitude in a text signals its fictionality – that overt massing of detail functions to shore up the edges of imagined characters.[25] This massing of detail can also, however, testify to the text's participation in a long tradition of empiricist observation, as it does in the case history.

The association of 'medical realism' with observation of detail appears in one of the few nineteenth-century medical texts to use the term (these are mostly American).[26] An 1899 letter published in the *Boston Medical and Surgical Journal* suggests that 'medical realism' would improve fiction,

---

[23] Roman Jakobson, 'On Realism in Art' (1921), in *Language in Literature*, ed. Krystyna Pomorska and Stephen Rudy (Cambridge, MA: Belknap Press, 1987), 19–27; Roland Barthes, 'The Reality Effect' (1968), in *The Rustle of Language*, trans. Richard Howard (New York: Hill and Wang, 1986), 141–8.

[24] See Kennedy, *Revising*, 54–86. For the scientific report, see Alan G. Gross, Joseph E. Harmon, and Michael Reidy, *Communicating Science: The Scientific Article from the Seventeenth Century to the Present* (Oxford: Oxford University Press, 2002).

[25] Catherine Gallagher, *Nobody's Story: Women Writers in the Marketplace* (Berkeley: University of California Press, 1995), 172–4.

[26] Well-reviewed medical texts could readily achieve a transatlantic readership, as with journals collecting and republishing extracts from foreign and British medical sources. In the literary world, despite transatlantic readership, American realism established a distinct tradition.

but only in certain genres.[27] This author criticizes the 'French school' of realism characterized by 'studies in sexual psychopathy and moral imbecility' (Zola). He mocks the idea of a truly realist fiction, noting, 'We feel that we would be driven to the verge of tears if it were to be revealed to us that charming Mrs. Swanly's graceful, bird-like habit of alighting upon her chair was the outcome of hemorrhoids.'[28] Even as he mocks the French realists for a tasteless and extreme aesthetic, his satiric revisions themselves enact a deflationary realism, and he encourages 'medical realism' if judiciously applied. In the 'pediatric department of novel writing', he says, 'the medical realist is really capable of accomplishing much good'. For example, a novel depicting family life may demonstrate that 'the offspring of a luetic and goitrous union bids fair to be far from robust'.[29]

Another turn-of-the-century physician also associates 'realism' with empirical observation. In his 1900 'Oration to the Massachusetts Medical Society', Arthur Tracy Cabot conventionally opposes 'Realism' to 'Idealism'. He defines 'Realism' as an inductive method based on close observation: 'theories are not allowed to stand unless they can be shown to rest on demonstrable facts'.[30] He reminds his listeners that the human 'senses are [also] fallible and often deceived', so 'the scientific spirit is one of skepticism'.[31]

According to Cabot's argument, he promotes realist work; but his rhetoric celebrates both realism and romance. He champions the years of 'patient, plodding' laboratory work producing the 'Golden Age' of surgery: 'plodding' suggests realist modes of accumulation, but 'Golden Age' calls forth romantic visions.[32] He comments that surgical anesthesia comes of Morton's 'brave, albeit reckless' venture, another romantic trope.[33] He tells his audience that, in surgery, 'we are constantly urged forward by the encouragement, Be bold; Be bold, and but rarely are checked by the admonition, Be not too bold'.[34] Cabot argues for the relentless power of realist accumulation: the slow building, the 'stepping forward constantly from fact to fact', underlying the great triumphs.[35] Indeed, he says, 'the

---

[27] 'Cynicus', 'Medical Realism in Fiction', Boston Medical and Surgical Journal 140:8 (1899), 199.
[28] Ibid., 199.   [29] Ibid.
[30] Arthur Tracy Cabot, 'Oration to the Massachusetts Medical Society', *Boston Medical and Surgical Journal* 142:24 (1900), 615–618; and 142:25 (1900), 647–50 (615). Franklin Staples adopts Cabot's view that realist medicine means combining clinical and laboratory work. In future, he suggests, 'the practicing physician and surgeon [...] may well have his own laboratory furnishings and appliances. [...] This is the time of rapidly approaching complete realism in practical medicine and surgery' ('Something of the Past and Present in the Progress of Medicine', *Journal of Medicine and Science* 6 [Aug 1900], 296–300 [300]).
[31] Cabot, Oration, 615–616.   [32] Ibid, 617–618.   [33] Ibid., 618.   [34] Ibid., 617–618.
[35] Ibid., 617.

nineteenth century has shown us that this patient piling of fact upon fact builds up structures of an interest and beauty before which the wildest dream of the idealist pales'.[36]

Physicians' and surgeons' growing interest in realism sparked innovations designed to promote better clinical observations. As practitioners formalized the clinical case history, they debated the best format to ensure a full, clear, accurate, precise, and reliable record of information and to facilitate the comparison and collation of data in the new era of 'numerical medicine'. Bennett set out standards of measurement and reportage for case records:

> All mention of size should be, according to its exact measurement, in feet and inches. Extent should be determined by proximity to well-known fixed points. All vague statements, such as large, great, small, little, etc., should be carefully avoided; and in recording cases, dates and references should always be given in the day of the month, and not in the day of the week.[37]

Enterprising physicians from George Fordyce to Arthur Sansome marketed blank case report forms – tabular or even body-shaped – to guide practitioners' note taking.[38]

As physicians accepted the methods of the laboratory, they adopted the systems used to train researchers to use technology, test instruments, and maintain standards while working asynchronously across long distances. Microscope test objects, for example – like the closely spaced markings of diatoms – revealed the quality of a microscope and challenged the expertise of the observer. Such guides for human ability served as a bound on human error, underwriting the project of clinical realism.

British practitioners were slow to accept the technologies of perception becoming available from the 1830s – the stethoscope, ophthalmoscope, thermometer, microscope, x-ray, and other instruments extending the human senses – but these eventually remade diagnostics and case writing. Victorian medical observation increasingly occurred via what we might call mediated realism: a realism developing in and through observation with devices. The human senses mediate our access to the world as well, of course, and human perception is necessarily partial and distorted, as Victorians were well aware. Eliot thus notes the mediating factors of

---

[36] Ibid., 616.   [37] Bennett, *Introduction*, 7.
[38] George Fordyce, 'An Attempt to Improve the Evidence of Medicine', in *Transactions of a Society for the Improvement of Medical and Chirurgical Knowledge* (London: Johnson, 1793), 243–93. Arthur Ernest Sansom, *Lectures on the Physical Diagnosis of Diseases of the Heart* (London: J. & A. Churchill, 1876).

observation: 'a faithful account of men and things as they have mirrored themselves in my mind' and 'tell you, as precisely as I can, what that reflection is'. The realist account is both faithful and error-ridden, marred by a 'defective [...] disturbed [...] faint or confused' reflection; it is both precise and inadequate, restricted by the limits of human ability.[39]

Practitioners use observational devices to compensate for sensory error and limitation, and to pursue the ideals of detachment that Lorraine Daston and Peter Galison have termed mechanical objectivity. However, using these devices introduces additional reframing, distortion, or error, because information about the world is mediated through the instrument. Thus, mediated observations are committed to detail and accuracy but conducted always in tension with the realist imperative for transparency and directness of reportage. Finally, these medical technologies bring observations closer to or into the body while they distance the practitioner from the patient, prompting concerns about impersonal, mechanical care.

Realism and Psychologism: Mimesis

Victorians were increasingly interested in the human psyche and its role in everything from cognition to convalescence. The increasing formalization of the case history demonstrates practitioners' awareness of individual bias and error in observation and note taking. Medical students were reminded to consider how individual psychological status might affect patient progress and disease outcome. The surgeon and pathologist Sir James Paget told his students that a healthy man often bears amputation poorly, less well than one 'utterly enfeebled by old disease of a joint' because healthy men usually come in for amputation after sudden trauma, a limb perhaps crushed during the workday. 'Their mental distress is much greater', he explained, 'than that of those who are relieved from disease; they are subjected to a great and sudden change of habits.'[40]

The term that twentieth-century scholars, following Erich Auerbach, often associated with the world-mirroring quality of realist representation – 'mimesis' – was not often used by nineteenth-century writers to refer to a literary quality.[41] Although 'mimesis' now suggests a realist aesthetic, it

---

[39] Eliot, *Adam Bede*, 159.
[40] James Paget, 'The Various Risks of Operation', *Clinical Lectures and Essays*, reprinted from *The Lancet* 2 (1867) (London: Longmans, Green, 1875), 1–50 (3).
[41] 'Mimesis' traditionally can refer to imitation or representation. Nineteenth-century writers used the term rarely, to refer to the Platonic/Aristotelian debate about the imitation of nature or to the imitation of spoken language via misspelling ('punkin' for 'pumpkin'). Coleridge influentially

most often appears in the Victorian period to discuss misleading or even false representation.[42] 'Neuromimesis', or neuro-mimicry, which starts to appear in medical texts in the 1870s, refers to a functional (non-physiological) disorder of the spine or joints, early identified by Paget in lectures at St. Bartholomew's Hospital.[43]

Howard Marsh, a surgeon at St. Bartholomew's who edited Paget's collected essays, offers a description of neuromimesis in his 1886 textbook *Diseases of the Joints*. In Marsh's description, the body displays symptoms imitating a physiological disorder: a joint or limb is paralyzed or wrenched, combined with pain and feeble circulation (cold, dusky skin) in the affected area. However, once the patient is put under anesthesia, the joint or limb readily resumes a natural position, normal appearance, and easy movement. Neuromimesis 'imitates' a structural (physiological) joint disorder by producing pain, stiffness, and/or distortion of the joint but usually without the inflammation, muscle atrophy, fever, or bone disjunction expected with a physical disorder.[44] Paget warns that neuromimesis can affect any of the 'invisible structures' of the body.[45]

Athena Vrettos discusses Victorians' fear that neuromimesis and other forms of sympathetic identification could spread moral epidemics.[46] Victorians associated neuromimesis with hysteria and with mental fragility and disorder, and with a difficult, deceptive diagnostic challenge. Paget does use Gothic language at times, as when he describes a muscle lump as 'a phantom, a mere mimicry of a tumour'.[47] But, overall, Paget defines neuromimesis in realist terms, refusing to mystify or demonize the disorder or patients. He describes neuromimesis as 'an unwilling imitation of organic disease', protecting patients from being disparaged as hypochondriacs or malingerers.[48] He argues that symptoms are physically felt; that patients' sufferings are due to a failed will ('I cannot will'[49]) and involuntary response to stimulus, not a deliberate deception. Paget also

---

distinguishes between art (imitation) and deceptive copying (representation). M. H. Abrams distinguishes between an eighteenth-century 'mirroring' model and a Romantic-era 'illumination' model of art; his Romantics use terms like 'overflow' or 'expression'. The term 'mimesis' was rarely used during the nineteenth century. See M. H. Abrams, *The Mirror and the Lamp* (Oxford: Oxford University Press, 1953).

[42] Twentieth-century writers like Walter Benjamin or Theodor Adorno reclaimed the term, distinguished from its classical aesthetic usage. They discuss mimesis not as realist representation but as a form of imitation in human and animal behavior or linguistics – as a means of relating to the environment.

[43] 'Nervous Mimicry', *Clinical Lectures and Essays*, 172–251.

[44] Howard Marsh, *Diseases of the Joints* (Philadelphia: Lea Brothers, 1886), 278–82.

[45] Paget, 'Nervous Mimicry', 174.   [46] Vrettos, *Somatic Fictions*, 83–90.

[47] Paget, 'Nervous Mimicry', 236.   [48] Ibid., 173.   [49] Ibid., 181.

distinguishes neuromimesis from mental disease. He does romanticize the 'neuromimete' or 'nervous mimic' as imaginatively or emotionally sensitive: 'You may, indeed, find among [them] some common-place people, with dull, low-level minds; but, in the majority, there is something notable, good or bad, higher or lower, than the average – something outstanding or sunken.'[50] However, he does not attribute it to imagination, overstrained attention, or insanity, pointing instead to 'erroneous workings of sensitive and motor nerve centres'. In fact, he says, 'there are many who cannot bring about a mimicry of disease by any effort of imagination or direction of the mind. Among these I am happy to count myself. I have tried many times, carefully, and with good opportunities, but have always failed.'[51]

While Paget defined neuromimesis in realist terms, as entirely physiological, his book influenced the surgeon Herbert W. Page's award-winning work on railway trauma, which argued that nervous mimicry could be voluntary or result from an affective or nervous shock, such as fright.[52] Page's 1883 book reintroduces romantic actors like desire, affect, and imagination into theories of the body's mimesis. This brief medical usage of 'mimesis' demonstrates the persistent entanglement, in Victorian writing, of realist and romantic tropes of mirroring, sympathy, and the mysteries of the psyche.

Totalizing Aesthetic

The view of realism as a totalizing aesthetic is rooted in Lukács's reading of the novel. In the rapidly modernizing, positivist world of nineteenth-century British allopathic medicine, doctors indeed figured knowledge as mastery and aspired to comprehensive reporting, despite the many residues and overlays of older, sectarian approaches. However, clinical realists would not necessarily have agreed that they used prose instrumentally or for rationalist aims. Association lectures would typically offer nods to both the 'art' and 'science' of medicine, mourning a loss in personal connection between patient and physician, as doctors regularized a model of formalized, detached practice. As medical training and practice were standardized across patients, institutions, and regions, outcomes demonstrably improved.

---

[50] Ibid., 188, 191, 179.   [51] Ibid., 183, 184.
[52] Herbert W. Page, *Injuries of the Spine and Spinal Cord without Apparent Mechanical Lesion, and Nervous Shock, in their Surgical and Medico-Legal Aspects* (London: J. & A. Churchill, 1883). See also Eric Caplan, 'Trains and Trauma in the American Gilded Age', in *Traumatic Pasts: History, Psychiatry, and Trauma in the Modern Age, 1870–1930*, ed. Mark S. Micale and Paul Lerner (Cambridge: Cambridge University Press, 2001), 56–77.

Physicians gained medical knowledge; but they feared a loss of empathy, intuition, and wisdom. Caldwell argues that the Foucauldian model (critiquing the positivist clinical gaze as totalizing) misrepresents British medicine. She describes a patient-centered, responsive clinical medicine from the nineteenth century through today. I argue that clinical realism, faced with a developing tension between the art and science of medicine, negotiated a balance between a detached, mechanical observation and the sympathetic, subjective insight that enlists humanistic intuition.[53] Most importantly, while nineteenth-century physicians sought a full knowledge of the body and an exact language to record it, they frequently voiced their humility before the impossible task.

Final Differences

Finally, although medical and literary texts may differ on these shared realist strategies for addressing readers, foundational differences lead literary and medical realism to different disciplinary trajectories by the end of the century. First, literary and medical authors work in very different relation to plot. Plot structure is not a hard determinant of literary genre, given the complicated mix of elements that make up a Victorian novel and the pressure of market expectations on a newly professional class of authors. However, plot strongly shapes the conversation that a novel enacts about the individual's relation to the world and how much either can change.

Romances may present a 'loss and restoration' (U-shaped or circular) plot structure, reinforcing class norms by depicting the fall and subsequent re-establishment of a noble protagonist and the social order. In contrast, literary realist texts often present a 'striving' or 'growth' plot structure (roughly arrow-shaped, enabling personal change or class mobility, as in the bildungsroman). In this or in Darwinian plots, the social order is not always absolute but, like the individual, can be re-formed and revised.[54] Or realist texts may employ an inverted-U-shaped plot structure as if inflating, then popping a bubble of romantic excitement; we follow the rise and fall of a non-noble or even ignoble protagonist, such as Trollope's Melmotte in

---

[53] See Kennedy, *Revising*, 123–4, 152–63.
[54] Gillian Beer, *Darwin's Plots: Evolutionary Narrative in Darwin, George Eliot, and Nineteenth-Century Fiction*, 3rd ed. (Cambridge: Cambridge University Press, 2009), 17–19, 42–3, 148–68. George Levine, *Darwin and the Novelists: Patterns of Science in Victorian Fiction* (Chicago: University of Chicago Press, 1992), 16–20, 185; George Levine, *Darwin the Writer* (Oxford: Oxford UP, 2011), 3–4, 24–9, 88.

The Way We Live Now (1875). Realist texts may also use the episodic or iterative plot structure of the picaresque, a genre which satirizes the existing social structure, as in Thackeray's *Vanity Fair* (1848).

A realist novel may be ethically motivated or historically influenced, but it is defined as *fiction*. Its plots may be shaped by generic convention and the expectations of publication and distribution channels such as *Blackwood's Edinburgh Magazine* or Mudie's Circulating Library, but they are free to follow authorial imagination. Medical realism, on the other hand, is defined by the effort to not be fiction. Cases were, of course, carefully crafted and framed by the underlying scaffolding supporting (and limiting) medical knowledge or by context, especially when the outcome was unexpected or the audience important. Nineteenth-century case histories were shaped by the practitioner's expectations about the trajectory of the case, and by the conventions of realist and romantic novel plots and characters describing illness, decline, amnesia, apoplexy, and the like. After poststructuralism, no historical narrative can be understood unproblematically as a mere record of fact. But a case history – while it is far from unmediated – is defined by the effort to achieve a referentiality unsought by the novel. It seeks to report factual events and to constrain itself by those events as they occurred and were observed by the author. Its 'plot' follows the arc of the patient's disease progression: what interventions were attempted, the patient's recovery or death – these things cannot be altered, or it is no history. The historian can use all the skill of the author to frame his point or moderate a tragic outcome, but he is bound by the play of the case (whether routine or dramatic) and the limitations of his skill as an observer.

Further, literary and medical realism define truth differently. Michael McKeon discusses the development of the novel as a complication/expansion of the concept of truth to include the as-if-true of verisimilitude and eventually mimesis. Gallagher emphasizes instead how this space – the space of the plausible or credible – emerges from the lie; how it trains modern readers in ironic assent to what is otherwise a modern condition of disbelief or skepticism. In either case, the realist text carves out a tenuous space between truth and falsehood. In a world shaped by the detached hermeneutic of the new clinical realism and the destabilizing research on human sensory and mental error, both literary and medical texts work to earn the reader's trust. But while literary rendering strives for a credible portrayal of fictional or fictionalized events, medical reportage works to present a truthful portrayal of real ones, as far as that is possible.[55] As

---

[55] Eliot's term in *Adam Bede* – 'faithful account of men and things' – could refer to either genre.

above, it is useful to make this provisional distinction about factual accountability. Case histories, generically, aim to be referential and accountable to external events. Since cases served as a repository of medical knowledge, a case that is not accountable perpetuates a medical untruth that could be used to guide patient care. Realist claims in medical texts are powerful and dangerous, with life-and-death effects in the real world. Skeptical of the possibility of full knowledge or transparency, nineteenth-century medical authors committed to history nonetheless.

Similarly, novels tell fictional stories, even when the realist novel portrays emotional, aesthetic, or ethical truths, or is based on historical events. If case histories, in order to work as a genre, need to be accountable to actual events, one can argue that even historical novels cannot be. In a realist novel, verisimilitude functions to evoke the sense that the events in the novel take place in a plausible world with a coherent internal logic, although they do not, ultimately, claim historical facticity. In Trollope's Barsetshire novels, the quotidian details of village and family life and church politics build a structure within which characters – like his warden, Septimus Harding – grow into complex, sympathetic persons. Verisimilitude renders a novel convincing and helps create a bond of identification between text and reader.

However, the realist text seeks to evoke belief, not credulity. In 'The Lifted Veil' (1859), Eliot schools the reader in differing modes of response, as the story 'performs and invites the same dual movement that mid-Victorian scientists were developing, a two-step of speculation and skepticism'.[56] Over-emphasis on the minutiae of documentary proof, as in Haggard's imperial romance *She* (1886), risks drawing attention to the mediated nature of the text, breaking the illusion of transparency that underlies the reader's belief.

Realist authors use a deflationary approach in this negotiation of belief; the narrator's declaration of skepticism signals that the narrative is trustworthy. When Ella Hepworth Dixon's *Story of a Modern Woman* (1894) describes *Antony and Cleopatra* (through a child's eyes) as 'a stout lady in long amber draperies, who kept throwing her arms around a tired-looking man with a brown face and a suit of gilt armour', the novel signals its intent to describe the world shorn of its artifice.[57]

---

[56] Meegan Kennedy, '"A True Prophet"? Speculation in Victorian Sensory Physiology and George Eliot's "The Lifted Veil"', *Nineteenth-Century Literature* 71:3 (2016), 369–403 (370).
[57] Ella Hepworth Dixon, *Story of a Modern Woman*, ed. Steve Farmer (1894; Ontario: Broadview, 2004), 54.

Trollope likewise balances a nostalgic with a realist eye when he sets *Doctor Thorne* (1858) in a county characterized by 'deep and shady and – let us add – dirty lanes' (5).[58] And although Frank Gresham does prove true to Mary Thorne, this does not prevent Trollope from poking fun at Frank's wooing: 'Oh, oh! Mary; do you love me? Don't you love me? Won't you love me? Say you will. Oh, Mary, dearest Mary, will you? won't you? do you? don't you?' (83). This, the narrator acknowledges, 'does not sound like the poetic raptures of a highly inspired lover' but conveys 'warmth, and a reality [...] not in itself repulsive' (87). Trollope accepted the melodramatic plot of *Doctor Thorne* from his brother, Thomas,[59] but at almost every point he deflects its sensationalism and deflates its pathos with realist or satirical detail. However, in describing Sir Roger's and Sir Louis Scatcherd's deaths from alcoholism, Trollope shifts strategy, bearing down on the grotesque or sensational detail in service to his gritty aim, in an almost naturalistic manner. These details shock in contrast to the detached tone elsewhere.

Sensational details caused controversy when Samuel Warren included them in his *Passages from the Diary of a Late Physician* (1837) because his readers mistakenly interpreted the narrative as fact, guided by Warren's misleading character names. His references to characters like 'Miss J—' and 'N—' suggested that these were real persons. Warren defended himself by pointing to medical journals using this technique to protect patient privacy. His use of this technique, however, falsely signaled that the stories were factual; and most 1830s novels had discarded the eighteenth-century strategy of claiming historical truth. Indeed, Gallagher argues that realistic naming conventions – using specific names instead of 'Mrs. St—' – anchored the novel's development as plausible fiction: if a narrative is nonreferential, then it can tell a new truth that is neither fact nor lie.[60]

As a result of these differences, by the 1890s, medical authors remained committed to a realist approach to narrative, albeit highly regulated and translated into tables and charts, while literary authors embraced the formal experimentation that becomes Modernism. Modernist literary experimentation grew from a Victorian anti-mimetic tradition that critiqued lowbrow fare but also prolific writers like Trollope for allegedly 'mechanical' technique. This romantic view of authorship valued originality, inspiration,

---

[58] Anthony Trollope, *Doctor Thorne*, ed. Ruth Rendell (1858; London: Penguin, 1991), 5.
[59] Ruth Rendell, 'Introduction' to Trollope, *Doctor Thorne*, viii.
[60] Catherine Gallagher, 'The Rise of Fictionality', in *The Novel: History, Geography and Culture*, ed. Franco Moretti, 2 vols. (Princeton and Oxford: Princeton University Press, 2006 (336–63), vol. 1, 341–2.

and intuition, privileging ethical and aesthetic authenticity over material verisimilitude. The anxiety over technique played out differently for medical and scientific authors, where the demands of mechanical objectivity and the increasing use of quantified and mediated realism actually favored a kind of automaticity. However, the drive toward clinical medicine elicited periodic moments of nostalgia for the 'art of medicine'. Nineteenth-century practitioners did not eliminate sympathy, insight, and intuition in medical practice, but they had to gain discernment in how to balance these qualities with clinical work.

Conclusion

The extent to which realism was associated with virtue and health is clear in G. H. Lewes's cheeky suggestion in 1858 that romantic writing is actually a form of parasitic illness. He notes that intestinal worms (entozoa) are 'epidemically rife' in German literati. We must, he says, 'restrain the too abundant copiousness of weak and watery idiom which flows from that body'.[61] Lewes rapidly sketches out an essential style for scientific and literary prose, saying, 'it can no more be required of a professor that he should write with felicity than that he should charm all beholders with his personal appearance; but literature requires that he should write intelligibly and carefully, as society requires that he should wash his face and button his waistcoat'.[62] He holds novelists to higher standards: 'Art always aims at the representation of Reality, i.e. of Truth; and no departure from truth is permissible, except such as inevitably lies in the nature of the medium itself. Realism is thus the basis of all Art, and its antithesis is not *Idealism*, but *Falsism*.'[63] Lewes argues that, in a poorly-written book, 'the characters and language, the motives and emotions are not real, because they are not true'.[64] But, while a novelist who relies on easy illusion risks critical scorn, a physician who does so hazards far more.

The contradictions of medical realism delineate a complex, independent written tradition. Medical authors were as sophisticated and skeptical as literary ones in their use of realist techniques. They took their writing as seriously as the earnest moralists of mid-century, who saw literature as a solution to the loss of faith, or the witty aesthetes of the *fin de siècle*, who proclaimed their allegiance to 'art for art's sake'. For a physician like

---

[61] G. H. Lewes, "Realism in Art: Recent German Fiction," *Westminster Review* n.s. v. 14, no. 2 (Oct 1858), pp. 488–518.
[62] Ibid., 273.   [63] Ibid.   [64] Ibid., 277.

Bennett, writing clinical realism combined aesthetic pleasure with moral and scientific duty. The struggle to achieve clear and detailed observation and reporting, the effort to maintain both sympathy and detachment, the drive to build professional vision through pragmatic practice. They also meant health and life for Victorian patients.

CHAPTER 2

'Dissecting Piece by Piece'
Experimentalism in Late-Victorian Fiction

Anne Stiles

Victorian prose fiction is not usually thought of as experimental in form or content, at least not compared to the philosophically and formally innovative Romanticism that preceded it or the stream-of-consciousness literary Modernism that followed. But the nineteenth century is widely acknowledged as a watershed period in the development of experimental science, including medical and biological sciences. It was also a period of unprecedented collaboration between science and literature. As scholars like Rick Rylance and Laura Otis have explained, the early- to mid-nineteenth century boasted a generalist intellectual culture in which disciplinary boundaries were far more permeable than they are today.[1] During this period, most scientific discoveries were made by gentleman amateurs. Their writings remained accessible to lay readers due to their largely observational character and lack of specialist jargon. Literary authors like George Eliot, Wilkie Collins, and Charles Dickens could thus comment with authority on the latest scientific discoveries. Moreover, many nineteenth-century periodicals published articles on scientific topics cheek-by-jowl with fiction, poetry, and literary criticism.[2] To cite only one example, an article by Robert Louis Stevenson appeared in the same issue of *Cornhill Magazine* as scientific popularizer Richard Proctor's 'Dual Consciousness' (1877), a coincidence that may have inspired Stevenson's exploration of multiple personalities in *Strange Case of Dr Jekyll and Mr Hyde* (1886).[3]

---

[1] Rick Rylance, *Victorian Psychology and British Culture, 1850–1880* (Oxford: Oxford University Press, 2000), 1; Laura Otis, Introduction to *Literature and Science in the Nineteenth Century: An Anthology*, ed. Laura Otis (Oxford: Oxford University Press, 2002), xvii.
[2] Otis, 'Introduction', xvii.
[3] Julia Reid, *Robert Louis Stevenson, Science, and the Fin de Siècle* (Houndmills: Palgrave Macmillan, 2006), 96; Anne Stiles, *Popular Fiction and Brain Science in the Late Nineteenth Century* (Cambridge: Cambridge University Press, 2012), 27–49.

This interdisciplinary openness contracted as scientific disciplines became more specialized, and predominantly observational scientific methods gave way to a climate of experimentalism. By the end of the century, many scientific fields – including emergent medical specialties such as neurology, bacteriology, cytology, and so forth – were practiced by trained professionals in universities, research hospitals, and government-funded laboratories, using highly specialized equipment and sometimes impenetrable disciplinary jargon. Their research privileged clinical human studies, vivisection, and microscopic examination of tissues, and it tended to appear in field-specific journals rather than mainstream venues. These changes happened later in Britain than in America or Continental Europe, due to greater antivivisection sentiment among the British public and to a medical culture that celebrated the general practitioner as 'Renaissance man'.[4] But the British scientific community ultimately followed the same trends seen in neighboring countries, such as France and Germany.

These sweeping changes in scientific practice and the medical discoveries they made possible actively shaped imaginative literature. This essay describes how late-Victorian authors engaged with experimental physiology in the form and substance of their work. Among the most responsive were literary naturalists like Thomas Hardy, George Gissing, and George Moore – British authors who adapted the self-proclaimed 'experimental' method of French novelist Émile Zola – and scientifically trained writers of genre fiction such as Arthur Conan Doyle, H. G. Wells, and Grant Allen. These authors crafted short stories and novels whose forms mimicked scientific methods and whose content engaged with physiological practices and discoveries, as I shall explain.

Collectively, the works of these avant-garde authors suggest a more deliberately experimental writing practice than we generally associate with the Victorians – one that veers away from didacticism, staid marriage plots, and sentimentality. Instead, these writers penned works deploying an allegedly scientific, objective, and utterly unsentimental form of realism that they called naturalism; scientific romances that tested an imaginative hypothesis (such as invisibility or time travel) against a convincingly ordinary suburban backdrop; and detective fiction in which scientific methods drove key developments in plot and character.

---

[4] Frank Stahnisch, 'On the Use of Animal Experimentation in the History of Neurology', in *History of Neurology*, ed. Stanley Finger, François Boller, and Kenneth Tyler (Amsterdam: Elsevier, 2009), 129–48 (139–42); Stephen Casper, *The Neurologists: A History of a Medical Specialty in Modern Britain, 1789–2000* (Manchester: Manchester University Press, 2015), 2.

While these fictions seemingly endorsed experimental practices, an equally vibrant body of literature reacted against the frightful implications of late-nineteenth-century physiology. Late-Victorian Gothic novels by Bram Stoker, Stevenson, and H. Rider Haggard created an atmosphere of horror by extrapolating from recent discoveries in neuroscience, sexology, criminology, and degeneration theory, as critics such as Kelly Hurley and I have argued.[5] Taken together, experimental genres like scientific romance, detective literature, and the Gothic have arguably had a greater impact on twenty-first-century fiction and popular media than some of the more conventional mid-Victorian forms (realism, melodrama, domestic fiction) that still receive the lion's share of critical attention.

Medical Backgrounds

Before launching into a study of experimental literature, I will begin with an extended example of the changes occurring in just one medical field – the study of the brain and nervous system – followed by a few briefer examples from other life-science disciplines during the Victorian era. In each of these fields, the transition from a predominantly observational to an experimental scientific method becomes apparent in hindsight, although the rate of change varied for each discipline.

Also apparent in retrospect is the messy process by which medical specialties defined their boundaries and evolved discipline-specific vocabularies and practices. In the case of neurology and related disciplines like psychiatry and psychology, even the terminology used to refer to these fields could be slippery. Coined by Thomas Willis in his 1664 treatise *Cerebri Anatome*, the term 'neurology' was seldom used before the late nineteenth century, first appearing in *The Lancet* in 1859 and in the *British Medical Journal* in 1861.[6] Neurology as an independent medical specialty, meanwhile, was not firmly established in Britain until after the First World War, as historian of science Stephen T. Casper explains.[7] This example highlights the perils of applying twenty-first-century disciplinary labels retroactively to nineteenth-century sciences that often resist such precise categorization.[8] This is particularly true of nineteenth-century mental sciences, which incorporated discoveries from fields we would now consider

---

[5] See Stiles, *Popular Fiction and Brain Science*, and Kelly Hurley, *The Gothic Body: Sexuality, Materialism, and Degeneration at the Fin de Siècle* (Cambridge: Cambridge University Press, 1996).
[6] Casper, *The Neurologists*, 5.   [7] Ibid., 2, 6.   [8] Otis, 'Introduction', xxvi.

pseudoscientific: phrenology, physiognomy, mesmerism, psychical research, and craniometry among them.[9]

In mid-nineteenth-century Britain, then, mental science disciplines and the modern professional networks that supported them existed only in embryo. Moreover, the kind of research considered 'scientific' by physicians and philosophers of mind was remarkably capacious in scope. Leaders in these fields included polymaths such as Herbert Spencer, Alexander Bain, and George Henry Lewes, as well as generalist physicians like William Carpenter, Thomas Laycock, and Henry Holland. These scientific writers freely cited poems, novels, and classical myths to support their arguments and to cement their authority with a non-specialist reading public. Mid-Victorian literary critics, meanwhile, pioneered a strain of physiologically oriented novel theory that focused on readers' pacing, attention, and somatic responses to fiction, as Nicholas Dames ably describes in *The Physiology of the Novel* (2007).[10] A related body of psychologically inflected poetry criticism attended to the bodily effects of verse on readers, as Jason Rudy explains in *Electric Meters* (2009). For these reasons, the mid-Victorian era has been more fully explored by scholars of literature and psychology than later decades, when medical research became more specialized.[11]

Later in the century, the mental sciences were increasingly dominated by university-trained scientists rather than gentleman amateurs. Their more specialized research favored clinical studies, quantitative analyses, and laboratory work with live animals over anecdotal evidence or philosophical speculation. This sea change was most pronounced on the Continent. In France, for instance, Paul Broca's cerebral localization work

---

[9] For instance, Jenny Bourne Taylor and Sally Shuttleworth's groundbreaking work *Embodied Selves: An Anthology of Psychological Texts, 1830–1890* (Oxford: Oxford University Press, 1998) includes excerpts from medical and psychological texts alongside writing on hypnotism, physiognomy, and other 'pseudoscientific' fields, thus demonstrating the scope and variety of mental sciences during this period.

[10] Nicholas Dames, *The Physiology of the Novel: Reading, Neural Science, and the Form of Victorian Fiction* (Oxford: Oxford University Press, 2007).

[11] See, for instance, Rylance, *Victorian Psychology*; Sally Shuttleworth, *George Eliot and Nineteenth Century Science: The Make-Believe of a Beginning* (Cambridge: Cambridge University Press, 1984), *Charlotte Brontë and Victorian Psychology* (Cambridge: Cambridge University Press, 1996), and *The Mind of the Child: Child Development in Literature, Science, and Medicine, 1840–1900* (Oxford: Oxford University Press, 2010); Jenny Bourne Taylor, *In the Secret Theatre of Home: Wilkie Collins, Sensation Narrative, and Nineteenth-Century Psychology* (New York: Routledge, 1988); Jason Rudy, *Electric Meters: Victorian Physiological Poetics* (Athens: Ohio University Press, 2009); Jill Matus, *Shock, Memory, and the Unconscious in Victorian Fiction* (Cambridge: Cambridge University Press, 2009); and Kay Young, *Imagining Minds: The Neuro-Aesthetics of Austen, Eliot, and Hardy* (Columbus: Ohio State University Press, 2010).

with aphasics during the 1860s linked the third frontal convolution of the left brain hemisphere to linguistic ability. In 1870, meanwhile, Prussian physicians Gustav Fritsch and Eduard Hitzig performed experiments on dogs in which brain lesions and electrical stimulations were used to pinpoint the location of the motor cortex.[12] Groundbreaking experiments like these sparked a trend towards cerebral localization research in Germany and France, and helped solidify the status of neurology as a discipline. In 1882, for instance, French physician Jean-Martin Charcot was honored with the first European professorship in neurology, an event many historians of science identify as the beginning of neurology as an independent field.[13]

Britain, too, boasted its share of watershed neurological developments during this era. In the 1860s, John Hughlings Jackson made important discoveries about the functions of the right cerebral hemisphere by observing patients who had sustained damage to this part of their brains. Jackson speculated that the right hemisphere was involved in spatial perception, facial recognition, and memory.[14] In the 1870s, meanwhile, Scottish physician David Ferrier (working at the West Riding Lunatic Asylum in England) electrically stimulated and damaged the brains of monkeys, cats, dogs, and rabbits to create detailed maps of the human cerebral cortex. These cerebral maps, published in Ferrier's landmark *Functions of the Brain* (1876), saved lives by helping surgeons locate brain tumors and hemorrhages without first opening the skull. Ferrier's experiments also incited controversy and resulted in his notorious trial for animal cruelty in 1881, not to mention his ominous afterlife in late-Victorian fictions such as Wells's *The Island of Doctor Moreau* (1896), Stoker's *Dracula* (1897), and Collins's *Heart and Science* (1882).[15] Ferrier's work and that of other localizationists also undermined revered theological concepts like the soul or individual will by suggesting that human beings are governed by their nerve impulses.[16]

---

[12] Stanley Finger, *Origins of Neuroscience: A History of Explorations into Brain Function* (Oxford: Oxford University Press, 1994), 38, 52.

[13] Christopher Goetz, 'Jean-Martin Charcot and the Anatomo-Clinical Method of Neurology', in *History of Neurology*, ed. Finger et al., 203–12 (203).

[14] Stanley Finger, 'The Birth of Localization Theory', in *History of Neurology*, ed. Finger et al., 117–28 (122).

[15] On Ferrier as a model for the mad scientist characters in Collins's and Wells's work, see Laura Otis, 'Howled out of the Country: Wilkie Collins and H. G. Wells Retry David Ferrier', in *Neurology and Literature, 1860–1920*, ed. Anne Stiles (Houndmills: Palgrave, 2007), 27–51. On Ferrier as an ominous presence in *Dracula*, see Stiles, *Popular Fiction and Brain Science*, ch. 2.

[16] Stiles, *Popular Fiction and Brain Science*, 2.

The controversies surrounding neurological experiments in Britain may explain why the field was slower to professionalize there than in America or on the Continent. British neurology arguably began to emerge as a specialized field in the 1870s, with the foundation of the journals *Mind* (1876–present) and *Brain* (1878–present), plus the formation of professional groups such as the Neurological Society of London (later, the Neurological Society for the United Kingdom), which first met in 1886.[17] With such developments, neurology began to distance itself from neighbor disciplines like psychology and psychiatry. Still, decades would elapse before British neurology assumed its modern form. As late as 1934, British universities had yet to appoint a single professor of neurology.[18]

This detailed information about Victorian neurology is intended to show the rapid rate of change in just one life-science discipline during this era, as well as the sweeping methodological shifts that led to a culture of experimentalism. I have also tried to indicate some effects of these changes on the lay public, many of whom grew increasingly suspicious of scientific culture as it became less accessible. But equally revolutionary developments and heated controversies occurred in other medical fields. In the study of heredity, for instance, Charles Darwin's theories of evolution – introduced in his 1859 bestseller *On the Origin of Species by Means of Natural Selection* and expanded upon in 1871 with *The Descent of Man, and Selection in Relation to Sex* – fundamentally challenged the prevailing creationist account of human origins and development. Perhaps because of his clearly written, jargon-free prose and his largely observational scientific practice, Darwin's works spawned widespread public debate in lay periodicals and scientific venues. Darwin's writings were also among the first scientific texts to attract attention from scholars of Victorian literature, beginning with classic studies such as Gillian Beer's *Darwin's Plots: Evolutionary Narrative in Darwin, George Eliot and Nineteenth-Century Fiction* (1983) and George Levine's *Darwin and the Novelists: Patterns of Science in Victorian Fiction* (1988).

Predictably, literary critics have been slower to embrace the more experimental, laboratory-based studies of heredity that helped found the modern field of genetics – perhaps due to their unfamiliar format and mathematical rigor. Take, for example, the work of Augustinian monk Gregor Johann Mendel, who grew generations of pea plants between 1857 and 1864 to demonstrate the heritability of traits such as height, color, and seed texture. Mendel's research was so avant-garde and

---

[17] Casper, *The Neurologists*, 36. [18] Ibid., 1.

mathematical in its orientation that even his contemporaries failed to understand it. His work would remain largely unknown until its rediscovery in the early twentieth century by geneticists.[19] In 1883, meanwhile, German evolutionary biologist August Weissman disproved Lamarckian theories of inheritance of acquired traits by cutting off the tails of five generations of mice – 901 animals in total – whose offspring stubbornly continued to grow tails.[20] While such groundbreaking genetic experiments have received scant attention from scholars of Victorian literature, novelists have creatively engaged with this pioneering work. For instance, Simon Mawer's entertaining book *Mendel's Dwarf* (1997) recounts how a dwarf geneticist, a distant relative of Mendel, isolates the gene for his form of dwarfism (achondroplasia).

In the Victorian era, the clinical applications of early genetic studies were still far in the future. By contrast, some medical discoveries had immediate impact. For instance, the advent of surgical anesthesia in the 1840s (using ether and nitrous oxide) and English surgeon Joseph Lister's antiseptic surgical practices, pioneered in the mid-1860s, made possible a range of delicate interventions on the human body that would have been inconceivable previously, when surgeries had to be performed speedily on patients who were writhing in pain.[21] The study of infectious disease also produced watershed discoveries. From the 1850s on, physicians like John Snow, Louis Pasteur, and others conducted research suggesting the existence of pathogens that caused specific diseases. During the London cholera epidemic of 1854, Snow traced the source of the infection to the water supply, contradicting the miasma theory of airborne contagion popular at the time. Snow's discovery led to the construction of the world's first modern sewer system in London. Also in 1854, Italian scientist Fillipo Pacini first sighted *Vibrio cholerae*, the bacterium that causes the disease – though his discovery was largely ignored at the time.[22] Two decades later, German microbiologist Robert Koch isolated the bacteria that cause

---

[19] Siddhartha Mukherjee, *The Gene: An Intimate History* (New York: Scribner, 2017), 47–53.
[20] Ibid., 57.
[21] Finger, *Origins*, 160–2. Novelist Fanny Burney's harrowing account of her mastectomy, performed in 1811 without anesthetic, vividly conveys the challenges surgeons and patients faced prior to the development of surgical anesthesia. 'When the dreadful steel was plunged into the breast – cutting through veins – arteries – nerves – flesh', Burney writes, 'I began a scream that lasted unremittingly for the whole time of the incision', which was approximately twenty minutes (Fanny Burney, *Journals and Letters, Selected with an Introduction by Peter Sabor and Lars E. Troide* [New York: Penguin, 2001], 442). Unlike many surgical patients of the day, who frequently succumbed to sepsis and death after operations, Burney survived another twenty-nine years.
[22] Steven Johnson, *The Ghost Map: The Story of London's Most Terrifying Epidemic – and How It Changed Science, Cities, and the Modern World* (New York: Riverhead Books, 2006), 99.

anthrax (in 1876) and tuberculosis (in 1882), placing the emergent germ theory of disease on a firmer scientific footing. Such developments transformed the theory and practice of medicine by ushering in a new era of specialization and experimentation across various medical fields.

As informed members of the general public, novelists could hardly ignore these crucial developments. In fact, some deliberately co-opted the language of experimental physiology to describe their writing practice and defend their controversial literary endeavors. The next section will discuss some of the most prominent naturalistic writers to take this approach, which began in France and migrated to Germany, America, and Britain.

Naturalism

The origins of literary naturalism in France are unsurprising, given that nation's permissive attitude toward animal experimentation. Among the most notorious vivisectors of the nineteenth century was French physiologist Claude Bernard, who proposed that scientific methods used in physics and chemistry be applied to medicine.[23] As he explained in his 1865 treatise *An Introduction to the Study of Experimental Medicine*, the scientist must take apart living beings so that 'the mechanisms of life can be unveiled'.[24] Bernard followed this principle by, for instance, draining the gastric juices from a living dog to analyze the processes of digestion independently from the body.[25] To justify his invasive animal experiments – typically performed without anesthetic – Bernard argued that 'we can save living beings from death only after sacrificing others'.[26]

It may seem strange that a novelist would seek to emulate these methods. But controversial French author Zola found common ground with Bernard after his novel *L'Assommoir* (1877) became an overnight *succès de scandale*.[27] *L'Assommoir* is the seventh installment in Zola's

---

[23] Diane Smith, 'Narrative Subversion in the Naturalist Novel: Three Novels of the 1880s', *Comparative Literature Studies* 29:2 (1992), 157–71 (158).
[24] Claude Bernard, An Introduction to the Study of Experimental Medicine (1865) in *Literature and Science in the Nineteenth Century: An Anthology*, ed. Laura Otis (Oxford: Oxford University Press, 2002), 203–8 (204).
[25] Lawrence Rothfield, *Vital Signs: Medical Realism in Nineteenth-Century Fiction* (Princeton: Princeton University Press, 1992), 128.
[26] Bernard, *Introduction,* 206.
[27] Robert Lethbridge, 'Introduction' to Émile Zola, *L'Assommoir*, trans. Margaret Mauldon (1877; Oxford: Oxford University Press, 2009), vii–xlvi. The title of *L'Assommoir* is typically left untranslated because of the difficulty in rendering the original French. The word 'assommoir'

twenty-volume Rougon-Macquart series, which traces the downward-trending fortunes of one extended family over several generations. To defend the novel's gritty depictions of working-class life, including its ruthlessly accurate portrayal of end-stage alcoholism, Zola cited Bernard's experimental techniques. In his treatise 'The Experimental Novel' (1880), Zola argued that the naturalist writer must 'dissect piece by piece' his characters to show how heredity and environment determine their actions.[28] The author aimed to 'prove [. . .] that if the experimental method leads to the knowledge of physical life, it should also lead to the knowledge of the passionate and intellectual life'.[29] In such passages, Zola tapped into the growing confidence and optimism surrounding late-nineteenth-century science to promote his controversial literary style.[30]

As critics have noted, Zola's experimental theories did not integrate seamlessly into his novelistic practice. Preserving an attitude of scientific detachment towards one's characters is difficult if not impossible for any novelist. More importantly, 'a writer can never actually set up an experimental milieu' in precisely the same manner as a scientist, as Lawrence Rothfield observes. The writer can only put forth a hypothesis and provide observations as supporting evidence.[31] Critics have also questioned how much naturalism truly differs from the realism that preceded it, since both genres share a commitment to mimetic representation. This distinction becomes especially blurry when considering realist authors with a strong thematic interest in science, such as Honoré de Balzac or Gustave Flaubert, whom Zola considered fellow naturalists.[32]

Zola's difficulty putting his theories into practice becomes apparent even in a ruthlessly clinical passage such as the conclusion of his novel *Nana* (1880), the ninth installment of the Rougon-Macquart cycle. *Nana's* eponymous heroine is a high-class prostitute of humble origins who succumbs to disfiguring smallpox:

---

was working-class slang for a cheap drinking establishment or the 'deadly liquor' served within (ibid., xi; Anthony Cummins, 'From *L'Assommoir* to "Let's ha' some more": Émile Zola's Early Circulation on the Late-Victorian Stage', *Victorian Review* 34:1 [2008], 155–70 [159]). It was also used 'to signify the mallet which is used in the slaughter-houses or abattoirs of Paris to kill animals', as one English critic explained (quoted in ibid., 159).

[28] Émile Zola, *The Experimental Novel and Other Essays*, trans. Belle Sherman (New York: Cassell Publishing, 1893), 25.
[29] Ibid., 2. [30] Smith, 'Narrative Subversion', 158. [31] Rothfield, *Vital Signs*, 126.
[32] Ibid., 123. The most useful definition of naturalism I have run across comes from Constance Harsh, who describes the genre as 'an essentially deterministic literature that focuses on the impingement of natural processes on human agency and consciousness'. Yet she wisely cautions that 'clear-cut generic definitions are notoriously difficult to make.' 'Gissing's *The Unclassed* and the Perils of Naturalism', *ELH* 59:4 (1992), 911–38 (912) 'Perils of Naturalism', 912.

> She was the fruit of the charnel-house, a heap of matter and blood, a shovelful of corrupted flesh thrown down on the pillow. The pustules had invaded the whole of the face, so that each touched its neighbour. Fading and sunken, they had assumed the greyish hue of mud [. . .]. Venus was rotting. It seemed as though the poison she had assimilated in the gutters, and on the carrion tolerated by the roadside, the leaven with which she had poisoned a whole people, had but now remounted to her face and turned it to corruption.[33]

While the opening lines of the passage transmit an aura of clinical accuracy and a wealth of observational detail, there is an obvious breakdown in authorial objectivity towards the conclusion, where Nana is blamed for the corruption of her blue-blooded customers or, alternatively, seen as an agent of working-class revenge upon the aristocracy. Either way, her significance as metaphor for social upheaval ultimately trumps her status as medical object.[34]

Despite such flaws, Zola's theoretical treatise and his widely read naturalist novels signaled that experimental science resonated with literary authors. Indeed, naturalism soon spread beyond French borders, though not without some resistance. In Britain, naturalism was slow to take hold, due to prevailing ideas about the novel's didactic function and the role of the novelist as moral authority. Critics of naturalism decried Zola's work as 'indecent, filthy, and contaminating'.[35] Of *L'Assommoir*, for instance, *The Athenaeum* warned that 'no words can be strong enough to paint [its] filthiness', while *The Saturday Review* dismissed the novel as 'six hundred pages of garbage'.[36] Henry Vizetelly, who published the first English translations of Zola's works in the 1880s, was jailed for 'trafficking in pornographic literature'.[37] While critics objected most forcefully to Zola's frank depictions of working-class vice, they likewise disapproved of his materialism, his scientific determinism, and his explicit comparison of his method to vivisection.[38]

Despite critical condemnation and the lack of available English translations of Zola's works, the British public flocked to popular dramatic adaptations of *L'Assommoir* as early as 1879.[39] As Anthony Cummins relates, at least twenty-eight different dramatic adaptations of *L'Assommoir*

---

[33] Émile Zola, *Nana*, trans. Victor Plarr (New York: Boni and Liveright, 1924), 504.
[34] Rothfield, *Vital Signs*, 7.
[35] Quoted in Harsh, 'Gissing's *The Unclassed* and the Perils of Naturalism', 913.
[36] Quoted in Cummins, 'From *L'Assommoir*', 155.
[37] Clarence Decker, 'Zola's Literary Reputation in England', *PMLA* 49:4 (1934), 1140–53 (1145).
[38] Harsh, 'Perils of Naturalism', 914.   [39] Cummins, 'From *L'Assommoir*', 158.

were produced throughout Britain that capitalized on the novel's salacious appeal.[40] Zola's style also found a few admirers within the British literary establishment. Among the earliest converts was Anglo-Irish novelist George Moore, the 'English Zola', who spent his teens and twenties studying art in Paris.[41] There, he absorbed the tenets of new artistic movements such as impressionism and naturalism, as he relates in his autobiographical novel, *Confessions of a Young Man* (1888):

> One day [...] I took up the *Voltaire*. It contained an article by M. Zola. *Naturalisme, la vérité, la science*, were repeated some half a dozen times [...] The idea of a new art based upon science, in opposition to the art of the old world that was based upon imagination, an art that should explain all things and embrace modern life in its entirety, be, as it were, a new creed in a new civilisation, filled me with wonder, and I stood dumb before the vastness of the conception. (94–5)[42]

Around the same time Moore found 'The Experimental Novel' in *Le Voltaire*, he also read and admired *L'Assommoir*. Longing to meet his literary icon, Moore made a pilgrimage to Zola's residence in Médan, a suburb of Paris. There, he was mildly shocked by 'Japanese prints depicting furious fornications' and found Zola 'terribly aloof and cold'.[43] Despite this unsettling reception, the two authors began a correspondence that lasted several years in which Moore referred to Zola as 'cher maître' [dear master].[44] Moore went on to write novels inspired by Zola's realistic depictions of working-class life. His early efforts in this vein, such as *A Modern Lover* (1883) and *The Mummer's Wife* (1885), were seen as 'French' and 'shocking' for exploring themes such as alcoholism, spousal abuse, and child neglect. These works were banned by British circulating libraries like Smith's and Mudie's, whose strict censorship Moore decried in his pamphlet 'Literature at Nurse: or, Circulating Morals' (1885).[45]

For Moore, critical acceptance and financial stability came only with his 1894 novel *Esther Waters*, widely considered to be his finest work.

---

[40] Ibid., 163. These dramatizations, such as Charles Reade's *Drink* (1879), admittedly sanitized and abridged the novel's controversial subject matter, so that some stage versions resembled mid-century temperance melodramas (ibid., 161).
[41] Ibid., 155.
[42] George Moore, *Confessions of a Young Man,* ed. Susan Dick (Kingston: McGill–Queen's University Press, 1972), 94–5.
[43] George Moore, 'My Impressions of Zola', in *Nana*, trans. Victor Plarr (New York: Boni and Liveright, 1924), v–xxiii.
[44] Moore, *Confessions,* 241n.
[45] David Skilton, 'Introduction' to George Moore, *Esther Waters* (1894; Oxford: Oxford University Press, 1983), vii–xxii (ix).

The novel, which describes a working-class mother's struggle to provide for her illegitimate son, was initially banned by the circulating libraries. But Smith's relented when Prime Minister William Gladstone voiced his approval of the novel in *The Westminster Gazette*. Moore's brief victory over censorship suggests that, in the shifting literary climate of the 1890s, naturalism was at last gaining a foothold on British soil, thanks in part to Moore's earlier literary efforts.[46] Ironically, by this time, Moore had distanced himself from his former literary idol. His 'Impressions of Zola', published the same year as *Esther Waters*, concludes with a denunciation of Zola's later work. 'Instead of [his] books becoming more and more beautiful, they have become larger, looser, and uglier', Moore opined, rating Zola's genius on the level of 'superior mediocrity'.[47]

Moore's change of heart notwithstanding, the 1890s ushered in a more genial climate for British naturalism. As Clarence Decker explains, the controversy over naturalism peaked around 1888 in England and gradually waned thereafter, so that 'by 1900, the naturalists [including Zola] were firmly established in the literary tradition'.[48] This attitude shift contributed to the rising literary fortunes of Gissing and Hardy. While neither author was especially invested in Zola or his experimental method – certainly not to the extent of Moore, at any rate – both produced gritty portrayals of working-class life that were sometimes described as naturalistic. Both likewise maintained a deterministic and pessimistic view of life influenced by recent advances in natural sciences, especially physiology. Moreover, critics who objected to the work of Gissing and Hardy often did so for the same reasons they repudiated Zola: a too-faithful rendering of working-class hardship that readers found inappropriately revealing, depressing, or both.

Gissing is an interesting, if problematic, exemplar of the literary naturalism of his era. While Gissing shared the low estimate of Zola's writing common in the 1880s, biographer Jacob Korg observes, 'it is precisely his novels written before [1889], those dealing with poverty, which are supposed by some critics to show a strong influence of Zola'.[49] Gissing also shared Zola's penchant for observing working-class life and taking copious

---

[46] Ibid., xiv.
[47] Moore, 'Impressions of Zola', xxiii, xv. On the breakdown of Moore's relationship with Zola, see also *Confessions*, 241–3n.
[48] Decker, 'Zola's Literary Reputation', 1148.
[49] Jacob Korg, *George Gissing: A Critical Biography* (Seattle: University of Washington Press, 1963), 128. Gissing would later revise his early impressions of Zola. The French novelist had become one of his literary heroes by 1898, thanks in part to his role in the Dreyfus affair (ibid.).

notes about his subject matter.[50] This attention to detail is evident in Gissing's most famous literary productions: novels such as *New Grub Street* (1891), *The Odd Women* (1893), and *The Whirlpool* (1897), which depict lower-middle-class life with unsentimental fidelity. Yet within such works, Gissing mocks the type of naturalist literature with which he was often associated. For instance, a minor subplot of *New Grub Street* concerns a writer, Harold Biffin, whose novel *Mr. Bailey, Grocer* displays 'the spirit of groveling realism'.[51] The book's title and the critique it elicits suggest Zola's and Moore's works and their hostile reception in England during the 1880s, the decade in which *New Grub Street* is set. Predictably, *Mr. Bailey, Grocer* is a financial flop, and Biffin commits suicide when starvation seems imminent. This fictional episode highlights Gissing's ambivalence towards naturalism, while epitomizing the fatalistic attitude so characteristic of the genre.

Like Gissing, Hardy was 'not a disciple of Zola', having remarked in 1895 that 'I am read in Zola very little.'[52] Yet Hardy's brand of realism or naturalism (depending on what you want to call it) has some important commonalities with Zola's method, especially their shared interest in physiology.[53] This interest becomes apparent, for instance, in Hardy's depiction of sexual assault in *Tess of the D'Urbervilles* (1892) and in his exploration of morbid psychology in *Jude the Obscure* (1895). Predictably, these works encountered strong public opposition and censorship, despite receiving high praise in some quarters. Early published versions of *Tess*, for instance, omitted the controversial rape scene that drives much of the plot, while the public outcry over *Jude*, Hardy wrote, 'completely cur[ed] me of further interest in novel writing'.[54]

Hardy drew his controversial observations about human nature from highly reputable scientific sources. As Suzanne Keen recounts, Hardy was exceptionally well versed in physiological psychology and philosophy of mind, not to mention evolutionary doctrine, having read the work of Darwin, Lewes, Spencer, and T. H. Huxley, among others, and made

---

[50] Ibid., 100.
[51] George Gissing, *New Grub Street*, ed. Bernard Bergonzi (1891; New York: Penguin, 1985), 522.
[52] William Newton, 'Hardy and the Naturalists: Their Use of Physiology', *Modern Philology* 49:1 (1951), 28–41 (29).
[53] On whether Hardy should properly be classed as a realist or a naturalist, see, for instance, Newton.
[54] Thomas Hardy, *Jude the Obscure* (1895; Ware: Wordsworth Classics, 1995), postscript. There is, of course, longstanding debate about whether Alec's sexual encounter with Tess should be characterized as rape or seduction, due to Hardy's circumspect language in this section.

copious remarks on these sources in his *Literary Notebooks*.[55] Hardy also met socially with scientific luminaries, including psychical researcher F. W. H. Myers and psychiatrist James Crichton Browne, the co-founder of the journal *Brain*.[56] Curiously, Hardy seems to have preferred scientific thinking that was anecdotal or theoretical in nature over the sort of experimental science he might have read in *Brain*. Keen speculates that this bias stemmed from Hardy's antivivisectionist leanings, suggesting another way in which the author differed from Zola.[57]

While British naturalist writers were not always strictly committed to experimentalism in the sense Zola intended, the family resemblance between their works – especially their shared emphasis on physiology and biological determinism – is an important feature of the genre as well as a sign of the times. A similar interest in scientific methods and practices is apparent in other late-Victorian genres, especially detective fiction, scientific romance, and the Gothic.

Genre Fiction

Perhaps the most obvious application of experimental science in late-Victorian literature can be found in the wildly popular detective fiction written during this period. In Conan Doyle's 'A Scandal in Bohemia' (1891), for instance, Dr. Watson describes Sherlock Holmes as 'the most perfect reasoning and observing machine that the world has seen', calling him a 'sensitive instrument' with 'high-power lenses'.[58] This curious description likens Holmes to 'a kind of camera', as Ronald Thomas suggests, or, perhaps, a microscope – that essential tool of experimental science.[59]

Conan Doyle, who received specialized training in ophthalmology, came by these sorts of visual metaphors naturally.[60] But one finds similar comparisons in lesser-known detective novels such as Allen's *Recalled to Life*, also published in 1891. Allen, a scientific popularizer, militant atheist, and author of New Woman fiction, depicts protagonist Una Callingham

---

[55] Suzanne Keen, *Thomas Hardy's Brains: Psychology, Neurology, and Hardy's Imagination* (Columbus: Ohio State University Press, 2014), 18.
[56] Ibid., 40. [57] Ibid., 42.
[58] Arthur Conan Doyle, 'A Scandal in Bohemia', in *The New Annotated Sherlock Holmes*, ed. Leslie Klinger, 2 vols. (New York: W. W. Norton, 2005), vol. 1, 5.
[59] Roland Thomas, *Detective Fiction and the Rise of Forensic Science* (Cambridge: Cambridge University Press, 1999), 171.
[60] Conan Doyle began a course of study in ophthalmology in Vienna in late 1890 (Thomas 167). His medical career, however, was spent as a general practitioner.

as a sort of human camera whose eye takes pictures of scenes that register as photographic 'negatives' in her brain.[61] When Una witnesses a horrific murder, she observes that 'no sensitive-plate could have photographed [the scene] more instantaneously, as by an electric spark, than my retina that evening, as for months after I saw it all'.[62]

While it makes sense that Sherlock Holmes or Una Callingham might use a microscope or flash photography to solve crimes – as each, in fact, does – why would their authors liken these characters to specific technologies? Conan Doyle does so, I suspect, to underscore the extent to which the logic of experimental science dictates the form and content of his tale. Indeed, literary critics have often observed how Conan Doyle employed techniques of medical diagnostics, biology, geology, or forensic science in his Holmes stories.[63] Holmes, who can identify a man's calling by his 'finger-nails, by his coat sleeve, by his boots, by his trouser-knees, by the callosities of his forefinger and thumb', as described in *A Study in Scarlet* (1887), has a discriminating visual faculty suited to any of these scientific fields.[64]

Holmes's extraordinary visual acuity – not to mention his status as human microscope – affiliates him with medical specialties that emerged in the late nineteenth century and gradually superseded old-fashioned general practitioners, represented by Dr. Watson (or by Conan Doyle himself, who was a 'respectable yet poverty-stricken' general practitioner before his literary career made him a household name[65]). Watson frankly admits Holmes's intellectual superiority, as if to acknowledge the dominance of experimental sciences over the primarily observational methods used by generalists such as himself.[66] The explosive popularity of the Holmes series – like the gradual acceptance of naturalism in the 1890s – testifies to more widespread embrace of these scientific trends.

Another important sign of the times was the emergence of the 'scientific romance', a term coined by writer Charles Howard Hinton to describe

---

[61] Stiles, *Popular Fiction and Brain Science*, 88.
[62] Grant Allen, *Recalled to Life* (Hard Press, 2005), 5.
[63] Thomas, for instance, argues that detectives are 'master diagnosticians', capable of reading pathological symptoms overlooked by others (*Detective Fiction*, 3); Lawrence Frank, meanwhile, suggests that 'the geologist and the detective [...] inhabit a world of signs that to the unseeing eyes of others do not exist' (*Victorian Detective Fiction and the Nature of Evidence: The Scientific Investigations of Poe, Dickens, and Doyle* [Houndmills: Palgrave Macmillan, 2003], 162).
[64] Arthur Conan Doyle, 'A Study in Scarlet', in *A Study in Scarlet and Sign of the Four* (New York: Berkeley, 1963), 23.
[65] Rothfield, *Vital Signs*, 142.   [66] Ibid.

the early science fiction produced by writers such as Jules Verne, Allen, M. P. Shiel, and Wells. In France, Verne dominated the field with popular novels such as *Journey to the Centre of the Earth* (1864), *Twenty Thousand Leagues under the Sea* (1870), and *Around the World in Eighty Days* (1873). In Britain, this genre was most closely identified with Wells, who surpassed his French predecessor with popular novels that employed a deliberately experimental method. In works such as *The Time Machine* (1895), *The Island of Doctor Moreau* (1896), *The Invisible Man* (1897), and *The War of the Worlds* (1898) – all produced within a remarkable three-year span – Wells used fiction as a 'mouthpiece for science', as he remarked in 1895.[67]

Specifically, Wells used his scientific romances to test fanciful hypotheses against a series of controls, as he explained in the introduction to a 1933 edition of his scientific romances. Each work concentrated on one hypothetical proposition, such as 'how would you feel and what might not happen to you [...] if for instance pigs could fly and one came rocketing over the hedge at you? [...] or if you became invisible?'. Wells then strove to '*domesticate* the impossible hypothesis' by making the rest of the story as realistic and commonplace as possible, thus tricking the reader into suspending disbelief.[68] For Wells, this 'domestication' usually involved a suburban London setting with ordinary middle-class characters, reflecting the environment of his childhood.[69]

Wells's adaptation of the scientific method for his romances was likely to have been inspired by his time at the Normal School of Science in South Kensington, where he studied under Darwin's apologist, T. H. Huxley.[70] But while Wells endorsed the scientific method, he did not necessarily approve of the uses to which it was put, as the calamitous adventures of his scientist heroes suggest. The eponymous villain of *The Island of Doctor Moreau*, for instance, conducts cruel vivisections that provide no clear benefit to humanity, while Griffin of *The Invisible Man* goes on a senseless killing spree. Even the more benign scientist characters in Wells's fiction –

---

[67] Quoted in Steven McLean, *The Early Fiction of H. G. Wells: Fantasies of Science* (Houndmills: Palgrave Macmillan, 2009), 2.
[68] H. G. Wells, 'Introduction' to *The Scientific Romances of H. G. Wells* (London: Victor Gollancz, 1933), viii.
[69] Marina Warner, 'Introduction' to H. G. Wells, *The Time Machine* (1895; New York: Penguin, 2005), xiii–xxviii (xix).
[70] Though Wells left the Normal School without taking a degree, he earned a BSc in zoology at the University of London in 1890.

such as the Time Traveler and the bumbling chemist Cavor of *The First Men in the Moon* (1901) – could best be described as observers who fail to influence the remarkable new worlds they encounter. Their powerlessness in the face of catastrophe suggests the limits of the scientific method and the hubris of those who employ it recklessly.

Like the Wellsian scientific romance, late-Victorian Gothic novels often appropriated elements of the experimental science of their day while condemning scientific discoveries and practices – a dynamic one might call 'complicitous critique', to use Linda Hutcheon's term.[71] Hurley suggests, for instance, that *fin-de-siècle* Gothic fiction maintained an opportunistic yet critical relationship to the biology, sexology, evolutionary narratives, and criminology of the era. These disciplines, she suggests, undermined any notion of a stable human identity, thus inspiring the 'slug-men, snake-women, ape-men, beast-people, octopus-sealmen, beetle-women, dog-men, [and] fungus people' that populate late-Victorian Gothic fiction.[72] Similarly, I have argued that many late-century Gothic romances critiqued neurological discoveries for destabilizing traditional Christian ideas about free will and the immortal soul. Chapter 21 of Stoker's *Dracula*, for instance, features an invasive and ultimately unsuccessful brain surgery using Ferrier's cranial maps. Moreover, the novel's vampire villain mimics neurological researchers like Ferrier by ruthlessly experimenting on living subjects and depriving victims of autonomy and their immortal souls. Robert Louis Stevenson, too, capitalized on anxieties about bilateral brain hemisphere asymmetry and resultant personality changes in *Jekyll and Hyde*.[73] In these ways, the Gothic registered popular anxieties that accompanied scientific 'progress', counterbalancing the scientific optimism prevalent in many areas of Victorian life.

These examples suggest why late-Victorian novels were, in fact, more 'experimental' than is typically thought – both in their indebtedness to experimental science and in their stylistic inventiveness. In some cases, these two things were related, as in Zola's cooption of Bernard's experimental vivisection as the inspiration for his prose style. Other authors were more ambivalent about science, yet they still borrowed scientific ideas or even stylistic features of scientific writing, such as the case-study format

---

[71] See, for instance, ch. 1 of Linda Hutcheon's *The Politics of Postmodernism* (1989; New York: Routledge, 2002), which describes this dynamic in the context of postmodern literature and art.
[72] Hurley, *Gothic Body*, 4.   [73] See Stiles, *Popular Fiction and Brain Science*, chs. 1–2.

alluded to in *Jekyll and Hyde*.[74] These examples should make us reconsider stereotypes about Victorian fiction as staid, sentimental, or moralistic, and rethink critically neglected genres that have proven resilient and adaptable in the present day. Those genres that are most studied are not necessarily those that cast the longest shadow.

---

[74] Ibid., 44–7.

CHAPTER 3

Exhibiting Bodies
Museums, Collecting, and Knowledge in Nineteenth-Century Literature

Verity Burke

The nineteenth century was party to a vast proliferation of museums, a result (amongst other things) of growing leisure time for the middle and working classes, the development of the Victorian empire, and an increasing focus on materiality in medicine and the natural sciences. Standing on the shoulders of an Enlightenment culture of ordering and collecting the natural world, Victorian museums progressively developed their institutions into places not solely of collection but increasingly of curatorial narration, interpretation, and public pedagogy. Alongside national museums, like the Hunterian at the Royal College of Surgeons, there was also significant growth in a number of other institutions that exhibited the human body, such as freak shows, popular museums, and outmoded cabinets of curiosity. Yet the nature of the material which the anatomy museum collected and displayed – including exhibits on generation, sexual disease, and 'monstrous' bodies – left it vulnerable to accusations of impropriety. The exhibition of the body-object to an unrestricted audience was considered by many to be 'deeply inappropriate', leading some popular medical museums to be castigated as 'sinks of iniquity'.[1] As Kate Hill notes, 'the combined effect of a tradition of attitudes to bodily objects coming into contact with new ideas about the dangers of body parts and their display created a difficult terrain for the collection and display of anything connected with the body',[2] one that museums attempted to navigate through the careful ordering and policing of displays, alongside the creation of a body of literature that made apparent their rationale.

By the 1850s, an enduring anxiety was developing around the respectability of the anatomy museum. Closely associated with, and used as a

---

[1] Kate Hill, 'Collecting and the Body in Late-Victorian and Edwardian Museums', *Bodies and Things in Nineteenth-Century Literature and Culture*, ed. Katharina Boehm (Basingstoke: Palgrave Macmillan, 2012), 157.
[2] Hill, 'Collecting and the Body', 157.

demonstration of, the professionalisation of medicine, anatomy museums and the bodies they displayed were also embroiled in a range of controversies from body-snatching to quackery, motivating a need to differentiate the bodies on show in museums from those in freak shows, fairgrounds, and rarees, places that revealed the body not to educate but to titillate. Claims that museums might be sites of titillation were not entirely unfounded; visitors to La Specola – the natural history museum in Florence – were apt to touch the wax genitalia of the anatomical Venus, while Kahn's Anatomical and Pathological Museum in London peddled quack cures for visitors' sexual diseases.[3] Samuel Alberti has evidenced that museum campaigners carefully represented their collections as sites of enlightenment and education, while medical schools and university colleges became more cautious about public access, 'seeking to cleanse [collections] of their associations with the circus and the fair'.[4] As Alberti acknowledges, however, popular and commercial anatomy museums were contrastingly keen to attract crowds and to turn a profit. Showmen-physicians such as Joseph Kahn, Signor Sarti, and J. W. Reimers foregrounded the moral and educational aspects of their institutions, places that one could visit to 'know thyself', signifying a problem for museum campaigners who were similarly attempting to position their institutions as sites of both serious study and educational recreation. This chapter intends to take what we might call two 'border cases' – Dr Joseph Kahn's Anatomical and Pathological Museum and Wilkie Collins's *The Law and the Lady* (1875) – to demonstrate the significant dialogue between literature and anatomical museums; in particular, I aim to demonstrate how the 'genres' of museums and literature borrowed techniques from each other to legitimise the potentially sensational body as a site of knowledge.

Kate Forde and Laurence Talairach-Vielmas have both noted that the professionalisation of doctors 'led to the desire for a medical monopoly on anatomy and resulted in deliberate attempts to categorise it as knowledge from which laypeople could be excluded on moral grounds'.[5] This was a particular problem for anatomy museums, whose mission was to educate

---

[3] A. W. Bates, 'Dr. Kahn's Museum: Obscene Anatomy in Victorian London', *Journal of the Royal Society of Medicine* 99:12 (2006), accessed 7 July 2016, www.ncbi.nlm.nih.gov/pmc/articles/PMC1676337/; Samuel J. M. M. Alberti, *Morbid Curiosities* (Oxford: Oxford Scholarship Online, 2011), 181.

[4] Samuel J. M. M. Alberti, 'The Museum Affect: Visiting Collections of Anatomy and Natural History', *Science in the Marketplace*, ed. Aileen Fyfe and Bernard Lightman (Chicago: Chicago University Press, 2007), 371–403 (372).

[5] Laurence Talairach-Vielmas, 'Morbid Taste, Morbid Anatomy and Victorian Sensation Fiction', *English Literature* 2:4 (2015), 257–74 (260) and Kate Forde, 'Staging Science at Wellcome

through the display of such specimens. The connection between museum content and impropriety was reinforced through various incidents, including the French tailor who 'decapitated his wife with a saw', allegedly after he had visited 'Kahn's exhibition to study the anatomy of the throat'[6] – details that would not sound out of place in a disreputable periodical like *The Terrific Register*. It was amidst this medical and museological climate that the sensation novel emerged in the 1860s, drawing on the same anxieties of impropriety and titillation, and with plots that mirrored the challenge of how best to convey knowledge through the body.

The issues facing 'sensational' museums like Kahn's – of respectability and the interpretation of various suspect bodies – were played with in sensation fiction, such as Wilkie Collins's *The Law and the Lady* (1875). Collins's engagement with anatomical, medical, and museum culture shapes his novel, in which characters are simultaneously represented as specimens and curators, with clues collected from 'curious' cabinets and house-museums, worryingly unstable pathology, and book–body hybrids.[7] Working with nineteenth-century anxieties about differences between respectable and 'illegitimate' displays of anatomy, and the nature of what is now termed anatomical intermediality (the interactions between a museum's specimens and the media that interpret them), Collins's textualised and substitute bodies allow for the revelation of secrets and negotiate the tensions of the anatomy museum. While the 'othered' bodies of characters like the 'half man, half chair' (206) antagonist Miserrimus Dexter derive from the imagery of pathology and teratology,[8] Collins's representation of the detective heroine Valeria Macallan and the collections of Dexter and Major Fitz-David will be discussed for the purposes of a close analysis alongside the ephemera of Kahn's Museum. Knowledge is acquired in *The Law and the Lady* through reconstructing bodies and interpreting objects and texts, problematising the supremacy of the objective method and legitimising this interpretative process as one from which valuable information can be drawn.

Collection: Anatomical Models in Context', *The Morbid Anatomy Anthology*, ed. Joanna Ebenstein and Colin Dickey (New York: Morbid Anatomy Press, 2014), 272–87 (280).

[6] Kate Summerscale, *The Suspicions of Mr Whicher, or the Murder at Road Hill House* (London: Bloomsbury, 2008), (106), quoted in Alberti, *Morbid Curiosities*, 193.

[7] Wilkie Collins, *The Law and the Lady* (1875; Oxford: Oxford University Press, 2008), 77. All subsequent references to this edition will be given in the text.

[8] For more on Miserrimus Dexter and teratology, see Katherine Angell, 'Miserrimus Dexter: Monstrous Forms of the *Fin de Siècle*', *The Male Body in Medicine and Literature*, ed. Andrew Mangham and Daniel Lea (Liverpool: Liverpool University Press, 2018), 48–63.

Joseph Kahn's Anatomical and Pathological Museum

Dr Joseph Kahn's Anatomical and Pathological Museum was one of the most popular public museums of the mid-nineteenth century, receiving approximately two thousand visitors each week.[9] Despite (or perhaps because of) this immense appeal, Kahn's museum faced questions about the propriety of its exhibits, which included the naked figure of the wax Venus, salacious examples of sexual disease, and lectures about the wondrous form of the human body. Kahn's museum attempted to navigate the issues of respectability surrounding the anatomy museum through a myriad of texts published in order to ostensibly educate the public (and, in actuality, also advertise and promote the premises), including maps; a miniature catalogue; and a more extensive introduction, guide, and catalogue billed as the *Illustrated Handbook to Dr Kahn's Museum and Gallery of Science* (1855).

The contemporary responses to Kahn's museum were not as universally pleasant as suggested by the propaganda of the *Illustrated Handbook*. As Alberti notes, 'Kahn's museum in particular was variously considered "horrible", "revolting, filthy and disgusting"'. He cites the outraged response of one particular medical student:

> DECEMBER 7th: Went to Dr. Kahn's Museum in the afternoon. A decidedly indecent pseudo-scientific affair, founded by quack doctor [...] Lecture on Deleterious Influences was of course disgusting.
>
> DECEMBER 8th: Had a rather serious attack of diarrhœa, a malady to which I am seldom subject. Can it have been bestowed on me by an all-wise Providence as a just punishment for my having visited that sink of iniquity, Dr. Kahn's Museum yesterday? Who knows?[10]

The student's anecdotal experience bears closer examination for, instead of the museum displaying bodies for pedagogical reasons, the student's situation suggests that the museum experience could affect the body of the visitor. Crucially, the medical student comes away with anxious questions, uncertain of the provenance of his illness, rather than with additional knowledge that might prove useful in diagnosis. Further to the furore surrounding the specimens of sexual pathology, the indecency of the museum is also connected with its 'pseudo-scientific' nature.

---

[9] Forde, 'Staging Science', 277.
[10] Alberti, *Morbid Curiosities*, 188. Alberti is quoting from an 1860s diary entry from Shephard T. Taylor, *The Diary of a Medical Student during the Mid-Victorian Period, 1860–1864* (London: Jarrold, 1927), 16.

The reputation of Kahn's museum suffered a rapid decline in the medical press, from worthy site of medical study to 'sink of iniquity' that used its respectable museum reputation to sell quack remedies for venereal diseases. *The Lancet*, keen to police the boundaries between the medical and the popular, and to increase the prestige of the medical profession, suggested that the museum itself 'might be prosecuted for obscenity, as were "filthy books"'.[11] Subsequent legal cases, opposition from members of the medical profession, and complaints over the morality of the anatomy museum eventually forced it to close.[12] The prosecution of the institution under the Obscene Publications Act of 1857 is especially interesting in its demonstration of the intermedial construction of the museum space and specimens, beyond the close connection of the anatomy museum with the lectures and pamphlets on the subject of sexual diseases. As A. W. Bates points out, the Act focused on material that encouraged 'conduct inconsistent with public morals', offering a way to regulate popular anatomy selectively, for 'books and pictures that were illegal if offered to the public would be acceptable to a professional audience'; medical professionals were capable of morally appreciating anatomical materials, whereas the lower classes and women were considered particularly vulnerable to corruption.[13] The successful prosecution of Kahn's museum 'branded all public display of anatomical specimens as potentially obscene' and 'anatomical education was restricted to medical professionals', while 'public anatomy survived only in sideshows'.[14] What was problematic about the anatomy museum was not solely the objects stored, but the interpretation and narration of this material.

It was in December of 1873, just over a year before *The Law and the Lady* was first published, that the new owners of Kahn's museum, Roumanielle, Davidson, and Dennison, pleaded guilty to offences under the Obscene Publications Act, leading to the destruction of the anatomical waxes, 'fragments of which were then handed back to the defendants, with the prosecuting Society for the Suppression of Vice claiming to have performed a moral duty in having the museum literally "broken up"'.[15] The dissolution of Kahn's establishment on the grounds that it broke a law about publications reflects the growing attempt to morally and medically

---

[11] Bates, 'Dr. Kahn's Museum'. Bates demonstrates that Kahn did not abandon the museum's supposed educational objectives, continuing to lecture on a number of topics that were physically embodied in the museum displays, perhaps hoping that his previous reinforcing of the museum's worth through education would be enough to save it.
[12] Ibid.   [13] Ibid.   [14] Ibid.   [15] Ibid.

police the anatomy museum, but also, and less overtly, to reinforce the close interrelation between textual and material bodies. The closure of Kahn's establishment 'effectively ended public anatomy museums as an arena for medical education in England', marking the success of the medical community in branding certain kinds of public museum as more entertaining than educational, with the Liverpool Anatomy Museum selling its specimens to Louis Tussaud's waxwork show, and the remainders of Kahn's collection being shown amongst 'sensational dime museums' in the Bowery of America.[16] The language of the medical press and the publications of the anatomy museums attempted to separate the clean clinical science of museums like the Royal College of Surgeons' Hunterian Museum from the earlier cabinets of curiosity as well as the 'gloomy sepulchre of pathological horrors' of more immoral attractions.[17] By the time Collins was to pen *The Law and the Lady*, the anatomical body would be understood as requiring careful recollection, display, and interpretation, but more than ever it demanded the rehabilitation of respectability, through an emphasis on scientific value and education.

The Anatomical Venus and the Sexualised Specimens of Kahn's Museum

The list of the objects displayed in this part of the museum and carefully detailed in the *Illustrated Handbook*'s descriptions advertises the kinds of specimens and models exhibited to any visitor willing to pay the entry fee; so although 'the generative system in particular featured prominently in anatomical displays', both in 'respectable museums as elsewhere',[18] one can understand the anxieties about who was viewing material literally dissected in the catalogue. There are remarkably few illustrations in the so-called *Illustrated Handbook*, creating distance from the material specimen; the clinical language both foregrounds individual aspects of the specimens to educate the reader and visitor, and draws attention to the sexual organs. The assertions made in the *Illustrated Handbook*, that 'the exquisite beauty of these preparations cannot fail to strike the most superficial observer' reinforce the troublesome impression that the bodies displayed in the

---

[16] Ibid.
[17] H. Burt-White, 'The Museum', *St Bartholomew's Hospital Journal* 40 (1933), 81–4. Quoted in Bates, 'Dr. Kahn's Museum'.
[18] Alberti, *Morbid Curiosities*, 134.

anatomy museum might titillate rather than educate.[19] Kahn's numerous versions of the Anatomical Venus – deconstructable models of naked women that could be bloodlessly dissected to reveal the inner workings of the body – were especially problematic: Joanna Ebenstein notes how these wax women provoked enduring anxieties, for they 'have seduced, intrigued and instructed [...] flickering on the edges of medicine and myth, votive and vernacular, fetish and fine art'.[20]

While 'private anatomy shows boasted of their glorious full-body "anatomical Venuses"',[21] as well as emphasised their scientific utility, the entries in Kahn's handbook place equal importance on the beauty of the wax women, stressing how 'every portion of the female figure is presented to view', positioning it as salacious as well as educative. The entry on Kahn's museum's '*Venus De Medici*' nods to the fact that these models were 'intentionally reminiscent of classical sculptures', a 'familiar and inoffensive representation of the human form' that would already have been familiar to museum visitors, recalling the classical statuary adorning the exterior of Kahn's museum.[22] It was, however, also the name of La Specola's well-known *Medici Venus*, a full-body figure of beauty displayed naked with both skin and organs on show to the visitor. Hinting at the full revelation and beauty of the figure, Kahn's handbook fleshes out the Anatomical Venus.

The entries for Kahn's Venus models emphasise the artistry rather than the science of the model, utilising poetry to foreground the Venus's classical associations:

> This figure is a most beautiful piece of artistic work, and has been recently completed at immense labour and cost. The external contour of the frame has been deemed by all who have seen it, so near an approximation to perfection in beauty – so truly in accordance with the highest conception which poets and artists have formed of the beautiful in the female form, that its qualities may be summed up in the admirable lines of Mrs. Eames, the American poetess: – 'Thou wert a worship in the ages olden, / Thou bright-veiled image of divinity, / Crowned with such gleams, imperial and golden, / As Phidias gave to immortality; A type exquisite of the pure ideal / Forth shadowed in perfect loveliness, / Embodied and existent in the real, / A perfect shape to kneel before and bless.' The abdomen of this magnificent figure is laid open, for the purpose of showing the position of the viscera,

---

[19] Joseph Kahn, *Catalogue of Dr. Kahn's Anatomical and Pathological Museum, 4, Coventry Street, Leicester Square; to which is added, a series of lectures, under the title of 'Shoals and Quicksands' of Youth, as delivered by Dr. Kahn* (London: W. J. Golbourn, 1851), 11.
[20] Joanna Ebenstein, *The Anatomical Venus* (London: Thames and Hudson, 2016), 15.
[21] Alberti, *Morbid Curiosities*, 147.   [22] Bates, 'Dr. Kahn's Museum'.

when displayed by the uterus in the later months of gestation. The period represented is about eight months, and it will be observed how enormously the womb is enlarged, and how, by its increase in size, it has changed the position of all the other organs situated in the abdominal cavity.[23]

The 'ideal' of beauty is 'embodied' in Eames's poem, but when the focus shifts from the beautiful external qualities of the body, the 'gleams, imperial and golden', the text attempts to strip back not just the flesh but any implication that the figure might be considered immoral. Despite the revelation of the sexual organs in both the specimen and its prose frame, the text is used to highlight the science behind the display of the female body. Other models used to illustrate and explain the reproductive system are similarly crowded with medical terminology, such as the '*Mammary Glands*', which are discussed purely in terms of their reproductive functions, as though the author believes this medical focus will distract the viewer from the potential impropriety of displaying female body parts.

The handbook is ambiguous in aim, however, as its ability to be widely disseminated positions it not only as an aid to better understanding the specimens of Kahn's museum but also as a window into the censored models in restricted sections; as an advert for Kahn's medical practice and the museum as a commercial attraction; and to reinforce impressions that the quack remedies for sexual diseases, sold in the museum, were efficient (a significant number of the handbook's descriptions of diseased specimens notes the perfect success Kahn has had in treating similar cases). The handbook becomes another problematic body open to public view. While attempts to use cataloguing, lecturing, labelling, and other textual methods to disseminate knowledge from the model body were adopted by the anatomy museum to legitimise its place as a scientific institution, these were problematised by 'popular', commercial, and potentially corrupt motivations. It is my argument that Collins's novel plays with this tension, representing numerous bodyobjects that can be both immorally titillating and capable of disseminating important information, depending on the interpretation of the characters and the readers. The interpretation of knowledge from these intermedial bodies is used in *The Law and the Lady* as a means of solving mysteries and renewing respectability.

---

[23] Anon., *Illustrated Handbook*, 23–4.

Wilkie Collins and Museum Culture

As Alberti notes, there were 'many opportunities to encounter the natural world on display in late nineteenth-century Britain', especially in 'collections of things that were once alive', whether in national museums or in more commercially driven ventures.[24] A large public museum could accommodate 'hundreds of thousands of visitors in a year' while a private medical collection could teach doctors and surgeons year after year.[25] The depth to which nineteenth-century museums and the bodies they displayed permeated the cultural landscape is reflected and explored in Wilkie Collins's sensational detective novel *The Law and the Lady*. Like the cataloguing and narration of museum objects, Collins's novel also plays with this use of education as a means of deflecting criticisms around the sensational content of his work.

Collins's interest in museums is well documented. The trips he took to the continent with Charles Dickens and Augustus Egg in the 1850s, during which he encountered the galleries and museums of Florence and Rome,[26] would have provided ample opportunity to visit the popular tourist destination of La Specola. Dickens's earlier trip with his family particularly notes Florence's 'Museum of Natural History [La Specola], famous through the world for its preparations in wax [...] gradually ascending through separate organs of the human frame, up to the whole structure of that wonderful creation, exquisitely presented, as in recent death', considering it an artistic memento mori rather than a celebration of science.[27] Collins's *Memoirs of the Life of William Collins* (1848) represents his father's enjoyment of classical statuary, including 'the divine loveliness of parts of the Venus de Medici'.[28] William Collins's recollection of 'the defect wrought [...] by modern repairs; among which, her arms especially impressed him as being too long' echoes the fragmentary anatomy of the anatomical Venus. Collins's personal interest in and experience of museums resurfaces time and again in his fiction; contemporary reviews of *Armadale* (1864–1866) compare Lydia Gwilt to 'a waxwork figure', the medical realism of the sensation novel turning 'sensational

---

[24] Alberti, 'Museum Affect', 371. [25] Ibid., 391.
[26] Lyn Pykett, *Wilkie Collins* (Oxford: Oxford University Press, 2009), 15.
[27] Charles Dickens, *The Complete Works of Charles Dickens: Pictures from Italy and American Notes* (New York: Cosimo, 2009), 175.
[28] Wilkie Collins, *Memoirs of the Life of William Collins, Esq. R.A.*, (London: Longman et. al, 1848), accessed 4 March 2015, www.web40571.clarahost.co.uk/wilkie/etext/Memoirs.html.

characters into medical specimens exhibited in anatomical collections', with Gwilt compared by Talairach-Vielmas to 'the anatomical Venuses whose body parts could be lifted so as to reveal inner organs'.[29] London's Royal College of Surgeons, the home of anatomist John Hunter's famous museum, is mentioned repeatedly as the stomping ground of *Heart and Science*'s (1882) surgeon Ovid de Vere. Collectors and collecting populate Collins's novels, from Frederick Fairlie's hoarding of pictures, prints, and coins in *The Woman in White* (1859–1860) and Mrs Lecount's aquarium in *No Name* (1862), to moth trapping in *The Guilty River* (1886).

As the debate around the legitimacy or quackery of Kahn and his museum remained intense in the 1860s, it was likely to have inspired sensational narratives; certainly Collins's *The Law and the Lady* suggests an appropriation of (and dialogue with) the concerns facing the anatomy museum regarding collecting, knowledge, and respectability. The language of the book's reviews foregrounds these anxieties, voicing concern that Collins 'dwells in a world of strange and lurid imaginings' instead of emphasising 'the beauties and phenomena of the natural world', mirroring divisive responses to the anatomy museum.[30] The gothicisation of the displayed body in Collins's novels evidences the pervasiveness of the concerns of museum culture, yet *The Law and the Lady* drives at the same means of resolving the anxieties played out in museums and their publications by harnessing curatorial techniques, legitimising the collection of the body as an object of knowledge, framed and represented by text. The partible anatomical bodies – reconstructed, ordered, and narrated in museums – are reflected in both the fragmentary bodies of *The Law and the Lady*, and in the way the novel frames its body-objects as divisible pieces to be collected as clues and interpreted to shape knowledge. Just as museum visitors made sense of the body-object when it was juxtaposed with models, images, and text, the novel's central mystery is resolved by detective Valeria collecting bodies that are comprised of various media; the novel's objects – from the Major's book of hair to Dexter's portraits of flayed saints – frequently recall the corporeal, whether the objects are material bodies or not, and Valeria adopts a scientific and curatorial process in the interpretation of them.

---

[29] Talairach-Vielmas, 'Morbid Taste', 265.
[30] Quotation from *The World* taken from Catherine Peters, *The King of Inventors: A Life of Wilkie Collins* (Princeton: Princeton University Press, 2014), 377.

Valeria Macallan as Anatomical Specimen

The generative system was displayed in both respectable and more problematic anatomy museums, with female sexual organs a favourite of both curators and visitors.[31] The criticisms of impropriety levelled at anatomy museums were similar to those raised in contemporary criticism of the sensation novel: detective novels in particular 'invited the readers to uncover the secrets of the female characters as in a morbid striptease', while 'sensation novels appealed to readers in the same way as freak shows or medical collections'. Like the anatomy museum's salacious models, 'they promised to show readers what lay beneath the skirts of some of their heroines and villainesses, strongly relying on medical diagnosis to access the truth'.[32] The construction of bodies becomes analogous to specimen preservation or model construction in the context of the novel: Major Fitz-David attempts to preserve his youthful appearance through the application of wig and painted cheeks; detective protagonist Valeria paints her face to appeal to lecherous collector Fitz-David; the villainous Dexter carefully maintains his appearance; and the latter's Gothic paintings represent anatomised bodies. The anatomical Venus, in particular, embodies this aestheticised body-object, presenting an 'idealized kind of human anatomy complete with real hair, sensuously parted lips and lambent skin' composed of 'several layers of dissection' to expose the secrets contained within the body.[33]

The relationship between bodies and body-objects, especially the salacious anatomical Venus, resurfaces in Collins's novel. Valeria's constant reminders to compose herself, and the scene in which she is 'made up' by her maid, distort the boundaries between the techniques used on specimens, those used on living bodies, and the life-like appearance of anatomical models, classical statuary, and mannequins. Valeria's anatomising of her physical appearance finds new resonance when read alongside Kahn's catalogue, with its dissectible Venus de Medici. The novel's introduction of the detective protagonist positions her as both a displayed and interpreted body, and a figure employing the museal strategies of narration and curation:

> What does the glass show me? The glass shows a tall and slender young woman of three-and-twenty years of age. She is not at all the sort of person who attracts attention in the street, seeing that she fails to exhibit the

---

[31] Alberti, 'Museum Affect', 134. [32] Talairach-Vielmas, 'Morbid Taste', 263.
[33] Forde, 'Staging Science', 275–6.

> popular yellow hair and the popular painted cheeks. Her hair is black; dressed, in these later days (as it was dressed years since to please her father), in broad ripples drawn back from the forehead, and gathered into a simple knot behind (like the hair of the Venus de' Medici), so as to show the neck beneath. Her complexion is pale: except in moments of violent agitation there is no colour to be seen in her face. Her eyes are of so dark a blue that they are generally mistaken for black [...]. The whole picture, as reflected in the glass, represents a woman of some elegance, rather too pale, and rather too sedate and serious in her moments of silence and repose – in short, a person who fails to strike the ordinary observer at first sight; but who gains in general estimation, on a second, and sometimes even on a third, view. (10–11)

The corpse-like pallor of a woman in repose, 'too sedate [...] serious [...] silent', likens Valeria's body to ones that are displayed and anatomised, such as the wax Venuses. Despite Valeria's assertion that she 'fails to exhibit', there is an invitation to gaze at the carefully catalogued body parts, each brought to the reader's visual imagination. The description functions as a dissection, in which the reader can learn about Valeria through her anatomised body, guiding the gaze and aiding in the correct interpretation of the body (her eyes are not black, for example, but blue). The body is foregrounded as a site of knowledge, one that can reveal the circulatory system, through the colour (or lack of it) in Valeria's skin, and one that is carefully constructed through form and text. Like the Venus de Medici, a statue whose attempts to conceal her modesty simultaneously draw attention to what remains on show, the collected parts of Valeria's body tread a careful line between respectability and salacious exhibition.

If Valeria is to gain access to the Major's house-museum, which she visits in her hunt for information about her husband's case, she must understand the importance of the beautification of the body. The appeal to the viewer is not solely moral and educational, but aesthetic, blurring the boundaries between the legitimate and illegitimate display of the body. Valeria consults a chambermaid to achieve the 'transformation of my face' (57), her deathly paleness brightened with a 'touch of colour' (56), artistically rendered to match the bodies that are 'exhibit[ed]' in the streets in her previous description, with falsely flushed cheeks and carefully coiffed hair. The chambermaid's 'box of paints and powders' draws on the corpse-like beauty of the anatomical Venus through the 'false fairness' of the hair, the 'false colour' of the cheeks, and most of all the 'false brightness of the eyes' (57), recalling the carefully reconstructed specimen and the glassy gaze of the wax Venus. Collins's positioning of the Venus statuary of the Major's collection in close proximity to Valeria's carefully painted appearance creates a link between displayed art objects, the female body, and the morbid specimen.

Major Fitz-David's Collection

Uncanny anatomical bodies and their surrogates re-emerge in the context of the Major's house-museum. Talairach-Vielmas has noted how Valeria 'uncannily resembles all the other women, as if her identity could not be dissociated from the other female figures of the novel':

> Valeria reminds Major Fitz-David of Madame Mirliflore because of her 'prodigious tenacity of purpose', she has the same 'carriage of the head' as one lady, and 'the same creamy paleness' as another. Most importantly, her figure seems a replica of Sara Macallan's, a 'reflection of the dead and gone', which enables her to get acquainted with Sara's unrequited lover Dexter.[34]

Talairach-Vielmas's examples also reflect the novel's re-articulation of various parts into new wholes, and the comparative techniques and substitutions that occur throughout the novel between bodies, objects, and narration. The motif of the substitute (and, as Talairach-Vielmas notes, particularly the double) recurs throughout the Major's collection. Valeria's curiosity leads her to:

> two antique upright cabinets in buhl; containing rows of drawers, and supporting two fine reproductions (reduced in size) of the Venus Milo and the Venus Callipyge. I had Major Fitz-David's permission to do just what I pleased. I opened the six drawers in each cabinet and examined their contents without hesitation. (77)

Valeria carefully catalogues the items in the cabinet and notes the material construction of the two Venuses, their reduced size and their reproduced nature.

Like the anatomy museum, Collins's novel contains numerous replicas of the female body, with Valeria's entry into this space evoking anxieties about the room reserved for 'medical men only' in Kahn's museum. Major Fitz-David exhibits several artefacts portraying the fragmentary female body, requiring Valeria's curatorial eye and methodical, semi-scientific expertise to interpret them. Examining a broken vase, Valeria realises that on it 'was painted with exquisite delicacy a woman's head; representing a nymph, or a goddess', and questions 'by what accident' it had become

---

[34] Laurence Talairach-Vielmas, *Moulding the Female Body in Victorian Fairy Tales and Sensation Novels* (London: Routledge, 2016), 163.

broken, as well as why 'Major Fitz-David's face changed when he found that I had discovered the remains of his shattered work of Art in the cabinet drawer' (81). The interplay of both bodies and objects that defy categorisation is reflected in the anatomised figures portrayed on the vase, fragmentary 'remains' that predict the recovery of a letter that will shed light on the novel's central mystery. Valeria is able to discard the 'portraits of ladies' in favour of analysing the contents of the bookcase, and she determines to systematically 'begin the work of investigation at the top shelves' (84). While many of the Major's 'costly curiosities' are artistic and cultural objects, the language surrounding them is bodily, specialist, speaking of 'disinterring' these 'specimens' with a focus on morphology and 'shape' (86), reconstructing the past through found relics.

Valeria's search leads her to an upper shelf, where she discovers 'in solitary grandeur one object only – a gorgeously-bound book' (86). She catalogues the item's appearance, laying it before the reader for analysis and appraisal:

> The leaves were of the finest vellum, with tastefully designed illuminations round them. And what did these highly ornamented pages contain? To my unutterable amazement and disgust, they contained locks of hair let neatly into the centre of each page – with inscriptions beneath, which proved them to be love-tokens from various ladies, who had touched the Major's susceptible heart at different periods of his life. The inscriptions were written in other languages besides English; but they appeared to be equally devoted to the same curious purpose – namely, to reminding the Major of the dates at which his various attachments had come to an untimely end. Thus, the first page exhibited a lock of the lightest flaxen hair, with these lines beneath: 'My adored Madeline. Eternal constancy. Alas: July 22nd, 1839!' [...] More shades of hair, more inscriptions followed, until I was weary of looking at them. I put down the book disgusted with the creatures who had assisted in filling it – and then took it up again, by an afterthought. (87)

Although presented as a romantic souvenir, the book literalises the intermedial representation of the specimen: composed of body matter, with leaves of vellum (parchment made from calf skin) prophesying the papery skin of a Marquis stored in Dexter's house, the book articulates disparate body parts into a legible, comprehensible collection. The interior of the book finds analogues with its exterior, an analysis of its anatomy revealing its secrets: the lock on the outside of the book is explicable in relation to the bodily nature of the locks of hair it contains. The private nature of the book is in tension with its revelation to the reader-as-visitor through Valeria's use of museal language like 'exhibited' and 'adorned' to parade the body parts in a lengthy description.[35] Valeria's 'disgust' at these collected 'creatures' parallels the repulsion of many viewers of the displayed anatomical body. Nor is the collection displayed with science or education in mind. The bodies within are framed in the language of the earlier mortality-focused displays by both Valeria and the Major, 'mourned appropriately' with 'alas', expressing the pain of an 'untimely end'. The bodies are identified, with each item labelled and itemised – an embodied catalogue, a truly intermedial collection – the material object understood through its textual frame, with the book positioned as an eerie memento mori. The different types of hair and their associated experiences are collected and placed in comparative sequence; yet despite the rigorous method of collection, labelling, and display, this synthesised object-text-body is explored in personal language, revealing the Major's relationships: while the specimens collected here may not be respectable, the intermedial techniques certainly form a core body of knowledge. Valeria's visit to the Major's collection, and her examination of the hybrid body-book sits at the edge of 'proper' behaviour just like visits to institutions such as Kahn's museum. Yet this impropriety is diffused through similar means to those employed by popular attractions, as these mortal remains are educational, and Valeria correctly interprets and learns about them.

Dexter's Museum

A number of critics have paid particular attention to the 'catalogue of nightmare items' that constitutes Dexter's 'cabinet of curiosities', or house museum, 'the degenerate collection, which parodies and twists the organisation and public facing ethos of the nineteenth-century museum'.[36] Collins plays with what makes a museum respectable, presenting body-objects and intermedial interpretation, for 'the things that Dexter presents are consciously displayed, and invite the gaze of the viewer, preparing them with attached information and signage, pivotal tools of information and effacement at the curator's disposal'.[37] Dexter's house museum troubles

---

[35] Talairach-Vielmas suggests that the medical curiosities visible in sensation novels frequently function as 'tell-tale devices, laying bare the mechanisms of the detective narrative and recurrently suggesting images of the body opened, dissected and exhibited'. Talairach-Vielmas, 'Morbid Taste', 261.

[36] Jessica Lauren Allsop, *Curious Objects and Victorian Collectors: Men, Markets, Museums* (unpublished PhD thesis, University of Exeter, 2013), 124.

[37] Allsop, *Curious Objects*, 124.

the tools available for the legitimisation of the museum, borrowing and gothicising its exhibitionary techniques – ordering, cataloguing, lecturing, and labelling – while strengthening problematic associations with grave-robbing, disorder, and crime. Nor are Dexter's displays traditionally educative; his curatorship and interpretation of art objects instead foreground their charnel nature, problematising the kinds of information that can be understood by viewing them. Valeria's curatorial eye must work to correctly 'read' and interpret his collection, to use it to gain knowledge, to validate the time she spends in dubious locations, and to restore respectability to her husband.

Valeria's close observation of Dexter's collection forms a secondary interpretation of the bodies that he has already composed and labelled:

> The first of the Passion-pictures illustrated Revenge. A corpse, in fancy costume, lay on the bank of a foaming river, under the shade of a giant tree. An infuriated man, also in fancy costume, stood astride over the dead body, with his sword lifted to the lowering sky, and watched, with a horrid expression of delight, the blood of the man whom he had just killed, dripping slowly in a procession of big red drops down the broad blade of his weapon. The next picture illustrated Cruelty, in many compartments. In one, I saw a disembowelled horse savagely spurred on by his rider at a bull-fight. In another, an aged philosopher was dissecting a live cat, and gloating over his work. In a third, two Pagans politely congratulated each other on the torture of two saints: one saint was roasting on a gridiron; the other, hung up to a tree by his heels, had just been skinned, and was not quite dead yet. (229)

Dexter's paintings, presenting bodies opened to the gaze of the viewer, evoke medicalised 'specimens' in which it is possible to discern the interpretative acts obscured by the clinical presentation of the body-objects in anatomy museums. Instead of the careful composition and beautification that Kahn's cataloguing lends the anatomical Venus, and in Valeria's own 'painting' of her face, Dexter's paintings recall the disordered 'curiosities' that haunted the reputation of the anatomy museum. By combining text with body, Collins acknowledges the importance of subjective interpretation, of the internal beyond the bodily, suggesting that this does damage to neither the educational experience nor the material scientific evidence but is instead in dialogue with it.

The tensions surrounding the display of bodies in the anatomy museum remain in Dexter's collection, however, with the sexualised, consumeristic 'insatiability' for horrors paralleled in the literal consumption of organic matter in Dexter's kitchen:

> The same insatiable relish for horrors exhibited downstairs by the pictures in the hall, was displayed again here. The photographs hanging on the wall, represented the various forms of madness taken from the life. The plaster casts ranged on the shelf opposite, were casts (after death) of the heads of famous murderers. A frightful little skeleton of a woman hung in a cupboard, behind a glazed door, with this cynical inscription placed above the skull – 'Behold the scaffolding on which beauty is built!' In a corresponding cupboard, with the door wide open, there hung in loose folds a shirt (as I took it to be) of chamois leather. Touching it (and finding it to be far softer than any chamois leather that my fingers had ever felt before), I disarranged the folds, and disclosed a ticket pinned among them, describing the thing in these horrid lines: – 'Skin of a French Marquis, tanned in the Revolution of Ninety-Three. Who says the nobility are not good for something? They make good leather.' After this last specimen of my host's taste in curiosities I pursued my investigation no farther. (247)

Dexter's kitchen replicates and redisplays the bodies of the anatomy museum, each object capable of illustrating the 'various forms' of obscured pathology, specimens of 'madness' that are ominously 'taken from the life'. His collection and exhibition of anatomical objects is decidedly that of the improper, illicitly and morbidly entertaining popular anatomy museum, yet the techniques used to display these objects remain the same as those of the more respectable national scientific collections. The plaster casts are 'ranged' on the shelf, although their particular arrangement does not appear to serve any illustrative purpose, evoking the waxwork show rather than the putative aim of the anatomy museum, and recalling the association between anatomy and the criminal punishment of dissection. Instead of enlightening the viewer, the skeleton is 'frightful'; it may reveal the 'scaffolding' of the human form, but the accompanying inscription recalls the memento mori of the outmoded cabinet of curiosity rather than the contemporary scientific institution. As with much of Dexter's half-lit, Gothic house, the skin of the marquis is displayed not to present a clear understanding of it as an object but to *require* the interpretative label to make sense of it; even so, the label taxonomises the marquis, not in scientific terminology but in order to memorialise and anonymise him.

These curiosities, displayed in cabinet-like cupboards, may be sensational but they are nonetheless educational: Valeria's 'investigation' here interrogates these body-objects as 'specimens' of Dexter's 'taste', collectable clues through which she can understand his morbidity and madness. Collins's intermediality demonstrates that sensational bodies can also educate, interrogating the tensions surrounding salacious displays of body-parts and reinterpreting them through detective fiction. The bodies of the novel are displayed to readers to entertain, but Valeria's and Dexter's activities also encourage attempts to discover a link between displayed human matter and the truth of the novel's mystery.

Kahn's *Illustrated Handbook* borrows literary techniques and genres, from narration that segues into medical terminology to the poetry that attempts to cloak the anatomical Venus in an aura of respectability. The ephemera of Kahn's museum also enlighten the visitor, and allow him or her to better understand objects through image and text. Collins's showcasing of curatorial techniques as detective work – Valeria's self-description and her cataloguing of the Major's museum – enlightens both Valeria and the reader, and correspondingly makes an examination of bodily objects a more decorous pursuit, while the dubious bodies on display in Dexter's collection can educate Valeria as to Dexter's taste, yet not be fully defused of their sensational potential. Literary techniques play a major part in shaping nineteenth-century objects and their meaning, not entirely mitigating anatomical anxieties but repositioning them into new and respectable circumstances, allowing them to impart knowledge and solve mysteries rather than remain mere curiosities.

CHAPTER 4

Anatomical Culture, Body-Snatching, and Nineteenth-Century Gothic

Laurence Talairach

> All kinds of carcasses I have cut up,
> And the judgment now must be –
> But brothers I took care of you,
> So pray take care of me!
> I have made candles of infants' fat
> The Sextons have been my slaves,
> I have bottled babes unborn, and dried
> Hearts and livers from rifled graves.
> And my Prentices now will surely come
> And carve me bone from bone,
> And I who have rifled the dead man's grave
> Shall never have rest in my own.
> Robert Southey, 'A Surgeon's Warning' (1796)

In a satirical etching by the Scottish artist Isaac Cruikshank, *Resurrection [sic] Men Disturbed, or a Guilty Conscience Needs No Accuser* (c. 1794), six men dig up corpses in a churchyard. The naked corpses, put into sacks, are carried to a nearby cart where cadavers have already been installed. The body-snatcher in the centre, with a wig and a tricorn hat, is undoubtedly a (Scottish) doctor, while his terrified accomplices, their hair standing on end, implore angels to protect them. On the left-hand side, a mule, bellowing, makes one of the diggers start with fear. Another digger, further, carries his own father on his back. William Austen's *The Anatomist Overtaken by the Watch . . . Carrying off Miss W– in a Hamper* (1773) is another example of eighteenth-century caricatures of anatomists in search of anatomical material. Hinting at William Hunter's lectures (a copy of which lies on the ground), the engraving features a gentleman, similarly wearing a tricorn hat and a physician's stick, who is running away, denounced by the body-snatcher who has just been arrested with his bounty. In another watercolour by Thomas Rowlandson, entitled *Resurrection Men* (n.d.), the anatomist is no longer caught in the act by the watch but by an animated skeleton; the word 'Resurgam' ('I will rise again') on the coffin lid in the foreground humorously blurs the boundaries between the fictional and often supernatural world of the Gothic and that of medical practice, ultra-realistic in its treatment of human corpses.

These three graphic examples linking the medical field with the body trade are stereotypical of popular views of medical professionals in the second half of the eighteenth century.[1] Indeed, if modern anatomy dates back to the early modern period and the work of the anatomist Andreas Vesalius, the creation of anatomy as a discipline in the long eighteenth century was part of the Enlightenment project, the discipline flourishing then as never before or since.[2] The College of Surgeons, founded in 1745 after the separation from the College of Barbers, was dissolved in 1796; a new Royal Charter established the Royal College of Surgeons in 1800. The last decades of the eighteenth century also witnessed the foundation of the great museum collections of anatomy and comparative anatomy, such as that of the Scottish surgeon and anatomist John Hunter, purchased by the government in 1799 and which founded the basis of the Hunterian Museum at the Royal College of Surgeons in London. The fast developments of anatomy in the eighteenth century were due to several factors: an increased interest in human anatomy and physiology, on the one hand, and the growth of medical schools, both public and private, on the other. These involved a rise in the demand for corpses: unlike the teaching hospitals, private anatomy schools taught anatomy by dissection without being legally entitled to have access to corpses.[3] Indeed, unlike many European countries, in England, just like in Scotland, Ireland, or North America, the bodies of criminals, prostitutes, or paupers could not be used for medical purposes before the 1832 Anatomy Act. The latter radically reformed anatomy, granting anatomists the right to use unclaimed pauper bodies from workhouses.

The beginning of anatomy legislation in Britain may be traced back to 1540, when Henry VIII allowed anatomists the use of the bodies of four hanged felons per year. This allowance was extended to six by Charles II,

---

[1] For more on late eighteenth-century caricaturists and medical practice see Fiona Haslam, *From Hogarth to Rowlandson: Medicine in Art in Eighteenth-Century Britain* (Liverpool: Liverpool University Press, 1996).

[2] On this point, see in particular Andrew Cunningham, *The Anatomist Anatomis'd: An Experimental Discipline in Enlightenment Europe* (Aldershot: Ashgate, 2010).

[3] As Ruth Richardson explains, private anatomy schools generally provided supplementary tuition of anatomy to students studying surgery at the hospital schools, the latter failing to deliver proper surgical training. Apothecaries who could not afford the hospital teaching fees also trained there. Ruth Richardson, *Death, Dissection and the Destitute* (1987; Chicago and London: The University of Chicago Press, 2000), 40.

until the 1752 Murder Act granted anatomists the use of all the criminals hanged at Tyburn and later Newgate from 1783. Even after the 1752 Murder Act, rioting scenes were frequent at the gallows as anatomists and surgeons struggled for the criminals' bodies, some of them having acquired the corpse even before the execution of the sentence and looking to prevent their bounty escaping in the hands of fellow practitioners.[4] Among the best known cases are those of Joshua Naples (the leader of a gang of resurrectionists in London[5]), of William Burke and William Hare (convicted of throttling sixteen victims to provide anatomical material to the Edinburgh anatomist Robert Knox[6]), and of John Bishop and Thomas Williams (sentenced to death in 1831 for the murder of a young Italian boy, who had been exhibiting white mice in the streets of London).

Although cases of body-snatching had been reported in Britain as early as in the seventeenth century,[7] in the last decades of the eighteenth century and early nineteenth century, and up until 1832, grave-robbery led to much public outcry (especially in Scotland where surgeons regularly stole the bodies of hanged criminals) and was reported in broadsides and newspapers.[8] The cases also regularly led to near-riot situations, the resurrectionists sometimes even asking to be put in gaol so as to escape from the violent mob.[9] William Hunter warned his students, for instance, that 'in a country where liberty disposes the people to licentiousness and outrage, and where anatomists are not legally supplied with dead bodies [...] it is to be hoped that you will be on your guard and, out of doors, speak with caution of what may be passing here, especially with respect to dead bodies'.[10]

---

[4] Ibid., 52.
[5] Joshua Naples was active as a body-snatcher from 1811 to 1832, supplying all the main schools of anatomy in London. When the Anatomy Act made his activity superfluous, Naples became a 'servant' in the dissecting room at St Thomas' Hospital (Richardson, *Death, Dissection and the Destitute*, 40, 61). Among the names of famous anatomists which appear in his diary are those of Abernethy, Brookes, and Bell. James Blake Bailey, *The Diary of a Resurrectionist, 1811–12, to which are Added an Account of the Resurrection Men in London and a Short History of the Passing of the Anatomy Act* (London: Swan Sonnenschein, 1896).
[6] Richardson, *Death, Dissection and the Destitute*; Tim Marshall, *Murdering to Dissect: Grave-Robbing, Frankenstein and the Anatomy Literature* (Manchester: Manchester University Press, 1995).
[7] Richardson, *Death, Dissection and the Destitute*, 54.
[8] See *The Trial of William Burke and Helen M'Dougal before the High Court of Judiciary at Edinburgh on Wednesday, December 24, 1828 for the Murder of Margery Campbell, or Docherty taken in shorthand by Mr. John Macnee* (Edinburgh: Robert Buchanan, William Hunter, John Stevenson; London: Balwick & Cradock, 1828), preface.
[9] Richardson mentions several cases, the police sometimes needing to escort the body-snatchers to the magistrate to avoid attacks by the mob. *Death, Dissection and the Destitute*, 85–90.
[10] William Hunter, *Two introductory lectures, Delivered by Dr. William Hunter, to his Last Course of Anatomical Lectures, at his Theatre in Windmill Street: as they were left Corrected for the Press by*

The burking cases and their trials took place against the backdrop of a change in the law that would grant anatomists access to the unclaimed bodies of the workhouse: the 1832 Anatomy Act. As Ruth Richardson contends, the Select Committee was appointed by the House of Commons in the spring of 1828 to 'inquire into the manner of obtaining Subjects of Dissection in the Schools of Anatomy', thus before the discovery of the Burke and Hare murders,[11] more as a reaction against the shortage of bodies for dissection than the issue of grave-robbing itself. The increase of anatomical material would limit the number of medical students fleeing to Paris for their education, where corpses available for dissection were much more numerous. The Act would also lead to a rise of medical students in the hospital schools and a decrease in private and provincial anatomical schools, since only the students' anatomical certificates delivered by schools and universities recognised by the Royal College of Surgeons through bye-laws passed in 1823 and 1824 were officially approved.[12]

It is especially in the 1820s that anatomists, such as John Abernethy and Thomas Southwood Smith, pressed for anatomy reform, highlighting the centrality of anatomical knowledge in medical science and the therapeutic applications of dissection.[13] In 1819, as Richardson explains, Abernethy 'had raised the idea of using paupers' bodies' in his *Hunterian Oration*.[14] For him, 'opportunities of dissection should [...] be afforded [to medical practitioners], 'anatomical knowledge [being] the only foundation on which the structure of medical science can be built'. 'Without this', he claimed, 'we should but increase the sufferings of those afflicted with diseases, and endanger their lives'.[15] A few years later, in an article published in *The Westminster Review*, Southwood Smith stressed as well the extent to which 'anatomical knowledge [was] the means of saving human life'.[16] The significance of anatomical knowledge and practice within the medical field typifies the shift to a much more empirical means of practicing medicine and underlines the rise of pathological anatomy.

---

himself. To which are Added, Some Papers Relating to Dr. Hunter's Intended Plan, for Establishing a Museum in London, for the Improvement of Anatomy, Surgery, and Physic (London: J. Johnson, 1784), 108–9. Quoted in Cunningham, *The Anatomist Anatomis'd*, 231.

[11] *Commons Journal* 22:4 (1828), 260, quoted in Richardson, *Death, Dissection and the Destitute*, 101.
[12] Ibid.
[13] John Abernethy, *Hunterian Oration* (London: s.n., 1819); Thomas Southwood Smith, 'The Use of the Dead to the Living', *The Westminster Review* 2 (1824), 59–97, reprinted in Thomas Southwood Smith, *The Use of the Dead to the Living* (Albany: Websters and Skinners, 1827).
[14] Abernethy, *Hunterian Oration*, 108.   [15] Ibid., 159.
[16] Southwood Smith, *The Use of the Dead to the Living*, 8.

That body-snatching was closely related to changes in definitions of the body and in the understanding of disease stands to reason; in the eighteenth and nineteenth centuries, dissection increasingly became synonymous with medical knowledge, as the Scottish George MacGregor made explicit in 1884:

> This practice of violating sepulchres, which must ever be regarded as one of the foulest blots on Scottish civilization, may be said to have had several contributing causes. The principal of these is admitted on all hands to have been the discovery on the part of the medical faculty that the knowledge they possessed of the human frame was founded rather upon uncertain tradition than upon empirical science; that they were practically ignorant of anatomy; and that if they hoped to make any advance in the art of healing human diseases they must devote more attention to a minute study of the dead subject.[17]

When the fashion for Gothic romances was launched, with the publication of Horace Walpole's *The Castle of Otranto* in 1764, and throughout the Romantic period, therefore, corpses were in constant need in the medical field. Gothic romances, especially those published by the Minerva Press, regularly mediated such uses and abuses of human bodies. As a case in point, Mrs Carver's *The Horrors of Oakendale Abbey* (1797) places body-snatchers at the heart of the Gothic plot with graphic horror and the corporeality of the cadaver replacing the supernatural. The evolution of the Gothic as a genre, on the one hand, and the increasing centrality of anatomy in medical science, on the other, gradually shaped what Michael Sappol terms 'an anatomical gothic' – the medical world and the Gothic making use of similar elements and tropes, notably related to life, death, and the boundaries of the self.[18] As a result, if fears of body violation are undeniable Gothic topoi, fears of having one's body stolen, manipulated, cut up, sold, and dissected did not solely belong to the province of Gothic literature from the end of the eighteenth century to the first decades of the nineteenth, especially (but not exclusively) in the years before the passage of the 1832 Anatomy Act.

On the literary scene, one of the most famous body-snatchers of the first decades of the nineteenth century is certainly Mary Shelley's Frankenstein, who haunts cemeteries and dissection rooms for body parts and fits the

---

[17] George Mac Gregor, *The History of Burke and Hare, and of the Resurrectionist Times* (Glasgow and London: Thomas D. Morison; Hamilton, Adams, 1884), 14.

[18] Michael Sappol, *A Traffic of Dead Bodies: Anatomy and Embodied Social Identity in Nineteenth-Century America* (2002; Princeton and Oxford: Princeton University Press, 2004), 303.

portrait of the enlightened anatomist to perfection. Though no material evidence confirms Shelley had knowledge of the pleas by Abernethy for reform,[19] Frankenstein's 'slippage between the surgeon, the dissector, the murderer'[20] indicates the author's awareness of contemporary debates over the figure of the anatomist and current anxieties related to anatomical practice. The Gothic atmosphere of the novel overtly draws upon fears related to medical practice at a time when the legislation regulating the uses of the human body became part of a public debate.[21] As his creature becomes a serial killer, Frankenstein feels, revealingly, guilty of the crimes ('the crimes which had their source in me';[22] 'they all died by my hands' [189]; 'I am the assassin of those most innocent victims; they died of my machinations' [190]). He is also eventually accused of the murder of his friend, Henry Clerval, before being freed from the criminal charge, like several anatomists of the time suspected of participating in a traffic in bodies. In addition, Frankenstein's experiment seems directly inspired by Giovani Aldini's (1762–1834) research on human corpses, especially when, on 17 January 1803, Aldini publicly experimented upon the corpse of the freshly hanged Thomas Forster at the Royal College of Surgeons in London, applying electrodes to various parts of his body and making the jaw quiver and one eye open.[23]

Although some of the details concerning Frankenstein's body-snatching often lack realism – such as when Frankenstein collects anatomical material over a few months in London before travelling to Scotland without caring about the effects of putrefaction – Frankenstein's traffic in bodies is most often presented indirectly, as when he appears as a body-snatcher in one of his dreams – or rather, nightmares – just after the creature's birth:

---

[19] Sharon Ruston, however, identifies links between Frankenstein and Abernethy, notably his vitalist notions. *Creating Romanticism: Case Studies in the Literature, Science and Medicine of the 1790s* (Basingstoke: Palgrave Macmillan, 2013), 126.
[20] Marshall, *Murdering to Dissect*, 13.   [21] This is the point that Marshall makes in ibid.
[22] Mary Shelley, *Frankenstein; or the Modern Prometheus*, ed. Maurice Hindle (1818/1831; London: Penguin, 2003), 189. All subsequent references to this edition are given in the text. Anatomists and surgeons were seen as the 'suspected accomplice[s] or encourager[s]', as in this 1829 article published in *Blackwood's Edinburgh Magazine* on Dr Knox's involvement in the Burke and Hare case: 'Dr Knox [...] stands', the writer argues, 'in that of the suspected accomplice or encourager of unparalleled murders'; 'Noctes Ambrosianae', *Blackwood's Edinburgh Magazine* 25 (1829), 371–400 (388).
[23] Anne K. Mellor, *Mary Shelley: Her Life, Her Fiction, Her Monsters* (1988; London: Routledge, 1989), 105. Shelley may have heard about the experiment through John William Polidori (1795–1821), who was Lord Byron's personal physician and travelling companion and who had studied medicine at Edinburgh (Mellor, *Mary Shelley*, 107).

> I thought I saw Elizabeth, in the bloom of health, walking in the streets of Ingolstadt. Delighted and surprised, I embraced her, but as I imprinted the first kiss on her lips, they became livid with the hue of death; her features appeared to change, and I thought that I held the corpse of my dead mother in my arms; a shroud enveloped her form, and I saw the grave-worms crawling in the folds of the flannel. (59)

The corpse of the mother, wrapped up in the shroud and already infested by worms, functions as an unconscious confession, suggesting that his theft of corpses may be what the narrative tries to repress.

Following in the footsteps of Shelley's doctor, several tales of terror published in *Blackwood's Edinburgh Magazine* in the 1820s and 1830s capitalised upon body-snatching and the underworld of Georgian medicine. Tales such as John Galt's 'The Buried Alive' (1821) underpinned the relationship between medical practice and body-snatching, establishing, in so doing, the clichés of the literature of terror which later marked Victorian popular fiction. In Galt's tale, the narrator, who suffers from catalepsy, is buried alive because of a medical misdiagnosis. Yet the protagonist is ironically rescued by resurrection men who take his body to an anatomist's for a demonstration. However, before dissecting the subject, the anatomist practises a galvanic experiment on the narrator's body, leading his eyes to open, while the knife piercing his bosom puts an end to his trance. The awakening of the patient on the anatomist's table, found both in fictional and real narratives, became a staple of the nineteenth-century tale of terror.

Megan Coyer's study of the relationship between medical culture and the periodical press in the early nineteenth century points out how some periodicals, such as *Blackwood's Edinburgh Magazine*, used contributors who were medical writers and who developed both their medical and literary careers, especially between the founding of the periodical in 1817 and the death of William Blackwood in 1834. Looking at the tale of terror as 'a form of hybrid "medico-popular" writing',[24] thereby blurring boundaries between literature and medicine, Coyer highlights the way in which the tale of terror provided a new perspective on the medical case histories that generally appeared in periodicals such as *The Edinburgh Magazine*, offering in particular the patient's viewpoint on trauma rather than that of an authoritative observer. As she argues, the stress on the Gothic in such first-person narratives, and the focus on the patient, both mark 'a significant shift in the treatment of medical subject matter' and

---

[24] Megan Coyer, *Literature, Medicine and the Nineteenth-Century Periodical Press: Blackwood's Edinburgh Magazine, 1817–1858* (Edinburgh: Edinburgh University Press, 2017), 37.

represent 'a significant innovation in Gothic form'.[25] By using a Gothic aesthetic (in particular through portraits of human suffering), these tales, Coyer contends, may be viewed as 'a subversion of the developmental trajectory of the medical case history of the nineteenth century'.[26] Coyer suggests, in addition, that the representation of more and more sensible physicians in such tales of terror paved the way for the medical man of the highest ideals typically found in Victorian literature,[27] bridging therefore the gap between Georgian satire on the medical profession and the Victorian idealisation, often misplaced – as we see in Keir Waddington's and Martin Willis's Chapter 7 analysis – of its practitioners.

Short stories hinging upon body-snatching often contrasted views on medical education and practice, however, blurring, in so doing, clear-cut portraits of contemporary medical practitioners. In 'On the Pleasures of Body-Snatching',[28] published in the *Monthly Magazine* in April 1827, the cold and clinical view of a student of anatomy on body-snatching is weighed against that of one of his accomplices, who is a stranger to the medical profession. From the title onwards, the short story promotes the therapeutic use of dissection. The characters set up a society of Resurrectionists, made up of young surgeons and students of anatomy, and the narrator gradually learns to become acquainted with body-snatching and used to encountering the corpses of people he knows on the anatomist's table. However, the end of the short story contrasts the reaction of the narrator with that of a sailor they have persuaded to help them steal more bodies. Unsurprisingly, the sailor, engaged to a young girl, Susan, soon realises that the corpse he has helped steal is that of his beloved:

> By the time we had got the coffin open, however, and its contents deposited in the sack, his spirit seemed to desert him altogether; and while we were filling up the grave, and putting matters *in statu quo*, he leant in silence against a tomb-stone. When we were preparing to depart, I went up and shook him violently, to rouse him from the trance in which he seemed to have fallen. '*It is a woman!*' said he, at length, in a whisper, so deep and

---

[25] Ibid., 43.
[26] Ibid., 47–8. Coyer draws on Meegan Kennedy's description of the rise of a clinical realist (and objective) discourse in medical case histories and a rejection of earlier sensational and Gothic narratives in medical writing. (Meegan Kennedy, *Revising the Clinic: Vision and Representation in Victorian Medical Narrative and the Novel* [Columbus: Ohio State University Press, 2010]).
[27] It is important to note here, however, that Coyer only refers to realist novels, from Martineau's *Deerbrock* (1839) to Trollope's *Dr Thorne* (1858) and George Eliot's *Middlemarch* (1871).
[28] Unsigned, 'On the Pleasures of Body-Snatching', *Monthly Magazine* 3:16 (1827), 355–65. All subsequent references to this text are given in the text.

horror-struck, that I instinctively let him go. [...] 'A woman, by G—!', cried he; 'aye, and a fair one, too – beautiful even in death! Her auburn ringlets hanging, in love-like languishment, over her neck of snow – her pencilled eyebrows – her dimpled chin – her modest lips, cold even as chastity!' At every disjointed sentence, the stranger advanced a step nearer: till, at length, when the fair and dead face came completely under his view, his hands met with a sound like the report of a pistol – and, in something between a shriek and a convulsive groan, he exclaimed, 'It is *Susan*!' – and fell senseless on the floor. (364–5)

The short story hence seemingly advocates the crucial part played by body-snatching for medical education and progress the better to focus on the feelings of the bereaved sailor and the callousness of body-snatchers – who are here all medical students eager to practise dissection. The contrast between the two points of view enables Galt to evoke sadism and necrophilia, forcefully galvanising thereby the Gothic narrative: although the narrator tells the sailor that 'a dead body [is] of no sex' (364), the horror-struck man is 'rouse[d]' from his trance when faced with the figure of his chaste Susan. The latter's body is painstakingly detailed, the dashes in the narrative constructing a blason which fetishizes even more the parts of the female body, as if anatomising it. This idea is further stressed by the mention of the sailor's 'disjointed sentence(s)', hinting as it does at the process of fragmentation. The focus on the hair and face, moreover, both recalls eighteenth-century Italian wax anatomical models (similarly constructed as 'languish[ing]' sleeping princesses with pencilled eyebrows and seemingly denying death[29]) and lets the reader imagine the rest of the naked body on the table, since the sailor's gaze is gradually sweeping down the corpse. The scene climaxes with the sailor's 'convulsive groan' and a fainting which both hint at sexual orgasm followed by the sailor's *petite mort*. Blurring pain and pleasure from the title on, the short story therefore plays with the eroticism of the 'fair and dead face', the female corpse both epitomising virginal femininity (safely protected from temptation by death, as 'cold even as chastity' suggests) and being eroticised.

The play with contrasting views on the practice of anatomy and body-snatching is fairly similar in another short story published in *Blackwood's Edinburgh Magazine* in December 1856. In 'A Recent Confession of an Opium-Eater', the narrator, intoxicated with laudanum, falls victim to

---

[29] Anatomical wax models were often represented as sleeping female bodies, especially the models from the Bologna and Florentine schools; wax modellers such as Joseph Towne (1806–1879), working at Guy's hospital in nineteenth-century London, proposed more ghastly reproductions of corpses.

body-snatchers. Taken to the resurrectionists' den, he reflects on the actual uses of his own body, as an opium-eater and therefore a potentially interesting medical case:

> The thrill of horror which now naturally passed through my heart, did not prevent me from seeing the case in all its philosophic bearings. My natural impulse was, of course, self-preservation; but still, as a philosopher, I was bound to consider also the interests of the public. I had every reason to believe that my organs and functions had become so vitiated by the use of opium, as to insure, to him who should lay bare, with scientific knife and anxious inquiry, this earthly tabernacle, the disclosure of the most remarkable phenomena. Had I then, as a citizen, the right to withhold this perishable frame, which would inevitably be dissolved in a few years, and perhaps under far less important conditions (for I might leave off opium, and, thus restoring my body to a healthy condition, render it comparatively valueless), when I might, by submitting to the fate designed for me, remain for ages, in spirits of wine, a monument of opium-eating?[30]

Informed by anatomical tropes (patent in the 'thrill' of horror, recalling the nervous system, or in images of penetration ['passed through']), the passage defines the body as the locus of secret knowledge ('lay bare', 'disclosure'). The narrator's 'philosophical' view of his own situation is significant in the way in which it promotes dissection and the practice of body-snatching by constructing the victim of medical practice as a valuable medical case forever displayed as a wet specimen. The irony which pervades the passage reaches a pinnacle at the end of the short story when the narrator, having managed to stupefy the resurrectionists with laudanum, escapes, but takes time beforehand to indulge in an opium trance. The final part of the short story re-works Thomas De Quincey's *Confessions of an English Opium-Eater* (1821), as the narrator offers his body for anatomical dissection as an interesting medical case.[31] The narrator imagines, indeed, that Escalupius, Galen, Hippocrates, Agrippa, Garth, Harvey, Hunter, and Astley Cooper are about to dissect his brain, liberating thereby his genius thoughts. Through the pleasure of the opium-eater in visualising his own dissection, as well as reflection on the benefits of dissection, the short story, narrated from the viewpoint of the victim, thus seemingly supports anatomy and the uses of human anatomical material

---

[30] Sir Edward Bruce Hamley, 'A Recent Confession of an Opium-Eater', *Blackwood's Edinburgh Magazine* 80:494 (1856), 629–36 (636).
[31] Like the tales of terror which made the fame of *Blackwood's*, De Quincey's *Confessions of an English Opium-Eater*, although published in the *London Magazine* in 1821, was originally intended for *Blackwood's*. Coyer, *Literature, Medicine and the Nineteenth-Century Periodical Press*, 37.

the better to play on the grotesque. Yet, with its shift from a terrified to an elated victim and its transformation of the victim into a megalomaniac, the short story also illuminates the evolution of medical Gothic narratives in the first decades of the nineteenth century. The blurring of clear-cut categories and the complexification of the roles of victim and/or villain are telling here, for they increasingly marked the figure of the Victorian body-snatcher, as shall be seen.

Indeed, around the time when the second edition of *Frankenstein* (1818) was published, Samuel Warren published short stories in *Blackwood's Magazine* from August 1830 to October 1837. Published in three volumes in 1838 under the title *Passages from the Diary of a Late Physician*,[32] the tales seemingly recorded various medical cases the narrator – a physician – was faced with. Among these cases is an episode of body-snatching. Entitled 'Grave Doings',[33] as if to play upon the physician's sense of responsibility, the tale nonetheless brings home the pivotal role of grave-robbing in medical research, education, and practice. It records the 'first and last exploit' of the medical practitioner 'in the way of body-stealing' (I, 321), but makes explicit the therapeutic part that dissection plays in medical research:

> My gentle reader – start not at learning that I have been, in my time, a resurrectionist. Let not this appalling word, this humiliating confession, conjure up in your fancy a throng of vampire-like images and associations, or earn your 'Physician's' dismissal from your hearts and hearths. It is your own groundless fears, my fair trembler – your own superstitious prejudices – that have driven me, and will drive many others of my brethren, to such dreadful doings as those hereafter detailed. Come, come – let us have one word of reason between us on the abstract question – and then for my tale. You expect us to cure you of disease, and yet deny us the only means of learning *how*! You would have us bring you the ore of skill and experience, yet forbid us to break the soil or sink a shaft! Is this fair, *fair* reader? Is this reasonable? (I, 321)

The stress on the significance of autopsy for medical progress highlights new theories on pathology and the localisation of the seats of disease (organs and tissues were interpreted rather than the constituents of the body, such as blood, and urine). Far from being a Gothic villain or

---

[32] Samuel Warren, *Passages from the Diary of a Late Physician*, 5th ed., 3 vols. (1834; Edinburgh: William Blackwood & Sons; London: T. Cadell, 1838). Subsequent references to this edition will be given in the text.

[33] Samuel Warren, 'Grave Doings', in *Passages from the Diary of a Late Physician*, vol. 1, 321–38.

vampire, the body-snatcher is no heartless or cruel being, and should not, as the physician begs, be 'dismiss[ed] from [his clients'] hearts and hearths'. This insight into the reality of the difficulties of medical practice aims to revise the readers' beliefs in medical practice (illuminated here by the Gothic paraphernalia, patent in terms like 'confession', 'fears', 'trembler', 'superstitious', or 'vampire'), and presents actual mysteries, such as the case of a heart disease that defies diagnosis, as the mysteries which ought to spur people's interest instead:

> A young and rather interesting female was admitted a patient at the hospital I attended; her case baffled all our skill, and her symptoms even defied diagnosis. *Now*, it seemed an enlargement of the heart – now, an ossification – then this, that, and the other; and at last it was plain we knew nothing at all about the matter – no, not even whether her disorder was organic or functional, primary or symptomatic – or whether it *was* really the heart that was at fault. She received no benefit at all under the fluctuating schemes of treatment we pursued, and at length fell into dying circumstances. (I, 322)

The slippery quality of the external symptoms makes the search for internal symptoms compulsory, thereby rendering the post-mortem examination essential. The patient's family, understanding that the surgeons wish to keep the patient in hospital until she dies in order to dissect her ask for the patient to be carried home. However, as the practitioners contend: 'we can get hold of her [. . .] as easily if she die with [her family] as with us' (I, 322). Body-snatching is thus presented as part of medical practice, and the narrator boasts about it as 'the *eclat* with which the successful issue of the affair would be attended among [their] fellow-students' (I, 323). The body-snatching episode is therefore ready to unravel. Yet, the thrilling adventure, set at midnight in the dark, becomes farce-like as the characters, believing they have been discovered, all run away in different directions, the porter even falling into a newly opened grave. The story thus ends with the narrator's swearing never to practise body-snatching again, the collection as a whole promoting an increasingly sensitive figure of the medical practitioner/body-snatcher.[34]

---

[34] This is what Coyer suggests in her reading of Warren's *Diary*. However, as I have argued elsewhere, the footnote added at the end of the short story undermines the medical practitioner's feelings of repentance. See Laurence Talairach-Vielmas, '"I have bottled babes unborn": The Gothic, Medical Collections and Nineteenth-Century Culture', *Gothic Studies* 17:1 (2015), 28–42. Moreover, as J. B. Bailey argues, claiming that the story was probably founded on fact, the short story stresses more the medical practitioner's interest in the valuable pathological specimen than his search for a corpse to dissect. Bailey, *The Diary of a Resurrectionist*, 15–16.

Warren's short story, although published after the passing of the 1832 Anatomy Act, shows that body-snatching, as an iconic Gothic motif, endured. Indeed, throughout the nineteenth century body-snatching failed to become that 'stuff of the old medicine',[35] before the closing down of private anatomy schools and the opening of the teaching hospitals. On the contrary, as a topos of the literature of terror emblematising fears related to the violation of the body and the fragmentation of the self, it continually resurfaced in mid-century Gothic. However, body-snatching was used more to purvey a social discourse than to emphasise the medical reality of the day, as the novels of G. W. M. Reynolds and Charles Dickens illustrate.

Famous for his supernatural novels, such as *Faust* (1845–1846), *Wagner, the Wehr-Wolf* (1846–1847), or *The Necromancer* (1852), Reynolds was also known for his urban Gothic series, *The Mysteries of London* (1844–1848) and *The Mysteries of the Courts of London* (1848–1856), which located horror in contemporary London. As a political activist much involved with Chartism, Reynolds gave shape to the type of urban Gothic that Dickens's novels later flourished on, offering a bleak and terrifying picture of London squalor and the living conditions of the working classes. In Reynolds's urban Gothic, the London underworld is a world of dirt, disease, and death, where body-snatchers prosper. Anatomical culture informs, indeed, *The Mysteries of London*, which pivots around the figure of Anthony Tidkins, the Resurrection Man, who persecutes the main male character, Richard Markham, throughout the first volume. Interestingly, the body-snatcher's trafficking in cadavers crystallises Reynolds's discussion of British commodity culture and political economy more generally.

Corpses (or 'stiff 'uns') proliferate throughout the narrative; they are stolen, exchanged, measured, examined by surgeons (or 'Sawbones') who become forensic experts to find out the causes of death; they are valuable commodities or dangerous decomposing matter.[36] Reynolds's series as a whole abounds with references to sensational cases of body-snatching, such as the 1831 case of the Italian boy, murdered by Bishop and Williams (I, 126), and the term 'burking' is used now and then (I, 838). Body-snatching enables Reynolds to combine graphic horror and sensational

---

[35] Ruth Richardson, *The Making of Mr. Gray's Anatomy. Bodies, Books, Fortune, Fame* (Oxford: Oxford University Press, 2008), 122.

[36] Plentiful details are given concerning the process of decomposition throughout the novel, from the 'body bugs' which come out of the corpse to the smelly 'fatty fluid' and gas produced by the putrefying cadaver. George W. M. Reynolds, *The Mysteries of London*, 2 vols. (Kansas City: Valancourt, 2012), vol. 1, 912–14. Subsequent references to this edition will be given in the text.

realism. Moreover, the narrative reflects contemporary medical practitioners' difficulty in having access to corpses,[37] even presenting surgeons who feel guilty about their body-snatching activities.

But if the medical practitioners do not appear that much as accomplices in crime, the Resurrection Man, as a clichéd Gothic villain, is nonetheless delineated in sometimes intriguing ways. The 'cadaverous-looking' body-snatcher, with his shaggy brows, is presented from the beginning as 'a villain stained with every crime – a murderer of the blackest dye – a wretch whose chief pursuit [is] the violation of the tomb' (I, 915). Yet, Reynolds's characterisation is telling through his allusions to Shelley's iconic Gothic villain. The Resurrection Man's story, located at the heart of the first volume, shapes Anthony Tidkins as a double of Frankenstein's Creature. Making complex as it does the roles of victim and victimiser – or mixing the figures of the resurrected creature with that of the resurrectionist – the embedded first-person narrative sheds a new light on the Gothic villain. For the narrative contains the record of Tidkins's struggle against poverty and alienation, shaping the body-snatcher as a victim of capitalist society forced into crime – as a product of a society that 'persecute[s]' (I, 545) the poor for fear they might rise against the rich. As a result, as Tidkins seeks to be avenged on the men who starved him, the figure of the body-snatcher undermines the construction of the Gothic villain and villainy more generally. As in *Frankenstein*, moreover, the network of Gothic motifs shapes Tidkins's quest for identity. The realm of anatomy and its use of nameless or stolen dead bodies and body parts become pivotal to the plot, since Reynolds locates the recognition scene of melodrama in the anatomy theatre when the resurrection man realises that his own beloved lies on the dissecting table:

> We carried the corpse into the surgery, and laid it upon a table. 'You are sure it is the right one ?' said the surgeon. – 'It is the body from the grave that you pointed out', answered my father. – 'The fact is', resumed the surgeon, 'that this is a very peculiar case. Six days ago, a young female rose in the morning in perfect health; that evening she was a corpse. I opened her, and found no traces of poison; but her family would not permit me to carry the examination any further. They did not wish her to be hacked about. Since her death some love-letters have been found in her drawer; but there is no name attached to any of them. [...] I am therefore anxious to make another and more searching investigation than on the former

---

[37] 'I would not for the world that the family of the deceased should learn that this tomb has been violated. Suspicions would immediately fall upon me; for it would be remembered how earnestly I desired to open the body, and how resolutely my request was refused' (I, 348).

occasion, into the cause of death. But I will soon satisfy myself that this is indeed the corpse I mean'. – With these words the surgeon tore away the shroud from the face of the corpse. I cast an anxious glance upon the pale, cold, marble countenance. My blood ran cold – my legs trembled – my strength seemed to have failed me. Was I mistaken? could it be the beloved of my heart – 'Yes; that is Miss Price', said the surgeon, coolly. All doubt on my part was now removed. I had exhumed the body of her whom a thousand times I had pressed to my sorrowful breast – whom I had clasped to my aching heart. I felt as if I had committed some horrible crime – a murder, or other deadly deed! (I, 540)

By displaying the 'nameless' body-snatcher's feelings and emotions (manifest in terms such as 'anxious', 'trembled', 'sorrowful breast', and 'aching heart'), the scene radically revamps the Gothic arch villain. The embedded narrative, climaxing as it does with the recognition scene (when the identity of the corpse –not of the body-snatcher/lover – is revealed), shifts the positions of Frankenstein and his Creature on the anatomist's table, Tidkins's feelings of guilt stressing even more his links with Frankenstein. Reynolds's play with the clichés of the literature of terror and his ironic and constant reversals literally anatomise his portrait of Victorian society and the London poor. The figure of the body-snatcher, informed by iconic Gothic texts, figures, and conventions the better to subvert them, functions thus within the text as a conspicuous *cliché* emblematising fear – an empty trope, or mere signifier, which repeatedly appears in the text (Tidkins constantly pops up throughout the episodes) to emphasise its artificiality, but whose meaning lies elsewhere. By the end of the first volume, the Resurrection Man appears, indeed, as a thing of the past – an 'abomination' – society is now rid of thanks to the passing of the 1832 Anatomy Act. If made redundant by the new legislation on the uses of the human body, the body-snatcher yet continually haunts Reynolds's narrative, but as a symbol of the widespread and legal forms of violence against the bodies of the weakest:

'But do you think there are such people as resurrection men now-a-days?'
'Resurrection men!' ejaculated the reverend visitor, bursting out into a laugh; 'no, my dear madam – society has got rid of those abominations'.
'Then where do surgeons get corpses from, sir?'
'From the hulks, the prisons, and the workhouses', was the answer.
'What! Poor creatures which goes to the workus!' cried Mrs. Smith, revolting at the idea.
'Yes – ma'am; but the surgeons don't like them as subjects, because they're nothing but skin and bone'. (I, 883)

Throughout Reynolds's novel, the traffic in bodies thus becomes a sensational way of merging his medical and social realism. Both persecuted by the (enduring) body-snatcher and discriminated by legislation, the 'poor creatures' and their appalling living and dying conditions lie at the heart of Reynolds's popular fiction.

Like Reynolds's *Mysteries of London*, Dickens's most famous body-snatcher, Jeremy Cruncher, in *A Tale of Two Cities* (1859), owes a lot to Shelley's *Frankenstein*. Both novels refer to the medical culture of the time and point to the lack of corpses for medical education and practice. Both novels unravel against a revolutionary backdrop, the French Revolution and the Reign of Terror informing Shelley's and Dickens's plots alike.[38] Tellingly, in both novels, the social revolution is metaphorised through images borrowed from the field of anatomy.

Dickens's historical novel relates a part of the French Revolution during the Reign of Terror, drawing parallels between France and Britain. On the one hand, France is characterised by the number of guillotined heads falling on the scaffold; on the other, Britain is the country where dissection flourishes and body-snatchers haunt churchyards in search of fresh material. The system of parallels and echoes between France and Britain is sustained throughout the novel and undergirds Dickens's social discourse. Dickens was known for his denunciation of the appalling living conditions of the lower classes in industrial cities, but many of his novels also drew attention to how the poor fell victim to the development of medical science and scientific progress more generally. In his 1836 short story 'The Black Veil', for instance, a mother has her hanged son's body stolen by body-snatchers and brought to a surgeon for reanimation. The motif of the body of the criminal sentenced to death is also found in Dickens's novels, such as *Barnaby Rudge* (1841) and *Great Expectations* (1861), while *The Pickwick Papers* (1836–37) shows medical students talking about dissecting corpses.[39] In fact, in both his fictional and non-fictional works, Dickens condemned the use of dissection in medical education as the ultimate means of accessing knowledge, such as in 'A Great Day for the Doctors' and 'Use and Abuse of the Dead', respectively published in *Household Words* in November 1850 and April 1858. Both texts highlight Dickens's plea for a more ethical regard for the bodies of the poor and his

---

[38] As Jean-Jacques Lecercle contends, the story is probably situated around the period 1792–1799. Jean-Jacques Lecercle, *Frankenstein: Mythe et Philosophie* (Paris: PUF, 1988), 55.

[39] Whether or not linked to the medical field, the issue of the objectification and commodification of human remains also permeates *Bleak House* (1852–1853) and *Our Mutual Friend* (1864–1865).

attack on a society which aligns the body of the murderer with that of the poor – therefore equating criminality and poverty.

A Tale of Two Cities is situated decades before the passing of the 1832 Anatomy Act. Jerry Cruncher, the resurrection man, whose name suggests dismemberment, haunts the Old Bailey waiting for the corpses of hanged criminals. His 'spiky hair looking as if it must tear the sheets to ribbons' (53) or much like the 'spiked wall' (60) of Newgate, binds the character to the world of both punishment and dissection, suggesting therefore the links between the legal and the anatomical realms. Dickens's novel was originally entitled *Buried Alive*. As we shall see, the motif of live burial encapsulates several different meanings which increasingly place the body and its uses at the heart of the narrative. The novel opens on the end of Dr Manette's eighteen years of incarceration in the Bastille. The physician's imprisonment is likened to a live burial (his release is compared to a digging out of the earth), while the prisoner's cadaverous face ('varieties of sunken cheeks, cadaverous colours, emaciated hands and figures' [18]) or his mysterious disappearance eighteenth years earlier, 'as if he had been spirited away' (27), present the surgeon as a corpse robbed by body-snatchers.

The comparison between Manette's imprisonment and the theft of his body is furthered throughout the novel. His 'haggard eyes' (41) and 'transparent' (42) bones suggest that Manette is a living corpse, or rather, a body hosting secrets which dissection only can reveal. Indeed, Manette suffers from monomania; the physician mechanically makes shoes, and his monomania resurfaces whenever an event recalls his buried past, such as when the French Charles Darnay, about to marry Manette's daughter, reveals that he is Monseigneur St Evrémonde's nephew – the cruel aristocrat who had Manette arrested. Hence, the secret at the core of the novel is both psychological (Manette's monomania) and political. The connections between Manette's monomania and anatomical culture (suggested by images of burial) are not coincidental. In fact, Manette's secret has been repressed/buried in his brain; the surgeon's brain thus functions as a double of the prison in which he was incarcerated and where he buried the missing piece of evidence: the letter which reveals the Marquis's crime and which leads to Darnay's second imprisonment.

Unsurprisingly, the Marquis is the villain of the narrative. The latter can dispose of people's lives at will, it seems, and he sends Manette to prison while living himself in a castle which reflects his crimes:

> For three heavy hours, the stone faces of the château, lion and human, stared blindly at the night. Dead darkness lay on all the landscape, dead darkness added its own hush to the hushing dust on all the roads.

The burial place had got to the pass that its little heaps of poor grass were indistinguishable from one another [...] Lighter and lighter, until at last the sun touched the tops of the still trees, and poured its radiance over the hill. In the glow, the water of the château seemed to turn to blood, and the stone faces crimsoned. (121)

The Gothic rhetoric of violence and death is intermingled with the historical narrative and, more particularly, Dickens's social discourse. The buried bodies ('little heaps of poor grass') are those of the 'poor' starved by the Marquis, their corpses bearing witness to the political regime before the Revolution. The use of indirect representation (the poor appear through the adjective in 'poor grass' or even 'little', simultaneously signalling their insignificance and their merging with the earth; crime is represented through the blood metaphor while the castle is personified) pinpoints the way in which meaning must systematically be decoded: identical metaphors build a network of associations which connect the two parts of the novel and the two countries/cities.

Indeed, at the beginning of the novel, France and Britain are compared through the image of two kings with large jaws ('There were a king with a large jaw and a queen with a plain face, on the throne of England; there were a king with a large jaw and a queen with a fair face, on the throne of France' [7]) 'carr[ying] their divine rights with a high hand' (9). The jaw (or mouth) metaphorises power, while, on the other hand, the citizens are starved ('starved fingers and toes' [32]), as if already dead ('cadaverous faces' [32]), placed naked on a dissecting table ('bare arms' [32]), and dismembered, as the synecdoche of the 'starved fingers and toes' intimates. As '[h]unger rattle[s] its dry bones' (33), the metaphor of the corpse circulates throughout the narrative, foreshadowing the moment when the French people surge up, as if resurrected from the earth, to claim vengeance.

Thus, the narrative draws parallels between France, where the king possesses 'the right of life and death over the surrounding vulgar' (116) and Britain, where people seem about to dislocate ('as if they were falling to pieces at the larger joints' [10]) and where medical practitioners use the bodies of the poor for research and education. This is the reason why the pauper's corpse, dissected on the anatomist's table, is never described, or is stolen but never visualised in the narrative: it is evoked indirectly through Dickens's system of parallels between the two countries; both monarchy in France and medical practitioners in Britain use the bodies of the poor, dismembering them or 'resurrecting' them. Dickens's echoes between France and England thus create corpses that only appear analogically. Just like young Cruncher, who only sees the coffin his father is digging out, the cadaver only materialises through the discourse of its representation. Thus, Dickens's medical realism – his use of body-snatchers and hints at anatomical dissection – remains, paradoxically enough, purely rhetorical, and artificial.[40]

By the end of the nineteenth century, body-snatching still reverberated with fear of the medical world. Yet it often hinted far more about medical research than it did about medical education. In Victorian realist novels, such as Harriet Martineau's *Deerbrook* (1839) or George Eliot's *Middlemarch* (1871), the many physicians suspected of body-snatching are those who are involved in medical research. As a late-century example, Robert Louis Stevenson's 'The Body-Snatcher' (1884) is a good instance of the ways in which tales of body-snatching may have been used to encapsulate types of discourse on medical research and a popular distrust of the medical profession. The horror tale was written in June 1881 to be published in *The Cornhill Magazine* but was refused and later published in *The Pall Mall* Christmas issue of 1884. This was a time when physiologists were experimenting on the live bodies of animals, culminating at the International Medical Congress in August 1881 when the pioneering Scottish physiologist/neurologist David Ferrier took part in the cerebral dissection of a living monkey. The physiologist's 1881 prosecution for the alleged cruelty involved in animal experimentations – and his acquittal – had been preceded by an important rise of the applications for licences and certificates to perform vivisection.

Stevenson's tale rewrites in part the 1828 Burke and Hare case, which had involved another Scottish anatomist – Dr Robert Knox.[41] It relates the medical experience of Fettes, as a sub-assistant of Knox's class, and of the young doctor Wolfe MacFarlane. Fettes receives 'subjects' ready for dissection – the 'unfriendly relics of humanity' or 'the raw material of the anatomists' – brought in (illegally) every night. Fettes and MacFarlane also regularly practise body-snatching themselves. The class is large and the students eager to dissect parts they have not practised on, such as Richardson, who longs for one of the subjects' head – perhaps echoing

---

[40] His network of correspondences, in fact, echoes Edmund Burke's anti-revolutionary rhetoric – reworked by Thomas Carlyle in *The French Revolution* (1837). Dickens was known to have travelled with *The French Revolution* in 1837. Chris Baldick, *In Frankenstein's Shadow: Myth, Monstrosity, and Nineteenth-Century Writing* (Oxford: Clarendon Press, 1987), 106.

[41] Rewritings of the Burke and Hare murders were not unfrequent. For a popular and sensational example (which hinges upon the ingredients which later made the fame of sensation novels, such as violent and brutal murders; stolen, concealed and recovered wills; illegitimate children; and forged documents), see David Pae, *Mary Paterson; or, The Fatal Error. A Story of the Burke and Hare Murders* (London: Fred Farrah, 1866).

here contemporary research into cerebral localisation. Hence some of the subjects are killed on purpose, like a woman whose face Fettes recognizes, while another – Gray – becomes anatomical material after a row with Fettes's medical fellow, MacFarlane.

At the end of the short story, however, as Fettes and MacFarlane believe they are transporting the body of a woman they have just 'resurrected', the 'thing' bumping between them turns out to be the body of Gray, whom they had dissected and whose head had been given to Richardson for dissection. The twist in the plot turns the Gothic tale of terror into a ghost story – the corpse which refuses to disappear ironically materialising the guilty conscience of the two body-snatchers.

Like that of his literary predecessors, Stevenson's Gothic constructs the medical world as a criminal realm, but rewrites the issue of guilt through a corpse which refuses to crumble into dust and decompose. The character's psychological obsession with Gray's corpse, which climaxes with the final delusion and the appearance of Gray's head on the female corpse the two body-snatchers have just dug up, do not result from any optical trick, as in many Gothic romances of the first phase (1764–1820).[42] Stevenson's ghost story illustrates rather the '"somatic" aspect of late-Victorian Gothic fiction',[43] as Robert Mighall terms it, showing how threat is increasingly located inside the individual by the end of the nineteenth century, paving the way for the psychiatric discourse later found in *Strange Case of Dr Jekyll and Mr Hyde* (1886) and in Bram Stoker's *Dracula* (1897). Indeed, Stevenson's late-Victorian Gothic posed questions related to medical ethics; yet his rewriting of clichés borrowed from early nineteenth-century tales of terror constructed horror first and foremost in physiological or biological terms, as 'embodied [...] monstrous bodies'[44] rather than the monstrous bodies earlier laid out on the dissecting table. By the last decades of the nineteenth century, therefore, the Gothic enabled writers to turn the world of medical experimentation upside down and to let readers dissect the very brains of the body-snatchers typically found in Blackwoodian tales of terror, so as to visualise (and vicariously experience) the physiology of guilt.

---

[42] *The Animated Skeleton* (1798) is an example, but optical delusions were mainstream, notably in Gothic romances published by the Minerva Press.
[43] Robert Mighall, *A Geography of Victorian Gothic Fiction: Mapping History's Nightmares* (Oxford: Oxford University Press, 1999), 130.
[44] Ibid.

PART II
Professionalisation

CHAPTER 5

Physic and Metaphysics
Poetry and the Unsteady Ascent of Professional Medicine

Daniel Brown

Deadly Doctors and Invigorating Verse

Poets and paradigms of a humane new science, Edward Jenner and Ronald Ross bookend a century of experimental collaborations and professional rivalries between medicine and poetry. Jenner proved the efficacy of vaccination against smallpox in 1796, and Ross identified the causes of malaria in 1897. Exemplary instances of scientific medicine, which led to hundreds of millions of lives being saved, their achievements have a parity that belies the erratic history of medicine that stretches between them. This history is discreetly and uniquely registered in poetry of the period. For some poets, such as Ross, verse was a mode of reflecting upon, or even hallucinating, their practice of medicine. For others, such as John Gibson, it was a medium for repudiating the new science. Gibson's 'Verses Composed upon that Sublime Subject the Cowpock Preached by Mr Lyons' (1803) presents vaccination not as an heroic new science for saving lives but as a hubristic attempt to frustrate the divine will: 'Let God alone the first infection give / Then should they die resigned to him you live.'[1] God has the privilege of 'the first infection', for just as Jenner's vaccination provokes a mild cowpox that prevents deadly smallpox, the deity can engender a mortal disease to protect against the more serious condition of damnation and ensure eternal life. Vaccination is cast as a religious trope to counter the hopeful new science of medicine it validates.

Also dating from 1803, the mock epic poem *Terrible Tractoration!!: A Poetical Petition against Galvanising Trumpery and the Perkinistic Institution* offers an outsider's perspective on the state of British medicine at the start of the nineteenth century. Written in London by the American Thomas Green Fessenden, *Terrible Tractoration!!* pits a modern therapy

---

[1] MS.8032, Wellcome Library, London. I would like to thank Dr Russell Hays for bringing his medical expertise to bear upon a draft of the following essay and for his improving suggestions.

from the New World against the British medical establishment, represented here by the protagonist and purported author of the poem, 'Christopher Caustic, M.D. LL.D ASS.', an 'Honorary Member of No Less than Nineteen Very Learned Societies'. The satire defends 'Metallic Tractors', a galvanic remedy that Fessenden's countryman Elisha Perkins had patented in 1796. These are a pair of metal rods, each made of a different alloy, which when alternately stroked over affected parts of the body supposedly influence 'hominal electricity'[2] to counter such conditions as arthritis, gout, haemorrhages, herpes, burns, and epilepsy: 'O'er the frail part a subtil fluid pour, / Drench'd with invisible Galvanic shower.'[3] In 1803 Perkins's son Benjamin established a charitable Institution in London 'for the use of the METALLIC TRACTORS, in Disorders of the Poor'.[4] Nathanial Hawthorne writes that it was 'at the request of Perkins [*fils*]' that Fessenden 'consented to make [the Tractors] the subject of a poem in Hudibrastic verse'.[5]

Fessenden defends Perkinism for what he sees to be its humanitarian motives, and accordingly has Caustic oppose it on these grounds in his satire. Identifying the Tractors with 'that pestiferous corps, / Who keep alive the paltry poor', 'curing those who ought to depend solely on "Death and the Doctor"',[6] Caustic sees Perkinian medicine thwarting a Malthusian hygiene. As an apologist and agent for a status quo in which disease and early death are common consequences of poverty, Caustic trusts in Death professionally as 'Our great and terrible Ally!'.[7] He has a like-minded colleague at the other end of the century, in the prison doctor of Oscar Wilde's *Ballad of Reading Gaol* (1898).

For most of the time he spent in prison from May 1895 to 1897, Wilde was held at Reading Gaol. In 1896 he became aware of a new prisoner, Charles Wooldridge, who was charged and promptly hung for murdering his wife. This history is re-worked in *The Ballad of Reading Gaol*, which Wilde wrote after his release, while living in exile in France. The doctor's place in the penal system, and in the larger system of Church and State, is neatly gauged by the following rhyme:

---

[2] Benjamin Douglas Perkins, *The Influence of Metallic Tractors on the Human Body* (London: J. Johnson, 1798), 92.
[3] Thomas Green Fessenden, *Terrible Tractoration!!: A Poetical Petition against Galvanising Trumpery and the Perkinistic Institution* (New York: Samuel Stansbury, 1804), xxxiv.
[4] Ibid., xxxiii.
[5] Nathaniel Hawthorne, *Tales, Sketches, and Other Papers*, in *Complete Works of Nathaniel Hawthorne*, 13 vols. (Boston: Houghton Mifflin, 1896), vol. 12, 251.
[6] Fessenden, *Terrible Tractoration!!*, 93, 60.   [7] Ibid., 73.

> The Governor was strong upon
> The Regulations Act:
> The Doctor said that Death was but
> A scientific fact:
> And twice a day the Chaplain called,
> And left a little tract.[8]

The Governor enforces the procedures for dealing and dispensing with the condemned man as they are specified by the 'Act'. The state's monopoly of violence is focused in this short, sharp, axe-like syllable, which the Doctor and the Chaplain each buttress with their authority and supplementary letters. While the Chaplain's 'little tract' sounds quaintly ineffectual and apologetic, the Doctor's forthright declaration, in which he equates the arbitrary 'Act' of a state killing with 'scientific fact', recalls Caustic's callousness, the alliterative alliance of 'Death and the Doctor'.

Caustic's poem culminates in the fourth and final canto, 'Grand Attack!'. In keeping with epic convention much of this canto is given over to catalogue. The doctors' armoury, 'all their weapons in possession',[9] are mobilised in the spirit not of the ancient Hippocratic Oath but the recent French Terror:

> Cram all the ninny-hammers gullets,
> With pills as big as pistol bullets;
> Then, Frenchman like, give each a glister,
> And next go on to bleed and blister.
> Dash at them escharotics gnawing,
> Their carcases to pick a flaw in;
>
> With fell trepaning perforator,
> Pierce every rascal's stubborn pate, or
> With chisel plied with might and main,
> Ope a huge hole in pericrane.[10]

Terrible Tractoration!! reports a brutal medicine, an ally of Death that lends itself to attack rather than healing, to warfare rather than wellbeing, with little means or indeed incentive to cure patients:

> Some fell by laudanum, and some by steel,
> And death in ambush lay in every pill;
> For save, or slay, this privilege we claim,
> Though credit suffers, the reward's the same.[11]

---

[8] Oscar Wilde, 'The Ballad of Reading Gaol', in *Oscar Wilde*, ed. Isobel Murray (Oxford: Oxford University Press, 1989), 548–66 (553).
[9] Fessenden, *Terrible Tractoration!!*, 93.   [10] Ibid., 171, 175.   [11] Ibid., 161.

Introduced at the start of George Crabbe's poem on 'Physic', which follows that on the lawyer in *The Borough* (1810), doctors are described as 'a graver Tribe', awarded an equivocal epithet that identifies them with dignity and dismal prospects. The pun's cloven characterisation is orchestrated in the balanced antitheses of the lines that follow, where doctors are described as learned without being efficacious, their diagnoses and treatments being matters of chance: 'Helpers of Men they're call'd, and we confess / Theirs the deep Study, theirs the lucky Guess.'[12] Such well-intentioned uncertainty leaves much scope for charlatans to fill the breach. Crabbe's discussion of doctors is accordingly brief, effectively forming a preface to the poem's long disquisition on quacks: 'Hence Sums enormous by those Cheats are made, / And Deaths unnumber'd by their dreadful Trade.'[13]

Crabbe is nevertheless optimistic about the future of medicine, believing that science can prevail over quackery: 'Then let us trust to Science – there are those / Who can their Falsehoods and their Frauds disclose.'[14] Fessenden is not so sanguine. *Terrible Tractoration!!* replies to accusations of quackery made against Perkinism by charging established medicine with hypocrisy. How can it demand a causal explanation of the Tractors, given the mystery surrounding its staple remedies?: 'this grave reasoning's all a hum, / Because the learn'd are in the dark / How opium, mercury acts, and bark [of Cinchona, Quinine]'.[15] The fragmented and unprofessional state of medicine at this time allows proponents of particular cures to each equally 'Tell the vile deeds by quackery done, / By every nostrum, save *thine own*.'[16]

One of the main targets of Fessenden's satire, Dr John Haygarth, does test the Tractors scientifically. In treating some of his patients at Bath, Haygarth secretly replaced the tractors with wooden facsimiles, which he found to be as efficacious in relieving the symptoms of rheumatism as the patented originals. From this experiment he concluded that the Tractors worked by harnessing the power not of electricity but of the imagination. Samuel Taylor Coleridge and Robert Southey included an entry on the 'The *Tractors*' as 'a mode of quackery' in *Omniana* (1812),[17] and probably knew Haygarth through the chemist Thomas Beddoes. Coleridge also read widely on the medical imagination, and would have

---

[12] George Crabbe, *The Borough*, 6th ed. (1810; London: Hatchard, 1816), 78.   [13] Ibid., 87.
[14] Ibid., 87.   [15] Fessenden, *Terrible Tractoration!!*, 125.   [16] Ibid., 154.
[17] Robert Southey and Samuel Taylor Coleridge, *Omniana, or Horae Otiosiores*, 2 vols. (London: Longmans, 1812), vol. 1, 191.

known Haygarth's book, *On the Imagination as a Cause & as a Cure of Disorders of the Body, Exemplified by Fictitious Tractors and Epidemical Convulsions* (1800).[18]

Having coined the term 'psychosomatic', Coleridge was convinced of the power of the imagination to both cause and cure disease. His holistic belief in the medical interactions of mind and body, of mental states and somatic feelings,[19] derives from an encompassing principle of Life that fascinated him and his peers, and impelled the conjoint development of new poetry and science. In his *Hints towards the Formation of a more Comprehensive Theory of Life* (comp. 1818; 1848), Coleridge describes a 'power' of Life, a continuous principle of motion impelled by 'the unceasing *polarity of life, as the form of its process*'[20] that articulates the interdependence of parts as a whole. Developed through his reading of Schelling and other German *Naturphilosophen*, this conception is consistent with the dynamic principle that Coleridge describes in his 1817 version of 'The Eolian Harp': 'O! the one life within us and abroad, / Which meets all motion and becomes its soul.'[21]

For Coleridge and his peers, imagination and poetry not only appreciate but also quicken the 'one life'. William Wordsworth sustains principles of medical mentalism throughout his poetry, championing the healing powers of joy, nature, and poetry itself. John Stuart Mill famously provides a personal testimonial for such claims, as, suffering from a severe depression in 1828, he found in 'Wordsworth's poems a medicine for my state of mind'.[22] In his 'Lines Suggested by a Portrait from the Pencil of F. Stone' (comp. 1834–1835), Wordsworth compares the power of his poetry to the pool described in John's Gospel (5:7), which will heal the first sick person to enter the water after it has been troubled by the angel:

> And I, grown old, but in a happier land,
> Domestic Portrait! have to verse consigned
> In thy calm presence those heart-moving words:
> Words that can soothe, more than they agitate;
> Whose spirit, like the angel that went down

---

[18] Jennifer Ford, *Coleridge on Dreaming* (Cambridge: Cambridge University Press, 1998), 187–8.
[19] Ibid., 175–6.
[20] Samuel Taylor Coleridge, *Miscellanies, Aesthetic and Literary* (London: Bell, 1885), 497.
[21] Samuel Taylor Coleridge, 'The Eolian Harp' (1796), in *The Complete Poetical Works of Samuel Taylor Coleridge*, ed. Ernest Hartley Coleridge, 2 vols. (Oxford: Oxford University Press, 1912), vol. 1, 100–2 (101).
[22] J. S. Mill, *Autobiography*, 3rd ed. (1873; London: Longmans, 1874), 148.

> Into Bethesda's pool, with healing virtue
> Informs the fountain in the human breast
> Which by thy visitation was disturbed.[23]

Poetic diction, those words 'to verse consigned', is implicitly paralleled with the powerful words of Christ in this episode as he heals the sick man by fiat, 'Rise, take up your pallet, and walk' (John 5:8). Wordsworth's lines turn upon the tension between the stasis of the portrait – 'thy calm presence' – and the agitation of the temporal medium of verse – the tranquil pool and its disturbed but vital form, the flow of poetic diction, described and demonstrated assonantly as 'Words that can soothe'. A poem is a contained organic form rhythmically pulsing, and the spirit of 'those heart-moving words' heals the human heart, as of a fibrillation, 'Informs the fountain in the human breast'. This physiological characterisation of soothing poetry recalls 'that serene and blessed mood' described in Wordsworth's 'Tintern Abbey' (1798), in which, 'even the motion of our human blood / Almost suspended, we are laid asleep / In body, and become a living soul', and 'see into the life of things'.[24]

Like Coleridge and Wordsworth, their friend the young chemist Humphry Davy also assumes that poetry, not medicine, is best able to describe Life. The tenor of a long draft poem he sent to Coleridge in 1800 can be grasped from its opening lines: 'Lo! o'er the earth the kindling spirits pour / The flames of life that bounteous nature gives.'[25] Originally titled 'The Spinosist', this paean to Life, both physiological and transcendent, received further revisions and a new title in 1808, when Davy was convalescing from an obscure but life-threatening illness.[26] The only reference the poem makes to the illness is its title, 'Written after Recovery from a Dangerous Illness', which accordingly mobilises these verses as a grateful tribute to the vital principle that on this occasion prevailed in the face of ineffectual medicine. The impotence of current medicine is also acknowledged obliquely in the closing lines of the poem, where death is figured as a cure for life, 'an awakening from a dream of pain'. Dr Caustic's alliance of 'Death and the Doctor', however, would be gradually countered by a scientific medicine that, sharing the precepts of the new science of biology, was dedicated to understanding and enhancing

---

[23] William Wordsworth, 'Lines Suggested by a Portrait from the Pencil of F. Stone', in *The Complete Poetical Works of William Wordsworth*, 9 vols. (Boston: Houghton Mifflin, 1919), vol. 9, 17–22 (22).
[24] William Wordsworth and Samuel Taylor Coleridge, *Lyrical Ballads*, ed. R. L. Brett and A. R. Jones (1798; London: Methuen, 1968), 114.
[25] John Davy, *Memoirs of the Life of Sir Humphry Davy*, 2 vols. (London: Longmans, 1836), vol. 1, 390.
[26] Ibid., 385.

the principle of Life that Davy lauds in his poem. Jenner's practice of vaccination furnishes the epochal instance of this new medicine.

The Normal and the Pathological: Saviour Scientists and Mad Poets

While Jenner did not discover vaccination, he established it scientifically, first by experiment and then, following its rapid and widespread adoption, with statistical analysis and epidemiological observations. The reach of vaccination in controlling infectious disease soon escalated the combative tropes used by medicine from those of individuals fighting for their lives to grand battles and campaigns. In 1808 the consumptive poet John Dawes Worgan, who lived with Jenner's family from 1806 to his death at the age of nineteen three years later,[27] wrote a verse 'Address to the Royal Jennerian Society'. It includes an account of a philanthropic expedition that King Charles IV of Spain commissioned, which from 1803 to 1806 vaccinated 230,000 people across the New World and Asia. The expedition included twenty-four male orphans aged eight to ten, none of whom had previously been exposed to smallpox or inoculated. They were used as incubators of the vaccine. The vesicle fluid was passed arm-to-arm from the ulcerated skin of one child to the next and extracted freshly, as required. Offering some redress for the Spanish conquest of 1519–1520, which had originally introduced smallpox to the Americas with catastrophic effects, the King's philanthropic expedition figures in Worgan's poem as a pacifist campaign and a secular holy war, a new form of paramilitarism that foreshadows the tropes that have become endemic to discourses of medical research and public health:

> See! at Philanthropy's divine command,
> Thy sons, Iberia, quit their native strand;
> With dauntless hope innumerous toils they dare,
> From pole to pole the vital gift to bear.
> No deep-mouth'd cannons thunder o'er the main,
> No sanguine fights the placid wave distain,
> But smiling Peace – her olive-branch displays,
> And faltering infants lisp their Guardian's praise,
> As on their arms the sov'reign shield they show,
> Whose heav'nly powers repel th' ERUPTIVE FOE,
> With mystic charm extend the fleeting breath,
> And blunt the direst of the shafts of death.[28]

---

[27] John Baron, *The Life of Edward Jenner*, 2 vols. (London: Colburn, 1838), vol. 2, 72–6.
[28] John Dawes Worgan, 'Address to the Royal Jennerian Society' (1808), in *Select Poems, &c.* (London: Longman, Hurst, Rees and Orme, 1810), 203–14 (207–8).

The children's arms are the armaments here. Figured as a 'sovereign shield', the rosaceous cowpox lesions are a preservative talisman and a military honour, a medallion issued by the King and an Enlightenment emblem of individual sovereignty – the right to life, for both the children and the otherwise subject people of the Spanish New World.

As well as furnishing a foundational story for modern medicine, Jenner also wrote poetry.[29] Along with Worgan, his circle included several other poets, amongst them Edward Gardner, who in the elegy he wrote after Jenner's death in 1823 describes the doctor as 'young-ey'd fancy's darling child', styling him as a romantic spirit that oddly recalls Keats's' Nightingale and Shelley's Skylark: 'Oft have I heard thee near thy glassy stream / Pour th' impassioned tones of genius wild.'[30]

Predicated upon romantic interfusions of poetry and science, Jenner's circle can be compared with Coleridge's better-known group in Bristol. The power of Jenner's science as a model for modern research-based medicine, however, has been instrumental in rupturing such holism, separating romantic ideas about Life from those of biology. This new scientific medicine increasingly distanced itself from poetry. Indeed it came to pathologise poets. While Baron's *Life of Jenner* often praises its subject for his 'imaginative fervour' and 'poet's tongue',[31] and indeed for the verses he wrote, it also reports that 'modern physicians have recognised in the delineations of the poet a real disease which they themselves witnessed'.[32] Jenner's scientific prowess presumably protected him from succumbing to this condition.

'In the course of the nineteenth century', Georges Canguilhem observes, 'the real identity of normal and pathological vital phenomena [...] became a kind of scientifically guaranteed dogma'.[33] Scientific medicine began to assert its authority and assume its professional prerogative of demarcating the normal and the pathological during the decades when some of its romantic peers were effectively offering themselves up as case studies. Opium consumption is conceptualised as addiction at this time, with Coleridge becoming 'the first Englishman to commit himself to the

---

[29] See Baron, *Life of Jenner*, vol. 1, 20–5.
[30] Edward Gardner, 'To My Absent Friend, Edward Jenner M.D. F.R.S.', Wellcome Library, MS.2069, 269.
[31] Baron, *Life of Jenner*, vol. 1, 14.   [32] Ibid., 206.
[33] Georges Canguilhem, *Le Normal et le Pathologique, Augmenté de Nouvelles Réflexions Concernant le Normal et le Pathologique*, trans. as *The Normal and the Pathological* by Carolyn R. Fawcett with Robert S. Cohen (1966; New York: Zone, 1991), 43.

full-time and long-term care of a surgeon for treatment of drug abuse'.[34] Lady Byron sought opinions about her husband's sanity from Dr Matthew Baillie and another doctor, Mr Le Mann, an episode that Byron alludes to in *Don Juan* (1819): 'For Inez call'd some druggists and physicians, / And tried to prove her loving lord was *mad.*'[35]

Writing in a time when medicine was gaining scientific credibility, John Gibson Lockhart opportunistically co-opted its discourse in his notorious defamation of John Keats in the fourth of his essays on 'The Cockney School of Poetry' (1818). Lockhart writes near the end of his essay, 'We had almost forgot to mention, that Keats belongs [also] to the Cockney School of Politics',[36] a passing reference to the real object of his attack, the poet's radical politics. By pathologising him through his poetry, Lockhart transubstantiates his private political opinion that Keats is socially harmful and undesirable into a pseudo-scientific observation, an almost unanswerable slur that casts him as a danger to public health and wellbeing. Lockhart's essay begins: 'Of all the manias of this mad age, the most incurable, as well as the most common, seems to be no other than the Metromanie.' He then goes on to argue that Keats 'has caught the infection'. Keats was an apprentice to an apothecary and surgeon for a year when he was fifteen and then a medical student at Guy's Hospital in London from 1811 to 1816, when he was awarded his apothecary's license. He decided, however, to forsake practising medicine in favour of writing poetry. Damning him with faint praise, Lockhart considers Keats to have 'talents which, devoted to the purposes of any useful profession, must have rendered him a respectable, if not an eminent citizen, [. . .] But all has been undone by a sudden attack of the malady'.[37] Keats has chosen artistic madness over professional sanity, to be a patient instead of a doctor.

Keats reaffirms his choice of poetry over medicine in his 'Ode to a Nightingale' (1819), where in the third and fourth stanzas he declares that he wishes to:

> Fade far away, dissolve, and quite forget
>   What thou among the leaves hast never known,
> The weariness, the fever, and the fret
>   Here, where men sit and hear each other groan;

---

[34] Clifford Siskin, *The Historicity of Romantic Discourse* (Oxford: Oxford University Press, 1988), 184.
[35] Lord Byron, *Don Juan*, Canto I (1819), in *Byron's Don Juan: A Variorum Edition*, ed. Truman Guy Steffan and Willis W. Pratt, 4 vols. (Edinburgh: Thomas Nelson, 1957), vol. 2, 35.
[36] [John Gibson Lockhart], 'The Cockney School of Poetry IV', *Blackwood's Magazine*, 3 (1818), 519–24, 524.
[37] Ibid., 519.

> Where palsy shakes a few, sad, last gray hairs,
>   Where youth grows pale, and spectre-thin, and dies;
>   Where but to think is to be full of sorrow
>   And leaden-eyed despairs,
>   Where Beauty cannot keep her lustrous eyes,
>   Or new Love pine at them beyond to-morrow.
>
> Away! away! for I will fly to thee,
>   Not charioted by Bacchus and his pards,
> But on the viewless wings of Poesy.[38]

Keats was familiar with suffering and death through the loss of his father in 1804, and then his mother in 1810 and brother Tom in 1818, both to the wasting illness of consumption that would claim his life, too. His medical training must also have informed the pessimistic description of human life he makes here, especially the specific references to fever, palsy, and consumption.[39] The third stanza makes an inductive leap from these medical conditions to its stark characterisation of human life in the 'Here' that we all inhabit. Its fourth line pivots about the connective 'and', which functions as a caesura that yields two half lines, and a structural parallel of 'Here' to 'hear' at the start of each. This positioning of the words facilitates their punning conflation, suffusing the spatial immediacy of the indexical with the visceral affliction of other men's groans: 'Here, where men sit and hear each other groan'. Carefully deployed, 'Here' is a keynote that gathers up and focuses the assonant modulations of the preceding line's 'The weariness, the fever, and the fret'. The word-sound is then itself varied in the series 'Here, where', inflected by the earlier 'weariness', a hypothesis that is vindicated by the lines that follow, where the word 'Where' takes the lead in cataloguing more miseries.

    Set against this grim depiction of human life, which advertises the failures of current medicine, poetry is attributed with life-enhancing qualities that directly contest Lockhart's mockery. The 'Ode' appears to make some pointed, or at least unapologetic, references to Lockhart's rhetoric, such as his essay's closing recommendation that Keats 'go back to the [apothecary's] shop', but 'be a little more sparing of extenuatives and soporifics in your practice than you have been in your poetry'.[40] The beginning of Keats's

---

[38] John Keats, 'Ode to a Nightingale' (1819), in *The Poems of John Keats*, ed. Jack Stillinger (London: Heinemann, 1978), 369–72 (370).

[39] See Donald C. Goellnicht, *The Poet-Physician: Keats and Medical Science* (Pittsburgh: University of Pittsburgh Press, 1984), 227–8.

[40] Lockhart, 'The Cockney School', 524.

poem is almost a retort to Lockhart's final words, as the poet becomes proxy apothecary to his own patient-like persona:

> My heart aches, and a drowsy numbness pains
>   My sense, as though of hemlock I had drunk,
> Or emptied some dull opiate to the drains
>   One minute past, and Lethe-wards had sunk.[41]

The second stanza introduces another form of Lethe water, 'a draught of vintage', 'That I might drink, and leave the world unseen, / And with thee fade away into the forest dim', a lyrical parallel to the emaciating 'extenuatives' Lockhart refers to, which then becomes the keynote to the third stanza, cited earlier: 'Fade far away, dissolve'. This stanza, of course, also includes a sobering reference to the involuntary extenuative of consumption, by which 'youth grows pale, and spectre-thin, and dies'. Hermione de Almeida notes that the word 'dissolve' had several scientific medical meanings at the time that Keats was writing, including the physiological sense of a release from life.[42] The various forms of fading, dissolving, and forgetting with which the poet tries to evade the groaning 'Here' of human life culminate in the sixth stanza's yearning for the oblivion of death: 'Darkling I listen; and, for many a time / I have been half in love with easeful Death.'[43] This life is met with 'easeful death', an almost anagrammatic reversal and undoing of *disease*. Implicitly disavowing Lockhart's normative ideas of sickness and health, Keats's humane and encompassing conception of life defies the critic's sarcastic diagnostics.

Keats's death by consumption at the age of twenty-five is well known, and known in many ways. Consumption was the lay term for *phthisis*, a broad diagnosis covering not only pulmonary tuberculosis but any wasting disease that had a pulmonary element. Finally demystified in 1882 with the discovery by Robert Koch of its pathogen, *Mycobacterium tuberculosis*, consumption was variously idealised and sexualised for much of the century. Keats became the definitive case of the creative consumptive, a hopeful but delusional association with the disease that the physician Sir William Osler names in an 1894 lecture marking the centenary of the poet's birth as 'the *Spes phthisica* that has carried so many consumptives cheerfully to the very gates of the grave'.[44] The 'Stethoscope Song' (1848),

---

[41] Keats, 'Ode', 369.
[42] Hermione de Almeida, *Romantic Medicine and John Keats* (New York: Oxford University Press, 1991), 83.
[43] Keats, 'Ode', 371.
[44] Harvey Cushing, *The Life of Sir William Osler*, 2 vols. (Oxford: Clarendon, 1925), vol. 1, 423.

by the American doctor Oliver Wendell Holmes, includes a description of 'six young damsels' who 'were getting slim and pale, / And short of breath on mounting stairs', and 'all made rhymes with "sighs" and "skies"'.[45] Consumption was also associated with syphilis and attributed to constitutional weakness, principally masturbation, while the paleness and delicacy it imposed upon its victims notoriously chimes in with nineteenth-century ideals of female attractiveness, instanced in such operatic heroines as Verdi's Violetta in *La Traviata* (1853).

Building upon the legacies of the first- and second-generation romantics in an age that was increasingly defined by masculinist cultures of empire, industry, and professional science, Victorian poetry was easily feminised and pathologised. This is clearly marked in commentaries on the Pre-Raphaelites, the poets who were most influenced by Keats's poetry and are credited with rediscovering it. Robert Buchanan's 1871 essay 'The Fleshly School of Poetry' finds in the poetry of Dante Gabriel Rossetti, as in his paintings, all the popular stigmatising symptoms of consumption, but leaves it to the reader to make the final diagnosis: 'the same morbid deviation from unhealthy forms of life, the same sense of weary, wasting, yet exquisite sensuality; nothing virile, nothing tender, nothing completely sane'.[46]

The reforming asylum doctor William A. F. Browne pioneered therapies of artistic self-expression for psychiatric patients. Late in life he conversely studied the relation of artists to mental illness, publishing his findings in the *Journal of Psychological Medicine and Mental Psychology* under the stark titles of 'Mad Poets' (1878) and 'Mad Artists' (1880). Wary of studies that only discuss poets deemed to have a mental illness, Browne wishes to locate pathologies that are endemic to the vocation itself. 'Mad Poets' accordingly examines a representative sample of canonical poets across the ages, 'that vast legion of ill-constituted, irregular, excitable, sentimental, sensitive, crotchety but clever and dreamy individuals who are seen in the twilight which connects the sunshine of right reason and the darkness of derangement'.[47] Browne embarks upon his study with a familiar romantic nosology:

---

[45] Oliver Wendell Holmes, *Poems* (Boston: Ticknor and Fields, 1864), 184.
[46] Joseph Bristow, ed., *The Victorian Poet: Poetics and Persona* (London: Croom Helm, 1987), 143. See also Max Nordau, *Degeneration* (London: Heinemann, 1898), 67–99.
[47] William A. F. Browne, 'Mad Poets, No. 1', *Journal of Psychological Medicine and Mental Psychology*, 4:2 (1878), 2.

There are manifold considerations which give to mad poets as a class a romantic interest, even a fascination, to scientific minds. Among these are the inquiries, first, whether the mental exaltation, excitement, the transcendental ecstasy, being carried above themselves, out of themselves, attributed to the stage of inspired composition, as the psychologist contends, or the hyperaemia, the blush of redundant blood which then suffuses the grey matter and the genetic cells which it contains, as the physicist believes, tend directly to the production of diseased thought and feeling; secondly, whether the descent, the original or acquired predispositions, the nurture, the situation, the surroundings of imaginative natures augment the proclivities to insanity; thirdly, whether the ideal world in which these inventors live and have their being [...] may not impart morbid tendencies to consciousness, even to their physical constitution.[48]

Cold Doctors and Warm Bodies

Browne's efforts to pathologise poets are reciprocated by poets who observe that doctors are subject to their own peculiar conditions and that medicine attracts or forms particular types of character. For some of these poets, the new professional medicine recalls Wordsworth's dictum 'We murder to dissect'[49] – it lacks the sympathetic imagination that the romantic ideology identifies with poetry. The prison doctor in Wilde's *Ballad of Reading Gaol* observes the condemned man's agony coldly for its physiological manifestations: 'some coarse-mouthed Doctor gloats, and notes / Each new and nerve-twitched post'.[50] Suffering is read by the doctor as bodily registered 'post', psychological torment relayed by the nerves, as by the reductionist analogy of telegraph wires. This sinister semiotic is itself observed by the poem, which in turn registers the doctor's sadistic job satisfaction in the crude chiming of 'gloats, and notes'.

Alfred, Lord Tennyson defends romantic ideology and Christian belief against scientific medicine. The Enlightenment origins and ideals of such science are presented in 'Locksley Hall Sixty Years After' (1886) as the utopian goals of a future state that will supersede 'the schemes and all the systems', once they fail and fall: 'All diseases quenched by Science, no man halt, or deaf or blind; / Stronger ever born of weaker, lustier body, larger mind?' The forthright declaration of this progressive platform is swiftly undermined by the question mark appended to it, yielding qualms about medical perfectibility that resonate with concerns about genetic

---

[48] Ibid., 1.   [49] Wordsworth, 'The Tables Turned', in *Lyrical Ballads*, 106.
[50] Wilde, *Ballad*, 550.

engineering in our own age. Tennyson finds in such homogenising rationalism not the promise of an egalitarian utopia but the enforced restraint and dissolution of nature's Blakean bounties: 'Every tiger madness muzzled, every serpent passion killed, / Every grim ravine a garden, every blazing desert tilled'.[51] Such opposed values interact allegorically in the figures of the nurse and new surgeon in Tennyson's 'In the Children's Hospital' (1880). The poem begins with the arrival of the new doctor, 'Fresh from the surgery-schools of France and of other lands',[52] his recent provenance clearly signalling the character of his medicine. The nurse, in whose voice the poem is written, responds intuitively to her first sighting of the surgeon: 'he sent a chill to my heart'.[53] This premonition of an icy continental rationalism prefigures her conjecture that he has no sympathetic imagination, indeed is a vivisector:

> I could think he was one of those who would break their jests on the dead,
> And mangle the living dog that had loved him and fawned at his knee –
> Drenched with the hellish oorali [curare].[54]

The antivivisection movement was galvanised during the 1870s when a French physiologist demonstrated the effects of injecting alcohol into dogs at the meeting of the British Medical Association, provoking outrage that British medical researchers were not only condoning such experiments but increasingly performing them, too. Pitting him against the English love of animals, the nurse identifies the surgeon with continental practices of experimental physiology. She accuses him of being 'happier using the knife than in trying to save the limb',[55] a charge that is upheld later in the poem by his willingness to perform a futile operation on one of the children, Emmie. Conforming to the caricature of the surgeon as butcher, he is also presented as physically crude, 'so coarse and so red', with 'big merciless hands'.[56] The surgeon meets with Enlightenment naturalism the nurse's suggestion that Christ be appealed to in order to help one of their dying children, as he proffers the rhetorical question 'can prayer set a broken bone?' and the further dismissive observation that 'the good Lord Jesus has had his day'.

Countering the godless materialism of the *sans culotte* surgeon, the children are identified with created nature, such 'works of the Lord' as

---

[51] Alfred, Lord Tennyson, 'Locksley Hall Sixty Years After' (1886), in *The Poems of Tennyson*, ed. Christopher Ricks, 3 vols. (London: Longman, 1987), vol. 3, 148–59 (155, 156).
[52] Alfred, Lord Tennyson, 'In the Children's Hospital' (1880), in *Poems*, ed. Ricks, vol. 3, 47–9 (47).
[53] Ibid.   [54] Ibid.   [55] Ibid., 47.   [56] Ibid.

the cowslip, wildflowers that 'freshen and sweeten the wards like the waft of an Angel's wing', but are each also allocated a pre-ordained fate. The children are figured with the Manichaean metaphor of 'spirits in prison',[57] waiting for release, while their identification with flowers naturalises their early deaths, as a sure way of preserving their innocent beauty. On the evening before she is to have her operation, Emmie overhears the kindly old doctor saying 'she'll never live thro' it'.[58] The intervening night becomes a battle to save her from the surgeon. Another child advises her to '"cry to the dear Lord Jesus" to help', and sleep 'with her arms lying out on the counterpane'[59] or bedcover, so that the Saviour can distinguish her from the other children in the ward. Her arms outstretched toward Christ, perhaps in *Imitatio Christi*, Emmie passes away during the stormy night, a dark night of the soul for the nurse, who 'dreams of the dreadful knife' and hears 'a phantom cry [...] , / The motherless bleat of a lamb in the storm'.[60] This lamb of God is saved from the knife, 'fears for our delicate Emmie who scarce would escape with her life',[61] oddly overcome by her death at the hands of Christ. 'In the Children's Hospital' reminds the reader that death is in God's gifting, much as Gibson does in his 'Verses Composed upon [...] the Cowpock'. The poem assumes the Christian doctrine of the Fall, a post-lapsarian world in which death is inevitable, but a good death and afterlife are not.

By introducing death, the Fall naturalises disease and so renders questionable modern medicine's goal of having 'All diseases quenched by Science'. In another late poem by Tennyson, 'Happy' (1889), a bride appreciates the body of her leper love as an honest emblem of man's postlapsarian state: 'This coarse diseaseful creature which in Eden was divine, / This Satan-haunted ruin, this little city of sewers'.[62] Drawn from the medieval *contemptus mundi* tradition, this trope of the body as a contested site and ruined structure is also used by the Jesuit priest Gerard Manley Hopkins in his sonnet 'Felix Randal' (comp. 1880), which commemorates the death of one of the poet's parishioners, a farrier, from pulmonary tuberculosis. The description of Randal's body focuses upon his build, 'his mould of man, big-bóned and hardy-handsome', a structure that is invaded and eroded, as 'reason rámbled in it and some / Fatal four disorders, fleshed there, all contended'.[63]

---

[57] Ibid., 48.   [58] Ibid.   [59] Ibid.   [60] Ibid., 49.   [61] Ibid.
[62] Alfred, Lord Tennyson, 'Happy: The Leper's Bride' (1889), in *Poems*, ed. Ricks, vol. 3, 189–94 (191).
[63] Gerard Manley Hopkins, 'Felix Randal' (completed 1880), in *The Poetical Works of Gerard Manley Hopkins*, ed. Norman H. Mackenzie (Oxford: Clarendon Press, 1990), 165.

In 'Happy' the male body represents the postlapsarian fraternity of sin and disease, a conjunction that Hopkins refers to obliquely by describing incarnate diseases as 'fleshed there' and having his own protocols for regulating his potentially sinful attraction to such bodies. He allows himself to express admiration for mature male bodies in his poetry once they have been absolved of sexuality by death. The poet-priest's attentiveness to the farrier's bodily physicality, 'his mould of man', resonates with his account of 'one sea-corpse cold', the dead sailor in 'The Loss of the Eurydice' (completed 1878): 'He was all of lovely manly mould.'[64] Having been made in God's image, the bodies described in these poems are now akin to Christ displayed on the Cross, the object of chaste admiration.

Recognised as a human and humane gesture that heals, touch is permissible for Hopkins through the priest's ministering and also metaphorically: 'touch had quenched thy tears, / Thy tears that touched my heart, child, Felix, poor Felix Randal'.[65] The yielding reciprocity and intimacy of the relations between the sick and the care-giver in 'Felix Randal' ('This seeing the sick endears them to us, us too it endears'[66]) is further observed in Walt Whitman's 'The Wound-Dresser' (1865). Like Hopkins, Whitman draws on personal experience for his poem, when as a hospital volunteer during the American Civil War he observed such men tending soldiers' injuries. The wound-dresser is introduced emblematically in an open and yielding stance: 'An old man bending I come among new faces.'[67] The poem comes into being as the protagonist yields to the curiosity of the young 'new faces', recalling for them his earlier experiences as a dresser, when he similarly approached the wounded 'With hinged knees', bending toward them, a habitual attitude that has since become fixed in the old man's kyphosis. In extremis, his patients too are yielding, 'the soldier bends, with curv'd neck, and side-falling head', and both dresser and his charges are reported to have found momentary refuge in physical contact and warmth, literally bracketed off from brutality and suffering for some moments in the poem's closing lines: '(Many a soldier's loving arms about this neck have cross'd and rested, / Many a soldier's kiss dwells on these bearded lips.)'.[68]

Hopkins was wary of Whitman. Writing in 1882, the priest confesses that 'I always knew in my heart Walt Whitman's mind to be more like my

---

[64] Gerard Manley Hopkins, 'The Loss of the Eurydice' (completed 1878), in *Works*, ed. by Mackenzie, 149–52 (151).
[65] Hopkins, 'Felix Randal', 165.   [66] Ibid.
[67] Whitman, *Leaves of Grass* (1855–1892; New York: Aventine, 1931), 316.   [68] Ibid., 319.

own than any other man's living', adding that 'As he is a very great scoundrel this is not a pleasant confession.'[69] While the physician to the soul is troubled by erotic subtexts to bodily physicality, Whitman finds desire implicit to healing touch. Tennyson's nurse asserts the healing power of love, but notably excludes physical contact as a means of conveying it, even to children: 'I am sure that some of our children would die, / But for the voice of Love, and the smile, and the comforting eye.'[70] The Christian association of the body with sin makes Hopkins and Tennyson cautious about touch. While 'In the Children's Hospital' identifies the new scientific medicine with coldness, a cognate naturalism licenses physical warmth in 'The Wound-Dresser', its final lines voicing what would be for Hopkins's and Tennyson's poems an unspeakable scandal of touch.

Touch became medicalised early in the nineteenth century, as diagnostics shifted from being a priori and physically aloof to being grounded in physical examination and sense data: inspection, palpation, percussion, and auscultation, most momentously, the enhanced mediate auscultation of the stethoscope, which was invented by R. T. H. Laennec in 1816. Such close and tactile practices were fringed with unease about sexual morality, and protocols were adopted for the new diagnostics. Pressures to extend this male prerogative to women incited waves of anxiety about sexual morality, when in the late 1860s and the early 1870s Sophia Jex-Blake led a campaign for women's rights to study and practice professional medicine. Bringing young men and women together to study the human body seemed a dangerous and immoral idea to many, while licensing women to take active roles over bodies, through such practices as surgery, palpation, and the direct diagnostic gaze of inspection, was variously seen as outrageous and titillating. Nevertheless, despite the often vicious efforts of her opponents, Jex-Blake's campaign was successful. The Medical Act of 1876 allowed medical professional bodies in Britain to accept qualified applicants irrespective of gender.

The advent of the 'Lady Doctor' in the final decades of the century was marked by a genre of light verse that airs the sorts of louche and trivialising assumptions about women that undergirded the controversy in the 1870s, but were not always expressed publicly. Most of these poems ignore the new doctor's professional skills, preferring instead to pay homage to the curative powers of her residual female charms. Such conventionally

---

[69] Claude Colleer Abbott (ed.), *The Letters of Gerard Manley Hopkins to Robert Bridges* (Oxford: Oxford University Press, 1935), 155.
[70] Tennyson, 'Children's Hospital', 47.

feminine qualities of 'voice [. . .], smile, and the comforting eye' that are inflected in a maternal register in Tennyson's nurse are often freighted with sexual interest and sly innuendo in other poems about nurses and in verses on female doctors. In John Godfrey Saxe's 'Guneopathy' (1856), the gent-protagonist describes with vaudevillian suggestiveness the efficacious presence and touch of a Lady doctor in remedying 'A kind of chronic chill':

> A lady came, – her presence brought
>   The blood into my ears!
> She took my hand – and something like
>   A fever now appears!
> Great Galen – I was all aglow,
>   Though I'd been cold for years.[71]

Nonsense, Decadence, and Deliverance

'Why must I sink all poetry in this prose, / The everlasting blowing of my nose?', Edward Lear asks in his 'Growling Eclogue: Composed at Cannes, December 9th, 1867' (1867).[72] Lear had recently met John Addington Symonds and his wife Catherine by chance at the popular winter resort town. On this occasion, however, Cannes was not popular with them, only wintry, and the 'Growling Eclogue' records their consequent illnesses and grumpiness. Rather than soaring in holiday sun, poetry is sunk in prosaic pathology, 'The everlasting blowing of my nose'. The opening lines find Lear's creative powers baulked and relegated to the tasks of nosology, as '*Edwardus*' asks '*Johannes*': 'What makes you look so black, so glum, so cross? / Is it neuralgia, headache, or remorse?' Categories of illness are dictated by the body of language in this poem, leaving Johannes protesting against their linguistic logic and necessity: 'Why must I suffer in this wind and this gloom? / Roomattics in a vile cold attic room?'[73] Succumbing helplessly to puns, he is plagued by rhymes and a heavy throbbing assonance:

> *Johannes*. Pain from a pane in one cracked window comes,
> Which sings and whistles, buzzes, shrieks and hums;
> In vain amain with pain the pane with this chord
> I fain would strain to stop the beastly *dis*cord![74]

---

[71] Ina Russelle Warren (ed.), *The Doctor's Window* (New York: Moulton, 1898), 68.
[72] Edward Lear, 'Growling Eclogue: Composed at Cannes, December 9th, 1867' (1867), in *The Complete Nonsense and Other Verse*, ed. Vivian Noakes (London: Penguin, 2002), 233–7 (233).
[73] Ibid., 235.   [74] Ibid., 236.

*Dis*ease is *dis*cord here, word and world sounds in which the decorous measures of verse and the healthy proportions of Vitruvian man are all out of kilter.

While Lear's poem begins tethered to the terms of nosology, they are the playful premise that generates the poem in Henry Savile Clarke's 'Lines by a Lunatic M.D.' (c. 1876). Written by a medical student turned dramatist, who is best known for his 1886 musical stage play of Lewis Carroll's *Alice in Wonderland*, the poem takes its cue from Latinate nomenclature for diseases, dignified names that lend themselves to reification. Titles fit for aristocrats or classical deities, their bearers share with these beings lives of leisure, which are similarly given over to amorous passions and rakish intrigues. Such liaisons are conducted within the grand edifice that these diseases hold in demesne, the human body:

> Oh! fair are the halls where stern *Peritonitis*
> Makes love to *Miss Asthma*, and courts the *Catarrh*.
> Where the bright *Influenza* is wooed by *Iritis*,
> And *Psora* joins *Measles* in 'Beautiful Star.'
>
> Oh! bright gleam the eyes of that flirt *Erythema*.
> And lightly *Pneumonia* whirls round in the dance.
> *Pleuritis* is madly in love with *OEdema*.
> And *Herpes* courts *Cholera* with amorous glance.[75]

All are healthy, fit for romance, biological agents that act nicely but naturalistically, oblivious to the consequences for their host organisms and vectors, the host of mere mortals who make the lives of these genteel agents of illness possible and pleasurable. The poem's dactylic and anapaestic tetrameters choreograph the *walpurgisnacht* waltz of the diseases. Within the fair halls of the respiratory system, *Pleuritis* and *OEdema* – diseases in which fluid accumulates in the pleural cavity and the lungs, respectively – are clearly meant to be together, adjunct to *Pneumonia*, which often causes these conditions. Although the pathogenic potential of *pneumococcus* bacteria was not demonstrated until the 1880s, the germ theory of disease was beginning to prevail in the 1860s and 1870s through the efforts of Louis Pasteur and Robert Koch, and is assumed by the poem. Savile Clarke's '*Pneumonia* whirls round in the dance' 'lightly' in the initial invigorating stage of contagion, as having entered the lungs she is eddied about by breaths of air.

---

[75] Henry Savile Clarke, 'Lines by a Lunatic M.D.' (c. 1876), in *The Comic Poets of the Nineteenth Century*, ed. W. Davenport Adams (London: Routledge, n.d.), 86.

The dizzying intoxication of the waltz also furnishes a trope for naturalism in Wilde's 1885 poem 'The Harlot's House', where the 'wheel and whirl' 'of the waltz'[76] describe the hedonistic abandonment of sexual lust. The 'ghostly dancers' in 'the house of Lust' represent a consumptive humanity that has lost its free will, 'Slim silhouetted skeletons', 'wire-pulled automatons'[77] who are governed by the overarching Darwinian exigency of species reproduction, the human sexual instinct that Sigmund Freud will theorise in the following decades. Another doctor, Freud's contemporary and compatriot Arthur Schnitzler, explores such themes in his play *Reigen* (*Roundelay*, 1900), which presents a cycle of ten sexual encounters, a serial saga of changing partners that relays syphilis across the social classes of *fin-de-siècle* Vienna. The play assumes that syphilis is caused by a pathogen. Whereas the miasma theory it despatched located the sources of contagious diseases externally and perceptibly in foul air, the new germ theory found them to be endemic to particular organisms, intrinsic to individuals, but imperceptible when most dangerous to others.

The convergence of sexual lust and the new germ theory, syphilis powerfully cathected *fin-de-siècle* anxieties. The invisibility of deadly pathogens encouraged hysteria, while a post-Darwinian *psychopathea sexualis* was identified with atavistic regression, 'decadence', and 'degeneration'. Max Nordau diagnoses *fin-de-siècle* culture 'as the confluence of two well-defined conditions of disease, with which [the physician] is quite familiar, viz. degeneration (degeneracy) and hysteria'.[78] He identifies Wilde as the primary pathogen of the age, a judgement that the courts concurred with, quarantining him from society with a two-year prison term. But physicians do not need Nordau as a mouthpiece, any more than Wilde did. They can speak for themselves, even within the constraints of an essay on poetry and medicine.

Fin-de-siècle scientist and poet, Ronald Ross identified the pathogen for malaria and its vector in 1897, disabusing the tropical disease of its etymological assumption, for – its name formed from the Italian for 'bad air' – it had long been seen to validate the miasma theory. His poem 'Vision of Nescience' (c. 1897) identifies its eponymous principle, 'the opposite of science',[79] with dreams and fantasies that are impelled by naturalistic drives. Its decadent 'vision of the night' recalls the richly coloured proto-surrealism of the Symbolists:

---

[76] Oscar Wilde, 'The Harlot's House' (1885), in Murray (ed.), *Oscar Wilde*, 539–40 (540).
[77] Ibid.   [78] Nordau, *Degeneration*, 15.   [79] Ronald Ross, *Memoirs* (London: Murray, 1923), iv.

> A ray of corruption, blue
> As in encharnel'd air
> On corpses comes. I knew
> A Death, a Woman there.
>
> Delirious, knee to knee,
> They drank of love like wine,
> He skeleton thin, and she
> Most beautiful, most divine.[80]

Later the poem discloses that the male lover is the devil, and, as 'The purple, fold by fold, / Fell from her', that the woman is a queen.[81]

The poem's decadent lovers are also inflected with a further characterisation redolent of the malarial pathogen and its blood-borne transmission that Ross was researching at the time he was writing the poem, naturalistic imagery in which they are compared to 'vultures sipping blood'. The implication of blood-borne infection hovers about the vision as it fades and unravels later in the poem, beginning with the wastage of its faux Helen of Troy, who is like the diseased malarial vector, the female *Anopheles* mosquito, followed by the male lover, 'Blood nourisht by her blood':

> I saw the Woman waste
> To nothing; and he, as tho'
>
> Blood nourisht by her blood,
> Grow grosser in the gloom
> And leprous like the toad
> That battens in the tomb.
>
> And both corrupted pined.[82]

A little further on from 'Nescience' in his chronologically arranged series of poems *In Exile* (1898), Ross includes a triumphant rebuke to this degenerate idol. On the evening of 21 August 1897, having proved his hypothesis about malarial transmission earlier in the day, Ross expresses his feelings of wonder and humility in poetry that is ostensibly 'bad' but genuinely affecting:

> This day relenting God
> Hath placed within my hand
> A wondrous thing; and God
> Be praised. At His command,
> Seeking His secret deeds
> With tears and toiling breath,

---

[80] Ronald Ross, *Philosophies* (London: Murray, 1911), 45. [81] Ibid., 46. [82] Ibid., 46.

I find thy cunning seeds,
O million-murdering Death.
I know this little thing
A myriad men will save.
O Death, where is thy sting?
Thy victory, O Grave?[83]

---

[83] Ibid., 53.

CHAPTER 6

Heroics, Devotion, and Erotics
Class, Sexuality, and the Victorian Nurse

Arlene Young

In a 1983 article in *Literature and Medicine*, Leslie Fiedler observes that 'nurses preside at the bedsides of males – privileged, even required, unlike other members of their sex, except for prostitutes, to touch, handle, manipulate the naked flesh of males'. As a result, he continues, nurses 'tend, therefore, to be portrayed also as erotic figures of a peculiar, ambiguous kind'.[1] While Fiedler was commenting on perceptions of nurses and on their cultural representations in the early 1980s, he identifies the precursors of the modern erotically ambiguous nurse as Victorian: the fictional Sairey Gamp and the historical Florence Nightingale. Just how the conflation of these two figures came to embody any kind of eroticism is not immediately obvious, and demands examination. The two figures could not be more dissimilar. Sairey Gamp, the famously disreputable monthly nurse who tends, in her way, to the medical needs of several characters in Charles Dickens's *Martin Chuzzlewitt* (serialised between 1842 and 1844) is a slovenly and dissipated menial. Florence Nightingale was an upper-class Victorian lady – refined, educated, and graceful by most accounts. Whence, then, the erotic power?

There is no question that Sairey would be conversant with all the exigencies of life and death, of birth, of illness and disease, and of every detail of the human body, male or female, young or old. She is the epitome of the worst kind of old-style Victorian nurse, a low-level servant assigned to some of the most disagreeable duties in the Victorian household. Without the benefits of sophisticated modern pharmaceuticals and equipment, nursing for women like Sairey was dirty, heavy work. Tending to the corporeal needs of the sick and dying, changing dressings, handling bodily fluids, and cleaning the sickroom all required physical stamina, not to mention a strong stomach. Nursing could also be dangerous; there were

---

[1] Leslie A. Fiedler, 'Images of the Nurse in Fiction and Popular Culture', *Literature and Medicine* 2 (1983), 29–90 (80).

no vaccines or effective treatments for communicable diseases, putting nurses at constant risk of contracting, and dying from, any number of illnesses. Like other household servants, the gamps of the early Victorian period received no formal training or certification. Florence Nightingale represented the polar opposite; she was the prototype of the new-style nurse who was trained in the latest techniques of medical hygiene and who approached her work as a vocation. She became an iconic figure of caring compassion and moral rectitude. Neither of these images is entirely fair or accurate, however, and together they do not constitute a plausible hybrid of the Victorian nurse.

As Fiedler acknowledges, the archetypes for the complex and enduring cultural figure of the nurse are varied and ancient – 'older even than the profession of nursing, as old as patriarchal society itself'.[2] In the Victorian period alone, that most formative era for nursing, the influences that cumulatively fashioned the popular figure of the nurse were legion and contradictory. The nurse most familiar to anyone at the time, or probably in any time, was a mother, a sister, or a wife who cared for ailing members of her family. As Nightingale herself attests in her *Notes on Nursing* (1860), 'every woman, or at least almost every woman, in England has, at some time or another of her life, charge of the personal health of somebody, whether child or invalid – in other words, every woman is a nurse'.[3] The domestic nurse, then, is commensurate with the Victorian domestic woman, and carries with her associations with the 'Angel in the House', the model of idealised Victorian womanhood immortalised in Coventry Patmore's poem. Nightingale was similarly elevated to the status of Angel in the Military Hospital, the ethereal Lady with the Lamp, immortalised in Henry Wadsworth Longfellow's poem as 'Santa Filomena', the vision of light that 'flit[s] from room to room', bringing comfort to suffering soldiers during the Crimean War.[4] While the real Nightingale undoubtedly worked indefatigably at the Barrack Hospital in Scutari, she was less a ministering angel than an efficient administrator, supervising the nurses, overseeing the organisation of the hospital, and fighting a battle of her own with the military establishment in order to obtain basic supplies for the soldiers under her care.

As a conflation of angel of mercy and hard-headed administrator, Nightingale had, in the words of a family friend, a *'strange & sexless*

---

[2] Ibid., 81. [3] Florence Nightingale, *Notes on Nursing* (New York: Appleton, 1860), 3.
[4] Henry Wadsworth Longfellow, 'Santa Filomena', in *The Poetical Works of Longfellow* (Boston: Houghton Mifflin, 1975), 197.

identity'; she was Joan of Arc *'come round again'*.⁵ This image is a departure from an earlier version of the military caregiver – the camp follower. Camp followers comprised civilians who accompanied troops on military campaigns, and included both men and women who worked as porters and as suppliers of food and other goods. Attitudes towards camp followers varied, and, while often sympathetic, were informed in the Victorian period by a sense of distain afforded by unfortunate necessity. 'Every great cause, like an army, must have its camp-followers', claimed an 1869 *Times* editorial. 'They hang about the skirts of the combatants, and when the battle is over pillage the slain.'⁶ Women camp followers undertook the same kinds of domestic duties they did at home – repair and laundering of clothing, meal preparation, and nursing care. They also provided sexual services, some as the legal or common-law spouses of individual soldiers and some as prostitutes.⁷ The association of the provision of nursing care with out-of-wedlock sexual contact – which in the Victorian period could only mean licentiousness and, for women, moral turpitude – tainted military nursing in the minds of the general public. Florence Nightingale was herself uneasy about the morals of the nurses in Scutari and accused them of 'flouting her rules of female decorum'. She had, according to Mark Bostridge, 'an abiding fear that an unoccupied nurse will inevitably fall into some kind of mischief, if not of a sexual nature, then stemming from the usual problems associated with excessive consumption of alcohol'.⁸ In other words, Nightingale's assessment of nurses at the battlefront was that they were much like Sairey Gamp and needed constant supervision in order to maintain an appropriate level of institutional decorum.

Nightingale's apprehensions about nurses in Scutari were limited to lay nurses. There was another group of nurses, however, that was above suspicion – the nurses of religious sisterhoods. The two groups of nurses were generally incompatible. The nursing sisters were uneasy about 'associating with "persons of doubtful character" who [...] were "almost daily intoxicated"'. The lay nurses in turn complained that the nursing sisters had 'pretensions beyond their status'.⁹ The disharmony between nursing

---

⁵ Quoted in Mark Bostridge, *Florence Nightingale: The Woman and Her Legend* (London: Viking, 2008), 262. Italics in original.
⁶ Unsigned, 'Every Great Cause, Like An Army', *The Times*, 22 September 1869, 6.
⁷ For a detailed summary of the roles of military camp followers in the pre-Victorian era, see John A. Lynn II, *Women, Armies, and Warfare in Early Modern Europe* (Cambridge: Cambridge University Press, 2008), 66–163.
⁸ Bostridge, *Florence Nightingale*, 234.   ⁹ Ibid., 231.

sisters and lay nurses in the Crimea paralleled a similar tension developing over new-style and old-style nursing in London hospitals, one that had been brewing for more than a decade before Nightingale drew public attention to nursing on such a grand scale. In the 1840s, around the same time that Dickens introduced the disreputable old-style nurse in the character of Sairey Gamp, there were attempts to reform nursing practice in programmes established by philanthropic and dedicated ladies of the upper classes. In 1840, Elizabeth Fry established the Protestant Sisters of Charity, later renamed the Institution of Nursing Sisters, to train respectable women from the working classes as nurses. Fry, like Nightingale after her, had been inspired by the pioneering nursing programme that was affiliated with the deaconess training institution in Kaiserswerth, Germany, which she visited for two days in May of 1840.

Although clearly associated with Protestantism, Fry's nurses were not part of a religious sisterhood, but several Anglican nursing sisterhoods established training programmes during the 1840s and 1850s.[10] These Anglican sisterhoods were modelled on existing Roman Catholic religious communities, many of which had been providing nursing care for the poor for centuries in institutions such as the Hôtel Dieu in Paris. Unlike Fry's institution, the sisterhoods recruited women from higher social classes, many indeed from the aristocracy, who were, like Nightingale, educated and refined; in the parlance of Victorian society, they were ladies. The ladies of the sisterhoods trained to be head nurses and nursing supervisors; they paid a premium to join the community, and their work was voluntary. The sisterhoods also admitted lay members, who trained to do basic nursing care; these nurses received room, board, and a small wage. This two-tiered system was obviously based on class, but within the sisterhoods appears to have caused little strife.[11] The sisterhoods' mission was initially to provide private and district nursing, but their superior abilities prompted several large London hospitals to contract individual sisterhoods to provide all in-house nursing services. St John's House, the most prominent of the sisterhoods, signed agreements with King's College Hospital in 1856 and Charing Cross Hospital in 1866. The All Saints Sisters of the Poor began providing nursing services at University College Hospital

---

[10] See Susan Mumm, *Stolen Daughters, Virgin Mothers: Anglican Sisterhoods in Victorian Britain* (London and New York: Leicester University Press, 1999) and Carol Helmstadter and Judith Godden, *Nursing before Nightingale, 1815–1899* (Aldershot: Ashgate, 2011).

[11] Judith Moore, *A Zeal for Responsibility: The Struggle for Professional Nursing in Victorian England, 1868–1883* (Athens and London: University of Georgia Press, 1988), 4.

in 1859.[12] Having charge of the all nursing care in large hospitals enabled the sisterhoods to develop systematic clinical training programmes. St John's House was especially successful in developing a system in which probationary students, under the supervision of trained sisters, rotated from ward to ward in order to develop clinical knowledge and skills in all areas of medicine and surgery. The non-denominational Nightingale Training School (later the Nightingale School of Nursing) opened at St Thomas's Hospital in 1860, and, while it has been recognised as the vanguard of modern nursing education, its system of nursing education and services in the Victorian period was not as progressive as that of St John's House. The Nightingale School prevailed, however, because of its secure finances from the endowment provided by the Nightingale Fund and the prestige afforded by its name. Florence Nightingale herself had only limited direct involvement in the school after its establishment. Although publicly supportive, she was, in fact, dubious about the training provided and about the terms of the contract with St Thomas's Hospital.[13]

Although Nightingale's vision for the school established in her name was to institute a programme that trained respectable working-class women in very basic nursing skills and very strong principles of hygiene and moral rectitude, the school eventually developed a two-tiered class system similar to that of the sisterhoods. In the mid-1860s, a new category of 'Specials' – lady volunteers who paid a premium – were admitted into the training programme. By the 1870s, the categories of 'Specials' had expanded to include different levels of premiums as well as 'Free Specials' – educated women of limited means who paid no premium and, in some cases, even received a small salary.[14] As with the sisterhoods, women from diverse classes in the Nightingale programme do not appear to have expressed animosity towards each other, although as Anne Summers contends, the lower-class nurse 'was, indeed, a Martha to the sister's Mary'.[15] That these women continued to work in relative harmony was perhaps the result of an ingrained acceptance of mistress–maid relations enhanced by the fact that lady probationers, like working-class ones, had to take on all the arduous duties associated with nursing the sick and dying. The class division did cause strife within hospitals, but that strife was

---

[12] Helmstadter and Godden, *Nursing before Nightingale*, 135, 148–9.
[13] Ibid., 194–5; Bostridge, *Florence Nightingale*, 447–9.
[14] Bostridge, *Florence Nightingale*, 367–8, 445.
[15] Anne Summers, 'The Mysterious Demise of Sarah Gamp: The Domiciliary Nurse and Her Detractors, c. 1830–1860', *Victorian Studies* 32:3 (1989), 365–86 (381).

generated by administrators and doctors, who had opposing views on the merits of old-style versus new-style nurses. Conflict arose both in hospitals affiliated with sisterhoods and in those that adopted similar reforms in the administration of nursing services, most notably Guy's Hospital.

While Victorian society in general was entranced by the mythology of Nightingale as the Lady with the Lamp and was therefore well primed to accept new-style nurses, responses to them and to their work were wildly divergent. The supposedly civilising effect of genteel ladies was much touted. In 1866, during an inquiry into nursing at the Middlesex Hospital in London, one surgeon lamented the regrettable conduct on the wards of his institution, noting that 'scenes of drunkenness, vice, and indecency had been such as to make the hair stand on end'. The physicians and hospital administrators taking part in the inquiry advocated for the appointment of a lady nurse as a remedy. 'The watchful care of an educated and intelligent nurse', according to one of the doctors, 'often did more for the recovery of a patient than the skill of the physician.'[16] Not all medical practitioners were so sanguine about the influence of lady nurses. Many doctors preferred the old system that allowed them to train the nurses they worked with in something more like an apprenticeship, a system that fostered the nurse's loyalty. One London surgeon accordingly questioned the efficacy of educated lady nurses: '[W]hat is there to learn', he demanded to know, 'that any active and sensible woman, trained in ordinary household work, cannot achieve under the guidance of a medical man?'[17] Because most of the new-style nurses were affiliated with religious sisterhoods, they were persistently accused of being more interested in the state of patients' spiritual, rather than physical, wellbeing. *The Lancet*, a respected organ of the medical profession, noted the 'oft-repeated cry of "proselytism"' with reference to nurses from the sisterhoods, but dismissed it as a 'foolish excuse for preferring the imperfections of former days to a system that embodies intelligence, the keenest sympathy, and refinement'.[18] That the supervising nurses on most wards in Britain were called 'sister' resulted in many nurses who were unconnected with sisterhoods also being suspected of proselytism. The rift between doctors and nurses became most acute at Guy's in 1880, prompting members of the medical staff and one brave lady nurse to fill the pages of London periodicals and

---

[16] Unsigned, 'Hospital Nursing', *The Times*, 30 July 1866, 12.
[17] George Barraclough, 'Nursing as a Career for Ladies', *Fraser's Magazine* 19 (1879), 468–79 (479).
[18] Unsigned, 'Volunteer Nursing', *The Lancet*, 8 September 1866, 271.

newspapers with sometimes intemperate attacks on the integrity of each other's profession.[19]

Many Victorians, both medical practitioners and general observers, continued to have faith in the nursing provided by lady nurses. A leader in *The Times* in 1883, reporting on the establishment of a government distinction for lady nursing in the military, praises the heroic nature of their work. Part of what distinguished the nurses being honoured was the aura of patriotism attached to their service, as well as the fact that their work, like that of the nursing sisters (but not the lay nurses), was voluntary. The association of nursing with military heroism coloured responses to all lady nurses, even those who, by the 1880s, were receiving pay for their work. '[T]he ladies who volunteer to minister to our sick and wounded soldiers and sailors are not worthier of decoration than the noble women who give themselves up to a life of self-abnegation in the great hospitals of London and other large towns', the leader affirms. 'Where the latter class of nurses are actuated by religion or philanthropy alone in their choice of a nurse's calling this is doubtless true, and even where the nurse receives remuneration, her choice of a career is noble enough.'[20] Countering this mantle of patriotism and philanthropy that ennobled the nurse in the Victorian imagination was the persistent conviction that nursing was degrading. George Barraclough, the surgeon who disparaged the training of lady nurses, voiced this opposing position succinctly. He warned of 'the horrible bad language' that genteel nurses 'may occasionally be compelled to hear from patients of the lowest class'. 'They who enter on the career of a nurse through the agency of an ordinary training institution', he cautioned, 'can hardly fail, in the course of years, to degenerate socially and intellectually.'[21] In the Barraclough school of thought, rather than the genteel lady nurses civilising the hospital culture and refining nursing practice, nursing would corrupt the genteel ladies.

The threads woven together to construct the character of the Victorian nurse, then, were, on the positive side, the genteel philanthropy of the lady nurse from the sisterhoods and the heroism of the military nurse. Both these identities still carried some negative connotations. The spectre of religiosity on the part of anyone associated with sisterhoods loomed large

---

[19] For in-depth analyses of the conflicts between nurses and doctors at Guy's and other London Hospitals in the 1870s and 1880s, see Arlene Young, '"Entirely a Woman's Question?": Class, Gender, and the Victorian Nurse', *Journal of Victorian Culture* 13:1 (2008), 18–41, and Moore, *Zeal for Responsibility*.
[20] Unsigned, 'The Royal Order, which Appear in Last Night's Gazette', *The Times*, 28 April 1883, 11.
[21] Barraclough, 'Career for Ladies', 471.

throughout the Victorian period. Military nurses, though largely freed from censure because of their association with the idolised figure of Florence Nightingale, still carried some of the stigma of their predecessors, the camp followers. And all of nursing still trailed clouds of ignominy courtesy of the ever-popular, and undoubtedly quite unfair, characterisation of Sairey Gamp. While nursing moved steadily, if not directly or effortlessly, towards professionalisation, misapprehensions about nurses persisted. The taint of intimate physical contact was still troubling, especially to the staid middle classes, whose daughters were entering training schools. Nursing's standing as a reputable calling further suffered from a series of public scandals in the late 1880s, beginning with the mistreatment of patients at Guy's, resulting in a charge of manslaughter against one of the new-style nurses and in accusations of 'inhumanity and carelessness' against another.[22] In the later 1880s, *The Times* reported on further charges of murder against nurses, in one case the beating to death of the accused's husband, in another the poisoning of the accused's eleven-year-old-daughter, a crime perpetrated by the mother in the hospital in which she worked.[23] The trustworthiness and moral probity of the lady nurse accordingly were not unassailable in late Victorian culture, and while public debates about reformed nursing and hospital organisation faded from the media, fictional representations of nurses embodied on-going cultural misgivings about the new-style nurse, just as Sairey Gamp had embodied unease about the old-style nurse. What emerges in these representations of new nursing practices and practitioners in the late nineteenth century is a curious and very Victorian fixation on sexuality. Although the media debates about nursing in the large public hospitals in the 1870s and 1880s had largely focused on the new forms of hospital organisation that new-style nursing entailed, most of the cultural resistance as expressed in fiction was explicitly or implicitly directed at the sexuality or the sexual roles of the women involved.

Fictional representations of nurses in the late Victorian period were in fact often positive, but even ostensibly favourable portrayals could be sexually charged, if perhaps indirectly, as in a narrative entitled 'The Story of a Nurse', published in *The Graphic* (later in a collection entitled *Tales of the Children's Ward*, 1894).[24] In this story, nursing is variously

---

[22] Unsigned, 'Guy's Hospital', *Saturday Review*, 30 October 1880, 546–7 (546).
[23] Unsigned, 'A Woman Charged with Beating Her Husband', *The Times*, 6 September 1885, 5; Unsigned, 'The Assizes', *The Times*, 24 February 1887, 10.
[24] Honnor Morten and H. F. Gethen, 'The Story of a Nurse', in *Tales of the Children's Ward* (London: Sampson, Low, Marston, 1894), 28–64. Subsequent references to this edition will appear in the

associated with all the most laudable qualities of the new-style nurse – philanthropy, heroism, and religion. When Dinah Lethmore, the nurse-protagonist, volunteers to work on a fever ward during an outbreak of typhus, the personal danger associated with her mission and that of her peers is cast in military terms, with the nurses outfitted in distinctive costumes and committed to quasi-battlefield discipline. Dinah and the other young nurses undertake their assignment as eagerly as heroic young men who enter the fray and sign up for an appointment to 'a dangerous post'. Dressed in special uniforms and red capes, their battleground defined by a 'cord of red braid', these courageous nurses are marked off from and admired by their peers (52–3). The emphasis in the capes and in the demarcating cord on the colour red – the colour of blood and of passion – and the elevation of these young women as superior to other young women in physical courage suggests their power as icons of heroism. They are, in a sense, untouchable in their bravery. Unlike the soldier, however, whose wounded body is the honoured emblem of his courage, the body of the nurse who tends the sick and dying on the fever ward is contaminated by her association with disease; her act of bravery renders her literally untouchable. Like the fallen woman, she is tainted and must be segregated from other women by the cord of red braid. The military connotations of the nurse's heroic work here carry with them inherent corruption.

Just as the by-now habitual associations of nursing with the military are here employed unconventionally, so, too does 'The Story of a Nurse' present a new take on the putative link between the new-style nurse and religion, depicted in a dream vision experienced by Dinah's suitor, Major Edis. That Edis is himself a soldier enhances his authority as someone attuned to the potential military connotations in the nurse's calling, which his dream calls into question:

> Major Edis was half asleep, and he saw a vision of the future. There was a great city stretched out before him, full of life and pleasure, and change and joy. All day long its streets were thronged by a hurrying crowd, who searched either for wealth or pleasure. And in the middle of the city, on a hill, was a great lonely temple surmounted by a golden cross. Every now and then some member of the hurrying crowd grew weary or sick of the rush of the streets, and turned aside and entered the temple. But unless

text. For an in-depth analysis of nurses in Victorian fiction, see ch. 3 of Arlene Young, *From Spinster to Career Woman: Middle-Class Women and Work in Victorian England* (Montreal, Kingston, London, and Chicago: McGill–Queen's University Press, 2019).

> injury or illness overtook them the crowd heeded not the great building in the centre of the city. And when a man went into the temple a sudden hush fell upon him, and he saw before him long aisles, but instead of pews there were rows of beds, and there was no music – the service was conducted in silence, and the ministers were women. It was a 'service' in the common acceptation of the word, for all the sick and weary who were worsted in the struggle without were here tended with love and sympathy, till healing was achieved. The ministers wore white robes, pure and unspotted; and when at rare intervals they went out into the streets, the crowd stood still while they passed, and bowed low before them. They were reverenced as were the Vestal Virgins in Rome. There seemed to be some Great High Priest in the Holy of Holies of the Temple; for when the ministers had done their most to secure healing, and pain and tiredness yet remained, round the bed of the sufferer gathered a kneeling group of the ministers, and a silent shadow shrouded the place, a darkness fell, and when the cloud passed away, and the ministers rose from their knees, the sufferer had also passed away, and gone to the Land of Perfect Health.
>
> It was a strange dream, and peculiarly vivid; Major Edis used to call it his vision of the religion of the future. It enabled him to see the nurses of to-day, not so much as soldiers as priests; and to understand why the rewards of this world were not for them. (42–3)

Major Edis rejects the nurse/soldier analogy and identifies nurses instead with priesthood in a curious 'religion of the future' that conflates aspects of Christianity, paganism, and a vague spiritualism. Edis envisions a future defined by a decadent modernity in which an urban populace rushes endlessly and seemingly mindlessly in search of 'wealth or pleasure'. The temple in the centre of the crowded city is unheeded by the crowd; it is a 'lonely' citadel approached only by the sick and weary. The link between church and hospital is obvious in the description of the interior of the temple, with its rows of beds in the hushed silence, and in the wordplay on 'service' and 'minister'. 'Service' here refers to attendance on the sick, rather than to a religious ceremony, and 'minister' refers to one who tends to physical needs, rather than to a member of the clergy. Ministering to the sick nevertheless takes on a religious aura in this vision, but there are almost none of the trappings of Christianity, except for the gold cross above the temple. The only overt religious reference is to Vestal Virgins, a curiously pagan association, but one that carries subtle Victorian domestic overtones, given that the Vestals were the priestesses of Vesta, goddess of the hearth. Sexual purity, implied by the comparison with the Vestals and echoed in the ministers' 'pure and unspotted' white robes, combined with loving and sympathetic servitude, define the ministers' moral character. The reverence afforded them by the deferential crowds is based solely on their service and devotion, not on religious fervour. While there is the supposition that there is a 'High Priest' and a 'Holy of Holies' in the temple, the only supreme power appears to be death and the only supreme good is Perfect Health. This oddly syncretic 'religion of the future' constitutes a kind of reverential secularism in which the only truly moral and respected beings are nurses. The menace of religiosity on the part of new-style nurses is negated by making them the locus of awe and respect.

Rather than being Fiedler's 'erotic figures of a peculiar, ambiguous kind', the nurses in Major Edis's dream are religious figures of a peculiar, ambiguous kind, and part of the ambiguity is the fixation on sexuality inherent in the almost obsessive insistence on purity, virginity, and unworldliness. The impossibility of such denial of the nurse's sexuality in the real world, however, where intimate knowledge and manipulation of bodies was an integral part of her work, continued to colour perceptions of nurses. Despite increased professionalisation and growing respect in the public at large, misgivings about nurses' motives and moral character persisted and were also registered in fictional representations. That these misgivings were patently unfair is nevertheless reflected in the fact that suspicions about nurses are almost always expressed by characters who are either unreasonable and ill-informed, or lower class (and therefore supposedly ignorant). In a novel entitled *Nurse Elisia* (1892), for example, the refined eponymous protagonist is employed to care for Ralph Elthorne, the ill-tempered patriarch of an affluent family who considers her to be simply 'a woman serving as a menial' whom he suspects of carrying on 'a contemptible flirtation' with one of his sons.[25] Elthorne's sister, Anne, manages to blend both the out-dated prejudices against gamps with mistrust of new-style nurses. Before meeting Elisia, Anne asserts that her 'experience of nurses is that they are dreadful women, who drink and go to sleep in sickrooms, and the patient cannot wake them, and dies for want of attention' (90). When the highly professional Elisia arrives, Anne's attitude changes, and she declares that she in fact 'would a great deal rather it had been one of those old-fashioned stout nurses who did not wear white starched caps and black dresses, just as if they were playing at being a nurse' (121). The servants in the household disparage Elisia as a 'beggarly nurse' who gives 'herself airs as if she was a lady' (141) or who, as a 'Horspittle' nurse, is '[d]ressed up like a nun out for a holiday' (113). Virtually every nineteenth-century prejudice against nurses – as disreputable,

---

[25] George Manville Fenn, *Nurse Elisia* (New York: Cassell, 1892), 216. Subsequent references to this edition will appear in the text.

immoral, supercilious, or pious – is accordingly directed against the forbearing Elisia, who turns out to be not only the 'principal lady nurse' at a large London hospital, but also the daughter of a Duke (117, 291). Even those who recognise Elisia's true refinement and professional expertise wonder about her motives. Elthorne's son Neil, a medical student in the hospital where Elisia normally works, wonders why she has become a nurse, why she is 'devoting herself to all those repulsive cases as if she were seeking by self-denial and punishment to make a kind of atonement for something which has gone before. What can have gone before?' (83).

The questions about Nurse Elisia are answered in the course of her story, revealing her to be dedicated and honourable. Elisia's story could in fact be interpreted as an endorsement of the evolving nursing profession, which, under the auspices of the newly formed British Nurses Association (founded in 1887), was working to establish standardised education and registration for qualified practitioners. Registration would, it was assumed, guarantee the quality of nursing care in Britain and eliminate uncertainty about any individual nurse's skills. Around the time of *Nurse Elisia*'s publication, however, nursing's reputation – not to mention that of publicly funded hospitals – suffered another blow with two scandals over the administration of the Eastern Hospital, a fever hospital in East London under the jurisdiction of the London Metropolitan Asylums Board. In 1885, the Asylums Board carried out an extensive investigation into unscrupulous financial practises on the part of the hospital's officers; in 1891, an even more intensive inquiry unveiled accusations of corruption, malpractice, and impropriety on the part of the administrators and the medical and nursing staffs. Covered in detail in the press throughout the British Isles, the proceedings of the inquiry aired the grievances of patients and some nurses over the mistreatment and neglect of the sick, the shockingly poor quality of the food, the scarcity of linens and supplies, the unprofessional conduct of some hospital staff, and the potential misappropriation of funds by administrators. Particularly shocking to Victorian sensibilities were revelations about the alleged drunkenness of the night nursing superintendent and about a late-night dance party held by the nurses on one of the children's wards.

The scandals at the Eastern Hospital created a national sensation, generating hundreds of articles in close to one hundred newspapers, including prestigious dailies such as *The Times* as well as local weeklies in remote counties in Britain and even Northern Ireland. As the *Weekly Irish Times* commented, the details revealed in the protracted inquiry of the first scandal put 'fiction utterly to shame'.[26] It is not surprising, then, that the incidents related during the second inquiry subsequently find their way into an early twentieth-century novel about life in a small provincial hospital at the end of the nineteenth century. *In a Cottage Hospital*, published in 1911, once again characterises nurses and nursing as morally and ethically suspect. The story is ostensibly based on the account 'related to the Author' by the 'broken-hearted mother' of the house surgeon at the centre of the story, a young man who died 'during the recent Boer War' – that is, the Second Boer War of 1899–1902. The events of the story, which precede the young surgeon's military service, date from the very end of the Victorian period and constitute a compendium of negative nineteenth-century stereotypes of nurses. In the preface, the author, George Trelawney, presents the story as true, the mother's narrative having been supplemented by the 'very carefully written account' compiled by the young doctor himself, by 'further particulars gathered from reliable sources, [and] by personal investigation'.[27] Trelawney also calls attention to the similarity of the events to the recent 'allegations of immorality and mismanagement' in Poor-Law Hospitals 'so sensational as to arouse the attention of the whole British Press' (viii). Although the Eastern Hospital scandals had occurred fifteen years previously, the parallels between the events in the novel and those revealed by the Asylum Board's inquiries are striking. By recalling prejudicial recent history, Trelawney reinvigorates the old prejudices about the character of nurses, and indeed the nurses in the cottage hospital in the fictitious town of Rebley make Sairey Gamp seem almost benevolent and decorous.

In both the Eastern Hospital scandal and in Trelawney's fictionalised version, it is not only the nurses who are corrupt but also the hospital's doctors, who are unethical and negligent, and its administrators, who divert funds for supplies, medicine, and food into their own pockets. However, part of the supposed advantage of introducing lady nurses in the mid-nineteenth century had been their civilising influence on hospital culture, an influence sorely lacking in Rebley Hospital. The only civilising potential resides in the character of James Kargill, the young doctor who arrives to take up the post of house surgeon, while among the relatively

---

[26] Unsigned, 'The Revelations at the Eastern Hospital, London', *Weekly Irish Times*, 1 August 1885, 6.
[27] George Trelawney, *In a Cottage Hospital* (London: Werner Laurie, 1911), vii. Subsequent references to this edition appear in the text.

youthful nurses at Rebley Hospital, the stereotypical disreputableness of the gamp is augmented by voluptuousness and sexual laxity. Kargill himself is unable to resist the flirtations of beautiful young May Patterson, to whom he becomes secretly engaged. May, however, like many of the other nurses, is carrying on an affair with one of the staff doctors. The nurses accord with Anne Elthorne's view of them as 'dreadful women' who drink and neglect their patients. 'Aw tell yer', one of the Rebley patients confides in Kargill, 'them nurses wot's paid ter look hafter us spends hall their time a'canoodlin', an' Gawd know what else in that blarsted sittin'-room downstairs'. (76). 'What else' turns out to be partying on the brandy and other spirits prescribed as stimulants for the patients. The prejudice against the potential religiosity of nurses also appears in *In a Cottage Hospital* in the characterisation of the matron, Miss Burroughs, who is enamoured of the (as it turns out, fraudulent) Reverend Mr Smally, who preaches and holds revival meetings at a nearby 'little tin chapel'. The matron ostentatiously flaunts her piety by praying over any morsel of food she arranges for Kargill and by 'holding prayer-meetings in her room, and making all the nurses come to them', much to their disgust (70).

Despite the author's claims about the veracity of his tale, the behaviour of the nurses and other members of staff at Rebley Hospital is so extreme as to be a veritable parody of Victorian medical practice at its worst and goes far beyond the improprieties alleged over the Eastern Hospital scandals. That Kargill will not turn a blind eye to the corrupt practices makes him a pariah, and when he is finally forced to leave, the doctors and nurses celebrate with a wild party in the nurses' sitting room, while the patients again languish unattended.[28] Even though the reader has by this time learned that alluring May Patterson has died as the result of a botched abortion, performed by her physician lover while he was intoxicated, and that this man's affluent lifestyle has been augmented by providing illegal abortions for wealthy society ladies, the orgy that closes the story of the hospital is a shocking read. Kargill, entering the hospital for the last time before his departure, comes upon the scene of a drunken revel:

> A strange scene met his astonished gaze. The table was laden with the remains of what had evidently been a tasty supper. Plates of oyster-shells, empty bottles of champagne, fragments of pies and pastry, jellies, trifle,

---

[28] The whistle-blower at the Eastern Hospital was a nurse, Diane Halkin, who was similarly reviled by her fellow nurses, who gathered at the entrance of the hospital (leaving patients unattended) to hiss and pelt flour at her as she left. See Unsigned, 'The Eastern Hospital Inquiry', *The Times*, 7 March 1891, 5.

cakes, sweets, fruit and innumerable dainties of various kinds were in distinct evidence. At the head of the table, smoking a large cigar and riotously dangling little Nurse Carson upon his knees, was [...] the chairman of the Hospital Committee. Next to him, in similar combined positions, were Sister Cross and old Dr Leary on one side, and Dr Arnold and Nurse Crabtree on the other [...]. Kargill stood at the door, too much astonished at the composition of this extraordinary party to say a word. They, on their part, were no less uncomfortably surprised and nonplussed. The girls jumped from the embraces of their respective admirers with very red faces, adjusted their disordered attire. But they were so flustered at the unexpected interruption that the adjustment was not as thorough as it might have been. Sister Cross had no apron on and her dress was unfastened; Nurse Carson's skirt appeared to reach only as far as her knees; and Nurse Crabtree's hair had come undone and was hanging in luxurious profusion all around her. (236)

The excessiveness of this scene speaks to the individual and institutional corruption at work in this cottage hospital, where funds are diverted from patient care to the debaucheries of the negligent caregivers, who leave the sick unattended. The nurses here are not just 'dreadful women' who drink and sleep in the sickroom; they are also dissipated sensualists whose sexual indiscretions are all the more blatant for their dismantling of professional attire and decorum. The eroticism here is peculiar only in the sense of being particular or special. The 'disordered attire' and unfastened hair that hangs 'in luxurious profusion' speak not just of very Victorian versions of sensuality, but more profoundly of the sensationalism of discredited respectability, of the exposure of rank hypocrisy.

In a Cottage Hospital is presented as a cautionary tale, not so much about medical practice in general, as about unregulated conditions in small regional institutions. The novel closes with an impassioned warning: '*Reader, there is many a Rebley Hospital in England, to-day!*' (241; italics in original). Kargill's frame of reference, however, is the large London teaching hospital where he trained, and such hospitals, along with their medical and nursing staff, were the benchmarks for up-to-date, well-regulated, and professional practice both at the time and in this novel. Both Kargill and the one nurse he finds trustworthy at Rebley trained and worked in large hospitals. That the nursing care at Rebley is discredited by means of out-dated negative stereotypes of nurses nevertheless remains telling. The prejudice against a cottage hospital is also revealing and subtly discredits some of the best nursing provided during the Victorian period. One of the most famous hospitals in Victorian England was the cottage hospital at Walsall, in the mining district of the Black Country, where terrible accidents in the pits demanded intense and expert nursing care.

The hospital's matron was Dorothy Pattison, known and beloved as Sister Dora, second only to Florence Nightingale as the most acclaimed and revered nurse in nineteenth-century Britain. Rebley, like Walsall, is in the centre of a mining district, and the name of the beautiful doomed love-interest of *In a Cottage Hospital*, May Patterson, is suggestively similar to the last name of Sister Dora.

The nurses at Rebley, despite their defects, are trained and maintain a veneer of professionalism with their smart uniforms and with the working schedules and treatment programmes they set up but do not follow. Like Anne Elthorne's version of hospital nurses, they wear starched white caps and uniforms, 'just as if they were playing at being' nurses, but their disordered uniforms only serve to eroticise them. The peculiar eroticism of the nurse here works as a facile tool to provoke public distrust and raise suspicions about the integrity of a still relatively new profession, and in so doing also directs attention to the possible inadequacies of small regional hospitals. In this critique of the hospital system, the first line of attack in questioning standards is the morally suspect nurse, rendered in all the shades of negative clichés popularised in the Victorian era.

The peculiar eroticism of the nurse, noted by Fiedler in the 1980s, was first consolidated in the Victorian period. The public perception of nurses over the course of the nineteenth century fluctuated radically in response to the disparate roles that they played in homes, in hospitals, in religious sisterhoods, and in military service. These roles and the perceptions they engendered were registered throughout the period in media reports and in fictional representations of both heroism and scandal, of good nurses and bad. Although Florence Nightingale and Sairey Gamp continued to be the most popular points of reference, no single version of the nurse dominated the public imagination at the time. The nurse was an unstable hybrid of feminine values and foibles – of devotion, of heroism, of veniality, and of unseemly sexual knowledge. The suggestion of professional impropriety and sexual availability dogged the profession for at least one hundred years, rendered in fictional representation of figures such as Nurse Ratched in Ken Kesey's *One Flew Over the Cuckoo's Nest* (1962) and in comic portrayals in the seemingly endless series of 'Carry-On' movies. In moving from the sensationalism of nineteenth-century melodrama to the low comedy of 'Carry-On Nurse', however, the trope of the eroticised nurse lost much of its sway. It is still the quasi-mythic Nightingale, the 'strange & sexless' hero who braved the dangers of war and disease to care for ordinary soldiers in the Crimean War, who remains the quintessential icon of modern nursing in the Western world.

CHAPTER 7

Pharmacology, Controversy, and the Everyday in Fin-de-Siècle Medicine and Fiction

Keir Waddington and Martin Willis

'There's no need for fiction in medicine,' remarks Foster, 'for the facts will always beat anything you can fancy. But it has seemed to me sometimes that a curious paper might be read at some of these meetings about the uses of medicine in popular fiction.'

'How?'

'Well, of what the folk die of, and what diseases are made most use of in novels. Some are worn to pieces, and others, which are equally common in real life, are never mentioned. Typhoid is fairly frequent, but scarlet fever is unknown. Heart disease is common, but then heart disease, as we know it, is usually the sequel of some foregoing disease, of which we never hear anything in the romance. Then there is the mysterious malady called brain fever, which always attacks the heroine after a crisis, but which is unknown under that name to the text books. People when they are over-excited in novels fall down in a fit. In a fairly large experience I have never known anyone do so in real life. The small complaints simply don't exist. Nobody ever gets shingles or quinsy, or mumps in a novel.'

Arthur Conan Doyle, 'A Medical Document' (1894)

Arthur Conan Doyle's capturing of a professional medical view of the features of late-Victorian popular fiction tells us something significant about *fin-de-siècle* medicine's literary representations. Doyle's mouthpiece, Theodore Foster, a prosperous general practitioner from the Midlands, speaks of the divergent incidence of the diseases practitioners encountered and the medical afflictions that occur in fiction. In doing so, he cannily notes that medical conditions are commonly used to provide or support melodrama and sensation but rarely to promote the kind of everyday occurrences that give definition to realism. Foster's conclusions – that it is the melodramatic and sensational aspects of medicine that are most common in late nineteenth-century fictions – are reflected in contemporary scholarship.

The exploration of medicine in fictions of the 1880s and 1890s has focused exclusively on the unusual and curious, and commonly within the genres of the Gothic or the romance.[1] While many of these illuminating works contribute to our understanding of the place of medicine at the *fin de siècle*, they miss – as does Theodore Foster (and Doyle) – those more quotidian representations of medical practice in popular fiction that also serve to position medicine in late-Victorian British culture. In this chapter, therefore, we explore first the relationship between fiction and medical controversy, and second the previously untrammelled representations of everyday medicine in late-Victorian fiction. Looking directly at the ordinary or commonplace, as well as considering it in relation to its much more common fraternity in the genres of romance, reveals not only the significance of the everyday for portrayals of professionalised medicine, but also shows, for the first time, how realist representation is a vehicle for emerging critiques of medical knowledge making and its claims to a new scientific basis. To do so, we move beyond the normal register of the anxieties generated by *fin-de-siècle* medicine to focus on the often overlooked territory of pharmacology: the description and use of prescribed drugs and dispensed therapeutics that play a central part in so many medical fictions. This is a particularly valuable area for study: it offers the opportunity to consider both the sensational controversies generated by new pharmacological treatments and the common, everyday drugs on which normal medical routines depended. By reading *fin-de-siècle* medical fictions through the sensational and the everyday, we consider how the formal elements of these texts enhanced their engagement with specific medical issues and how an understanding of their generic features offers important insight into contemporary medical debates. To provide further definition we focus our attention on two groups of short fictions: Doyle's series collected under the title *Round the Red Lamp* and first published in 1894, from which our epigraph is taken, and L. T. Meade's *Stories from the Diary of a Doctor*, serialised in *The Strand Magazine* from July 1893 to December 1895.

---

[1] See Michael Davis, 'Incongruous Compounds: Re-reading Jekyll and Hyde and Late-Victorian Psychology', *Journal of Victorian Culture* 11:2 (2006), 207–25; Christopher Pittard, *Purity and Contamination in Late Victorian Detective Fiction* (Aldershot: Ashgate, 2011); Laurence Talairach Vielmas, '"I Have Bottled Babes Unborn": The Gothic, Medical Collections, and Victorian Popular Culture', *Gothic Studies* 17:1 (2015), 28–42.

Doyle, Meade, and Their Medical Contexts

L. T. Meade, the pen name of Elizabeth Thomasina Toulmin Smith, had built her career on the strength of her ability to 'gauge the literary marketplace'. In 1893, she sought to capitalise on the success of Doyle by moving into writing medical detective fictions for the *Strand*. 'My First Patient', the first in the twenty-four-part series *Stories from the Diary of a Doctor*, appeared in July 1893 alongside Doyle's 'The Adventure of the Crooked Man'.[2]

Before Meade made her debut in the *Strand*, she had written *The Medicine Lady* (1892), a novel about a woman who acquires a vaccine for tuberculosis and administers it with fatal consequences. Inspired by the recent controversy surrounding tuberculin as a failed treatment for tuberculosis, *The Spectator* considered parts of the novel 'the best work' Meade had produced, and noted that 'the tale, it appears, owes something to the inspiration of a medical friend'.[3] In her medical detective fiction, Meade made claims to such medical authenticity and, in the second series, explicitly advertised *Stories from the Diary of a Doctor* (1893–1895) as a collaboration between herself and Clifford Halifax, MD, 'a medical man of large experience' and the hero of the stories.[4] While Halifax was a fiction, Meade did consult with Metropolitan Police Surgeon Edgar Beaumont, and the influence of current medical debates is apparent throughout her work. Woven through the *Stories from the Diary of a Doctor* are topical socio-medico concerns: from the benefits of bacteriology and the need for doctors to certify death, to the dangers of hypnotism and the hypodermic syringe. Meade's adherence to the genre of romance led to predictable criticisms from the medical press. In responding to one of Meade's earlier stories in 1892, *The Lancet* felt moved to dismiss Meade's fictions as 'by no means as realistic as they might be'.[5] Yet, as the journal recognised, such stories had the potential to bring medical issues to a wider audience. As Meade's work reveals, many of these issues went beyond the familiar anxieties about experimental science or degeneration to examine issues of professional etiquette and prescribing, as well as the connections between physical and mental health.

---

[2] L. T. Meade, 'My First Patient', *Strand Magazine* 6 (1893), 91–102 (91).
[3] Unsigned review of *The Medicine Lady* (1982) by L. T. Meade, *The Spectator* (11 February 1893), 24 (24).
[4] L. T. Meade, 'Creating a Mind', *Strand Magazine* 9 (1895), 33–47 (33).
[5] Unsigned review of *The Medicine Lady* (1892) by L. T. Meade, *The Lancet* (17 December 1892), 1394.

The stories in Doyle's *Round the Red Lamp* similarly combined the sensational with the ordinary and, as *The Lancet* later commented, were of 'distinctly medical interest'.[6] Doyle had begun to write stories with a medical setting when he moved to London to set himself up as an eye specialist. The first, 'A Physiologist's Wife', had been published in September 1890. *Round the Red Lamp* included these earlier stories and a further series originally intended for Jerome K. Jerome's magazine, *The Idler*. Jerome had originally asked for 'something very strong' and, in a letter to an American friend, Doyle explained how in the fifteen tales which formed *Round the Red Lamp* he was attempting to 'treat some features of medical life with a certain amount of realism', addressing both the positive and the darker sides of medicine. The aim, Doyle continued, was to 'startle the reader out of his usual grooves of thought', to shock 'him into seriousness'.[7]

Doyle's and Meade's doctors embody notions of knowledge, training, education, and class that were held up as crucial to late nineteenth-century medical practice as practitioners negotiated 'a careful and complicated balance between gentility and financial interests'.[8] Furthermore, the two collections of short fictions show general practitioners at work with numerous therapeutic products. It is the consequences of the use (and abuse) of these therapeutics that often drive the plots and lead the stories towards their conclusions and commentaries. In making therapeutics so central to their narratives both Meade and Doyle were capturing something of contemporary medical culture, which, as the next section will show, was continually alert to the advantages and disadvantages of new, laboratory-based pharmacological knowledge.

Drugs, Distrust, and Controversy: Fin-de-Siècle *Therapeutics*

Writing in 1804, William Williams looked forward to the advances which would result from 'the memorable alliance between Medicine and Chemistry'.[9] The anaesthetic properties of synthetic chemicals, such as

---

[6] Unsigned, 'Conan Doyle', *The Lancet* (12 July 1930), 90.
[7] Cited in Richard Lancelyn Green and John Michael Gibson, *A Bibliography of Arthur Conan Doyle* (Oxford: Clarendon Press, 1983), 82; Arthur Conan Doyle, *Round the Red Lamp and Other Medical Writing*, ed. with an introduction and notes by Robert Darby (1894; Kansas City: Valancourt Books, 2007), ix, 2.
[8] Lori Loeb, 'Doctors and Patent Medicines in Modern Britain: Professionalism and Consumerism', *Albion* 33:3 (2001), 404–25 (407).
[9] William Williams, *A Concise Treaty on the Progress of Medicine since the Year 1573* (Ipswich: n.p., 1804), 58.

chloroform and then morphine, stimulated interest, but looking back from the vantage point of the 1880s and 1890s, practitioners were less sanguine about this alliance. Popular accounts produced in response to Queen Victoria's Golden (1887) and Diamond (1897) Jubilees associated medical advances with surgery, the laboratory, and new diagnostic technologies.[10] While such commemorations were deliberate acts of construction aimed at highlighting England's contribution to medical progress, some significant advances in therapeutics were reported. Accounts highlighted the decline of heroic dosing and its replacement by physiologically-based chemical remedies as part of a broader emphasis on the application of science to the art of medicine, approaches visible in *Stories from the Diary of a Doctor* and *Round the Red Lamp*.[11] Commentators drew attention to how chemistry and the development of synthetic drugs were beginning to place pharmacology on a new footing.[12] Immunology was gradually being superseded by chemotherapy, as new pharmacological and therapeutic substances began to appear in the 1880s, often as by-products of the German chemical industry's experiments to find new anaesthetic agents through a combination of bacteriology and immunological research. Phenacetin and phenazone were, for example, both synthesised in 1887 and were widely used for the relief of fever in the 1890s. The discovery of diphtheria antitoxin in 1891 and Paul Ehrlich's theory of chemotherapy stimulated pharmaceutical companies, such as Burroughs Wellcome & Co, into producing new vaccines and anti-toxins. Meade's 'The Hooded Death' and 'The Strange Case of Captain Gascoigne' make explicit reference to such therapeutic breakthroughs, the first in relation to anti-venom, the second related to anti-toxins, both of which were lauded as areas of medical advance.[13]

When new drugs and new pharmacological substances were announced, they were often hailed as triumphs. For instance, throughout the 1860s numerous papers extolled the benefits of hypodermic injections of

---

[10] Malcolm Morris, 'The Progress of Medicine during the Queen's Reign', *The Nineteenth Century* 41 (1897), 739–58.
[11] See R. Brudenell Carter, 'Medicine and Surgery', in *The Reign of Queen Victoria*, ed. T. H. Ward (London: Smith, Elder & Co., 1887), 388–444; Benjamin Ward Richardson, 'Medicine under Queen Victoria', *Asclepiad* 4 (1887), 201–73; John Eric Erichsen, 'Recent Advances in Surgery and Medicine', *Edinburgh Review* 168 (1888), 5491–515 (5511).
[12] Mark Weatherall, *In Search of a Cure: A History of Pharmaceutical Discovery* (Oxford: Oxford University Press, 1990); Unsigned, 'Chemistry in Relation to Therapeutics', *The Lancet* (19 June 1897), 1688–9.
[13] L. T. Meade, 'The Hooded Death', *Strand Magazine* 9 (1895), 416–32; 'The Strange Case of Captain Gascoigne', *Strand Magazine* 10 (1895), 290–304.

morphine for a wide range of conditions.[14] Cocaine was equally lauded in the medical and popular press. Quickly associated with a varied range of applications, from removing pain and acting as a mild antiseptic to being used as a tonic in digestive disorders, cocaine was hailed as a wonder drug connected with modernity.[15] In the 1890s, serum therapy was seen to mark the arrival of 'scientific therapeutics'.[16] As Meade noted in one story, the future of therapeutics was in the 'marvellous success which has already attended to the treatment of disease by the elaboration and discovery of new forms of inoculation'.[17]

While contemporary practitioners might rhetorically emphasise advances in therapeutics to a public audience, in the last quarter of the nineteenth century, therapeutics and pharmacology were often criticised. As the pharmacologist Walter Langdon-Brown later remembered, 'it was curious that the most materialistic age in science should have been the most sceptical in the use of drugs'.[18] Despite protest from doctors, controls on the content and quality of drugs and patent medicines were minimal, with early attempts at regulation focusing on concerns about poisons and adulteration. Proprietary medicines were widely advertised and sold, much to the ire of medical practitioners, who vociferously attacked the trade and called for greater controls while also prescribing them.[19]

In this climate of scepticism and concern, new pharmacological substances proved controversial. Although lauded as breakthroughs, the increased use of morphine and the role of the hypodermic syringe divided medical practitioners.[20] Although an early advocate, Thomas Clifford Allbutt became convinced that 'injections of morphia, though free from the ordinary evils of opium eating, might, nevertheless, create the same artificial want and gain credit for assuaging a restlessness and depression of which it was itself the cause'. His views provoked resistance.[21] Throughout the 1870s the attendant dangers of hypodermic injections of morphine were debated, and, by the

---

[14] See, for example, Arthur Evershed, 'On the Hypodermic Injection of Morphia', *Medical Times and Gazette* (1 May 1869), 463; Thomas Clifford Allbutt, 'The Use of the Subcutaneous Injections of Morphia in Dyspepsia', *Practitioner* 2 (1869), 341–6; J. Constable, 'Case of Persistent and Alarming Hiccough in Pneumonia Cured by the Subcutaneous Injection of Morphia', *The Lancet* (21 August 1869), 264–5.
[15] See James E. Pilcher, 'Cocaine as an Anaesthetic', *Annals of Surgery*, 3 (1886), 51–66.
[16] Unsigned, Untitled, *The Practitioner*, 58 (1897), 591.   [17] Meade, 'Captain Gascoigne', 290.
[18] Unsigned, 'Obituary: Walter Langdon-Brown', *The Lancet* (12 October 1946), 546–8.
[19] See Loeb, 'Doctors and Patent Medicines', 404–25.
[20] See Virginia Berridge, *Opium and the People: Opiate Use and Drug Control in Nineteenth and Early Twentieth Century England* (London: Allen Lane, 1981), 135–70.
[21] Thomas Clifford Allbutt, 'On the Abuse of Hypodermic Injections of Morphia', *Practitioner* 5 (1870), 327–31; George Oliver, 'On Hypodermic Injection of Morphia', *Practitioner* 6 (1871),

1880s, the idea that levels of morphine addiction were increasing among the middle and upper classes engendered alarm.[22] Morphine was not alone in the controversy it generated. Two years after the effects of cocaine on mitigating pain had entered the public consciousness, the *British Medical Journal* explained in 1886 how 'this sweet rose of our therapeutic bouquet has its bitter thorn'.[23] Such concerns about the addictive properties of morphine and cocaine were built on alarm about the role of medical practitioners as purveyors of dangerous substances, and touched on long-standing professional concerns about the risks of self-medication and 'domestic drugging', which intensified in the 1880s and 1890s.[24]

At the same time, experimental chemists and general practitioners also reminded their colleagues that these controversial therapeutics were only part of the story of 1890s medicine. Science, and especially the science of bacteriology and pharmacology, may have been lauded, but it also aroused unease as a certain class of practitioner feared that the art of medicine would be replaced by laboratory science.[25] Just as vital as the new therapies associated with experimentation and the laboratory, many argued, were the more everyday considerations of patient engagement, careful diagnosis, and cautious use of common remedies. For research chemist turned Edinburgh-trained physician, Gordon Sharp, writing concurrently with Meade and Doyle in 1894, the 'therapeutist, to be a successful man' needs to take laboratory methods and the knowledge they create to the 'patient's bedside and see if the latter agrees with the two former'.[26] Indeed, he went on to argue, it was in the commonplace interactions with patients that pharmacological advances had often been made: 'many therapeutic triumphs have been the result of the bedside observations of the general practitioner, and much of the success'. Samuel West, physician at

---

75–80; F. E. Anstie, 'On the Effects of Prolonged Use of Morphia by Subcutaneous Injection', *Practitioner* 6 (1871), 148–57.

[22] See James Braithwaite, 'A Case in which the Hypodermic Injection of Morphia was Suddenly Discontinued After its Use Daily in Large Doses for Seven Years', *The Lancet* (21 December 1878), 874; W. C. Cass, 'Another Extraordinary Morphia Case', *The Lancet* (25 March 1882), 503–4; Percy Boulton, 'An Extraordinary Morphia Case', *The Lancet* (8 April 1882), 343–4; Philip E. Hill, 'A Case of Morphia Poisoning by Hypodermic Injection; Recovery', *The Lancet* (30 September 1882), 527–8.

[23] Douglas Small, 'Masters of Healing: Cocaine and the Ideal of the Victorian Medical Man', *Journal of Victorian Culture* 20:1 (2016), 3–20; Unsigned, 'United States [From a Correspondent]', *British Medical Journal* (2 January 1886), 40.

[24] Stanley Melville, 'Domestic Drugging: A Case of Antipyrin Poisoning', *The Lancet* (22 December 1894), 1515.

[25] See Steve Sturdy, 'Looking for Trouble: Medical Science and Clinical Practice in the Historiography of Modern Medicine', *Social History of Medicine*, 24:3 (2011), 739–57.

[26] Gordon Sharp, 'Principles of Therapeutic Progress', *The Lancet* (23 June 1894), 1557.

St Bartholomew's and at the Royal Free Hospital, pushed this further. West argued that the new science of pharmacology was little more than a 'new word', which registered nothing other than a change in the rhetoric of medical science.[27] Although not valued in the terms of pharmacology, which West sees as often disseminated to general practitioners 'rich in scientific promise', it is 'common remedies' that continue to offer the most practical results.[28]

As *fin-de-siècle* debates reveal, therapeutics did not always require drugs. Throughout 1894 there was considerable discussion in *The Lancet* of the use of 'mental therapeutics', the title given to an article by the German physician A. T. Schofield, which found purchase among Britain's medical community. Schofield began by asking a simple question: 'Students listen with rapt attention to the powers of [...] well-advertised modern drugs, but how often is their attention directed, save in ridicule, to this mighty curative agent that in its powers pretty well balances the whole pharmaecopeia – the mind?'[29] Schofield's call for a consideration of the role of the mind as a therapeutic agent was a practical call for the management of patients' beliefs and expectations. During a period when claims and counter-claims were made about the validity of medical power, Schofield promoted everyday practitioner authority as just as likely to lead to improved health as any form of chemical therapy. What was required was gaining the confidence of the patient and then, with 'simple methods', enabling them to change their own behaviours so as to improve their prognosis.[30] Schofield's mental therapeutics resonated with general practitioners. One Australian GP wrote to *The Lancet* to note that 'several cases have occurred in my practice which were certainly cured by mentally impressing upon the patients the certainty that the treatment I intended to adopt would cure them'.[31] Similar curative powers are given by Meade to Dr Halifax, whose powerful authority and conviction often engenders relief for patients previously unable to alleviate their symptoms. This is especially true in the first series of stories where Halifax is called upon to deal with a variety of extreme mental conditions, from dipsomania through hysteria to kleptomania.[32] It is also a key element of Doyle's

---

[27] Samuel West, 'Rational Therapeutics and the Use of Common Remedies', *The Lancet* (30 May 1894), 1474.

[28] Ibid., 1475. [29] A. T. Schofield, 'On Mental Therapeutics', *The Lancet* (3 February 1894), 262.

[30] A. T. Schofield, 'Mental Therapeutics', *The Lancet* (2 June 1894), 1401.

[31] W. J. Barkas, 'Mental Therapeutics', *The Lancet* (24 November 1894), 1246.

[32] See L. T. Meade, 'Trapped', *Strand Magazine*, 7 (1894), 465–80, and 'The Ponsonby Diamonds', *Strand Magazine* 7 (1894), 606–26.

'The Doctors of Hoyland', where the new, female doctor impresses her patients 'by the firmness of her manner'.[33]

Both Meade's and Doyle's fictions are immersed in this culture of medical therapeutics and contemporary pharmacology. In the next section we consider some of the representations of the more dramatic therapeutics of the late-Victorian period, and show through extended analysis of two stories how both Meade and Doyle investigate contemporary medical culture's use of new pharmacological products. In doing so, we draw parallels to the genre of romance, linking the grand effects of such therapies to archetypal characters and the domestic extremes of sensation fiction.

Medical Melodrama in Meade and Doyle

In 'The Wrong Prescription', Meade creates a vivid portrait of the 'morphia-maniac', which mirrored contemporary medical debate.[34] The trajectory of 'The Wrong Prescription' sees Halifax uncover and treat Miss Frances Wilton's morphine addiction, returning her to the young woman capable of adoration she had been six months earlier, and thus saving her from the common fate of fictional sensation heroines of the 1860s, whose obsessions usually end in death and disgrace.[35] Although the dangers of the hypodermic syringe and morphine had been sensationalised in an 1887 issue of *Nineteenth Century* by the physician Seymour Sharkey, Meade's short story prefigures populist Edwardian accounts which Parssinen and Kerner suggest informed cultural understanding of addiction.[36] In doing so, Meade presents a medicalised image of morphine addiction that could have come straight from a medical textbook, highlighting both the use of the drug and the syringe in medical practice and its physical and moral dangers.[37]

With the same shifting terminology present in medical writing, Miss Wilton emerges as a 'morphia-maniac': a 'victim of morphonism' suffering

---

[33] Doyle, *Round the Red Lamp*, 304.
[34] See, for instance, *Report from the Departmental Committee on the Treatment of Inebriates PP (1893–94) XVII; First Report of the Royal Commission on Opium: with Minutes of Evidence and Appendices* (London: HMSO, 1895).
[35] L. T. Meade, 'The Wrong Prescription', *Strand Magazine* 6 (1893), 600–63.
[36] Seymour Sharkey, 'Morphinomania', *Nineteenth Century* 22 (1887), 335–42; Terry M. Parssinen and Karen Kerner, 'Development of the Disease Model of Drug Addiction in Britain, 1870–1926', *Medical History* 24:3 (1980), 287–8.
[37] See William Osler, *The Principles and Practices of Medicine* (London: Pentland, 1892), 1005; Richard Quain, ed., *A Dictionary of Medicine*, 2 vols. (London: Longmans, 1894), vol. 2, 627; Thomas Clifford Allbutt, *Systems of Medicine*, 8 vols. (London: Macmillan, 1897), vol. 2, 886.

from 'the awful storm of abstinence'. The moral implications of 'such a vice' for the respectable are repeatedly stressed, but so too is the contested model of addiction as a physiological illness popularised by Norman Kerr, the leading British authority on addiction.[38] With the narrative focusing on the secret habits of the addict, lies, and deception, the path to Wilton's dependency on hypodermic injections of morphine emerges as a familiar one. Wilton's route to addiction comes via an earlier medical treatment for a 'feverish attack', which had brought sleeplessness and 'agonies of pain from neuralgia'. Just as in so many contemporary medical cases described in *The Lancet* and *The Practitioner*, the original medical practitioner had prescribed Wilton small doses of morphine injected 'in the usual way with a hypodermic syringe' to treat her fever and neuralgia. Although her symptoms improved, Wilton 'acquired a certain liking for the drug'. Within a short space of time 'she could not live without the drug'.[39] These connections were familiar ones by the 1890s: contemporary medical writing stressed how 'morphonism' was acquired through medical prescription and the apparent willingness of practitioners to hand over control for injections to either a nurse or the patient.[40] The story's shift from a common complaint to a disastrous addiction parallels the trends of sensation fiction, where domestic environments both hide and enculture the kinds of actions from which ruinous behaviour emanates.

If the dangerous consequences of medical practitioners giving up responsibility for treatment were stressed in medical writing and by Meade, middle- and upper-class women were believed to be particularly susceptible to morphine addiction, just as they were the subject of romance plots from the emergence of the first wave of Gothic fiction in the later eighteenth century to the kinds of adventure romances more common in the 1890s. Not only was morphine a relatively expensive drug, but, as *The Lancet* explained, 'Given a member of the weaker sex of the upper or middle class, enfeebled by a long illness, but selfishly fond of pleasure, and determined to purchase it at any cost, there are the syringe, the bottle, and the measure invitingly to hand, and all so small as to be easily concealed, even from the eye of prying domestics'.[41] In 'The Wrong Prescription', Meade reinforces this stereotype, stressing not only the moral dimension prevalent in medical writings but also the link

---

[38] Meade, 'Wrong Prescription', 603–4; 605; Norman Kerr, *Inebriety or Narcomania*, 3rd ed. (1st ed. 1888; London: H. K. Lewis, 1894).
[39] Meade, 'Wrong Prescription', 604, 610.
[40] Berridge, *Opium and the People*, 145; Allbutt, *Systems of Medicine*, 886.
[41] Unsigned, 'Hypodermic "Dram-Drinking"', *The Lancet* (11 October 1879), 552.

between addiction, class, gender, and nervous disorder. In doing so, morphine addiction is confirmed as a disease of the will and an inherently female disorder.[42] Wilson emerges as a beautiful, yet neurotic and morally damaged woman in a representation that was already familiar from the works of Mary Elizabeth Braddon and Wilkie Collins, and would be captured again in French paintings of the sexualised female morphine addict. After procuring morphine from a former nurse, Wilton appears 'unquestionably the most beautiful girl in the room. Her fine dark eyes, generally so dull in expression, were now bright and sparkling. There was not the least doubt that she was under the influence of a powerful dose of the poison'.[43] Such beauty, however, is quickly eroded. Wilton takes on the appearance of the addict as her habit robs her of youth and vitality. In asserting Wilton's corruption and moral failings, just as in medical writing, Meade highlights Wilton's mental instability as caused by her addiction. Making reference to the fashionable gendered condition of 'acute neurosthenia [sic]', Wilton's withdrawal reduces her to 'complete nervous prostration'.[44]

Halifax's response to the crisis follows an approach which was beginning to become recognisable: rather than a method of sudden withdrawal described as the 'English treatment', Halifax initially administers small doses of morphine to address Wilton's immediate collapse – an approach recommended in Edward Levinstein's authoritative text *The Morbid Cravings for Morphia* (1878) – a treatment Halifax combines with rest, nourishment, and the type of psychological encouragement advocated by Schofield and others.[45] Halifax is, of course, the archetypal romance hero of this story: the medical man who combines pharmacological knowledge with high social graces and incorruptible moral standards. Rather than bringing disaster as initially feared, through Halifax's quick thinking the 'awful discovery' later in the narrative that Wilton has been given 'another prescription' containing strychnine brings a resolution. Although a poison, strychnine offers a tonic to 'ward off the extreme weakness of the heart' to restore Wilton, although not without an appropriate and morally satisfying painful period of withdrawal.[46] As Doyle explained to the readers of the *Hampshire County Times:* 'The whole science of medicine is by the use of a mild poison to counteract a deadly one.'[47] While Halifax successfully treats Wilton, the implications are clear: just as in medical texts, morphonism is

---

[42] Berridge, *Opium and the People*, 148.   [43] Meade, 'Wrong Prescription', 607.   [44] Ibid., 607.
[45] Ibid., 603.   [46] Ibid., 612.   [47] Doyle, *Round the Red Lamp*, 280.

shown to be curable, and doctors other than the heroic Halifax are guilty of enabling drug dependency in their patients.

We can look more closely at the generic particularities of representing dangerous pharmacological practices in a study of Doyle's 'The Los Amigos Fiasco', a story which also centres on therapeutic excess. The narrative tells the story of the outlaw Duncan Warner, who is captured by the authorities and sentenced to death by electrocution. Despite the large dosage he is given, Warner not only survives but is enhanced by the process, gaining ever greater strength from each attempt to put him to death. Although efforts are made to complete the execution by other means, Warner resists them all. His dosage of electricity has, as one Los Amigos resident explains, 'increased this man's vitality until he can defy death for centuries'.[48] The story is not one that attempts to say something about electro-therapies as such, but rather is a satiric comment upon contemporary pharmacological science that resonates with contemporary medical commentary on homoeopathy and dosages. Indeed one character is even made a mouthpiece for this understanding of the story when he notes that he understands the size of the dose of electricity 'by analogy [...] all drugs increase their effect when they increase their dose'.[49] As becomes clear, the story cautions against the use of drugs without the necessary understanding of their power or efficacy. For Doyle, the primary culprits are laboratory experimenters rather than general practitioners. Even the most knowledgeable electrician in the story is characterised as a 'crank' who is 'eternally working with wires and insulators and Leyden jars' but who 'never seemed to get any further, or have any results worth publishing'.[50]

The excesses of the dosage are matched also by genre excess. 'The Los Amigos Fiasco' begins as an adventure narrative, placed on the same American frontier that Doyle explores in 'A Study in Scarlet'. As the narrative moves towards the gargantuan dosing of the captured outlaw, both the language and the action push adventure first to its limits and then beyond that into farce and fantasy. The reader's introduction to Los Amigos, given by the doctor-narrator, notes that the town's electrical works are 'on a very large scale', and does so in the register of many later nineteenth century realist–melodramatic tales of rural life.[51] But as discussions of the large electrical dosage to be administered to Warner advance, so too do the generic features begin to expand. What is first known as Warner's 'electrocution' becomes a 'blasting of flesh and blood', its power

[48] Ibid., 287. [49] Ibid. [50] Ibid., 283–5. [51] Ibid., 287.

described as 'the essence of ten thunderbolts'.[52] The largesse of the language is matched by farcical narrative content; Warner's extraordinary resistance to the electricity, which leaves him 'radiant with the glow of perfect health', extends to his defiance of two attempts at hanging and to being shot six times. The story concludes with claims that Warner is likely to 'wear out' the 'new gaol' in which he is incarcerated, and he will not be able to be executed for another 'fifty years'.[53] The adventure anti-hero, whose early characterisation was as a lion-headed outlaw, is now the bald and glowing figure of a fantasy (almost a science fiction) of super-heroic immortality. The generic travel of the narrative parallels the commentary on the dangers of excess dosages: genre is employed both to illuminate issues of overdosing and to reveal its effects within the form of the fiction.

A similar sympathy between genre and pharmacology is apparent in the use of common remedies across Meade's and Doyle's fictions. In the next section we investigate the importance of everyday medicines in developing realist narratives and enabling Meade and Doyle to offer further commentary on the role of the *fin-de-siècle* practitioner and the nature of everyday medical practises.

Common Remedies: Meade, Doyle, and Everyday Medicine

Historians have become increasingly interested in the everyday as a category of analysis, not only drawing on de Certeau and Lefebvre to explore how the everyday is external to (or eludes) the discourses and techniques of power, but also to shed light on lived experiences.[54] However, scholars working on late-Victorian medicine have been less attuned to everyday medical encounters. As Doyle reminds us in 'The Curse of Eve', while we and the patients in his stories might experience events 'which seemed so appallingly important', we also need to be sensitive to how medical fictions can reveal 'the merest everyday matter of business to the medical man'.[55] We can see the everyday nature of prescribing in both Meade's and Doyle's

---

[52] Ibid., 287, 282.   [53] Ibid., 293–4.
[54] Alf Ludtke, 'Introduction: What Is the History of Everyday Life and Who Are Its Practitioners?' in *The History of Everyday Life*, ed. Alf Ludtke, trans. Willam Templer (Princeton: Princeton University Press, 1991), 3–40; J. Brewer, 'Microhistory and the Histories of Everyday Life', *Cultural and Social History* 7 (2000), 87–109; Ben Highmore, ed., *The Everyday Life Reader* (London and New York: Routledge, 2002); Joe Moran, *Reading the Everyday* (London: Taylor and Francis, 2005).
[55] Doyle, *Round the Red Lamp*, 62.

work, not least in how Halifax has medicines to hand as he always travels with 'a small medical case' – his 'bag of drugs and instruments'.[56]

In rendering the 'everyday matter' of prescribing and administering drugs to patients, Meade and Doyle were in tune with the contemporary medical view. Notwithstanding the controversies associated with new developments in pharmacology, which give a view of dynamic therapeutic change, there was an enduring sense that, as one general practitioner looking back on his career noted, 'progress seemed at a standstill [...]. Diagnosis may have been frequently correct, but [...] treatment was empirical'.[57] The changes associated with anatomy, physiology, pathology, and bacteriology, often held up as markers of progress in nineteenth-century medicine, did not produce distinct changes in doctors' ability to treat disease. The period may have seen the introduction of new painkilling and fever-reducing drugs, but older remedies based on plant extracts, mineral salts, and inorganic chemicals not only survived but also continued to be actively used. Often, prescribing was more about managing symptoms than curing disease, with prescription books from contemporary general practices highlighting how polypharmacy was the norm. Much of this polypharmacy was routine during a period when, as critics noted, the doctors' 'education in pharmacy, chemistry and Materia Medica is totally inadequate and recognized to be so'.[58] It took less time or knowledge than the adoption of new or dramatic procedures, notwithstanding contemporary images in sensational and Gothic texts that medical practitioners were ardent experimenters.

Doctors' prescribing hence looked as much to the past as it did to the future: practitioners might mix traditional remedies with new drugs, such as morphine or chlorodyne. If Meade could make explicit reference to the modern therapeutics gradually being marketed to general practitioners by her reference to Halifax's 'Burroughs and Wellcome medical case', more often traditional and modern drugs were finely balanced, a balance found in *Stories from the Diary of a Doctor* and *Round the Red Lamp*.[59] As Doyle told the medical students at the opening of the new academic session at St Mary's Hospital in 1910, practitioners had a 'very copious and hard-worked pharmacopoeia. There were noble prescriptions in those days – I don't know if they are quite extinct now [...]. Wondrous was

---

[56] Meade, 'Hooded Death', 424; 'Wrong Prescription', 603.
[57] E. R. Furbes, *London Doctor* (London: n.p., 1940), 16–17.
[58] *Report of the Select Committee on Patent Medicines* (London: HMSO, 1914), 534.
[59] L. T. Meade, 'The Small House of Steven's Heath', *Strand Magazine* 10 (1895), 512–26 (513).

the science which combined so many powerful drugs.'[60] Often individual prescriptions and personalised remedies, as seen in Meade's 'Little Sir Noel', were integral to a doctor's practice and a matter of professional pride.[61] For instance, in Doyle's 'The Curse of Eve', the local doctor sends for his 'A.C.E. mixture' when a patient is weakened from a lengthy labour.[62] Doctors often combined new and powerful remedies with stock mixtures, which they would dilute 'down into the bottle of medicine'.[63] Doyle later recounted how he had known a country practitioner who 'used to empty all the bottles which had not been claimed into one huge jar, from which he occasionally dispensed droughts for his more obscure cases', explaining how 'It's like grape-shot [. . .]. If one misses, another may hit.'[64]

A lack of effective drugs ensured that some acute conditions could become chronic long-term conditions, and their on-going management was part of a practitioners' work. This is common in Meade's stories: Halifax's attentions to the long-term conditions that trouble his largely elite patients focus on prosaic management of health, age, and bodily comfort. Indeed, as Anne Digby suggests, 'prescriptions of medicine served functions other than a strictly clinical treatment of disease'.[65] They met the expectations of patients that they receive some kind of treatment, acting as a form of reassurance, or as a marker that the practitioner was doing something to treat the condition. Such practises formed part of the mental therapeutics that were considered a necessary part of the practitioner's skill.

In the fictions of both Meade and Doyle pharmacological substances often appear as generic drafts, restoratives, sedatives, or narcotics, reflecting the range of common preparations available. Sometimes self-administered but in most cases prescribed by a general practitioner, the nature of the drugs given is often glossed over or summed up in the simplest terms as a 'stimulant', 'a cooling dose', 'a simple dose', 'restoratives', or 'soothing remedies'.[66] For instance, in Meade's 'Creating a Mind', a story that deals primarily with an experimental surgical procedure performed on the 'beautiful idiot' grandson of a squire, the medical treatment the squire receives for a spinal injury at the start of the narrative is summed up in a

---

[60] Arthur Conan Doyle, 'The Romance of Medicine', *St Mary's Hospital Gazette* 16 (1910), 100–6.
[61] L. T. Meade, 'Little Sir Noel', *Strand Magazine* 9 (1895), 649–63.
[62] Doyle, *Round the Red Lamp*, 65.
[63] Quoted in Anne Digby, *The Evolution of British General Practice, 1850–1948* (Oxford: Oxford University Press, 1999), 197.
[64] Doyle, 'The Romance of Medicine', 100–6.
[65] Digby, *Evolution of British General Practice*, 198.
[66] See, Doyle, *Round the Red Lamp*, 33, 50; L. T. Meade, 'The Silent Tongue', *Strand Magazine* 9 (1895), 325–39 (327); 'Hooded Death', 425–6.

simple sentence. After examining the squire and confirming to him that 'the paralysis will pass off before long', Halifax explains to the daughter: 'now there is nothing to be done but to apply the simple remedies which I have ordered, and to watch him'.[67] In Doyle's story of hereditary syphilis, 'The Third Generation', the ravages and moral taint of syphilis on subsequent generations is explored, but the treatment prescribed is equally normalised into a mixture (probably containing mercury), a powder to be taken every morning, and an ointment applied to the affected legs.[68] As with contemporary medical practice, the aim of such prescribing was to soothe and manage, rather than to cure. As Meade repeatedly shows, often what matters more is not therapeutics but the calmness of the sickroom and the need to avoid undue mental excitement. Prescribing and administering such everyday medicines was a matter-of-fact business.

The ordinariness of these medicines and their use should not hide their importance in narrative terms. They achieve two things: first, they enable narrative realism, which in turn offers an opportunity for commentary on contemporary medical culture, and, second, they illuminate the interesting relations of power between doctors and patients and between the genres of realism and romance during a period when conflicting images of medical authority were being presented. Doyle's 'The Doctors of Hoyland' is a particularly apposite example of how these different functions work together. Doyle draws upon everyday pharmacological products to provide verisimilitude to the narrative of the conflict between the established male doctor, James Ripley, and the medical interloper, the female doctor Verrinder Smith, reflecting everyday concerns regarding women practitioners. This is captured neatly in a description of disagreement over treatment, where Ripley's prescribing is bested by Smith's:

> And soon there were tangible proofs of her powers upon the country side. Farmer Eyton, whose callous ulcer had been spreading over his shin for years back under a gentle *regime* of zinc ointment, was painted round with blistering fluid, and found, after three blasphemous nights, that his sore was stimulated into healing.[69]

The treatments described are either commonplace (the zinc ointment) or so everyday as to remain unnamed (blistering fluid). Their mundanity is part of the realist narrative of medical practice that is being developed. But they also help to promote realism in another way: they are the matter-of-fact foundation for the anti-romance between Ripley and Smith that goes

---

[67] Meade, 'Creating a Mind', 34.   [68] Doyle, *Round the Red Lamp*, 38.   [69] Ibid., 305.

on to become the cornerstone of the narrative. This is made thoroughly clear to the reader in a later confrontation between the two protagonists. Ripley, at last won over by Smith's doctoring, begins to imagine her as his wife. Doyle skilfully manages this part of the narrative so as to allow the language of romance to emerge: 'Her dainty skill, her gentle touch, her sweet presence, the community of their tastes, had all united to hopelessly upset his previous opinions [...] he asked her if she would be his wife.'[70] Smith's negative response sees a shift back towards realism:

> If I had known what was passing in your mind I should have told you earlier that I intend to devote my life entirely to science. There are many women with a capacity for marriage, but few with a taste for biology [...]. I came down here while waiting for an opening in the Paris Physiological Laboratory. I have just heard that there is a vacancy for me there.[71]

The change in language, including the reference to the real laboratory outside of the text, locates this passage back in the genre of realism. It undermines, indeed brings to an abrupt close, the romance narrative that Smith had unwisely begun. The narrative inclusion of the everyday, then, is the method by which Doyle instantiates an analysis of alternative structures of power in a story of gendered medicine.

Meade uses everyday drugs for similar purposes in a story from March 1895, 'The Silent Tongue'. The narrative opens as a romance: Halifax is invited to visit an old friend on the occasion of the marriage of his daughter. He arrives to find his friend, General Romney, unwell, and narrates a scene of commonplace prescription, mixing of medicine, 'a simple dose' made 'from ingredients [...] close at hand', and application.[72] The dose has the effect of partially steadying the nerves of the aging General, leading Halifax to note that 'his eyes were still too excited, though, to please me, and I purposely led the conversation to every-day subjects'.[73] Halifax's measured efforts to restore health succeed for a time, until the romance plot reaches its zenith with a suspicious death, which points to the unlawful activity of the daughter's fiancé. These events lead the General to collapse and enter what appears to be a final illness, which Halifax diagnoses as a 'progressive paralysis of the brain'. The narrative oscillates, then, between realist medical practice that acts as a curative – the everyday prescribing Halifax details – and the romance plot that tends towards illness. Through the opposing genres of the story, Meade explores

---

[70] Ibid., 313.   [71] Ibid., 314.   [72] Meade, 'Silent Tongue', 327.   [73] Ibid., 328.

the place of everyday remedies, as the general practitioner seeks to offer either alleviation or management of his patient's symptoms.

This story illuminates the important role played by those modest mental therapeutics that were highlighted by Schofield and other practitioners as just as vital to the doctor's armoury as the new, heavily promoted pharmacological inventions. While Halifax's leading of the General to conversation on 'every-day subjects' is one very good example of those common mental therapies, it is at the conclusion to the narrative that Halifax's expertise in this area becomes most obvious. As the General's health declines, Halifax recognises that the 'expression in [the General's] eyes' is a desire to communicate before he dies.[74] The remaining narrative focuses on the use of oxygen gas to revivify the General in order for him to impart his information. Oxygen gas was a common therapy in the 1890s, having been in use in medicine for nearly eighty years, and the scene is narrated in everyday terms: 'I got the apparatus quickly into order, mixed the chemicals, and soon had the satisfaction of seeing the bag slowly fill with pure oxygen gas.'[75] This closing sequence might easily have been narrated in Gothic terms, as was the revivifying of a patient, for example, in George Eliot's short story 'The Lifted Veil' (1859). That Meade did so in a realist mode indicates her desire to connect everyday medical practices with realism. Further, this allows her to promote the value of the general practitioner's experience and expertise in mental management. This is the kind of alternative source of power, outside the realm of the scientific pharmacopeia, that a focus upon the everyday brings to light.

From Controversy to the Everyday

While scholars have become used to referring to the anxieties and controversies produced by medicine and reflected in medical fictions in the *fin de siècle*, and have accepted this as the normal register for how authors engaged with medical debates, a closer examination of the position of pharmacological substances and remedies in literary texts reveals a different dynamic. As we have shown, Meade's and Doyle's medical fictions are products not only of *fin-de-siècle* fashions in literary production but also of Britain's medical culture. Their fictions do not simply reflect that culture. Instead, they interrogate medical advances in pharmacology from a variety of perspectives, considering in detail the use of new drugs and their effects on patients and on general practice. Moreover, both authors show a

---

[74] Ibid., 337.   [75] Ibid., 338.

considerable understanding of how general practice sought to resolve the tensions between new drug use and traditional therapeutic methods. While medical professionals, like those writing for *The Lancet*, might have scoffed at Meade's fictions as 'hopelessly inaccurate', it is the literary critical knowledge of these medical practitioners turned reviewers that is revealed as perfunctory.[76] These reviewers miss the fact that the stories offer a fascinating intervention into medical culture at the level of its practical politics.

What these fictions also importantly reveal is how both Meade and Doyle employ the formal elements of their fictions to enhance their engagement with specific medical issues. The heightened debates on drug use and abuse within medical communities were communicated through melodrama and sensation, while common remedies and practices were captured by realism. Often, as we expose in our study of specific short stories, these different generic features were placed in active conflict with one another, in ways similar to those found in external medical debates. Previous scholarly work has revealed the relation between fictional form and medical writing: Meegan Kennedy and Monika Class, for example, have both shown how published medical case notes were influenced by literary genre.[77] There has, however, been no work before now to show that *fin-de-siècle* literary texts used generic features of fiction to offer insight into contemporary medical debates. Future study of genre, and particularly of realism at the *fin de siècle*, needs to balance our tendency to focus on the curious and the unique with the everyday to give a different picture of medicine's relation to fiction and its forms. Certainly, scholarship on late-Victorian medicine's representation in various narrative forms would be advanced by extending the focus to the quotidian nature of medical practice that we have begun here. Undertaking this work will enable us to determine with much greater clarity the traffic between different disciplines communicating through different narrative forms; to decipher, for instance, the complexity behind Dr Foster's claim, in the same story as we drew upon for our epigraph, that 'I'm not romancing [...] this is absolute fact.'[78]

---

[76] Unsigned, 'Literary Table', *The Lancet* (31 October 1896), 1235.
[77] Meegan Kennedy, *Revising the Clinic: Vision and Representation in Victorian Medical Narrative and the Novel* (Columbus: Ohio State University Press, 2010); Monika Class, 'Introduction: Medical Case Histories as Genre: New Approaches', *Literature and Medicine* 32:1 (2014), vii–xvi.
[78] Doyle, *Round the Red Lamp*, 208.

PART III

Responses

CHAPTER 8

Disorders of the Age
Nervous Climates

Sally Shuttleworth and Melissa Dickson

> A human life, I think, should be well rooted in some spot of a native land.
>
> George Eliot, *Daniel Deronda*[1]

George Eliot's observation in *Daniel Deronda* is redolent with nostalgia. Her vision of psychological and moral rootedness, of 'a spot where the definiteness of early memories may be inwrought with affection', is an articulation of absence (15). Gwendolen Harleth, with her life spent roving from place to place, is the epitome of the modern restless soul, her overcharged nerves a reflection of her literal lack of groundedness. The idea that mind, body, and soul take their imprint, or 'nourishment' in Eliot's phrase (16), from their surroundings is one that became increasingly dominant in the late nineteenth century as writers, medics, and social commentators sought to explore the consequences for body and mind of the emerging forms of a pressured, deracinated society. This essay focuses on Eliot's *Daniel Deronda* (1876) and George Gissing's *The Whirlpool* (1896), looking at how they engage with medical discourses of the era. Both offer pessimistic case studies of the ways in which pathological forms of economic and social life are imprinted on the mind and body, from the gambling salon and debased culture of the health spa in Eliot's novel, to Gissing's engagement with *fin-de-siècle* discourses of degeneration.

Daniel Deronda *and the Disorders of Modern Life*

Eliot's engagement with contemporary medical culture was both theoretical and intensely material. As she was finishing the last sections of *Middlemarch* in 1872, she fell (as was frequently the case) into a state of nervous disorder. Writing to Alexander Main on 13 September 1872, she observed:

---

[1] George Eliot, *Daniel Deronda*, ed. Graham Handley, intro. K. M. Newton (Oxford: Oxford University Press, 2014), 15. Further references to this edition will be given in the text.

> We start in search of health this afternoon. Our destination, to be reached about the end of next week, is Homburg, where we shall not gamble but drink the waters and cultivate repose of mind. I am at a very low ebb and during the last week I have run down at a quicker rate into a nervous condition in which the chirping of the grasshopper – if it were to be heard in these parts – would be a noticeable addition to the sounds already irritating me.[2]

Eliot and Lewes had frequently sought health in spas or resorts before: in Baden-Baden, for example in 1868,[3] while in 1870, when Lewes was diagnosed with nervous exhaustion, they charged across England, from Cromer up to Harrogate (where they took the waters) and Whitby, following their doctor's orders that they should seek 'bracing air and rest from brain-work'.[4] Homburg was much advertised in British newspapers, journals, and travel guides, boasting an unrivalled summer climate and the perfect conditions for curing nervous conditions: 'The mountains' pure and bracing air contributes largely to invigorate the system and is very beneficial in nervous affections.'[5] Eliot travelled to Homburg, not merely as a tourist but also as a patient seeking cure, intending to take the waters, and to overcome her nervous prostration brought on by the strains of mental labour.

Once arrived, Eliot and Lewes found the air, waters, and plantations to their liking, but, as is well known, were disturbed by the scenes of gambling in the Kursaal. Eliot records her horror at the sight of

> the dull faces bending round the gaming tables, the raking-up of the money, and the flinging of the coins towards the winners by the hard-faced croupiers, the hateful, hideous women staring at the board like stupid monomaniacs [. . .]. Hell is the only right name for such places.[6]

---

[2] Gordon Haight, *George Eliot Letters*, 9 vols. (New Haven: Yale University Press, 1954–1978), vol. 5, 309. When Eliot finished *Felix Holt* Lewes recorded in his diary (1 June 1866), 'The continued ill health of the last months, the dreadful nervousness and depression made her writing a serious matter.' George Henry Lewes Manuscript Diary, Beinecke Rare Book and Manuscript Library, Yale University.

[3] G. H. Lewes notes in a letter from Baden-Baden in 1868, that while there they took Morris's 'Delightful Poem "The Earthly Paradise" into the woods to read', trying to recreate the 'golden age', which Morris framed as the very opposite of the driven, capitalist culture of the era. *The Letters of George Henry Lewes*, 2 vols., ed. William Baker (Victoria: English Literary Monographs, University of Victoria, 1995), vol. 2, 129. Letter from Lewes to George Smith, 8 June 1868.

[4] *Letters*, vol. 5, 101–11.

[5] The Homburg Baths were advertised repeatedly from the 1850s on in *Bradshaw's Illustrated Handbooks*, and from the early 1870s across a range of journals such as the *Dublin University Magazine* or the *Saturday Review* (6 June 1874), and also in specific advertisements designed for medical men, for example the *Lancet Advertiser* (24 June 1876).

[6] Letter to Mrs William Cross, [25 September 1872], *Letters*, vol. 5, 312.

In particular, she was disturbed by 'the play of Byron's grand niece, who is only 26 years old, and is completely in the grasp of this mean, money-raking demon. It made me cry to see her young fresh face among the hags and brutally stupid men around her'.[7] Although Eliot complained that there was 'little of dramatic "Stoff" to be picked up by watching or listening', the arresting opening scene of *Daniel Deronda* is clearly here in germ, where we, as readers, view through Daniel's eyes the reckless play of that 'problematic sylph', Gwendolen Harleth in the fictionalised German spa of Leubronn.[8]

Daniel Deronda gives symbolic centrality to the health spa, as an expression of the economic, social, and psychological disorders of the age. The irony of situating gambling and financial speculation in the Kursaal, or cure-hall, is not lost on George Eliot. Just as the oppressive salon becomes a 'condenser' (3) of the human breath exhaled in this 'scene of gas-poisoned absorption' (5), with its promiscuous mingling of European classes and cultures, so the resort itself becomes a generator of disease, offering a condensed expression of the ills of modern life. Gwendolen's startling poise at the gaming tables, her belief in herself as a 'goddess of luck' (6), proves as friable as that of the financial markets and the bank of Grapnell and Co, who 'also thought of reigning in the realm of luck' (129–30) and whose unexpected failure sets in train Gwendolen's own subsequent descent into nervous disorder. In preparing to write her novel, Eliot had immersed herself not merely in Jewish history and culture but also in texts exploring the problems of modern life, such as James Thomson's *City of Dreadful Night* (1874) and Trollope's *The Way We Live Now* (1875), as well as works on political economy, and, through G. H. Lewes, the latest developments in psychology and neurology.[9] Eliot focuses on the inner psychological turmoil of her characters, caught up in the trammels of social and economic disorder and instability. Gwendolen's life spent 'roving from one foreign watering place or Parisian apartment to another' (17) is symptomatic of a wider malaise, and she, like her fellow exiles, Daniel and Mirah, registers its effects in the nervous tissues of body and mind.

---

[7] Letter to John Blackwood, 4 October 1872, *Letters*, vol. 5, 314. [8] Ibid.
[9] Eliot wrote to James Thomson on 30 May 1874 to express her admiration of *The City of Dreadful Night* (*Letters*, vol. 6, 53). Lewes records that they read *The Way We Live Now* in January 1874, before she had started the novel, and again in August of that year, immediately after Eliot had finished the first chapter of *Daniel Deronda*. Manuscript Diary, 1874, Beinecke Library. Eliot's heavily annotated copy of J. E. Cairnes, *Some Leading Principles of Political Economy* (1874), is in the Dr Williams's Library, London.

On returning from Homburg, Eliot had immediately plunged into reading the manuscript of Lewes's first volume of *Problems of Life and Mind* (1874), the work which he believed would transform understandings of the inter-relations of body, mind, and the social realm.[10] Both also read aloud their respective works to each other, and the copies of the early volumes of *Problems of Life and Mind* in Dr Williams's Library, which are extensively annotated by Eliot, show her deeply engaged in the arguments. 'Mind', Lewes claimed, 'cannot be explained without constant recognition of the statico-dynamical relations of Organism and Social Medium', a passage which might lie behind the unsettling effects on Deronda of Gwendolen's 'dynamic' glance.[11] Drawing on the recent work of David Ferrier and John Hughlings Jackson, and their counterparts in Germany, on neurology, Lewes argued that there was no mental phenomenon without a corresponding neural phenomenon, and, pushing the implications of this idea further than others, he suggested that 'every neural phenomenon involves the whole Organism'.[12] As a model of being, and of selfhood, it corresponds at an individual, somatic level to Eliot's model of the minute interconnections and transmissions of the social body. Commenting on a passage in *Problems of Life and Mind*, which argues for the inseparability of cause and effect, and for viewing all phenomena as 'embodied histories', Eliot writes, 'admirable here'.[13] In *Daniel Deronda* she explores, at a deeper level than before, the 'embodied histories' of her characters, the imprinting on the nerves and tissues of the body of every tremor of social and psychological experience, whether Daniel's extreme sensitivity and dread associated with his unknown parentage, Mirah's suicidal impulses when 'my thoughts were stronger than I was' (185), or Gwendolen's 'fits of spiritual dread' (52).

In the much neglected 'Hand and Banner' section of the novel, the 'laboratory assistant' Marrables observes that ideas 'may act by the distribution of gases [...] instruments are getting so fine now, men may come to register the spread of a theory by observing changes in the atmosphere and corresponding changes in the nerves' (442). Even now, in the age of

---

[10] Eliot letter to Alexander Main, 4 November 1872, *Letters*, vol. 5, 323–4.
[11] G. H. Lewes, *The Foundations of a Creed. Problems of Life and Mind. First Series*, 2 vols. (London: 1874), vol. 1, 161. The copy owned by Lewes and Eliot and now housed in the Dr Williams's Library is heavily annotated, with multiple annotations and line markings, with Eliot frequently commenting, where she either agreed with arguments, or was continuing a discussion with Lewes when she differed in opinion. This is one of the sections she has marked, noting, 'The organism and its conditions of receptivity or gradual preparation or historical receptivity'.
[12] Lewes, *Foundations*, 112. Lined passage.   [13] Ibid., 358–60.

sophisticated neuroscience, such a precision of measurement is not within sight, but the observation is testimony to the excitement generated in the early days of neurology, when it seemed like the slightest impulses of the mind could be recorded and measured, in parallel with the physiological chemistry of the body and its processes of interchange with the surrounding atmosphere. The remark takes us back to the opening of the novel, to 'Science, the strict measurer' invoked in the epigraph, and to the condensation of human breath into the 'dull, gas-poisoned absorption' of the gamblers, who are literally and symbolically poisoning mind and body, reducing human potential to the condition of a drug-induced stupor which 'compelled the brains of each to the same narrow monotony of action' (5). It also takes us forward to the 'strange spiritual chemistry' (266) of Grandcourt's mind, and to the second invocation of 'strictly-measuring science', where Mordecai's 'visionary excitement' is linked to 'the sensibility of the artist [that] seizes combinations which science explains and justifies' (433). Throughout *Daniel Deronda,* George Eliot is in detailed dialogue with contemporary sciences of the mind, drawing on recent findings, but with the 'sensibility of the artist', both seizing combinations and creating her own distinct language of 'spiritual chemistry', which cannot be contained within the strict measurements or theories of neural science.

Critics exploring psychology within *Daniel Deronda* have tended to focus primarily on Gwendolen, and have variously outlined intersections with contemporary theories of monomania, hysteria, trauma, or the unconscious.[14] David Trotter has shown convincingly the link between Gwendolen's fits of spiritual dread, and terror of solitude in open spaces, with that eminently modern disorder, agoraphobia, identified by Carl Westphal in 1871.[15] As a diagnosis of seemingly inexplicable fear, exhibited not by the mad but, in Westphal's initial cases, by otherwise eminently rational middle-class men, it caused a sensation in European medicine, spawning numerous other identifications of phobic forms, which were repeatedly linked to the pressured and disorientating

---

[14] Simon During, 'The Strange Case of Monomania: Patriarchy in Literature, Murder in Middlemarch and Drowning in Daniel Deronda', *Representations* 23 (1988), 86–104; Athena Vrettos, *Somatic Fictions: Imagining Illness in Victorian Culture* (Stanford: Stanford University Press, 1995), 57–80; Jill Matus, *Shock, Memory and the Unconscious in Victorian Fiction* (Cambridge: Cambridge University Press, 2009), 121–59; Jane Wood, *Passion and Pathology in Victorian Fiction* (Oxford: Oxford University Press, 2001), 141–62.

[15] David Trotter, 'The Invention of Agoraphobia', *Victorian Literature and Culture* 32:2 (2004), 463–74; Terry J. Knapp and Michael T. Schumacher eds., *Westphal's 'Die Agoraphobie'* (Lanham: University Press of America, 1988).

conditions of modern life. On their visit to Berlin in 1870 the previous year, Lewes had spent considerable time with Westphal, visiting the psychiatric wards at the Charité, and he and Eliot had dined at Westphal's house, meeting leading lights of both physiology and psychiatry.[16] Although Eliot appeared to suggest in a letter that she could not share Lewes's sympathy for this 'hideous branch of practice', she was increasingly drawn in to this new dimension of his work, and indeed on return from Berlin she and Lewes visited Oxford, where, she records, they had 'an interesting morning with Dr Rolleston who dissected a brain for me'.[17]

While absorbing such work on the intersections between physiology, neurology, and psychiatry, Eliot did not confine herself to one theory or diagnosis, but sought rather to produce her own imaginative guide to the 'unmapped country' of the mind (233). She adopts in *Daniel Deronda* a narrative form which, like the operations of the unconscious, proceeds by chains of symbolic association, whether the picture of the 'upturned dead face' (20) which presages Grandcourt's death, the image of throttling hands, or the twinned tropes of gambling and jewels which open the novel. From Gwendolen's necklace, recklessly lost and redeemed, to Mrs Glasher's vindictive gift of the diamonds, and finally to Lapidoth's ultimate betrayal in the theft of Deronda's ring, jewels track symbolically the inner pathways and outer social transmission of emotional energy and affect. Thus Gwendolen's gambling (a language which Eliot also uses to describe her engagement to Grandcourt) is mirrored in hideous form by Lapidoth, with his 'hysterical excitability' (654) and the 'imperious gambling desire within him, which carried on its activity through every other occupation, and made a continuous web of imagination that held all else in its meshes' (663).

---

[16] In his Journal for 28 March 1870 Lewes records: 'At 9.30 Westphal came and took me to the Charité where we visited the section of Nervous Diseases.' He takes extended notes on the 'interesting cases' he saw of aphasia, hysteria, hallucinations, and other disorders. MS Journal, Beinecke Library. He and Eliot also dined at Westphal's, where she records meeting some of the leading medical figures in Berlin: Letter to Mrs Richard Congreve, 3 April 1870, *Letters* vol. 5, 86–7.

[17] Ibid. Margaret Harris and Judith Johnston, eds., *The Journals of George Eliot* (Cambridge: Cambridge University Press, 1998), diary entry 26 May 1870, 140. George Rolleston was Linacre Professor of Physiology and Anatomy, and Physician to the Radcliffe Infirmary. She also visited the laboratory of the chemist Sir Benjamin Brodie and was shown new forms of chemical measurement. Lewes's records of reading show his interest in the work on the brain being produced at the West Riding Asylum by Ferrier, Hughlings Jackson, James Crichton Browne, and their old friend Clifford Allbutt. From 1874 Hughlings Jackson, who had moved to London, became a regular guest at the Priory Sunday gatherings.

The description echoes that of Gwendolen on the boat with Grandcourt, 'at the very height of her entanglement in those fatal meshes which are woven within more closely than without' (563). Similarly Lapidoth's thought processes which prepare for the theft, when 'his desire at once leaped into the thought (not yet an intention)' (665), echo Gwendolen's 'I only know that I saw my wish outside me' (586). Whilst Gwendolen, in her halting confession, depicts her action as 'leaping away from myself' (586), Lapidoth merely confirms the established habits of a lifetime, his entrapment in the repetitive cycles of desire. In the watches of the night Mordecai's warning words had been like those of an 'insubstantial ghost' while his mind focused on '*Roulette*', and the 'numbers and movements that seemed to make the very tissue of [his] consciousness' (656). Gwendolen, by contrast, confesses to Deronda that 'I wanted to make my gain out of another's loss – you remember? – it was like roulette – and the money burnt into me' (583). The parallels, almost excessive in nature, register Eliot's original disturbance at Homburg: Gwendolen, the young, fresh-faced heroine, is granted a limited form of redemption through Deronda, whilst Lapidoth, the inveterate gambler who would have sold his own daughter, embodies the psychology of addiction in its 'final imperious stage': 'the unjoyous dissipation of demons, seeking diversion on the burning marl of perdition' (651). Like the demonic Grandcourt with his imperious will to power, Lapidoth is granted no quarter: both represent the perverted psychologies of a rootless, degraded age. In light of such behaviours, spiritual dread appears a rational response.

The Whirlpool, *Market Culture, and Psychological Disintegration*

The social and economic forces that drive the market culture of the late nineteenth century are, Eliot's novel makes clear, not only seductive and exciting, but also precarious, exhausting, and potentially overwhelming. Bankers and financiers were, alongside politicians and 'too laborious scholars', amongst those professional classes deemed by the eminent British physician Benjamin Ward Richardson to be suffering from unprecedented levels of worry and mental strain in the late nineteenth century.[18] In his 1876 work, *Diseases of Modern Life*, Richardson outlined the various forms of malady which he had identified as the primary afflictions of those engaged in commercial occupations: people, he noted, who regularly subjected themselves to broken rest, irregular meals, confinement in the

[18] Benjamin Ward Richardson, *Diseases of Modern Life* (London: Macmillan, 1876), 123.

office, competitive struggles, excessive anxiety, and mental shocks. The resultant depletion of the human nervous system, Richardson argued, induced a series of irreversible conditions:

> They who live solely for gain are amongst the acutest physical sufferers in the world. Every penny earned, by excess of hard strain for it, is grasped at a cost of vital power that never comes back. Disorganized heart, disorganized brain are the physical evils, – described in the chapter on worry and mental strain, – with which the prize, when it comes, is won.[19]

Stress and financial uncertainty, it seemed, took their toll on both the body and mind of the Victorian banker. Furthermore, an extreme reversal of fortune was, Richardson claimed in his *Discourses on Practical Physic* (1871), the most common cause of intermittent action of the heart in the wider population.[20] Subject to the turbulent economic landscape of metropolitan modernity, which saw innumerable crashes on the stock exchange and the collapse of several banks, the nervous body seemed to teeter constantly on the verge of collapse.

It is not surprising, then, that sudden losses of wealth, such as that experienced by the collapse of the bank of Grapnell and Co in *Daniel Deronda*, and the subsequent medical conditions that these shocks induced, became staples of Victorian fiction, prompting the suicides of financiers and speculators, like Merdle in Dickens's *Little Dorrit* (1857), and Dobbs Broughton, Ferdinand Lopez, and Augustus Melmotte in Anthony Trollope's *The Last Chronicle of Barset* (1867), *The Prime Minister* (1876), and *The Way We Live Now* (1875), respectively. In George Gissing's 1897 novel *The Whirlpool*, which is explicitly set within an economic environment of risk and speculation, everyone in the metropolis seems to have been inescapably drawn into the vicissitudes of Victorian market culture. The collapse of Bennet Frothingham's company – the rather expansively titled Britannia Loan, Assurance, Investment, and Banking Company – in the opening pages of the novel not only drives Bennet Frothingham to suicide and leaves his wife and children socially disgraced, but its material and psychological effects extend across the social networks of London's middle-class investors. One of these investors, the overworked and neuralgic journalist Edgar Abbott, commits suicide by a morphine overdose. Frothingham's wife is left guiltily attempting to use her private capital to restore some of the lost fortunes of the Abbott family,

---

[19] Ibid., 418.
[20] Benjamin Ward Richardson, *Discourses on Practical Physic: On Physical Disease from Mental Strain* (London: J & A Churchill, 1871), 55.

while his daughter, Alma, pursues her ambition to become an acclaimed professional musician despite 'the dishonour darkening upon her name'.[21] It is as though, as the male protagonist Harvey Rolfe observes, 'we were all being swept into a ghastly whirlpool which roars over the bottomless pit' (48). Here, the currents of industry and economy are indelibly imprinted on the mind and body, as 'round and round they go; brains humming till they melt or explode' (157).

Gissing's image of the dizzying whirlpool of metropolitan life, in which inhabitants live constantly at high pressure, subject to the demands of modern consumer capitalism, is a symbolic distillation of contemporary anxieties. The previous year, he had published a short story entitled 'At High Pressure' (1896), which featured an unmarried young woman named Linda Vassie, whose life was a whirlwind of cabs, trains, periodical reading, and committee meetings, as 'from morning to night – often, indeed, till past midnight – Linda was engaged, at high pressure, in a great variety of pursuits'.[22] Beyond Gissing's own fiction, the whirlpool was a concept deployed in many contemporary explorations of the increasingly demanding physical and psychological conditions of modern life. In 1895, the eminent English physician T. Clifford Allbutt had written an article for the *Contemporary Review*, entitled 'Nervous Diseases and Modern Life', in which he evoked the whirlpool metaphor in order to present, and critique, the popular perception that new forms of nervous disease were being inculcated by the conditions of modernity. Allbutt noted that various maladies, from 'nervous debility, to hysteria, to neurasthenia, to the fretfulness, the melancholy, the unrest due to living at high pressure, to the whirl of the railway, the pelting of telegrams, the strife of business, the hunger for riches, the lust of vulgar minds for coarse and instant pleasures', were frequently understood to be either induced or aggravated by the pressures of an urban environment.[23] 'Life at high pressure' was, according to the London-based physician Thomas Stretch Dowse, 'the prominent feature of the nineteenth century', and he declared in his 1880 study of brain and nerve exhaustion that 'we cannot be surprised when we find that the so-called nervous diseases and exhaustions, dipsomania and insanity,

---

[21] George Gissing, *The Whirlpool* (1897; London: Sidgwick and Jackson, 1911), 63. Subsequent references to this edition will be given in the text.
[22] George Gissing, 'At High Pressure' (1896), in *Human Odds and Ends: Stories and Sketches* (London: Lawrence and Bullen, 1898), 277–83, (278).
[23] T. Clifford Allbutt, 'Nervous Diseases and Modern Life', *Contemporary Review* 67 (1895), 210–31, (214). Allbutt insisted that, despite this popular perception, the number of nervous disorders afflicting the population was not on the increase.

are increasing beyond all proportion to the rapid increase of the population'.[24] Max Nordau's *Degeneration* (1892), first published in English in the same year as Gissing's 'At High Pressure' made explicit reference to 'the vertigo and whirl of our frenzied life' as inevitable causes of neurasthenia and fatigue.[25] In keeping with the fate of many of Gissing's characters, Nordau insisted that the human body was not fit for the increasingly fast pace of urban life, which he characterised by its 'vastly increased number of sense impressions and organic reactions, and therefore of perceptions, judgements, and motor impulses, which at present are forced into a given unity of time'.[26] The bombardment of new information and excessive external stimuli was, he argued, a cause of significant wear and tear on the body and brain, and he voiced concerns over the possible corruption of the race by such influences.

Gissing recorded in his diary of March 1895, during the period he was writing *The Whirlpool*, that he had finished reading Nordau's *Degeneration*. In September the following year, while still drafting the novel and evidently pursuing his concern with the potentially deleterious effects of urbanism, capitalism, and industrialism, he noted that he had read *English Men of Science* (1874) by the psychologist, anthropologist, and later eugenicist Sir Francis Galton.[27] Galton's purpose in this work had been to evaluate the relative contributions of heredity and environment – what he referred to for the first time as 'nature and nurture' – to the individual differences in eminent men of science through an extensive assessment of the anthropometric data that he had gathered on the racial, religious, social, physical, and psychological characteristics of nearly 200 fellows of the Royal Society. Through these case studies, Galton set out to examine the significance of hereditary traits and the import of 'every influence from without that affects [man] after his birth'.[28] Gissing, whose

---

[24] Thomas Stretch Dowse, *On Brain and Nerve Exhaustion: 'Neurasthenia', Its Nature and Curative Treatment* (London: Ballière, Tindall, and Cox, 1880), 40. Janet Oppenheim has explored the extended medical debates of the Victorian and Edwardian eras that surrounded the condition variously known as shattered nerves, nervous collapse, nervous disorder, and neurasthenia in *Shattered Nerves: Doctors, Patients, and Depression in Victorian England* (Oxford: Oxford University Press, 1991).

[25] Max Nordau, *Degeneration* (1892; London: William Heinemann, 1896), 42.   [26] Ibid.

[27] Pierre Coustillas, ed., *London and the Life of Literature in Late Victorian England: The Diary of George Gissing, Novelist* (Hassocks: Harvester Press, 1978), 365, 422. David Glover makes this point about Gissing's reading in his study of the similar concerns regarding neuroses triggered by the vertiginous nature of modern consumer capitalism in 'Sex and the City: Gissing, Helmholtz, Freud' in *George Gissing: Voices of the Unclassed*, ed. Martin Ryle and Jenny Bourne Taylor (Aldershot: Ashgate, 2005), 77–91.

[28] Francis Galton, *English Men of Science: Their Nature and Nurture* (London: Macmillan, 1874), 12.

own preoccupation with heredity is apparent from his diaries and letters at this time, drew this discourse into *The Whirlpool*, exploring the potential complications of those hereditary traits passed from parent to child as they emerge in the private, domestic dramas of the middle class.

Degeneration theories like Nordau's illuminated what J. Edward Chamberlin and Sander L. Gilman have referred to as the 'dark side of progress'.[29] The supposed advancement of the human race was understood to be constantly threatened with potential reversals through collapse, deviancy, or decay. The ability of individuals to withstand the excessive strain placed upon their nerves by modern city life became of increasing importance, and it is a concern explicitly brought into Gissing's novel. In its early pages, we meet Mrs Abbott, a former school teacher who, we are informed, has given birth to only one child, a constitutionally weak creature who 'struggled through a few months of sickly life, and died of convulsions during its mother's absence at a garden-party' (29). Appropriately, Mrs Abbott sits reading *L'Hérédité Psychologique* (1875) by the French psychologist Théodule Ribot. Gissing himself was very familiar with Ribot's study, noting in his diary on 31 October 1889 that he had '*worked* at Ribot' throughout the day.[30] The notion of his actively 'working at' rather than simply 'reading' the text is suggestive of considerable mental exertion and intellectual engagement on Gissing's part, and he certainly made careful notes in his commonplace book of Ribot's main arguments regarding the immediate transmission of characteristics from parents to their children, the potential preponderance of one of the parents in hereditary transmission, atavism, and potential exceptions to the laws of heredity.[31] That the ideas contained in Ribot had, to some extent, being plaguing Gissing is suggested by his diary entry over a week later, on 9 November 1889, that he had spent his evening 'in a troubled state of mind, occasionally glancing at "Darwin's Origin of Species"' in what he termed 'a queer jumble of thoughts'.[32] Anxious reflections on evolution and heredity similarly percolate throughout *The Whirlpool*. Ribot's book, a material symbol within the novel of Mrs Abbot's interest in the mental conditions that might be transmitted from one generation to the next, has presumably influenced her assessment of the two young children who were

---

[29] J. Edward Chamberlin and Sander L. Gilman, *Degeneration: The Dark Side of Progress* (New York: Columbia University Press, 1985).
[30] Coustillas, ed., *London and the Life of Literature*, 170. Italics added.
[31] Jacob Korg, ed., *George Gissing's Commonplace Book: A Manuscript in the Berg Collection of the New York Public Library* (New York: New York Public Library, 1962), 59–61.
[32] Coustillas, ed., *London and the Life of Literature*, 170.

simply abandoned by their father (a relative by marriage) and left in her care. 'They are anything but *nice* children', she observes to Rolfe as he interrupts her reading, but 'what could one expect with such a father?' (29). These vulgar and 'luckless brats' are, in Mrs Abbott's view, the unwitting products of hereditary degeneracy.

Harvey Rolfe, who is living very comfortably off inherited wealth, seeks to remain aloof from the whirlpool of existence, and responds to Mrs Abbott that 'that kind of thing doesn't interest me much' (29). He professes himself to be 'merely a looker on' (45), entirely indifferent to the increasingly stressful rhythms and demands of the modern world. Deriding any emotional attachment to the young as mere 'sentimental rubbish', he is content (at least hypothetically) to allow weak, nervous, or sickly children – those anti-progressive signs of national degeneration – to be destroyed by the pressures of existence rather than to bequeath their weakened constitutions to succeeding generations:

> People snivel over the deaths of babies; I see nothing to grieve about. If a child dies, why, the probabilities are it *ought* to die; if it lives, it lives, and you get survival of the fittest. We don't want to choke the world with people, most of them rickety and wheezing; let us be healthy, and have breathing space. (13)

Ironically, Rolfe is unwittingly articulating an argument outlined by Ribot in a chapter on 'Heredity and the Law of Evolution' in *L'Hérédité*. Asserting that the influence of heredity may be an indirect cause of degeneration through the gradual accumulation of physical and moral attributes transmitted from one generation to the next, Ribot notes that the intervention of modern medicine and familial affection ensures the survival of those declining types who would otherwise have become extinct:

> In our day, paternal affection, with the assistance of medical science, more certain, and possessed of more resources, makes more and more certain the future of children, by saving the lives of countless weak, deformed, or otherwise ill-constituted creatures that would surely have died in a savage race, or in our own a century or two ago. These children become men, they marry, and by heredity transmit to their descendants at least a predisposition to imperfections like their own.[33]

---

[33] Théodule Ribot, *Heredity, A Psychological Study of Its Phenomena, Laws, Causes, and Consequences* (London: H. S. King, 1875), 303. Gissing made a note of this particular argument in the summary he made of Ribot in his commonplace book. Daniel Pick makes use of this passage from Ribot in his discussion of the parallels drawn between East and West in degenerationist discourse. See Daniel Pick, *Faces of Degeneration: A European Disorder, c. 1848–1918* (Cambridge: Cambridge University Press, 1999), 41.

Despite casually advocating a kind of eugenicist philosophy of selective breeding for the improvement of the human race in keeping with such philosophies, Rolfe nonetheless finds himself confronting issues of heredity within the domestic sphere. This manifests particularly in his concerns for the health and development of his own fragile son, and in his relationship with his increasingly neurotic wife Alma, whose own hereditary nervous temperament has left her peculiarly susceptible to the 'whirlpool way of life' (117).[34]

As he contemplates his infant son's large head, little face, and emergent 'vocabulary of his own' (143), Rolfe reflects upon the forces of evolution and hereditary transmission that render his child at once a 'fresh and young' sixteen month old, and a 'wondrously old' creature with the same inherited traits, 'the same music of earliest human speech, the same ripple of innocent laughter, renewed from generation to generation' (143). Like the tragic Father Time in Thomas Hardy's *Jude the Obscure* (1895), published only two years earlier, this child is a figure who, in the context of widespread concerns regarding the transmission and accumulation of morbid qualities, inhabits both old age and infancy.[35] With 'the burden of all time' and human history weighing upon him and his offspring, Rolfe finds that 'he must needs ponder anxiously on his child's heritage', turning to his biological past in order to intuit his future health or pathology, and 'use his weary knowledge to cast the horoscope of this dawning life' (143). Overwhelmingly, the 'sanguine humour, traceable perhaps to a paternal source' (228), of his child's mother and the nervous excitement that she seemingly inherited from her own mother (who died suddenly after a night of over-stimulation at the theatre) point to an extremely troubling biological inheritance. Alma has, Rolfe believes, an 'inevitable taint', exacerbated by her female constitution, which may manifest itself in his son in due course.[36]

It is in the character of Alma Frothingham that the tensions between nature and nurture, and between biological theories of determinism and

---

[34] Rolfe's anxious contemplation of the future health or pathology of his son find a parallel in Gissing's reflections on the nature of his own child, of whom he wrote in August 1896, 'what a terrible lesson is the existence of this child, born of a loveless and utterly unsuitable marriage' (Coustillas, ed., *London and the Life of Literature*, 418).

[35] For a discussion of Father Time in the context of childhood at the *fin de siècle*, see Sally Shuttleworth, *The Mind of the Child: Child Development in Literature, Science, and Medicine, 1840–1900* (Oxford: Oxford University Press, 2010), 335–52.

[36] On the discourses of specifically female pathology at work in Gissing's novel, see William Greenslade, 'Women and the Disease of Civilisation: George Gissing's "The Whirlpool"', *Victorian Studies* 32:4 (1989), 506–23.

anxieties surrounding the pernicious effects of modern life, are brought most anxiously to the fore. Alma, Gissing makes clear, is not musically gifted, and her struggle to establish a musical career in the metropolis is motivated not by a love of music but rather by her neurotic ambition to be widely loved and admired. Her struggle for public recognition nonetheless identifies her as a part of the rapidly rising trend of professionally-trained female violin-players of the eighteen nineties. The professional female violinist, as Paula Gillett has argued, was associated at this period with the figure of the New Woman who 'turned away from the restrictions associated with traditional mores, sometimes denounced marriage as an oppressive institution and embraced such novelties as smoking, public speaking, and club life'.[37] The New Woman sought, in the words of the British psychiatrist Henry Maudsley, to 'contend on equal terms with men for the goal of men's ambitions', and was frequently understood – within the context of evolutionary, neurological, anthropological, and psychological theory – to over-exert herself at great risk to her own nervous system, as well as the social and moral structures of the Victorian family.[38] Gillett, like Sophie Fuller in her study of female musical creativity in Victorian fiction, demonstrates the inherently transgressive nature of a woman's pursuance of a professional career in music in this period. Such efforts were, according to Fuller, largely met with the distinct undermining of female agency. To this end, creative musical women in nineteenth-century novels ranging from Elizabeth Sara Sheppard's *Charles Auchester* (1853) and *Counterparts* (1854), to George Meredith's *Sandra Belloni* (1864), Marie Corelli's *A Romance of Two Worlds* (1886), and E.F. Benson's *Dodo: A Detail of the Day* (1893) suffer various forms of mockery, illness, death, and the loss of their music. Unlike the genuinely musical and demure Mirah Lapidoth, whose voice is noted to be appropriately domestic and best suited to a space no larger than a private drawing-room (485), Alma's attempts to live at high pressure are shown by Gissing to be socially transgressive and symptomatic of maternal inadequacies. She undermines the harmony of the domestic sphere by

---

[37] Paula Gillett, *Musical Women in England, 1870–1914: 'Encroaching on All Men's Privileges'* (Basingstoke: Macmillan, 2000), 122–3.
[38] Henry Maudsley, 'Sex in Mind and Education', *Fortnightly Review* 15 (1874), 466–83 (467). Jane Wood explores Alma's disruption to both the public and private spheres of nineteenth-century London in her detailed discussion of the New Woman fiction of the *fin de siècle* in order to demonstrate the extent to which late nineteenth-century biological and physical sciences fostered a culture of unease around questions of sexual equality. See Wood, *Passion and Pathology*, 163–215.

refusing to nurse her sickly child, in addition to deliberately engineering a miscarriage. She also indulges in a series of increasingly compromising social encounters.

Alma is shown mentally and physically to be distinctly ill-adapted to the stresses and strains of public life: in her attempt to move from amateur to professional status she becomes increasingly disturbed and suffers from severe headaches and nervous disorders. Like the unnamed musical heroine of Corelli's *A Romance of Two Worlds*, whose 'dull throbbing weight of pain' in her head is accompanied by nervous terrors and 'fragments of my own musical compositions' that 'hummed in my ears with wearying persistence', her affliction is both physical and psychological, as 'a strain of music hummed incessantly on her ear, till inability to dismiss it made her cry with half-frenzied wretchedness' (263).[39] Highly strung nerves and physical deterioration are, it seems, the inevitable consequences of the female artistic temperament and its tendency towards excessive mental and physical exertion in the pursuit of creative production.

The figure of the female musician whose nerves have been shattered by excessive devotion to musical training and performance operates more broadly as a metaphor for those external forces and vibrations of modern life that play upon the body of the New Woman as though it were a musical instrument. Just as Hardy's Sue Bridehead in *Jude the Obscure* is figured as a 'harp which the least wind of emotion could make to vibrate', so Tess, in his 1891 novel *Tess of the D'Urbervilles*, is made to '[undulated] upon the thin-notes of the second-hand harp', The instrumental nature and inherent vulnerability of the female body is understood to palpitate, vibrate, and tremble involuntarily in response to external forces while stimuli carry distinct sexual, physiological, and psychological dangers.[40] In literature, the possibility of a violent and insidious infiltration of the female body through music was most fully and famously realised by the malevolent mesmeric conductor Svengali in George Du Maurier's 1894 novel *Trilby*. Here, music is explicitly associated with hypnotic powers and the physical and psychological possession of a young woman's body and mind, as Svengali seizes control of the young Trilby's consciousness in order to

---

[39] Marie Corelli, *A Romance of Two Worlds* (New York: W. M. L. Allison, 1886), 20.
[40] Thomas Hardy, *Jude the Obscure*, ed. Patricia Ingham (Oxford: Oxford University Press, 2002), 268. Thomas Hardy, *Tess of the D'Urbervilles*, ed. Simon Gatrell (Oxford: Oxford University Press, 2005), 139.

conduct her extraordinary singing performances.[41] In the case of Alma Frothingham, however, it is the hypnotic whirlpool of London society itself that infiltrates her mind and destroys her nervous system. Her musical talent and social poise prove as unstable as the financial markets that destroyed her father: she neglects her son, mismanages her husband's finances, and becomes embroiled in an accidental homicide.

Ultimately, it is not through striving to realise an artistic ideal that Alma strains her nervous system and mental faculties to the extreme; rather, it is her commodification of musical talent and of herself on the ever-vacillating London market. Alma's musical talent – which might formerly have been nurtured only within the safe, domestic spaces of the middle-class parlour and drawing-room – is for her, the narrator observes, 'not an end in itself' but rather a means by which she might compete in the market economy and attain 'a place of distinction above ordinary handsome girls and heiresses' (245). In this, Alma resembles Eliot's Gwendolen Harleth (as opposed to Mirah) and Rosamond Vincy, whose soulless, imitative musical performances are manipulatively deployed in order to sustain a desire for attention and admiration comparable to the 'anti-social ego-mania' that had been identified by Nordau as serving 'only to gratify vanity, or an aesthetical instinct of small importance and easy to control'.[42] In Alma's case, so great is the effort of mastering 'mere manual difficulties', securing performance opportunities, and maintaining the pose of an artist through 'lofty cant and sounding hollowness' (246), that she begins increasingly to manifest degenerate symptoms of nervous exhaustion, neurosis, psychosis, and general debility derived from prolonged exposure to the urban environment. Finally, entirely unnerved and on the verge of collapse without the artificial vitality induced by a 'little bottle of something in repute for fashionable disorder of the nerves' (305), Alma becomes gradually habituated to ever-increasing doses of her euphemistically titled 'draught of oblivion' (314) in a counter-intuitive attempt to offset these symptoms. Her death by morphine overdose replicates the tragedy of her father's suicide, in an affirmation of her hereditary weakness, and the self-destruction and premature bodily and mental decay that is inherent in living life at high pressure.

---

[41] Gissing recorded in his diary entry of 3 May 1896 that he had read 'with scant satisfaction, the notorious "Trilby"' (Coustillas, ed., *London and the Life of Literature*, 409), though he did not expand on what it was that he had found wanting.

[42] Nordau, *Degeneration*, 318.

The medical registration of the problems of modernity and nervous overstrain, coupled with contemporary Darwinian narratives of evolution and degeneration, were the inspiration for myriad medical and cultural fantasies in the late nineteenth century. As a consequence, a close reading of novels such as *Daniel Deronda* and *The Whirlpool* in this context offers us a new perspective on the nineteenth-century culture of nerves and the perceived vulnerabilities of the human mind and body in the modern age. With their personal and familial destinies dictated by the ebb and flow of the financial markets, their fits of nervous dread, and their marked descents into psychological turmoil, these over-stimulated, nervous, rootless creatures of the modern age are shown to be increasingly vulnerable to the pressures of their urban environments. These instances of mutually-affirming interaction between literary and medical discourses proffer rich, fictional case-studies of neurosis and mental decline before Freud. Literature, as it moves between the self and its environment, between pathologies of the body and the broader dynamics of social, cultural, and economic exchange, performs a crucial intermediary role in establishing and exposing new, medicalised assumptions about the operations of society and identity. Late-nineteenth-century theories and treatments of the diseases of modern life and of cultural and hereditary degeneration were not only deeply embedded in social and cultural operations; the category of modernity itself was actively constructed and deployed within medical and literary discourse.

CHAPTER 9

Medicine, Sanitary Reform, and Literature of Urban Poverty

Andrew Mangham

In his famous descriptions of London's poor for *The Morning Chronicle*, Henry Mayhew used a descriptive reportage style that would come to typify one of the dominant features of the Victorian social-problem novel. On Jacob's Island, the Bermondsey slum that had provided a setting for Dickens's exploration of a criminal underworld in *Oliver Twist* (1837–1839), Mayhew writes:

> On entering the precincts of the pest island, the air has literally the smell of a graveyard, and a feeling of nausea and heaviness comes over any one unaccustomed to imbibe the musty atmosphere. It is not only the nose, but the stomach that tells how heavily the air is loaded with sulphuretted hydrogen [...]. The water is covered with a scum almost like a cobweb, and prismatic with grease. In it float large masses of green rotting weed, and against the posts of the bridges are swollen carcasses of dead animals, almost bursting with the gases of putrefaction. Along its shores are heaps of indescribable filth, the phosphoretted smell from which tells you of the rotting fish there.[1]

According to Sheila M. Smith, it was a chief aim of writings like Mayhew's 'to present a "true object"', to

> enlarge their readers' sympathies by means of a sensuous response to people and objects not previously scrutinized for the purpose of fiction [... or for] social, philosophical, and scientific endeavour. The pursuit of "truth about" physical fact is outstanding in this period.[2]

That Mayhew's reports have a commitment to the pursuit of fact is clear from his mode of writing: the prose involves descriptions of journeys the author himself has taken and the 'sensuous response' is captured in the

---

[1] [Henry Mayhew], 'A Visit to the Cholera Districts of Bermondsey', *Morning Chronicle* (24 September 1849), 4.
[2] Sheila M. Smith, *The Other Nation: The Poor in English Novels of the 1840s and 1850s* (Oxford: Oxford University Press, 1980), 23.

smells, tastes, and visceral reactions of the narrator. Smith's *The Other Nation: The Poor in English Novels of the 1840s and 1850s,* published in 1980, is typical of the historical and literary scholarship that, at the beginning of a new, cultural-materialist interest in the social-problem questions of the nineteenth century, argued that descriptions like Mayhew's opened up a world 'not previously scrutinized' in both the fiction and non-fiction of the period. In fact, by the time the major authors associated with social-problem literature and reportage journalism (Mayhew, Dickens, Gaskell, Kingsley, and Disraeli) wrote in the style that came, in many ways, to define them, urban poverty had been a prominent discussion for decades. The New Poor Law of 1834 was the culmination of years of debate about what should be done with the nation's growing pauper population, and the plights of the urban poor had been the subject of endless reports like Mayhew's, as well as street ballads, blue papers, reform manuals, and political tracts. By the hungry 1840s, poverty had become *terra pernota* rather than *terra incognita.* Joseph W. Childers suggests, indeed, that the reports of social investigators like Mayhew were actually 'compilations of similar instances and observations that together discursively solidif[ied] a representation of the reality of the poor'.[3] What Mayhew's laboured descriptions tell us, notwithstanding, is that the idea of confronting the reader with detailed, sensory accounts appeared to remain important even without the pressure of introducing a topic which was unfamiliar. Childers adds:

> Resolving the problems of the lower classes – both the problems the lower classes possess and the problems they pose for the middle and upper classes – [was seen to depend] on 'better and scientific' attention to the mechanisms by which the poor [were] observed and their destitution alleviated. [...] Edwin Chadwick's work] suggests that reliable representations of the conditions of the lower classes thus depend on observers' willingness to attend closely to what may be both painful to witness and difficult to describe.[4]

For Childers, this 'better and scientific' method involved 'unrelenting "fidelity to reality"', the establishment of that 'truthfulness of representation' which 'the tradition of realist fiction' would itself be based upon.[5] The Victorians, he concedes, 'knew full well that language was constitutive and that words could just as easily misrepresent [...]. Whether or not they expressly took up the problems of representation, the issue most

---

[3] Joseph W. Childers, *Novel Possibilities: Fiction and the Formation of Early Victorian Culture* (Philadelphia: University of Pennsylvania Press, 1995), 82.
[4] Ibid., 73. [5] Ibid., 81, 82.

concerning these writers was how to represent accurately what they saw.'[6] What I would suggest is that the ordering of this last argument can be inverted and that, considering how often social-problem writers would resort to non-realist elements in their fiction (Gaskell's love stories, Dickens's grotesques, Kingsley's heroic plots), the better question is: regardless of whether or not these authors took up the problems of accurate description, how did their works concern themselves with the nature of representation? Take, for instance, Mayhew's description of Jacob's Island. Instead of telling us facts such as the air is heavy with sulphuretted hydrogen and there are rotting fish in the water, the author concerns himself with the evidence upon which those facts are known: 'It is not only the nose, but the stomach that *tells how* heavily the air is loaded with sulphuretted hydrogen', 'the phosphoretted smell [. . .] *tells you* of the rotting fish there'. These are not simply evocative representations; they are outlines that have the question of how we know the facts about poverty built in.

In Mayhew's case, it is the odours and the physiological reactions of the stomach that register truth. In his descriptions of the people living in Jacob's Island, there is a greater attention to the range of symptoms which betray the effects of the poisoned air and water:

> We crossed the bridge, and spoke to one of the inmates. In answer to our questions, she told us she was never well. Indeed, the signs of the deadly influence of the place were painted in the earthy complexion of the poor woman. [. . .] The blanched cheeks of the people that now came out to stare at us, were white as vegetables grown in the dark [. . .]. As we left [one] house, a child sat nursing a dying half-comatose babe on a door step. The skin of its little arms, instead of being plumped out with health, was loose and shrivelled, like an old crone's, and had a flabby monkey-like appearance more than the character of a human cuticle. The almost jaundiced colour of the child's skin, its half paralyzed limbs, and state of stupor, told it was suffering from some slow poison; indeed the symptoms might readily have been mistaken for those of chronic poisoning from acetate of lead.[7]

The opening of this passage reminds us how Mayhew's social commentaries were based on interviews with the working and pauper classes. His journalistic maps of London life were built, indeed, upon a system of question-and-response with the city's inhabitants, and such is clear, not only in the dialogues he has, but in his silent interactions with their bodies as well. He sees in this woman's complexion, for example, the '*signs*' of

---

[6] Ibid., 81. [7] Mayhew, 'Cholera Districts', 4.

deadly influence; also, the state of a child's body *tells him* that it is 'suffering from slow poisoning'. Detail, in Mayhew's work, is not only a means of achieving a level of truthful representation; it is a means of exhibiting and exploring the means through which social-problem realism is achieved through a focus on bodies and the environments that shape, infect, and destroy them.

The striking examples of cholera-infested bodies in the *Morning Chronicle* series highlight how Mayhew worked alongside a milieu in which medical ideas on sanitation, and strategies for thinking about signs of poverty scientifically, were becoming increasingly dominant. Underpinning the century's cleanliness campaigns, the statistics and medical descriptions of men such as Thomas Southwood Smith, Samuel Farr, and Edwin Chadwick, turned, as Eileen Cleere has argued, a 'seemingly instinctive sensitivity to filth into ideological [...] coherence'.[8] While Cleere follows a Foucauldian track in seeing this 'ideological coherence' as an attempt to recast 'social power' as a 'natural human desire for beauty over ugliness',[9] my own concern is with how such discursive coherence was created, or at least approximated, through an exchange of ideas that took place across medicine and the literatures of social investigation. It is beyond the limits of this chapter to offer a comprehensive account of all such interactions, but it *is* possible to focus on specific, fertile hubs of activity that developed in the nineteenth century – places and discourses, that is, where writers from a range of disciplinary backgrounds interacted, disagreed, shared ideas, and learned from each other's strategies of representation. Two such ferments I will consider here, largely through the figure of William Gaskell – dissenting minister and husband to the author of *Mary Barton* (1848) and *North and South* (1855). These 'ferments' are the city of Manchester and the working-class family periodical.

Manchester

It is worth remembering that, if Manchester became fully aware of its problems with poverty, poor health, and bad sanitation – an awareness we see in works like *Mary Barton* and *North and South* – it also recognised a concomitant need for solutions. Its people came up with countless discussions through its philanthropic and religious associations, mechanics'

---

[8] Eileen Cleere, *The Sanitary Arts: Aesthetic Culture and the Victorian Cleanliness Campaigns* (Columbus: Ohio State University Press, 2014), 4.
[9] Ibid., 5.

institutes, Sunday schools, missionary societies, and church organisations.[10] There is certainly discernible a link between the health and social needs of Manchester's booming population, and the desire to find better health services through knowledge of how industry impacted on the body. Although by mid-century, for example, the central Manchester Infirmary had become so ramshackle that Florence Nightingale would recommend its immediate demolition,[11] the institution had been, in the early years of the century, a hub of medico-scientific enlightenment – 'the most comprehensive medical service in Britain', according to John Pickstone, it featured a 'fever hospital linked with a board of health, a voluntary body that promoted civic public health regulations and collected medical information on fever and its treatment'.[12] In autopsies performed at the Infirmary in the 1830s, the surgeon John Leigh noted 'the presence of "black carboniferous material in the lungs"' of some of Manchester's dead.[13] Encouraged by Chadwick's *Report on the Sanitary Condition of the Labouring Population of Great Britain* (1842), Leigh produced 'On Some Circumstances Affecting the Sanitary Condition of the Town of Manchester' (1844), in which he argued that 'heavy fuel consumption in these areas was the primary cause of the polluted and unhealthy state of the atmosphere of the town'.[14]

A number of civic institutions argued the same point, especially the Manchester Statistical Society and the Manchester and Salford Sanitary Association, inaugurated, respectively, in 1833 and 1855. The Reverend William Gaskell was a member of both these associations. He was also Minister of the Unitarian chapel in Cross Street for much of his life, and his wealthy congregation, according to David Thiele, had 'immense power and prestige' when it came to Manchester's sanitary and social reforms.[15] The chapel was linked to both the Literary and Philosophical Society and The Manchester Academy; it was also home to the Cross Street Domestic Mission. William sat on the board of the Mechanics' Institute, the Working Men's College, the Home Missionary Society, the Literary

---

[10] For an outline of these developments see Robert H. Kargon, *Science in Victorian Manchester: Enterprise and Expertise* (Manchester: Manchester University Press, 1977).
[11] John Pickstone, 'Manchester's History and Manchester's Medicine', *British Medical Journal* (19–26 December 1987), 1604–8, 1606.
[12] Ibid., 1605.
[13] John Leigh, 'On Some Circumstances Affecting the Sanitary Condition of the Town of Manchester' (1844), quoted in Kargon, *Science in Victorian Manchester*, 69.
[14] Kargon, *Science in Victorian Manchester*, 69.
[15] David Thiele, '"That There Brutus": Elite Culture and Knowledge Diffusion in the Industrial Novels of Elizabeth Gaskell', *Victorian Literature and Culture* 35 (2007), 263–85, 266.

and Philosophical Society, the Portico Library, the British Association for the Advancement of Science, the Unitarian New College, and the Lower Mosely Street Sunday Schools. Along with his wife, he was involved in the relief missions set up during Manchester's cholera epidemics of 1848–1849 and 1854, as well as the Lancashire Cotton Famine of 1862.[16] In 1852 and 1855, respectively, he is likely to have been at two lectures delivered to the Manchester Literary and Philosophical Society by the chemist Robert Angus Smith. Smith coined the term 'acid rain' after witnessing the effects of air pollution on the urban environments of Britain's major industrial cities. In one of his Manchester speeches he said that the Lancashire capital was 'a proverb, by giving its rivers and canals such blackness as not only to render them disagreeable, but to cast a shade of gloom on all who come into the town'.[17] The problem, according to another commentator writing much in the same spirit, was that 'in the north, [. . .] the extension of the towns [had] been so sudden [. . . that] the mode of their increase [was] peculiarly unfavourable to the most salutary conditions'.[18]

In Smith's lectures, it is science that offers hope of remediation: it 'has now certainly made us see what before was quite invisible' and thus 'a new era has begun'.[19] If science has allowed us to see, however, there were still plenty of important and significant people who were determined to remain sightless:

> With us the sanitary movement has for a time been very active, and the knowledge of many necessary conditions of public as well as private health has been disseminated among all the reading public, so as to be now proverbially true; but their adoption by the unreading and unthinking has to follow.[20]

What is crystallised in this short passage is something I would like to term the Manchester way of thinking: borne out of complex intersections

---

[16] See Jenny Uglow, *Elizabeth Gaskell: A Habit of Stories* (London: Faber and Faber, 1993), 300, 504; Barbara Brill, *William Gaskell, 1805–84* (Manchester: Manchester Literary and Philosophical Publications, 1984), 88, 94.

[17] Robert Angus Smith, 'On Sewage and Sewage Rivers', in *Transactions of the Manchester Literary and Philosophical Society* 12 (1855), 155–75, 161.

[18] R. Arthur Arnold, *The History of the Cotton Famine* (London: Saunders, Otley, 1864), 436. See also John Leigh's 'On Some Circumstances Affecting the Sanitary Condition of the Town of Manchester' (1844). Leigh wrote the paper in response to Edwin Chadwick's *Report on the Sanitary Condition of the Labouring Population of Great Britain* (1842).

[19] Robert Angus Smith, 'Some Ancient and Modern Ideas of Sanitary Economy', in *Transactions of the Manchester Literary and Philosophical Society* 11 (1854), 39–89, 39.

[20] Smith, 'Sanitary Economy', 65.

between the perceived effects of modern industry and scientific endeavour, it is a form of intellection, similar to that we saw in Mayhew's London reportage, characterised by its ability to read and to think critically – to pull apart the meanings of signs and symptoms, and to question the knowledge that underpins the social-problem mission. Smith's exasperation about the lack of engagement from the 'unreading' and the 'unthinking' suggests that the age of social-problem literature, the years that produced *Mary Barton*, *Hard Times* (1854), and *North and South*, was an age in which the burden of urban improvement had evolved into a recognition of the need to know and analyse the languages, literatures, and sciences of industrial life.

William and Elizabeth Gaskell

In spite of his extraordinary range of activity, William Gaskell is a far more elusive historical figure than his wife is. Very private in his personal affairs, he kept no diaries and burned all his letters. Yet we know from the correspondences of his wife and various other documentary records relating to his ministry and volunteer work that he was a man with a vast amount of energy when it came to schemes of social improvement. He also developed an expertise in poetry and local dialects, which may seem like a very different sort of focus, yet, in its interest in the ways in which information is transacted, moulded, even distorted by local knowledge, Gaskell's fascination with poetry and language is likely to have introduced him to the kinds of analytical tools that we find medical men using alongside their more material approaches to health and wellbeing. In 1838 Elizabeth Gaskell wrote to her friend Mary Howitt:

> My husband has lately been giving four lectures to the very poorest of the weavers in the very poorest district of Manchester, Miles Platting, on 'The Poets and Poetry of Humble Life.' You cannot think how well they have been attended, or how interested people have seemed.[21]

She continues:

> We once thought of *trying* to write sketches among the poor, *rather* in the manner of Crabbe (now don't think this presumptuous), but in a more seeing-beauty spirit; and one – only one – was published in *Blackwood*, January 1837.[22]

---

[21] Elizabeth Gaskell, letter to Mary Howitt, 18 August 1838, in *The Letters of Elizabeth Gaskell*, ed. J. A. V. Chapple and Arthur Pollard (Manchester: Mandolin, 1997), 28–34, 33.
[22] Ibid. Italics in original.

With this sketch, entitled 'Sketches among the Poor, No. 1', 'the Gaskells planned to paint a community and to draw moral lessons through portraits of individuals as Crabbe had done thirty years earlier in 'The Parish Register' [1807] and *The Borough* [1810]'.[23] The poem would get recycled by Elizabeth, ten years later, as Alice Wilson's story in *Mary Barton*. It concerns another Mary, a character 'who had come to Manchester from the Lake District as a young girl. An exile in the city, far from her family, Mary always hopes to return home, but is kept in the alien streets by her work and her concerns for others.'[24] With elements of Wordsworth as well as Crabbe, the verse looks beyond the sooty streets of Manchester and develops a nostalgic, elegiac style which has the effect of ennobling rural poverty:

> The brook went singing by, leaving its foam
> Among the flags and blue forget-me-not;
> And in a nook, above that shelter'd spot,
> For ages stood a gnarled hawthorn-tree,
> And if you pass'd in spring-time, you might see
> The knotted trunk all coronal'd with flowers,
> That every breeze shook down in fragrant showers.[25]

Notwithstanding William's scholarly interests in the shape and texture of local dialects, there is an obvious difference between the descriptions in this sketch of rural poverty and the more analytical portraits that would come to define the social-problem genre. Written in the Romantic style, this early verse is descriptive in order to be evocative of a certain type of beauty; in that sense it is the opposite of the social-problem style. The poem shares with Mayhew an aim to capture a reality through sensory detail, yet it presents nothing of the exploration of how things are known to us: 'if you pass'd [...], you might see', it is said, suggesting that truths remain static whether they are experienced by a human being or not. In Mayhew's interrogation of Jacob's Island, by contrast, we are given a Berkeleyan sense that facts would not exist without being brought to light by the investigator; the subjectivity of the observer is not only active, it is constitutive. The same would be said by linguists interested in local dialects: how we say things determines how we understand them. In the Gaskells' early poem, however, both observation and articulation are incidental – they work through memory yet fail to address what such a

---

[23] Uglow, *Elizabeth Gaskell*, 101–2.   [24] Ibid., 101.
[25] [Elizabeth Gaskell and William Gaskell], 'Sketches among the Poor, No. 1', *Blackwood's Edinburgh Magazine* 41 (1837), 48–50.

conceptual distance means in terms of clarity and truth. This important distinction highlights how social-problem writing developed a use of detail, especially – as we shall see – corporeal detail, in order to be critical, in the analytical sense, of the epistemological strategies that underpin writing on poverty. The Gaskells are central to this exploration because of the way their work evolved, from a Romantic and moralistic fable of the 1830s, to an analytical detailism influenced by the social-reform activities and medical texts of mid-century Manchester.

Temperance Rhymes

'The Sketches of the Rural Poor' project was likely to have been disrupted by William Gaskell's work on a new collection of poems entitled *Temperance Rhymes* (1839), which was written with the aim of promoting moderation in drink among 'the working men of Manchester'. Identified by the collection's dedication, the workers are a force that 'may act as another small weight on the right end of that lever which is to raise them in the scale of humanity'.[26] The volume was praised by no less a luminary than Wordsworth; he wrote to Gaskell: 'I have read your Temperance Rhymes with much pleasure and cannot but think that they must do good.'[27] What he liked in particular, he said, was the collection's creation of poems 'that present pictures of the good and virtuous, by way of contrast to the wretched whom you would deter from continuing in a course that must end in death, and if not repented of, in misery unspeakable'.[28] Living in Manchester and being a member of numerous philanthropic programmes involving the poverty-stricken, William would have experienced how the working classes were not the reckless mob portrayed in the Malthusian philosophies that had underpinned the New Poor Law. He portrayed the working classes as a rather complex and powerful force comprising both good and bad. More than anything else, however, Gaskell was interested in how the working men and women of British industry were prey to environmental forces beyond their control. One would expect a book on temperance, written by a priest, to be catechistic in tone, and *Temperance Rhymes* fails to surprise us here. It doles out, in no modest quantities, judgements and forebodings on the perceived predilections for

---

[26] William Gaskell, *Temperance Rhymes* (London: Simkin, Marshall, 1839), dedication.
[27] William Wordsworth, letter to William Gaskell, 22 July 1840, in *Letters Addressed to Mrs Gaskell by Celebrated Contemporaries*, ed. Ross D. Weller (Manchester: Manchester University Press, 1935), 34.
[28] Ibid.

alcohol among the poorer classes. And yet, as Elizabeth Gaskell does with characters like John Barton, William provides a portrait of temperate working people having their lives blighted by the hardest of industrial situations. One poem's narrator exclaims:

> Oh! hard it is to think,
>   That what might comforts buy
> Is wasted all in one vile sink,
>   Where hell's pollution's lie.[29]

Howitt's Journal *and Thomas Southwood Smith*

Eight years later, Gaskell would place one of his temperance rhymes in the newly established *Howitt's Journal*. Set up and edited by William and Mary Howitt, the periodical was aimed, primarily, at working-class readers: 'Amid the million', the opening editorial address proclaimed, 'there lies enormous need of aid, of comfort, of advocacy, and of enlightenment; and amongst the million, therefore, we shall labour, with hand and heart, with intellect and affection.'[30] Based in Surrey, the well-to-do Howitts had a circle of friends which included some of the period's dignitaries, among them Tennyson, Dickens, Leigh Hunt, Richard Henry Hone, Anna Jameson, Elizabeth Barrett Browning, Thomas Southwood Smith, and Elizabeth and William Gaskell. Radical in their political outlooks, the Howitts were also dissenters, like the Gaskells, and advocated the provision of education for working men and women. A major objective of *Howitt's Journal*, therefore, was 'to promote their education, and especially their self-education – a process full of the noblest self-respect and independence'.[31] It was also motivated by 'the cause of Peace, of Temperance, of Sanatary Reform, of Schools of every class – to all the efforts of Free Trade, free opinion; to [the] abolition of obstructive Monopolies, and the recognition of those great rights which belong to every individual of the great British people'.[32]

---

[29] Gaskell, *Temperance Rhymes*, 25.
[30] William Howitt and Mary Howitt, 'William and Mary Howitt's Address', *Howitt's Journal* 1 (1847), 1–2, 1. For more on Quaker periodicals in the nineteenth century, see Geoffrey Cantor, 'Friends of Science? The Role of Science in Quaker Periodicals', in *Culture and Science in Nineteenth-Century Media*, ed. Geoffrey Cantor, Gowan Dawson, Richard Noakes, Sally Shuttleworth, and Jonathan R. Topham (Aldershot: Ashgate, 2004), 86–93.
[31] William and Mary Howitt, 'Address', 1.   [32] Ibid., 1–2.

That education was considered to be one such 'great right' in *Howitt's* can be seen in the varied range of topics covered, especially 'literature, art and science'.[33] The first volume featured Elizabeth Gaskell's first prose story, 'Libbie Marsh's Three Eras' (1847), as well as one of her husband's poems and an article on sanitary reform by the physician Thomas Southwood Smith. In her recent study *Literature and Medicine in the Nineteenth-Century Periodical Press* (2017), Megan Coyer notes that 'contributing to periodicals, even quasi-anonymously, could be advantageous to men of science', like Southwood Smith, 'in developing their reputations [...]. Conversely, anonymous contribution to popular periodicals could provide a certain freedom from culpability' in subjects that might prove controversial.[34] Gowan Dawson, Richard Noakes, and Jonathan R. Topham add that 'periodicals allowed publishers to develop relationships with particular groups of readers',[35] a factor that was also likely to have motivated scientific authors like Southwood Smith to contribute to a magazine like *Howitt's*; his sanitary work stood to have a greater impact in the pages of a working-class family periodical than in the parliamentary reports, government blue books, and specialist (and expensive) treatises he also drew up. Here he could work independently of the boards, commissioners, and consultants funded by the government – men, like Chadwick, who had contributed to legislative programmes like the New Poor Law. In response to the cholera epidemic of 1826–1837, he was appointed by the Poor Law Commissioners to write a report on the health and sanitary conditions of the East End of London. The report, entitled 'Report on the Physical Causes of Sickness and Mortality to which the Poor are Particularly Exposed, and which are Capable of Prevention by Sanitary Measures' (1837), said much of what the Commissioners wanted to hear: that 'some of the severest evils [...] are the consequences of improvidence', and that many 'evils are capable of being remedied [...] by bringing the poor under the influence of the inducements to forethought and prudence'.[36] And yet, contrary to the Commissioners' belief in the inevitability of urban misery, a belief built upon their faith in Malthusian

---

[33] Ibid., 2.

[34] Megan Coyer, *Literature and Medicine in the Nineteenth-Century Periodical Press: Blackwood's Edinburgh Magazine, 1817–1858* (Edinburgh: Edinburgh University Press, 2017), 29–30.

[35] Gowan Dawson, Richard Noakes, and Jonathan R. Topham, 'Introduction' to *Science in the Nineteenth Century Periodical*, ed. Geoffrey Cantor, Gowan Dawson, Graeme Gooday, Richard Noakes, Sally Shuttleworth, and Jonathan R. Topham (Cambridge: Cambridge University Press, 2004), 8.

[36] Quoted in Gertrude Hill Lewes, *Dr Southwood Smith: A Retrospect* (Edinburgh and London: Blackwood and Sons, 1898), 61.

theory, Southwood Smith stressed, as its title makes clear, 'the preventibleness of this dreadful state of things' – of the possibility of bringing about health and wellbeing through 'wise attention to the laws of health'.[37]

In his less-constrained 'Address to the Working Classes of the United Kingdom, on their Duty in the Present State of the Sanatory Question' (1847), published in the very first number of *Howitt's*, Southwood Smith presented a grim, though not entirely unexpected, set of statistics:

> It appears not only that the rate of mortality in the whole of England at the present day is deplorably high, but that there is an extraordinary excess of mortality over and above what is natural, supposing the term at present attainable, to be the natural term of human life. The statement of this excess present to the mind an appalling picture. From accurate calculations based on the observation of carefully recorded facts, it is rendered certain that the annual slaughter in England alone, by causes that are preventable, by causes that produce not only one disease, namely, typhus fever, is more than double the loss sustained by the allied armies in the battle of Waterloo; that 136 persons perish every day in England alone, whose lives might be saved; that in one single city, namely, Manchester, thirteen thousand three hundred and sixty-two children have perished in seven years over and above the mortality natural to mankind.[38]

I noted that these statistics are not entirely unexpected because similar sets of figures had been presented in a range of publications and reports, including, most famously, Chadwick's report of 1842. Though based, as Christopher Hamlin has illustrated, on 'statistical rigour', Chadwick's text appeared to confirm its author's belief 'that there was no such thing as an innocent pauper'.[39] Excess, in Chadwick's mind, signalled individual failings; the working classes were living immoderately, with a lack of attention to basic principles of cleanliness. Hamlin notes:

> At heart Chadwick was a social engineer who would rationalize systems to rationalize people, while [Southwood] Smith was a liberate theologian and a compassionate doctor. Chadwick thought of populations, Smith of individuals. If, as Benthamites, both were concerned with happiness, Chadwick's happiness was a condition delivered by (and defined by) a scientific state, while Smith's was felt by real people.[40]

---

[37] Ibid., 65.
[38] Thomas Southwood Smith, 'An Address to the Working Classes of the United Kingdom, on their Duty in the Present State of the Sanatory Question', *Howitt's Journal* 1 (1847), 3–4, 3.
[39] Christopher Hamlin, *Public Health and Social Justice in the Age of Chadwick: Britain, 1800–1854* (Cambridge: Cambridge University Press, 1998), 99, 23.
[40] Ibid., 112.

'Extraordinary excess' in Southwood Smith's contribution to *Howitt's Magazine* is certainly different to Chadwick's interpretation of the same. The former's use of the term 'annual slaughter' is reminiscent of Engels's famous reference to urban poverty as 'social murder' in *The Condition of the Working Class in England,* a work that had been penned just two years earlier in 1845.[41] Engels's work has in common with Southwood Smith's address to the working-class readers of *Howitt's* a use of statistical data for the purpose of radical suggestion. Southwood Smith advises his readers:

> You should rouse yourselves and show that you will submit to this dreadful state of things no longer. Let a voice come from your streets, lanes, alleys, courts, workshops, and houses, that shall startle legislature. [...] Petition both houses of Parliament. Call upon the instructed and benevolent men in the legislative body to sustain your just claim to protection and assistance. Petition Parliament to give you sewers; Petition Parliament to give you constant and abundant supplies of water; supplies adequate to the unintermitting and effectual cleansing both of your sewers and streets, and which will afford you the easy means of substituting universally the water-closet for the filthy and the fever-generating cess-pool: petition Parliament to remove – for it is in the power of Parliament universally and completely to remove – some sources of poison that surround your dwellings, and that carry diseases, suffering, and death into your homes.[42]

These were powerful words in 1847 because they were written soon before a number of political revolutions in Europe and the Chartist march to London. Southwood Smith's repetition of the word 'Parliament', indeed, hints at the incendiary notion that it is the government, not the working class, who is to blame for the alarming excesses in mortality rates. What he succeeds in doing, in this passage and in the article as a whole, is interweaving descriptions of urban squalor (similar to, and contemporaneous with, those of Mayhew) with a rousing call to accept such conditions no longer.

The physician proves himself more liberal than Chadwick, to be sure, but I am not sure about Hamlin's intimation that Chadwick's social philosophy was defined by 'a scientific state', while Southwood Smith's was not. While Chadwick had trained as a lawyer, Southwood Smith had taken a medical degree from the University of Edinburgh in 1816. He worked at the London Fever Hospital and published, in 1830, the highly influential *Treatise on Fever*. He based his research on his experiences as a

---

[41] Friedrich Engels, *The Condition of the Working Class in England*, ed. Victor Kiernan (1845; London: Penguin, 1987), 70.
[42] Southwood Smith, 'Address', 4.

clinician and insisted on his approach being founded on sound scientific principles. We see this, in the *Howitt's* contribution, in his determination to make 'calculations based on the observation of carefully recorded facts'. The word 'natural', he is aware, carries a certain amount of ambiguity. Thus, he qualifies, let us suppose 'the term at present attainable, to be the natural term of human life'. What this self-critical approach reveals, I argue, is a type of research that is not only more in touch with the people but is also more reflexive about how one forms expert descriptions and comes to vital conclusions about health.

In his *Introduction to Medical Literature* (1813), surgeon Thomas Young, a fellow of the Royal Society of Physicians, wrote:

> Medicine not only comprehends so very extensive a range of knowledge, but its truths are often so profound, and so much concealed from a cursory inspection, so intricate, so much disguised, distorted and obscured by a multitude of delicate and invisible causes, that nothing less than the all-commanding eye of the most enlightened understanding, than the all-penetrating and all-searching power of genius, can possibly recognise that which is hidden in darkness, can follow that which is remote into the last traces that it imprints, can distinguish certainty from opinion and probability, can separate the essential from the accidental, and finally, can analyse and develop any subject of investigation so completely as to leave no further doubt respecting any of its properties which are cognisable by human means.[43]

When Young's book was published in 1813 with the intention of guiding medical students through the medical textbooks available to them, Southwood Smith was undertaking his degree in Edinburgh. It is a reasonable supposition that he encountered Young's portentous instructions; certain it is that his later writings acknowledge the burdens and potential pitfalls involved in interpretation. Even at his most heated, in the pages of *Howitt's Journal*, Southwood Smith is mindful of the subjective nature of interpretation. In *The Philosophy of Health* (1836–1837), a two-volume study published around the same time as the East London report, he argued that some knowledge of the medical sort 'may be useful to those who have no intention to practice physic, or to perform operations in surgery; may be useful to every human being, to enable him to take a rational care of his health, to make him observant of his own altered sensations, as indications of approaching sickness'.[44] Key words, when it comes to Southwood

---

[43] Thomas Young, *An Introduction to Medical Literature* (London: Underwood and Blacks, 1813), 7.
[44] Thomas Southwood Smith, *The Philosophy of Health*, 2 vols. (1836–1837; London: C. Cox, 1847), vol. 1, 4.

Smith's thinking, are 'wise attention' and 'rational care'. They signal how, in practice and theory, he strives for the kind of careful attention to detail that had been advocated by Young. In his East End report, despite agreeing with the Commissioners' general sense that the poor were to blame for their lack of health, Southwood Smith's unpacking of his own methods and modes of description signal a solemn responsibility in the methods of the professional explorer. In an early biography of Southwood Smith, it is noted:

> In order to make the Report more full and impressive, Dr Southwood Smith writes an exact account of what he saw. He went personally over the greater part of the Bethan Green and Whitechapel districts. 'I traversed', he says, 'a circle of them from six to seven miles in extent. I wrote the account of the places I am about to notice on the spot; I entered many of the houses and examined their condition as to cleanliness, ventilation, as well as the state of the people themselves, who were at the time labouring under fever'.[45]

'I traversed', 'I wrote', 'I am about to notice', 'I entered' – these are the words of a man interested in his modus operandi almost as much as he is in the sick people he is charged with investigating. He appears to subscribe to the view of Thomas Young that medicine's subjects are 'concealed from a cursory inspection', are 'intricate', 'disguised', 'distorted', and often 'obscured by a multitude of delicate and invisible causes'. His Report's recognition of its methods of investigation appears to be aspiring to what Young called 'the most enlightened understanding' – the 'all-penetrating and all-searching' medical investigation, which is able to 'distinguish certainty from opinion and probability, [and] can separate the essential from the accidental'.

Temperance in Howitt's

The poem that William Gaskell published alongside Southwood Smith's address on sanitation was likely to have been chosen for its thematic intersections with the physician's piece. As has been observed by Geoffrey Cantor, Gowan Dawson, Richard Noakes, Sally Shuttleworth, and Jonathan R. Topham in their book *Culture and Science in the Nineteenth-Century Media* (2004), 'periodical content [was] never self-contained or isolated; instead [it] constantly point[ed] beyond [itself], either to other articles in the same periodical or to pieces published in rival journals'.[46] The poem was also immediately succeeded by 'literary

---

[45] Lewes, *Dr Southwood Smith*, 62–3.
[46] Geoffrey Cantor, Gowan Dawson, Richard Noakes, Sally Shuttleworth, and Jonathan R. Topham, eds., 'Introduction' to *Culture and Science*, xviii.

notices' of two medical works, Erasmus Wilson's *Healthy Skin, or the Management of the Skin* (1845) (which was dedicated to Chadwick) and John F. South's *Household Surgery, or Hints on Emergencies* (1847). While the overall tone of Gaskell's poem is didactic, its key tableau is a medical one. It instructs a night 'reveller' roaring a song in the streets to 'hush [his] boisterous strain!' and

> Seest thou that upper light?
>   There, by the sick man's bed of pain,
>   They're watching through the night.
>
> Ah! There are eyes filled to the brim,
>   That dare not yet o'erflow;
> With feigned hope they hide from him
>   The truth full well they know. [...]
>
> Oh! Could those walls but open now
>   And show thee what I saw,
> Thy soul perforce would trembling bow
>   In penitence and awe. [...]
>
> Sad was that face to look upon,
>   Where pain its stamp had set,
> The eye so bright, the cheek so wan,
>   As Life and Death there met.[47]

While it is moral rather than sanitary reform that this poem seeks (not that the Victorians were in the habit of making much of a distinction between these), it has some of the hallmarks of the medical investigations that became central to reform. Rather than simply outlining the narrative of the dying man as he and his wife had done with Mary in 'Sketches of the Rural Poor', Gaskell frames the moment with numerous references to seeing, looking, and observing. The scene is presented as a set piece of theatre, almost, where death is a spectacle defined by its symptoms. The poem is reminiscent of Southwood Smith's 'I wrote [...] I noticed [...]' and Mayhew's 'signs of deadly influence' in the way it creates moral purpose through attention to how misery is witnessed. We see a blurring of the boundaries between observation and feeling when the dying man is watched by 'eyes filled to the brim', not only with tears, but with 'truth'. The poem fits with the sanitary reformer's sense of good as coming, in part, through an understanding of the mechanics of interpretation.

---

[47] William Gaskell, 'A Temperance Rhyme', *Howitt's Journal* 1 (1849), 308.

Cottonopolis

Two years before his death in 1884, William Gaskell published his final work, *Cottonopolis* (1882). Appearing as a single volume, it is a relatively lengthy poem whose epigraph, *ex fumo dare lucem* (light from smoke), seems to sum up the Manchester way of thinking. It begins:

> In Cottonopolis I dwell,
> And on the whole I love it well,
> And fain a helping hand would lend
> Some of its obvious faults to mend.
>
> Imprimis, then, its clouds of smoke
> Often my righteous wrath provoke, [...]
> This morning, as to town I came,
> I felt it was a burning shame
> That two huge chimneys puffing kept
> Heaven's blessed light to intercept,
> And with their noxious fumes distressed
> My tender throat and delicate chest.[48]

Although it cannot claim to be a great work of literature, *Cottonopolis* shares with *Temperance Rhymes* a presentation of its subject that has some recognition of the means of observing and exploring. Two enormous chimneys frame the metropolis and register their bad work on the throat and chest of the narrator. At another point, 'The other night, at latish hour', the speaker comes across a poverty-stricken boy:

> A little lad so piteously
> To buy a paper begged of me
> I felt unable to refuse,
> And took a copy of the *News*.[49]

Hearing the boy's 'artless story' of how he sells newspapers on the street corner, the narrator wishes to learn more about his life and follows him home:

> Leading me through a dark back street,
> Whose smells were anything but sweet,
> The laddie brought me to a room,
> Where a faint fire half broke the gloom.
> But shewed me such a filthy den
> As I had never seen till then.

---

[48] [William Gaskell], *Cottonopolis* (Manchester: Johnson and Rawson, 1882), 3.   [49] Ibid., 6.

> Of furniture it was quite bare,
> Except a three-legged stool and chair,
> And on the floor a ragged bed
> On which two little girls were laid,
> And stretched beside them, closely pressed,
> Father and mother, half undressed.[50]

The suggestion that the speaker had never seen 'such a filthy den till then' proves that Gaskell uses a fictional narrator – the author himself would have witnessed many such scenes of misery during his years of missionary work. The use of a naïve speaker allows the poem to foreground its process of discovery. Like Henry Mayhew, Thomas Southwood Smith, and other slum explorers, Gaskell's narrator is led through a labyrinth of dark and filthy streets where he registers the smells and sights of poverty. The street vendor's father and mother, half undressed, are censured heavily, yet, as in *Temperance Rhymes,* there is some recognition of how 'the vile spot where [these people] had birth / Is a contentious hell on earth'.[51] Responsibility is shifted, to a large extent, from the dejected to the civic authorities whose charge it is to relieve the most miserable:

> Sometimes [these problems] make me ask for what
> A City Council we have got,
> If such a nuisance they allow
> As this from which we suffer now.
> Surely, if so inclined they might,
> Perhaps, not remedy it quite,
> But means devise, at any rate,
> Its present foulness to abate.[52]

There is another significant shift in focus from the faults of the indigent to the wider lack of interest in the means of remedying Manchester's problems. Rather than just listing solutions, the poem advocates exploration of, or at least an interest in, urban poverty:

> Again, it is a burning shame,
> And anxious thought should surely claim,
> That underneath five years of age
> Thousands of children quit this stage,
> And make the death-rate stand so high
> [...] We [should] demand the reasons why [...]
>
> I've given you now both rhyme and reason,
> And hope 'twill prove a word in season,

---

[50] Ibid., 7. [51] Ibid., 9. [52] Ibid., 3.

> And serve attention to direct
> Where it may have a good effect.[53]

Gaskell's evangelical focus gives way, tellingly, to an interest in high death rates and their reasons. In line with what Southwood Smith saw as central to the practice of medicine, he also suggests that 'reason' and 'attention' must be central to any such investigation. To the readers it is addressed:

> If you would have your pity stirred,
> Be not by selfish ease deterred,
> But go to Market Street at night
> Where blazes the electric light,
> And there, unhappily, you'll see
> As sad a sight as well can be –
> Poor little savages half-clad,
> Too surely 'going to the bad.'[54]

The dialogue between light and darkness, real and metaphorical, is fascinating here. In contrast to the thousands of sentimentalised children created by the Victorians, Gaskell presents 'savages' with prominent bodies 'half-clad' – no less deserving of high feeling (as the adjective 'poor' makes clear) despite all their barbarity. As the epigraph promises light from smoke, and the opening of the poem worries about the light of heaven being obscured by the two massive chimneys, the author stresses some need for clarity of vision, for a trip to Market Street where the electric lights allow the material realities of poverty to be seen in full, and where the critical faculty of the onlooker will be allowed to do its vital work.

Insistent in its appeal to the emotional and moral nature of destitution and squalor, William Gaskell's poetry is thus a product of nineteenth-century Manchester: written in the heart of the textile metropolis, the writing demonstrates something of the intricate and reciprocal inspirations that moved between literature and the sciences of sanitary reform. It does this by landing upon a critical approach to bodies and their environments. In the earlier context of the popular family magazine, Gaskell's voice joined that of Southwood Smith in drawing attention to the importance of a careful, more critical, approach to the nature of perception. Inspired by medicine's increasing sense that accuracy and detail are vital to the successful pursuit of social improvement, this more analytical interest illustrates the features shared by the period's social-problem literature and its sciences of sanitary reform.

---

[53] Ibid., 10, 13.   [54] Ibid., 5–6.

CHAPTER 10

Flexible Bodies, Astral Minds
Gendered Mind–Body Practices and Colonial Medicine
Narin Hassan

In his biography of Shivapuri Baba (Swami Govindananda Bharati), John G. Bennett records that between 1896 and 1901, the Swami had several meetings with Queen Victoria where he taught her meditation techniques. Bharati, who supposedly lived to the age of 137, was a Nepali mystic who began a solitary pilgrimage around the globe on foot beginning in 1870. His encounters with the Queen have received little critical attention apart from biographical sources such as Bennett's, although they have been noted in contemporary magazines and websites. For example, in *Yoga International* 15 May 2015, Georg Feuerston writes: 'Because of Queen Victoria's interest in him, Shivapuri Baba and his message were well received in certain exclusive circles in Europe', arguing that he

> appears to have been the first modern yoga master to transplant the wisdom of India to the West. He was blessed with a very long life, and after his awakening at the age of fifty, he dedicated it entirely to the spiritual welfare of others. He had no fewer than eighteen audiences with Queen Victoria, who considered him a friend.[1]

Very little is recorded of what took place in these meetings, but they suggest that Queen Victoria sought advice from the sage and may have engaged with meditation practices later in her life. Howard Murphet considers him an 'advisor' to Queen Victoria,[2] and Bennett notes that Shivapuri Baba received an invitation from the Queen's Indian Secretariat and 'visited the Queen eighteen times – "at various castles" as he put it', and the visits 'were no doubt scrupulously entered in the

---

[1] Georg Feuerston, 'The Lost Teachings of Yoga', *Yoga International*. https://yogainternational.com/article/view/the-lost-teachings-of-yoga.
  Feuerston originally published this *Yoga International* piece in 2002, and it was reprinted in the May 2015 edition. Feuerston was a prolific scholar of yoga studies, and refers to John Bennett in his list of sources on Shivapuri Baba.
[2] Howard Murphet, *Practical Yoga for Everyone* (Hyderabad: Orient Longman, 2001), 68.

Queen's diary, and equally scrupulously cut out by Princess Beatrice when she carried out only too well the task of editing them'.[3]

While information regarding these meetings is vague or somewhat veiled (and, perhaps, exaggerated by biographers eager to show the impact of Shivapuri Baba's techniques), these interactions coincide with the publication of a number of late Victorian texts addressed to women around topics of health, which, as I will soon discuss, revealed a widening interest in various forms of exercise, breathing, and meditation rooted in South Asian cultures. They are also timed soon after the visit of Swami Vivekananda to Chicago for the Parliament of Religions in 1893, an event that exposed transatlantic audiences more fully to Indian methods of healing through breath work and meditation.[4] Vivekananda's publication, *Raja Yoga* (1896), highlighted yoga as a system that had evolved beyond the acrobatic movements that were associated with lower-class Indian 'fakirs' and presented the practice as a more complex, respectable, and attainable spiritual method that could provide mental and physical improvement. The text also spread understandings of yoga as a spiritual practice to readers in the West.[5]

While through much of the nineteenth century colonial spaces such as India were largely viewed as 'the tropics' – and as sites of disease in need of European intervention – the late nineteenth century also saw a growing interest in Eastern philosophies and practices as potentially beneficial to the body and good health. As the century progressed, self-care guides,

---

[3] John G. Bennett, *The Long Pilgrimage: The Life and Teaching of Sri Govindananda Bharati* (London: Hodder and Stoughton, 1965), 25.

[4] A number of scholars, including Srinivas Arumavudan (*Guru English: South Asian Religion in a Cosmopolitan Language* [Princeton: Princeton University Press, 2009]) and Mark Singleton ('Transnational Exchange and the Genesis of Modern Postural Yoga', in *Yoga Travelling: Bodily Practice in Transcultural Perspective*, ed. Beatrix Hauser [Switzerland: Springer, 2013], 37–56), have written about the impact of Vivekananda's presence and speech in Chicago for the Parliament of Religions, and highlighted how it exposed Western audiences to the practices of yoga more widely. Stefanie Syman, in her book *The Subtle Body: The Story of Yoga in America* (New York: Ferrari, Straus, and Giroux, 2010), notes that the audiences at this event were largely female (49).

[5] Mark Singleton describes how the image of the 'fakir', like that of the sannyasin or yogi, was associated with the lower classes and did not meld with the notion of Indian respectability that Vivekananda was trying to project 'for a dignified Indian cultural revival' (40). He writes of Vivekananda's *Raja Yoga* (1896): 'part practical manual, part commentary on Patanjali's Yogasutra, [*Raja Yoga*] was immensely important in the development of Western understandings of yoga. Many of the popular yoga guides published in Britain and America during the succeeding decades bear traces of his influence, and in some ways Raja Yoga can be considered the public face of the transnational yoga renaissance' ('Transnational Exchange', 40). Stefanie Syman traces how Vivekananda's text focused upon meditation and yoga philosophy and influenced American women such as Sarah Farmer, Sara Chapman Bull, and Blanche Devries, who set up organizations and initiatives related to his teachings (*Subtle Body*, 46–9, 63–71, 99).

exercise manuals, and travel handbooks, often directed at women, began to integrate Eastern traditions of physical and spiritual guidance with medical advice. These texts shaped cultural attitudes related to health and the body and functioned alongside novels, travel narratives, and memoirs to address the relationship of travel and empire to health and medicine. The late Victorian period also witnessed a transnational convergence of evolving medical interest in the capacities of the brain and its relationship to the body.[6] My interest is in how these movements reflected new ideals of the healthy and productive female body and, further, how they intersected with Eastern philosophies and practices, particularly those practiced in India – a site that was intimate and central to British imperial efforts. In particular, I trace the ways that European and American women became increasingly intrigued by and immersed within practices that were becoming more available to Western audiences, such as meditation, yoga exercises (asana), and breathing methods (pranayama). Engagement with these activities was accessible through travels to India and was also encouraged through the more widely-available health guides and manuals that provided access to these techniques. I suggest that, for some European women, travels to India and access to the ancient philosophies of yoga and meditation provided an antidote to the evolving theories of Western allopathic medicine, which focused largely upon a divide between mind and body and categorized female bodies and minds as weaker and more susceptible to disorder.

Tracing connections between gender and empire, I consider how engagement with Indian yogic philosophies offered women alternatives to Western medicine – an increasingly institutional system from which they were often excluded. In a culture where medical and scientific practices increasingly limited women's participation and sometimes stifled their capabilities and experiences, many European and American women turned to foreign spaces as sites of healing and participated within alternative systems of self-care, often arguing for them as scientifically informed therapeutic practices. Unlike the often-regimented and prescriptive advice

---

[6] Critics, including Anne Stiles, Peter Logan, and many others, have explored nineteenth-century knowledge around the brain and nervous system, while Jan Tod, Bruce Haley, and others have traced the ways that notions of the healthy body and physical cultures were shaped during the period. See Anne Stiles, *Popular Fiction and Brain Science in the Late Nineteenth Century* (Cambridge: Cambridge University Press, 2012); Peter Logan, *Nerves and Narratives: A Cultural History of Hysteria in Nineteenth-Century British Prose* (Oakland: University of California Press, 1997); Jan Todd, *Physical Culture and the Body Beautiful Purposive Exercise in the Lives of American Women, 1800–1870* (Macon: Mercer University Press, 1998); Bruce Haley, *The Healthy Body and Victorian Culture* (Cambridge, MA: Harvard University Press, 1978).

women would receive at home – largely the result of an increasingly industrialized, professionalized, and masculine public sphere – foreign spaces and the healing systems they offered tended to present more flexible and intuitive modes of thinking and understanding the body. Often these more exotic, alternative systems provided a respite from the mundane, promising the potential for energetic spiritual and physical transformation. I explore how women turned to Indian traditions and practices for forms of self-improvement and healing that could challenge Western scientific theories and redefine conceptions of the body and mind. The figures I discuss emphasized yoga as a science and represented its practice as therapeutic and transformative and as challenging hierarchical distinctions of the mind and the body.

I come to this topic through an interest in analyzing twenty-first-century 'mind–body' practices that include yoga, mindfulness, meditation, and a variety of holistic health practices. While I am interested in the ways that yoga and related practices function as a global and gendered phenomenon in our contemporary moment, the late nineteenth century witnessed a similar convergence of Indian spiritualism with the practices and discourses of self-care, body management, and exercise as well as medical investigations of the nervous system and brain. While much of the scholarship on the Western attraction to India as a spiritual site of healing and transformation focuses upon the twentieth century (and particularly upon the movements of the 1960s), my goal is to trace a longer history, and to examine the ways that women in the *fin de siècle* engaged in the process of disseminating and, at times, producing practices connected with Indian traditions and situating the colonial location as a space of potential mental and physical rejuvenation. Our readings of literature and medicine in the nineteenth century can be expanded as we consider the more fluid boundaries between medicine and spirituality, and as we examine the wide variety of texts that were being produced in the period on these topics. Increasingly global networks and cultures of travel towards the end of the century supported new ways to think about the body and health and gave women greater access to Indian texts and traditions. These could inspire women to imagine and create an expanded sense of empowerment and health. Yoga and meditation were methods of healing associated with South Asia, but they also became shaped in new and more hybrid forms as they came into contact with travelers. Evolving forms of wellness were shaped through the intermingling of European women with various methods and forms of yoga and meditation in India at the turn of the century. This process of engagement allowed women to participate within colonial realms and also challenge the dominant discourses of colonial medicine and science.

Tracing Gender, Colonialism, and Medicine in the Nineteenth Century

Scholarship on gender, medicine, and empire has been largely focused upon tropical and colonial spaces as sites of disease and disorder. Work on colonial medicine tends to emphasize how exotic locations were a marker for illness or contagion, and address the ways that colonial efforts focused upon the reorganization of medical practices and disease prevention. Often, this research focuses upon colonial efforts to eradicate disease and establish the authority of Western medicine. For example, focusing upon the case of India, Gyan Prakash has shown how colonial contexts further intensified the authority of Western science and medicine and also helped to uphold institutional inequities within colonial contexts.[7] Many of the fictional and literary works of the period – novels, travel journals, and poems – established foreign spaces with lack of order and disease. Fictional examples include the representation of Bertha Mason with the disorder of the tropics in Charlotte Brontë's *Jane Eyre* (1847) and Rochester's claim that 'the fresh wind from Europe' was a healing force against his demise in the West Indies. *Fin-de-siècle* texts such as Stoker's *Dracula* (1897) also associate foreign and primitive spaces as degenerative, as do Anglophone stories such as Frances Hodgson Burnett's *The Secret Garden* (1911) and Flora Annie Steel's *Voices in the Night* (1900). Both texts present India as a site of potential disease and highlight ways that Europeans can be weakened in the tropical climate. Medical guidebooks such as Edward Tilt's *Health in India for British Women, and on the Prevention of Disease in Tropical Climates* (1875) warn readers of the dangers of the Indian climate and its debilitating impact upon European bodies, particularly upon the bodies of women and children. Tilt feared that India could not be effectively colonized without minimizing what he termed 'the blood tax'[8] and claimed 'that Europeans when residing in a tropical climate are thereby made more liable to diseases of the reproductive organs scarcely

---

[7] See Gyan Prakash, *Another Reason: Science and the Imagination of Modern India* (Princeton: Princeton University Press, 1998).
[8] Edward Tilt, *Health in India for British Women, and on the Prevention of Disease in Tropical Climates*, 4th ed. (London: J & A Churchill, 1875), 4.

requires proof'[9] and 'children must be sent home or grow up sickly in mind and body'.[10] Doctors such as Tilt focused upon ways to maintain the health of Europeans within the debilitating climates of spaces like India, and also argued that effective colonial impact could only be sustained if the health and sanitation of the region were improved. Travel narratives often posed the tension of foreign spaces as simultaneously healing or as unhealthy and disease ridden. Accounts by women, such as Harriet Martineau's *Eastern Life Present and Past* (1844), presented domestic spaces as unhealthy for women and children and in need of reform – for Martineau the Egyptian harem is a site of sickness, malaise, and bad ventilation as it is in the accounts of Emmeline Lott, who depicted the Indian 'zenana' as a similar site of laziness and disease. The zenana, as numerous scholars have shown, is a particularly loaded site as it represents the core of primitivism with women being secluded and also unhealthy.[11] On the other hand, texts such as Lucie Duff Gordon's *Letters from Egypt* (1862) represent the dry air and warm climate of Egypt as an antidote to the cold, damp climate of England and depict journeys as healing. Such accounts are shared by other women travelers, including Marianne North, who suffered ailments at home and found refuge and cures in her journeys around the globe. As I have argued in other work, the colonies were also envisioned as productive spaces for medical research, experimentation, and practice – particularly for women. India was a site where early women doctors including Mary Scharlieb and Edith Petchey could study and practice when they were barred from medical schools in Britain, and, typically, once established as doctors, they could become representatives of the authority of Western medicine, particularly as a force to shift traditional practices and 'uncover' the zenana. Women doctors in colonial realms typically participated in discourses that situated native peoples and their health care resources as primitive and in need of repair. They became involved in the development of clinics and hospitals, and, as I have also argued, gained their own authority within colonial spaces, both as amateur

---

[9] Ibid., 53.   [10] Ibid., 3.
[11] We see this depiction of the zenana as unhealthy as a trope in travel writing of the period. See, for example, representations from Harriet Martineau, Emmeline Lott, and many others. For critical references, among others, see Inderpal Grewal, *Home and Harem: Nation, Gender, Empire, and Cultures of Travel* (Durham: Duke University Press, 1996); Ali Behdad, 'The Eroticized Orient: Images of the Harem in Montesquieu and His Precursors' *Stanford French Review* 13 (1989), 109–26; Indira Ghose, *Women Travellers in Colonial India: The Power of the Female Gaze* (Delhi: Oxford University Press, 1998). Ghose notes, 'Nowhere is the range of the traveller's gaze more clearly shown than in the descriptions of visits to the zenana' (11).

'doctors' and as professionally trained medical women.[12] Thus, the colonies could be a space of empowerment as well as self-growth, as women could have more vocal impact abroad.

Yet, rethinking this work, I suggest that the colonies could also be sites of discovery in new ways, especially as medicine became increasingly institutionalized and continued to limit women. While colonial spaces were often imagined as sites in need of reform and European intervention, I ask that we also consider them as spaces that could stimulate knowledge and function as sites of healing. How, then, were colonial spaces also a site for hybrid and shared forms of knowledge? How did women engage with mind and body practices that they encountered through colonial travel, and how did these practices and methods travel themselves at the turn of the century? How did a variety of textual forms, such as guidebooks, function in hybrid ways to shape notions of health and healing and also to widen our sense of the culture of literature and medicine in the period?

Props and Exercise: India in Victorian Conceptions of the Physical Body

Although many readings of Victorian culture link idealized femininity with domesticity and the containment of the female body – a connection that was indeed prevalent in the period – this was also the age when an expanding physical culture for women was firmly in place, and when the possibilities of travel and global exploration became more open to women. An evolving culture of self-care and physical exercises that could be practiced at home presented an alternative for European women that challenged the confinement of the zenana and its symbolic references to Eastern femininity and potential sickness. Yet, many of the manuals and guides addressed to women incorporated aspects of Indian props and exercises as they presented ways for women to strengthen their bodies and health through simple exercises. Earlier in the period, Donald Walker published *Exercises for Ladies* (1837), which opened with the claim that 'few women are exempt from some degree of deformity. This always increases with age, unless means of prevention are either intentionally or accidentally employed.'[13] Walker's prescription was for women to engage in gentle exercises, often with the use of light Indian clubs and other props,

---

[12] See Narin Hassan, *Diagnosing Empire: Women, Medical Knowledge, and Colonial Mobility* (Hampshire: Ashgate, 2011).
[13] Donald Walker, *Exercise for Ladies* (London: Thomas Hurst, 1837), xi.

suggesting that such activity 'prevents that troubled sensibility and nervous irregularity that we observe frequently in many indolent women'.[14] In the same year, William Coulson published a medical manual on deformities of the chest that argued that Indian exercises gave 'the fullest expansion of the chest'.[15] Indian 'clubs' or 'scepters' were originally used by Indian soldiers but became popular exercise props within Europe by the middle of the century, when doctors began to write about their benefits for both men and women. Exercise guides such as *Madame Brennar's Gymnastics for Ladies* (1870) included illustrations of women exercising with barbells, and, by the middle of the nineteenth century, exercise props such as dumbbells and Indian clubs were introduced and marketed to women as tools that could increase lung capacity, build muscle strength, and encourage spinal flexibility. At the turn of the century, Margaret Noble traveled to India to study yoga, and Mollie Bagot Stack created the popular 'Stretch and Swing' system that was designed for women to stay mobile and develop physical strength. Cassell's 1881 household guide included calisthenic routines for women with props such as Indian clubs and commentary that highlighted the enormous potential of exercise to increase the power of the female body as well as establish a sense of routine and organization:

> As soon as women experience the benefits of physical education a general desire arises to share in its advantages, among which we may reckon a sense of power of action, an increased cheerfulness, and general vigour; for whatever bodily organs are properly exercised become strong, though irregular exercise is worse than none at all. What bodily training will do is best seen by the manner in which a slouching plough-boy is transformed into a smart soldier.[16]

While such references clearly highlighted the physical benefits of exercise for women, they also associated proper alignment and bodily care with spiritual growth and responsible female behavior – establishing how physical alignment combined with spiritual and emotional strength and proper household management. I am interested in how these new systems and methods of exercise targeted to women were influenced by early yogic and meditative practices in India. The study of yoga as a cultural practice

---

[14] Ibid., 256.
[15] William Coulson. *Deformities of the Chest and Spine* (London: Thomas Hurst, 1837), xi. Coulson also notes that the covering of Indian women's bodies could 'preserve the beauty of the bosom to a very advanced age' (237).
[16] Unsigned, 'Calisthenics for Ladies', *Cassell's Household Guide to Every Department of Practical Life* (London, Paris, and New York: Casser, Petter, Galpin, 1881), 231.

and global phenomenon has begun to be examined by religious scholars and anthropologists, including Joseph Alter, Suzanne Newcombe, Mark Singleton, and others. Singleton addresses the ways in which the late nineteenth century witnessed more philosophical, cultural, and technological exchanges regarding the body and exercise and how the health of the body was viewed in relation to the nation. He discusses how the practice of yoga and physical culture emerged in the late nineteenth century:

> Across Europe and Asia, people were embracing new technologies for building the body in the interests of the nation. India was no exception, and the decades either side of 1900 saw a dramatic rise in the popularity of modern physical culture. Many borrowed European techniques of gymnastics and bodybuilding and merged them with indigenous practices. One eventual result of such mergers was the now dominant mode of postural yoga practice.[17]

Singleton also notes how 'in Europe and America the newly emerging forms of postural yoga began to be assimilated into already present traditions of women's gymnastics'.[18] Patricia Vertinsky reveals that the convergence of medicine with practices of exercise had a long-standing history:

> In England, a steady stream of popularized and increasingly scientific medical commentaries had developed during the nineteenth century related to female health and posture, incorporating wider anxieties about eugenic practices and maternal health as the century wore on.[19]

While Vertinsky, Alter, Singleton, and others have begun to trace the ways that physical and spiritual practices intersected in the nineteenth century and developed as a precursor to the popular yoga practices we now recognize, I suggest that the culture of exchange was particularly open to women at this time, and women participated in the cross-cultural aspects of physical culture as both mediators and practitioners.

Breath, Mind, and Movement: Manuals of Meditation and Healing by Genevieve Stebbins

One key example is a handbook by Genevieve Stebbins, entitled *Dynamic Breathing and Harmonial Gymnastics* (1892). Initially trained as an actress,

---

[17] Singleton, 'Transnational Exchange', 39.   [18] Ibid., 39.
[19] Patricia Vertinsky, '"Building the Body Beautiful" in the Women's League of Health and Beauty: Yoga and Female Agency in 1930s Britain', *Rethinking History. The Journal of Theory and Practice* 12 (2002): 517–42, 523.

Stebbins was influenced by the work of Delsarte Ling, and other men who were beginning to establish movement and expression systems. She developed exercise and breathing methods that appear strongly influenced by elements of Eastern spirituality, dance, and systems of meditation. Stebbins's book is a practical exercise manual and an esoteric guide to health that references philosophy, religion, and health practices across the globe. She opens the book with a focus upon breath and the connection of beings to the universe, noting that 'the breath is the life and the power of breathing is the ability to indraw the invisible essence of continued existence'.[20] Along with mentioning astronomy and the power of the air and sun early in the text, she writes:

> And seeing that every orb in space is dependent upon every other orb, that the thrilling pulsations of one must of necessity, according to the doctrine of the conversation of force create corresponding pulsations amid the countless orbs of this infinite universe, we can by the wondrous creative powers of the mind, distinctly perceive the might outrush from, and the influx to, each creation of this invisible but potential essence across conceivable distances of the interstellar spaces in one continuous rhythmic harmony of life in the inbreathing and outbreathing breath of God.[21]

Stebbins alludes to Buddhist philosophies regarding the interconnectedness of all living things, as well as theories about astral planes and energies that flow within the universe. For her, the power of the mind and breath lead the efforts of the body and ensure its effective functioning. She provides a full chapter on the power of respiration, reminding readers that 'rhythmic breathing can stimulate the mental powers to their highest capacity',[22] and then produces a chapter on 'dynamic breathing', arguing that deep, rhythmic breathing combined with a clearly formulated image or idea in the mind

> produces a sensitive, magnetic condition of the brain and lungs, which attracts the finer ethereal essence from the atmosphere with every breath, and stores up this essence in the lung cells and brain convolutions in almost the same way that a storage battery stores up the electricity from the dynamo or other source of supply.[23]

As she develops her theories, Stebbins refers to the work of 'Hindu metaphysicians', 'Bhuddha', 'Mahomet', and various other religious figures,[24]

---

[20] Genevieve Stebbins, *Dynamic Breathing and Harmonic Gymnastics: A Complete System of Psychical, Aesthetic and Physical Culture*, 2nd ed. (New York: Edgar S. Werner, 1892), 4.
[21] Ibid., 5.   [22] Ibid., 19.   [23] Ibid., 52.   [24] Ibid., 42–3.

as well as the activities of 'whirling dervishes, shamans, and Hindoo tribes', who use the power of breath to create hypnotic states.[25] Stebbins writes that

> the system of pyscho-physical culture and the various exercises for the same given in this work are based chiefly upon those just mentioned, combined with others more occult and mystic in their nature, which have been taken from those ideal and charmingly beautiful motions of sacred dance and prayer practiced by various oriental nations for certain religious and metaphysical effects, while the whole is blended with a system of vital, dynamic breathing and mental imagery.[26]

Throughout her text, Stebbins alludes to the perfect equanimity that can be achieved in the body through the movements which she suggests bring together the balance of 'oriental' practices and mystical experiences. She argues that it is this synergy that creates health in the body and mind:

> this perfect combination stimulates to healthy, vigorous action every power and molecule of the brain, so as to produce, by mental reaction, a life giving stimulating ecstasy upon the soul – the psyche; hence the true meaning of this especial system which is, in very truth, psycho-physical, and affects, simultaneously, the body to vigorous health, the brain to powerful mental action, and the soul to higher aspiration.[27]

Stebbins is fascinated by the twists and curves of Arab houris and Indian dancing girls, noting that these dancers 'go through the most wonderful and graceful evolutions, producing everything that is possible to the harmonic poise and the spiral line'.[28] This 'spiral line' is the focus of many of the exercises she recommends to her readers, but, even as she emphasizes the importance of gesture and movement, she reminds readers that the brain is the 'grand centre of physical life'.[29] She also argues that 'every motion in our exercises is ancient'[30] and *the storing of oxygen is a mystic force, and the one we are trying to know more of*.[31] Thus, her methods go both forward and back in time – connecting to ancient and mythical forms, and also connecting with ideas that were evolving around the relationship of the brain and nervous system to human behavior – and she brings together physical movement with a call for her readers and students to develop a mental (and often mystical) practice. This emphasis on the mystical or esoteric was not always well received, as a reviewer from the *Journal of Education* in 1893 argued:

---

[25] Ibid., 53.   [26] Ibid., 59.   [27] Ibid., 59.   [28] Ibid., 65.   [29] Ibid., 61.   [30] Ibid., 66.
[31] Ibid., 72. Italics in original.

There is plenty of good sense in her theories of deep breathing, but when she carries them into the realms of psychology and mysticism, and descants on 'hypnotic spectrophobia' and 'dynamic essences of the sentient soul' the ordinary reader will be more than likely to close the volume convinced of his utter inability to follow the tortuous, mysterious, five-syllabled paths which lead to an understanding of the author's meaning.[32]

While Stebbins briefly mentions props like Indian clubs, her method of exercise is primarily focused upon the relationship of the brain and the breath to the body and the practitioner's ability to focus and control both breath and movement without the assistance of props. She emphasizes how mental strength and alignment and the 'psycho-physical' aspects of being are the key to longevity and good health. Although her critics may have found the approach unusual, Stebbins's method asks the reader to try to assume a meditative state, and her methods emphasize the importance of attaining the balance of combining mental awareness and physical movement to produce a trancelike or hypnotic experience. At the same time, as she encourages dynamic breath and movement to create more awareness of the body and its relationship to the environment, she also alludes to the possibility of breath work to transport the practitioner to elevated realms beyond the everyday – and much of her emphasis is upon the power of the imagination to elevate the body and perception to a higher plane. Describing the 'Phenomena of Respiration', she writes:

> First that various states and conditions of respiration in the natural state are due to certain manifestations of the mind. Secondly, that seeing that certain states of respiration are the outcome of, or are favourable to, certain mental conditions, are in fact, the invariable accompaniments of each other, we are led irresistibly to infer that with the powerful aid of the imagination and a systematic rhythmic breathing we can stimulate the mental powers to their highest capacity, artificially remove much of the discord in life which results from inharmonious mental states and scientifically produce, in a systemic manner, the most beneficial results.[33]

Stebbins concludes that breath and mind are intricately connected and establishes that her manual produces scientifically effective results for powerful and productive breathing and mental capacity. Her other work, *Genevieve Stebbins' System of Physical Training* (1899), focuses more specifically upon bodily movements and physical exercises, but in Lesson

---

[32] Unsigned review of Genevieve Stebbins's *Dynamic Breathing and Harmonic Gymnastics*, *Journal of Education* 37:16 (1893), 251.
[33] Stebbins, *Dynamic Breathing and Harmonic Gymnastics*, 19.

One of the text she notes that 'the body is the plastic image of the soul'.[34] She argues that breath 'recuperates' mental exhaustion and includes a chapter on 'Eastern Medical Drills' that are 'adapted from various forms of Oriental worship'[35] and include having the arms rise up and the hands held in prayer in much the same way a yoga sun salutation would include movements.

Stebbins's work precludes the movement of physical asana and practice that begin in the early twentieth century, and introduces nineteenth-century audiences to ancient theories of meditation and breath that she describes as powerful and illuminating. Her manual provides a challenge to Western theories of the boundaries of mind and body, instead re-conceptualizing these terms and focusing upon the potential power of merging and redefining them. Such concepts of bringing the physical body to a healing state through the power of the mind, breath, and meditation, were concepts that were also being practiced within India, by European women who were inspired to both travel and immerse themselves within the ashrams that existed there.

Indian Journeys: Western Women and the Scientific Cultures of Yoga

Two literary figures, Annie Besant and Margaret Noble (Sister Nivedita), traveled to India at the turn of the century and became deeply immersed in Indian culture by producing yogic concepts related to health and healing. They produced a variety of texts, ranging from autobiographical works to travel accounts and critical essays, and published reflections upon Indian culture and imperial politics. These women argued for yoga as a powerful, scientific practice that was critical to healing and to creating a just society. For example, in her *Introduction to Yoga*, a publication of her lectures to the Theosophical Society on their anniversary held in Benares in December 1907, Besant notes:

> These lectures are intended to give an outline of Yoga, in order to prepare the student to take up, for practical purposes, the Sutras of Patanjali, the chief treatise on Yoga [...]. They may, however, also serve to give the ordinary lay reader some idea of the Science of sciences, and perhaps to allure a few towards its study.

---

[34] Genevieve Stebbins, *The Genevieve Stebbins System of Physical Training* (New York: Edward S. Werner, 1898), 15.
[35] Ibid., 84.

She then emphasizes how yoga is a critical science:

> Yoga is a science. That is the second thing to grasp. Yoga is a science, and not a vague dreaming drifting or imagining. It is an applied science, a systematized collection of laws applied to bring about a definite end. It takes up the laws of psychology, applicable to the unfolding of the whole consciousness of man on every plane, in every world, and applies those rationally in a particular place. This rational application of the laws of unfolding consciousness acts exactly on the same principles that you see applied around you every day in other departments of science.[36]

Later in her text, Besant emphasizes that 'yoga is a science of psychology'[37] and also describes yoga as a system for living, which addresses ways to purify both mind and body and provides prescriptions for 'regulating the physical body in all its activities', including understanding the quality of foods.[38] She became active in Indian resistance movements, and part of her investment in Indian culture was related to her immersion within the spiritual realms of yoga – systems which she believed could be beneficial for her readers. Serving as the President of the Theosophical Society in India, Besant, like her predecessor Madame Blavatsky, focused upon the spiritual elements of the practice – focusing upon ancient Indian philosophy as a powerful way to gain access to the soul and to higher levels of consciousness. But her goal was to integrate conceptions of mind and body and to establish Indian philosophical systems such as yoga as scientific. In her recent reading of Besant's scientific experiments on 'Occult Chemistry', an essay in which Besant explores her clairvoyant research into the atom with Charles Leadbetter, Sumangala Bhattacharya notes how the author's time in India allowed her to engage in alternative forms of research that she argued were a valid science:

> Although mainstream science, with its increasing emphasis on laboratory-intensive experimentation, was closed to Besant because of her notoriety, Eastern thought offered an alternative route to knowledge production [...]. Besant's study of arcane Hindu philosophies in India contributed to her conviction that Indian occult practices could be harnessed in ways that intersected with, and even transcended, the work of conventional Western science.[39]

---

[36] Annie Besant, *An Introduction to Yoga* (Madras: Minerva, 1908), 9–10.   [37] Ibid., 78.
[38] Ibid., 125–6.
[39] Sumangala Bhattacharya, 'The Victorian Occult Atom: Annie Besant and Clairvoyant Atomic Research', in *Strange Science: Investigating the Limits of Knowledge in the Victorian Age*, ed. Shalyn Claggett and Lara Karpenko (Ann Arbor: University of Michigan Press, 2017), 197–214, 199.

Like these experiments on chemistry and atomic knowledge, Besant's engagement with the still loosely defined concept of 'yoga' allows her to create an authoritative voice for herself in India and also represent Indian philosophies as powerful and scientifically valid – her *Introduction to Yoga* is presented as a practical manual for living that can provide readers with a more fulfilling and healthy life.

Other women of her generation were also deeply invested within yoga ashrams, and sought to highlight how yoga practices could bring health and benefit to society. For example, Margaret Noble, who spent her childhood in Ireland, became a disciple of Swami Vivekananda and spent much of her adult life in India opening schools and spreading the philosophies of Vivekananda through charity work. She was known in India as 'Sister Nivedita' and published several works in which she highlighted local Indian medical practices as beneficial and also traced the ways that Raja yoga could provide mental focus to control the physical body in beneficial ways, claiming that 'there is a habitual, almost an instinctive, recognition in India of the fact that the mind is the controlling element in life, and it has become a second nature with them to appeal directly to it'.[40] Presenting a challenge to the work of 'lady doctors' trained in Western medicine as necessary, she writes:

> It is easy to point out flaws in Indian village medicine midwifery, and whatnot, but how do we account for the great dignity and suppleness of the general physical development and for the marvelous freedom of the race from skin blemish of any kind? This too in a country where the germ fauna is at least as dangerous as that other fauna of the jungle which includes the tiger and the cobra. In urging these points, I am not denying that modern science can aid, but only that it has no right to despise village lore.
>
> Every system of course mistrusts any other. This is the superstition of party. To this fact I trace the phenomenon, detailed by the medical missionary sometimes, of men of sufficient means saying 'if you can cure her for 20 s (about ten rupees) you may do so' – alluding to a wife or some woman member of the speaker's household. The Christian charity of the lady doctor rushes immediately to the conclusion that his wife or mother's health is a matter of complete indifference to her client.[41]

Further, in her *Studies from an Eastern Home* (1913), Noble highlights the benefits of Indian herbs and medicines with a chapter honoring the native neem tree and outlining the healing qualities of its leaves, bark, and roots.

---

[40] Margaret Noble, *The Web of Indian Life by the Sister Nivedita (Margaret Noble) of Ramkrishna Vivekananda* (London: William Heinemann, 1906), 65.
[41] Margaret Noble, *Select Essays of Sister Nivedita* (Madras: Ganesh, 1911), 54–5.

She also makes a case for the work of local women healers, writing: 'When the patient first succumbs to the malady, there is many a village wife whose diagnosis is as valuable as the physician's or the priest's' (145). Noble's references to the beneficial aspects of native medicines and of local healers is a contrast to earlier references in travel narratives and medical guides that often highlighted the dangers of local midwives and doctors, and encouraged Europeans to seek Western doctors. Indeed, the rise of the 'lady doctor' that Noble mentions was encouraged through arguments for the need for women to transcend the boundaries of the 'zenana' or harem and provide medical advice and care to Indian families. Here, Noble presents the 'lady doctor' as rushing to offer services prematurely and making incorrect assumptions about the needs of local families. Like Besant, she suggests that there is scientific value in Indian methods. She connects Indian traditions linked to yoga, such as controlling breath and mind through careful practice, as being valuable and beneficial beyond the borders of India. Finally, Noble seems to challenge the divide between religion and science:

> In spite nevertheless of the relative non-development of natural science in India, it is the perfect compatibility of the Hindu religious hypothesis with the highest scientific activity, that is to make that country within the present century the main source of the new synthesis of religion for which we in the West are certainly waiting.[42]

Here Noble suggests that Indian culture provides a remedy for the tensions between scientific inquiry and spirituality, imagining a more holistic and productive fusion between the two.

Both Besant and Noble produce works that can be considered guides for living and that also provide readers with alternative ways of thinking about the body and health. For example, Besant writes:

> But yoga, for its practical purposes, considers man simply as a duality – Mind and Body, a Unit of consciousness in a set of envelopes. This is not the duality of the Self and the Not-Self. For in Yoga 'Self' includes consciousness *plus* such matter as it cannot distinguish from itself, and Not-Self is only the matter it can put aside.

And later in the text she writes:

> The unfolding of powers belongs to the side of consciousness; purification of bodies belongs to the side of matter. You must purify each of your three

---

[42] Noble, *Web of Indian Life*, 262.

working bodies – mental, astral, and physical. Without that purification you had better leave yoga alone. First of all, how shall you purify the thought-body? By right thinking. Then you must use imagination, your great creative tool, once more. Imagine things, and imagining them, you will form your thought body into the organisation that you desire. Imagine something strongly, as the painter imagines when he is going to paint. Visualize an object, if you have the power of visualization at all, if you have not, try to make it. It is an artistic faculty of course, but most people have it more or less [...] by strengthening your imagination you will be making the great tool with which you have to practice yoga.[43]

While Annie Besant, in her *Introduction to Yoga* encourages readers to focus upon the meditative aspects of the practice (and in fact, she and figures including Helena Blavatsky and Margaret Noble both minimize the physical aspects of Indian yoga techniques in favor of spiritual exploration), Stebbins attempts to converge mind and body to enhance the capabilities of both. By the turn of the century, other figures, including Indra Devi (Eugenie Peterson) and Mirra Alfassa began to expand the practice of yoga in a transnational context between India, Europe, and the United States. These European women traveled to India, became immersed in yoga ashrams, and eventually taught exercise and meditation programs themselves. For these women, influenced by and integrated within Indian culture, the philosophy and practice of yoga was imagined to provide an alternative way of thinking about mind and body – their work challenged the divide between these concepts and suggested a fusion of the two. In turn, addressing the hybrid and shifting forms of mind, body, and spirit, they appropriated yoga as a form of living that could challenge Western medicine and scientific inquiry.

In his reading of cosmopolitanism and South Asian religious forms, Srinivas Aruvumadan traces how Indian religious philosophies migrated West, and describes the success of Vivekananda, one of the primary Indian yogis to share his knowledge in the United States at the Chicago World's Fair in 1893. Aruvumadan describes the adulation he received during his visit, and his description of Hinduism as a universal and unifying religion:

> each race has a peculiar bent [...] each race has a peculiar mission to fulfill in the world [...]. Let the Persian or the Greek, or the Roman, or the Arab, or the Englishman march his battalions, conquer the world, and link the different nations together, and the philosophy and spirituality of India is

[43] Annie Besant, *Introduction to Yoga*, 13, 123–4.

ready to flow along the new made channels into the veins of the nations in the world [...] India's gift to the world is the light spiritual.[44]

This 'spiritual light', I argue, shone brightly during the late nineteenth century, and was particularly attractive to women who sought new forms of physical and spiritual healing. Although the *fin de siècle* was a period marked by theories of degeneration, the waning of colonial power, and the exhaustion of a period of industrial expansion, it also marked the burgeoning of new physical practices, and the desire to restore the strength of mind and body. In this moment, the potential for healing and for transformation comes from the 'primitivism' and mythology of the East – in a reversal of colonial circulation, Indian techniques of physical and mental sustenance provide glimpses of recovery and support through the convergence of global practices of self-care. While women were increasingly targeted as consumers of physical exercise programs and props (as indeed they are now), some of the manuals they encountered also encouraged them to explore and experience new ways of thinking about the potential of their bodies, their breath, and their minds. The programs that Stebbins and others created were, then, much more than exercise systems – they were a call to action that could also provide readers with a space for mental growth, transformation, and perhaps an escape from limitations and regimented routines. Perhaps, then, Queen Victoria, like others in this period, benefitted from the power of meditative exercise and practice as a way to transcend reality – perhaps for her, and for the other women who engaged with the methods that appear very close to the practice we now call yoga, such a form of healing and exercise could be the perfect escape from the chaotic, or banal, qualities of everyday life.

[44] Aramuvadan, *Guru English*, 10–11.

CHAPTER 11

The Other 'Other Victorians'
Normative Sexualities in Victorian Literature
Pamela K. Gilbert

> Sexual unspeakability does not function simply as a collection of prohibitions for Victorian writers. Rather, it affords them abundant opportunities to develop an elaborate discourse – richly ambiguous, subtly coded, prolix and polyvalent.
> William A. Cohen, *Sex Scandal: The Private Parts of Victorian Fiction*[1]

Over the last thirty years, our understanding of Victorian sexuality has diversified immensely. From the early days of Steven Marcus's reading of pornography, through feminist readings of women's sexuality as both repressed and demonized, we have moved into queerer readings of homosexual subtexts and homosocial bonds, and finally into an exploration, simultaneous with the rise of queer scholarship, into normative masculine sexualities. Yet, with all this at our disposal, our understanding of sexuality in Victorian fiction sometimes seems not to have progressed much beyond the repressive hypothesis. Even as we denounced a generation of historians and scholars for thinking Victorians were repressed, we canonized a literature based on heteronormative courtship narratives and traditional gender roles. We then critiqued that literature for adhering to – or championed it for subverting – those traditional narratives. This is perhaps particularly true of narratives of feminine sexuality. When the process of feminist recovery began, we sought out literature that seemed to challenge those narratives, but in insisting on this 'subversive' feminist content, whether we found it explicitly in New Woman fiction or implicitly in sensational fiction that we could read as critical of patriarchy, we looked for dialogue with these traditional narratives. In fact, Victorian fiction was always wilder and woollier than we gave it credit for being.

Often, this fiction is simply not concerned with what has become our vision of sexuality, and, while we hunt for endorsement or critique of that

---
[1] William A. Cohen, *Sex Scandal: The Private Parts of Victorian Fiction* (Durham: Duke University Press, 1996), 3.

vision, we miss the far more interesting and inclusive range of representations available. And that range, while present throughout Victorian literature, is often more visible in popular fiction. For example, *The Mysteries of London* (1844–1846) offers portrayals of prostitution, cross-dressing, and other sexually non-normative behaviors that do not result in the death or ostracization of the heroine.[2] The class of a character can also mediate reception: servant Afy Hallijohn in *East Lynne* (1861) is comic when she does exactly what Lady Isobel experiences as tragedy – that is, she becomes the mistress of the rake Francis Levinson. So can the class of the publication and implied class of the reader. This was true outside of fiction, as well. Camilla Townsend noted that when a cross-dressing working woman who had married another woman was arrested in 1865 for attempted murder, local working-class papers either found her gender transgressions uninteresting or they supported her, whereas middle-class venues found her behavior scandalous and incomprehensible.[3] Our focus on mainstream middle-class fiction reinforces assumptions that all fictional portrayals of eroticism exist in a direct relation to a heteronormative courtship plot that the original range of readers may have found less relevant than we think. Even in mainstream fiction, references to a richer set of sexual possibilities often are 'hiding in plain sight'.

Sharon Marcus showed in 2007 that women's relationships, often including what we would consider lesbian sex, were not considered transgressive (and not simply because no one realized that they were having sex).[4] For the Victorians the clear boundaries between lesbian sexuality and heterosexuality, or even sexual/non-sexual activity, were qualitatively other than ours. And I want to argue that heterosexual extramarital relations were defined along this same range from admirable to acceptable to eyebrow-raising to clearly transgressive (though the possibility of pregnancy drew a somewhat clearer line in the sand). Despite the advances made by queer theory, however, it is only recently that scholars have actually begun to be able to apply these insights to the sexuality of an earlier historical period and to get beyond the binaries that we 'other Victorians' are trapped within – in this case, not that of masculine–feminine merely, or even of homo–hetero, but of sexual–non-sexual.

---

[2] See Ellen Bayuk Rosenman, *Unauthorized Pleasures: Accounts of Victorian Erotic Experience* (Ithaca: Cornell University Press, 2003), and Cohen, *Sex Scandal*.
[3] Camilla Townsend, '"I Am the Woman for Spirit": A Working Woman's Gender Transgression in Victorian London', in *Sexualities in Victorian Britain*, ed. Andrew H. Miller and James Eli Adams (Bloomington: Indiana University Press, 1996), 214–33 (228).
[4] Sharon Marcus, *Between Women: Friendship, Desire and Marriage in Victorian England* (Princeton: Princeton University Press, 2007).

Conversely, we should not assume that the Victorians believed that the heteronormative marital relationship was the most central one for most people, though it was, of course, significant for both financial and reproductive reasons. Mary Jean Corbett's provocative *Family Likeness* (2008) shows that the early nineteenth century inherited a tradition of endogamous marriage that gradually became defined as transgressive, leading to a model of intimate relations between strangers that became the foundation of fictional marriage plots.[5] But Davidoff and Hall's classic *Family Fortunes* showed back in 1987 that cousin marriage persisted well into late-century.[6] As Talia Schaffer shows in *Romance's Rival* (2016), novels of the period, far from valorizing the exogamous marriage of passion, tended to confirm the less exciting, but safer (often endogamous) marriage as the preferable choice. For example in Charlotte Mary Yonge's novels, although filled with apparently excruciatingly self-sacrificing females mated to variably annoying men, the marital/erotic relation is shown to be less significant in many ways than the kinship relationship between female in-laws and siblings. And Schaffer shows that this is not unique but representative of a pervasive suspicion and even rejection of the erotic motive for marriage. In part, Schaffer observes, this has been invisible to literary critics because of our presentist tendency to read all plots through the lens of the simple masculine–feminine gender opposition and the marriage plot to which we like to believe Victorians adhered.[7] Holly Furneaux in 2009, 'rejects a false logic that places marriage and the biological family as central to thinking about the Victorian [...] in favour of [...] other forms of intimacy, affinity and family formation'.[8] Like Sedgwick, Butler, and especially Marcus, Furneaux aims to show that the binaries we now consider normative were not yet 'conceptually fixed' and that Victorians accepted non-reproductive family formations and erotic relations.[9] Richard Kaye, in his excellent study *The Flirt's Tragedy* (2002), focuses on courtships that do not come to what we might imagine as fruition at all. He points out that the flirt generates plots and often serves the marital plot, but is in no way reduceable simply to an instrument of that plot.

---

[5] Mary Jean Corbett, *Family Likeness: Sex, Marriage, and Incest from Jane Austen to Virginia Woolf* (Ithaca: Cornell University Press, 2008).
[6] Leonore Davidoff and Catherine Hall, *Family Fortunes: Men and Women of the English Middle Class, 1780–1850* (Chicago: University of Chicago Press, 1991).
[7] Talia Schaffer, *Romance's Rival: Familiar Marriage in Victorian Fiction* (New York and Oxford: Oxford University Press, 2016).
[8] Holly Furneaux, *Queer Dickens: Erotics, Families, Masculinities* (Oxford: Oxford University Press, 2009), 9–10.
[9] Ibid., 10.

Posing flirtation as 'managed desire' against the more abandoned impulses of erotic love, Kaye points out that flirtation provided energies 'inassimilable to plots of marriage', which have been overlooked. This, he notes, revises a generation of theories of the novel based on the importance of marriage to closure, national identity, and realist form.[10] What the more recent work of Schaffer, Corbett, and others show us is that marital plots, also, are stories of managed desire. The management of desire is key to the entire field of Victorian culture, and its fiction, also, in its multifold forms, depends on various kinds of desire being fulfilled, deferred, and very often, as Schaffer points out, frustrated altogether.

That does not mean that the novel, or the Victorians who wrote and read it, rejected sex and eroticism as a primary driver of human motivation and social connection. Indeed, from philosophers to scientists, sexual desire was considered central to social and biological life, and the whole formation of society and propriety as necessary to corral and direct sexuality. Part of the problem of working within the history of sexuality is that once one posits that sexuality is culturally constructed, it is hard to know what exactly one is studying. Is a practice what we think it is? And even if it is the practice we think it is, was it *sex*? Havelock Ellis famously writes of a woman, active in the purity movement in the late nineteenth century, thrown into a spiritual and psychological crisis by learning after a lifetime of peaceful pleasure that she had been happily practicing the dreaded act of masturbation without knowing that is what it was.[11] Whether one takes this story at face value or reads it cynically, it highlights the extent to which interpretation of the sexual can vary.

Beyond reproduction and biopolitics, historians have shown that what counts as sexuality has been interpreted very differently over time, even within the same culture (or by different individuals in the same time). After the Regency, often thought a period of upper-class license, scholarship has tended to focus on what was thought to be a Victorian middle-class concern with governmentalizing reproduction and pathologizing nonreproductive sexuality in the period from the late 1830s roughly through the 1880s. Much of the range of today's scholarship on sexuality, especially in the sciences and social sciences, is still continuous with the work done by sexologists and by Freud; like their work, it tends to emphasize sexuality as central to identity, and seeks both to taxonomize

---

[10] Richard A. Kaye, *The Flirt's Tragedy: Desire without End in Victorian and Edwardian Fiction* (Charlottesville: University Press of Virginia, 2002), 39.
[11] Havelock Ellis, *Studies in the Psychology of Sex*, 7 vols. (Philadelphia: F. A. Davis, 1910), vol. 1, 164.

sexual behaviors by their adherence to norms and understand them in a cultural and historical context. Incorporating Foucault's critique, current scholarship on sexuality and culture, largely from the humanities and social sciences, tends to critique that continuity, emphasizing the constructed nature of such taxonomies and questioning the very notions of instinct or a core self.

Literary scholarship on the period has recently tended to move in a few directions, toward transgressive sexualities, queer family constellations, or pornography. By the *fin de siècle*, the rise of sexology, depth psychology, and eugenics took up a distinctive set of sexual subcultures, and New-Woman feminist critiques of normative sexuality and marriage. Many of these novels set up queer family groups, some of which are also explicitly erotic. But (with the exception of Furneaux's work on Dickens), the novels that scholars have most addressed are late-century works of critique and opposition, consciously proposing alternatives to the normative sexualities of the day. Because of the history of the field, heteronormative sexuality has been least studied in recent scholarship on literature and sexuality, outside of some discussions of marriage and reproduction. I want here to focus on the mid-century, and its casual references (always a bit muted, and polite) to the range of ordinary, if potentially risky, practices.

So let me look first at two very different books (in period and in readership) that each offer a vision of sexuality outside the typical courtship plot. Harrison Ainsworth's *Jack Sheppard* (1838–1840) foregrounds a pubescent sexuality marked within the text as normative. Wilkie Collins's *The Law and the Lady* (1875) foregrounds a sexuality marked for us as perverse but still legible. Phillipe Aries in the 1960s and Jim Kincaid's *Child-Loving* in 1992 enabled a fuller exploration of the period's representations of child sexuality, yet, despite this promising beginning, we still tend to conceptualize all representations of child sexuality as either victimization through genital sexuality with adults or as psychoanalytically informed unconscious (pre-genital) sexuality. This has an unfortunate double effect – to eliminate from view forms of child sexuality that are not explicitly genital and to code all forms of non-genital sexuality, even among adults, as immature.

In *Jack Sheppard*, twelve-year old Jack appears in a pub, drunk, in the company of his two historically famous doxies, Poll and Bess:

> There sat Jack, evidently in the last stage of intoxication, with his collar opened, his dress disarranged, [...] receiving and returning [...] – the blandishments of a couple of females [...]. The younger [...] could not be more than seventeen, though her person had all the maturity of twenty.

Nor, remarks the narrator, 'was Jack by any means the only stripling in the room'.[12] The women call Jack their little 'fancy man' and are referred to later as his two wives, and again his mistresses, and are accepted as such without demur by the other characters. The women are clearly also represented as a continuing couple after Jack's death – although Poll suggests that they pillage his possessions when he is executed, there is no suggestion that they would steal from him while he lives, nor do they seem to compete over either man or money. This representation is no doubt at least in part tied to nineteenth-century beliefs about the licentiousness of prior periods and of prostitutes. But what is striking is the easy assumption that dissolute Jack is old enough at twelve to engage in a long-term erotic relationship with these two women. Other youths in the novel are similarly described in erotic terms.

Although this is not simply an example of ephebophilia, it certainly participates in that tradition. There is a long cultural tradition in Europe and elsewhere of seeing children and youths as appropriate objects of erotic appreciation, though not necessarily equally or as targets of actual erotic engagement. Indeed, as the work of Kincaid and others has suggested, the portrayal of the Victorian child may well have been recognized not only as an invention of a category to refuse and contain sexuality by formulating a category of innocence, but as a way to heighten erotic appreciation of emerging concepts of latency by defining and cordoning adolescence off from adulthood. In that way, the portrayal of sexually active children in an earlier period (here the 1700s) is addressed to a sensibility that understood children (particularly of the lower classes) as potential erotic objects, but also to salve any concern about that appreciation by pointing to an historical (and here gendered) difference in their availability. It is the same gesture in reverse that Dickens engages in by placing *The Old Curiosity Shop*'s (1840–1841) Little Nell ('fourteen [...] but small'[13]) in perpetual sexual jeopardy, while repeatedly describing, and then killing her off, as still a virginal 'child'. This kind of representation largely ceases in the early 1840s, with references to children as sexual objects (let alone subjects) becoming more carefully coded.

If the ephebe was, for respectable Victorians, considered an erotic object to be admired from a distance, adult relationships were marked as much by

---

[12] William H. Ainsworth, *Jack Sheppard*, ed. Manuela Mourão and Edward Jacobs (Peterborough: Broadview Press, 2007), 226–8.
[13] Charles Dickens, *The Old Curiosity Shop*, ed. Elizabeth M. Brennan (1840–1841; Oxford: Oxford University Press, 1997), 61.

erotic courtship without conventional consummation as by that consummation itself. Moving to a later novel for a middle-class audience, *The Law and the Lady* provides two interesting cases of adult sexuality outside the marriage plot. The first, a very common one, but perhaps one scholars have not spent enough time on, is the heterosexual courtship relations, often multiple, between a man and various women not seeking marriage and often already married. Although genital violation of the sanctity of marriage through intercourse was severely sanctioned when acknowledged (and still happened all the time), various kinds of eroticism were clearly tolerated and in some cases encouraged; in short, for a married woman to have 'followers' was normative to a degree. Collins manages to both support the marriage plot by having his heroine, Valeria, engage in investigations to clear her husband of a false accusation and save her marriage, and to sideline it by having the husband disappear in the first few pages of the novel and not return until the end. Thus, Valeria is free to interact as a virtuous married woman, with access to the sexual knowledge and unchaperoned company that implies, without the incumbrance of a husband present. Her husband's friends, with whom she interacts to gain insight into his case, are all roués who have engaged in affairs with married women, and she is immediately adopted by them as one of their admirers; in turn, she flirts shamelessly to gain her own ends.

While mainstream novels are full of flirtations that are less harmless – think of Will Ladislaw and Rosamond Vincy – many either present these relationships dichotomously as non-sexual or as extremely dangerous, especially if the woman appears to be conscious of an erotic component in the attraction. However, Collins's novel endorses Valeria's behavior, and endorses such relationships more generally, while monogamous marriage is depicted as much more dangerous. Heteronormative love destroys two men who are initially depicted as happy with alternate forms of sexuality: the first, the Major, a flirt with a whole harem of women to admire from the aristocratic mistress to the working-class girl he is training as a singer (the latest in a string of such women), ends by his marrying the latter, which instantly ages and immiserates him. The other man, Misserimus Dexter, having assaulted Valeria, reveals that he was in love with her husband's first wife, whom Valeria resembles, and, in an effort to seduce the first wife, drove her to suicide. The guilt from this finally drives him to madness and death.

The Major is a recognizable Victorian character; novels and lives of the period are full of those like him, sending *billets doux*, hanging about married women, and keeping lower-class mistresses who are not seen as competing with the upper-class women whom he also openly admires. The Major is overtly sensual, praising female beauty and declaring himself a victim of women's charms, and a collector of conquests, saving locks of hair in an album tabulating names and dates. What these locks of hair signify in terms of actual sexual acts is unclear. Valeria estimates him as someone who must have been 'dangerous' to women when he was young; but does this mean simply dangerous to their peace, as the expression ran, or dangerous to their social standing because he crossed the line with them into actual infidelity? Dexter calls him a 'lap-dog' and despises him as (sexually) harmless.[14]

The period is more tolerant of extramarital 'crushes' than the canonical novel seems to give it credit for, and it is quite possible that a fairly respectable and experienced male lover – or better, multiple lovers – hanging about might have seemed like good insurance for a marriage from the family's perspective, with the assumption first that marriage was not sufficient to contain the eroticism of couples and secondly that all players knew where the boundaries were. Such relationships may indeed have been seen as supportive to heteronormative marriage, but they may also have been seen as an important part of the extended social life to which the status of being married gave women access, even as access to married women was an advantage for men whose attentions to an unmarried girl would have been unacceptable.

In *The Ordeal of Richard Feverel* (1859), Richard is portrayed as foolish because he cannot grasp the harmlessness of his wife's relationship with the Marquis, who certainly intends to seduce her, though he does not succeed. Richard himself ends up in trouble because he cannot distinguish the appropriate uses of extramarital heterosexual friendships with a kept woman and a proto-New Woman, respectively. His wife, however, makes better use of her extramarital relations: while the Marquis hopes to seduce her, she uses him to read to her (and thus Richard's unborn child) in the hopes of improving the baby's intellect. Her cross-class homosocial relationship with Richard's old wet nurse, Mrs. Berry, supports her marriage as well. In this scene, Mrs. Berry discovers the wife's pregnancy and pledges to help her regain the company of her dilatory husband:

> 'You been guessing a boy – woman-like', she [Mrs Berry] said. Then they cooed, and kissed, and undressed by the fire, [...] both praying for the unborn child; [...] and thereat Lucy closed to her, and felt a strong love for

---

[14] Wilkie Collins, *The Law and the Lady*, ed. David Skilton (1875; London: Penguin, 1999), 242.

her. [...] Berry leaned over her, and eyed her roguishly, saying, 'I never see ye like this, but I'm half in love with ye myself, you blushin' beauty! [...] 'Ye look so ripe with kisses [...].' [...] Then they lay in bed, and Mrs. Berry fondled her, [...] and hinted at Lucy's delicious shivers when Richard was again in his rightful place, which she, Bessy Berry, now usurped; and all sorts of amorous sweet things.[15]

Bessy spends her time in bed with Lucy talking up the joys of marriage, and her time out of bed trying to get the couple back together. This seems to offer a good example of Sharon Marcus's thesis. Mudie's refusal to stock *Ordeal* when it was published may reflect concerns about sexual frankness generally, but it may also be linked to Meredith's permissive attitudes about non-normative eroticism in relation to marriage. In any case, this book neatly links my two themes: the appeal of the sexually desirous ephebe (the multitudinous adult characters of the novel anxiously contemplate and the reader enjoys the boy Richard's awakening desire), and the role of extramarital homosexual and heterosexual flirtations – both addressing the appropriate management of desire prior to, or outside of, marriage.

Nineteenth-century courtship that did not progress to a definite engagement might include quite a bit of sexual play. Historian of sexuality Michael Mason notes that William Hazlitt writes of his interactions with his landlady's daughter, Sarah Walker, who sits on his lap, rubbing his erection 'for half a day together' or for 'an hour, while I poked her up'.[16] Conversations between Sarah, the below-stairs staff, and others about comparative penis size were apparently common, provoking Hazlitt's anxiety, yet he also describes her as 'refined'.[17] Americans seem to have been surprised by the uninhibited conversation 'at all levels' of English society,[18] and outside of Mudie's and the licensed theaters, both conversation and entertainment were often rather frank. London music halls offered such comic songs as 'The Deserted Penis'[19] and 'The Bride', which declares the singer's fealty to his 'hot, wheedling, coaxing' bride's 'C–' over 'every randy whore'.[20]

The pervasiveness of sexually charged relationships beyond marriage, of course, is not news to anyone who has ever read a French novel from the same period. And Kaye examines some of this ground. But given that it is a

---

[15] George Meredith, *The Ordeal of Richard Feverel*, ed. Edward Mendelson (1859; New York: Penguin, 1998), 430.
[16] Michael Mason, *The Making of Victorian Sexuality* (Oxford: Oxford University Press, 1994), 129.
[17] Ibid.   [18] Ibid., 130.   [19] Ibid., 164.   [20] Quoted in ibid., 220–1.

part of the mainstream landscape of the period, it is astonishing how little attention these kinds of eroticism have been given in the literary scholarship. Some of the heterosexual polyamorous relationships hinted at in the Deceased Wife's Sister's Bill, or in the ending of *The Woman in White* (1859–1860), have been mentioned, but have received little detailed treatment. Both heterosexual 'platonic' and erotic friendships run throughout the period, yet few have yet received the attention that their homosocial and homosexual counterparts have from literary scholars. Nor have the polyamorous relationships across class that constitute and seem to sustain the relations between upper-class males and their female and male beloveds received attention. Moreover, if it is true that most novels that successfully passed, in three-volume form, through Mudie's, were written with the cheek of the Young Person in mind, such might explain why the theme of adult sexuality is less pervasive in British fiction than in its continental sibling. All the more reason, then, to look beyond the middlebrow mid-century three-volume novels critics have traditionally canonized.

Returning to Collins's characters, Misserimus Dexter represents a more dramatically non-normative sexuality. He is childlike in his actions and impulsive egotism, yet explicitly sexual with the heroine. He is literally 'half of a man' – a beautiful head and trunk, strong arms, hair of almost feminine loveliness, and no legs at all, resulting from a birth defect. Dexter's interest in 'normal' heterosexual relations scandalizes some of the characters, who decry his desire for marriage and who feel that he presumes on his disabled status to be 'impudent' to women.[21] Repeatedly, the text hints coyly at what is 'missing' under his lap-blanket, but also suggests that he may be genitally capable. Valeria is told that she is not safe alone with him, and, in fact, he 'grossly insult[s]' her: 'He caught my hand in his, and devoured it with kisses. [...] He twisted himself suddenly in the chair, and wound his arm around my waist. In the terror and indignation of the moment, vainly struggling with him, I cried out for help.'[22]

Nor is this the only physical expression of Dexter's desires. On another occasion, he asks Valeria to beat him, supposedly to punish him for his behavior; he also beats his cousin, Ariel (a developmentally impaired 'idiot', who is obsessively devoted to him). Ariel in turn also asks Valeria to beat her as a proxy to absorb her anger at Dexter. Dexter is physically sadistic in other ways with this cousin as well, who is nonetheless proud to be the object of his attentions:

---

[21] Collins, *Law and the Lady*, 271.   [22] Ibid., 280.

The unfortunate Ariel was standing before a table, with a dish of little cakes placed in front of her. Round each of her wrists was tied a string [...] held in Miserrimus Dexter's hands. 'Try again, my beauty!' I heard him say [...] 'Take a cake.' At the word of command, Ariel submissively stretched out one arm toward the dish. Just as she touched a cake with the tips of her fingers her hand was jerked away by a pull at the string, so savagely cruel in the nimble and devilish violence of it that I felt inclined to snatch Benjamin's cane out of his hand and break it over Miserrimus Dexter's back. [...] His eyes fastened on me with a fierce, devouring delight. 'Come in! come in!' he cried. [...] '[...] When I am in my malicious humors I must tease something. I am teasing Ariel.'[23]

In short, the novel is full of (largely male–female) eroticism, sometimes framed as explicitly sexual and sometimes not, outside of normative pairings, despite a superficial nod to a marriage that is the plot device holding the text together.

Like the erotic potential of acceptable courtship of a married woman by a male 'family friend', some of the pleasures we can detect in these texts are either non-penetrative and/or non-orgasmic. Dexter's teasing of his cousin is about prolonging her desire (for the cakes) and his pleasure in frustrating and hurting her – but not badly enough to end the play. It ends not with climax on his part, but, when he is tired, he simply stops. Though she does eventually get the cakes, she claims that her pleasure is in *his* pleasure, not in obtaining the supposed objects of her desire. That is, the eroticism is heightened and prolonged by the avoidance of various forms of consummation, and then, even when ending, consummation is not reached – the teasing is the end in itself. To riff on a way of thinking about form that was popular in the eighties, the classic form of the novel is thought to follow a sexual pattern traditionally coded as masculine: setting up a situation, complication, growing tension, a 'climax', and a post-climax denouement that settles down quickly. But that pattern, of course, is not valid for periodical publications in picaresque form, such as the feuilleton. And even within the traditional three-volume novel tied by a single, often courtship, plot, various subplots follow a different logic and structure. The fact that, by the 1870s, this story may be told in the three-volume novel using disabled or aged characters who are figured as inappropriate for heteronormative adult courtship may be significant – in earlier popular texts, this is not the case.

---

[23] Ibid., 305.

Victorian courtship in fact, and at least partially in literature, was defined as much by non-consummation as by consummation. First, there was a long period of courtship without commitment, or, as Eliot puts it in *Mill on the Floss* (1860),

> that stage of courtship which makes the most exquisite moment of youth [...] when each is sure of the other's love, but no formal declaration has been made, and all is mutual divination, exalting the most trivial word, the lightest gesture, into thrills delicate and delicious as wafted jasmine scent. The explicitness of an engagement wears off this finest edge of susceptibility; it is jasmine gathered and presented in a large bouquet.[24]

Even after an explicit engagement, when couples were left more to themselves, there might be several years of sexual activity without traditional consummation – even among quite decorous couples. Bundling – or the practice of courting couples to spend the night in the same bed (but clothed) – was still common in some areas until 1870 or so (Mason 169).[25] As one of Havelock Ellis's informants remembers his mid-century courtships:

> At the age of 25 I married the daughter of an officer, a beautiful girl with a fully developed figure and an amorous disposition. While engaged, we used to pass hours wrapped in each other's arms, practising mutual masturbation, or I would kiss her passionately on the mouth, introducing my tongue into her mouth at intervals, with the invariable result that I had an emission and she went off into sighs and shivers. After marriage we practised all sorts of fancy coitus, coitus reservatus, etc., and rarely passed twenty-four hours without two conjunctions, until she got far on in the family way, and our play had to cease for a while.[26]

– at which point he took up with an old schoolfellow, and practiced mutual masturbation. Once his wife died, he moved in with that partner for the rest of the other man's life.

If the traditional courtship narrative is all about deferral followed by consummation, these other narratives are even less concerned with orgasm, with denouement. The stories continue for a while – charged with erotic possibility – and then they stop, rather than end, inconclusively drifting out of the plot. While we pay attention to the courtship narrative, and the form of the traditional story arc – erotic attraction between marriageable couple, complication(s), near disaster, then climax of the reunion – and

---

[24] George Eliot, *The Mill on the Floss*, ed. Gordon S. Haight (Oxford: Oxford University Press, 1980), 338.
[25] Mason, *Victorian Sexuality*, 169. [26] Ellis, *Studies*, vol. 3, 303.

tend to see any other sexual narratives as in service to or defeated by this one, they may be read in quite other ways. And in literature that is less dependent on a single story arc, as the mid-Victorian three-volume novel tended at least partially to be, and as popular serial fiction was not, we might see quite different themes, plots, and even formal properties through the lens of a non-heteronormative eroticism.

As Kaye suggests, flirtation disrupts our typical understanding of the novel in this period and privileges deferral rather than consummation – a point to which more attention must be paid. Claire Jarvis more recently addresses what she calls 'exquisite masochism', a 'charged' scene of 'sustained stasis' in which 'description thickens, and a glance, gesture, or object takes on heightened relational significance' in order to read 'non-genital sex as central to Victorian erotic life'.[27] This is a good insight, although it is not clear that many of the scenes she reads are in any usual sense of the term masochistic (or even sexual). Jarvis sees this as the novel's way of narrating sexual tension that it cannot describe directly – but, in fact, the novel does a pretty good job of narrating sex. Richard Kaye's study of flirtation is more supple on the ways that suspension and deferral are important not only to the structure of the novel but to sexuality in the period. He also shows that this pattern is ubiquitous, rather than operating as an alternative to the novel's narrative.

Although the three-volume novel is usually explicit only about verbal flirtation, Havelock Ellis refers to the wider range of such behavior as being common in England and the United States: 'modern civilized conditions [...] make actual sexual intercourse dangerous as well as disreputable. Flirtation adapts itself to these conditions.'[28] Instead of simply being the preliminary stage of courtship up to the point where the participants are considered to have committed themselves,

> it is developed into a form of sexual gratification as complete as due observation of the conditions already mentioned will allow. In Germany, and especially in France where it is held in great abhorrence, this is the only form of flirtation known; it is regarded as an exportation from the United States and is denominated 'flirtage.' Its practical outcome is held to be the 'demi-vierge,' who knows and has experienced the joys of sex while yet retaining her hymen intact.[29]

---

[27] Claire Jarvis, *Exquisite Masochism: Marriage, Sex, and the Novel Form* (Baltimore: Johns Hopkins Press, 2016), vii.
[28] Ellis, *Studies*, vol. 6, 519.   [29] Ibid., 518.

This 'degenerate' practice, includes all sexually exciting activities, 'coitus being always excepted'.[30] It includes behavior from 'a provocative look or a simple apparently unintentional touch' to 'pressure or friction of the sexual parts, sometimes leading to orgasm'.[31] Dancing, Ellis notes, if done skillfully, can cause orgasm in the male partner. But, 'most usually the process is that voluptuous contact and revery which, in English slang, is called "spooning." [...] Neither party is committed to any relationship with the other beyond the period devoted to flirtage'.[32] This could include discussion of 'erotic and indecorous topics', a practice novels more often reference. Tim Hitchcock in his history of sexuality in England from 1700–1800 notes that a good deal of erotic play, whether to the point of orgasm or not, was common among both males and females from youth through adulthood, but was not considered 'serious' – that is, tending to commitment – unless heterosexual penetration was involved.[33] Masturbation, and mutual masturbation, as well as intracrural intercourse (between the thighs or buttocks) was common between members of the same sex and of different sexes, and was sometimes not recognized even as sexual, and certainly not as the kind of either transgression or commitment that genital penetration was understood to be.

Among courting couples, erotic activity with a 'respectable' partner was sometimes, for men, supposed to be ancillary to full intercourse with other partners, whereas women, it was thought, could wait longer. Still, many men seem to have restricted themselves to non-consummatory activity with a beloved partner, despite a popular belief that seminal ejaculation in full intercourse was desirable and even necessary for health. Mason notes that medical 'practitioners who felt strongly that unmarried men should be chaste often complained' about colleagues 'recommending release with prostitutes or mistresses'.[34] One informant reported by Ellis confesses that as a youth, 'Every time I received the sacrament [...] I repented of my intention of whoring at 18 – as a man "must" do – and afterward I relapsed to the expectation.'[35] (He seems, however, not ultimately to have done so.)

William Acton has cast a long shadow over a general understanding of medical attitudes towards women's sexuality in the period, despite the efforts of historians of sexuality to contextualize his as a single voice. Havelock Ellis sums up what has become a mainstream view of

---

[30] Ibid.   [31] Ibid., 519.   [32] Ibid.
[33] Tim Hitchcock, *English Sexualities, 1700–1800* (Basingstoke: Macmillan, 1997), 30–3.
[34] Mason, *Victorian Sexuality*, 183.   [35] Ellis, *Studies*, vol. 3, 337.

Victorian sexology: 'In ancient times men blamed women for concupiscence or praised them for chastity, but it seems to have been reserved for the nineteenth century to state that women are apt to be [...] peculiarly liable to sexual anesthesia.'[36] He cites several nineteenth-century works, including Acton's, as examples of this kind of thinking, but counters these with a long history of citations from several countries showing the widespread belief that women have more powerful sexual feelings than men. But many mid-Victorian thinkers also insisted on women's sexual nature; doctor Elizabeth Blackwell writes that a woman remaining sexually inactive, 'after thirty years of age is often injured in mind or body. [...] As sex is a natural and most powerful human force, there is risk of injury in permanently stifling it.'[37] As Mason points out, medical practitioners were far from monolithic in their training or levels of influence,[38] and many doctors honored – or simply shared – the perspectives of the laity. Mason remarks that Acton's position is, in fact, 'without a parallel in the sexual literature of the day', and suggests that it has been read out of context – a book directed to men worried about sexual problems, in which it is offered as reassurance to those fearing that they cannot satisfy a wife.[39]

Literary critics, however, despite a generation of debunking from historians, sometimes still fall prey to the notion that the Victorians believed women – at least 'nice' women of the middle class – to be less sexually desirous than men. Part of this widespread belief comes from Havelock Ellis himself. Ellis cites Balzac's comparison of the 'average husband to an orang-utan trying to play the violin', and lectures Englishmen on their insensibility to women's sexuality.[40] He cites Richard Burton's observation that Eastern men delay orgasm to ensure the woman's pleasure: 'Europeans devote no care to this matter, and Hindoo women, who require about twenty minutes to complete the act, contemptuously call them "village cocks."'[41] Ellis also summarizes a range of authorities to remind his readers of a widespread belief that a woman's strongest sexual feelings were in maturity, linked to the periodicity of the menses and the

---

[36] Ibid., vol. 3, 193–4.
[37] Elizabeth Blackwell, *Counsel to Parents on the Moral Education of Their Children in Relation to Sex* (London: Hirst Smith and Son, 1878), 77–8.
[38] Mason, *Victorian Sexuality*, 179.   [39] Ibid., 195, 196.   [40] Ellis, *Studies*, vol. 6, 539–40.
[41] Ibid., vol. 3, 237.

climacteric.[42] Ellis writes that women's full 'erotism' appears in adulthood, and that novels reflect this: while

> English novelists, who have generally sought to avoid touching the deeper and more complex aspects of passion, often choose very youthful heroines, French novelists, who have frequently had a predilection for the problems of passion, often choose heroines who are approaching the age of 30.[43]

Believing that 'the sexual instinct has increased rather than diminished with the growth of civilization', Ellis argues for the acceptance of what he terms 'variation', on the grounds that civilized taste demands less 'coarse and monotonous food' than 'the peasant'. Whereas peasants are 'monogamous, [...] civilized people, with their more versatile and sensitive tastes, are apt to crave for variety'.[44]

Despite critics' focus on the central courtship plot of the mid-century tale of domestic realism, such texts are also filled with references to sexual situations considered common and not unduly transgressive, if suffused with the danger of becoming so. The mature but unsatisfied wife or widow is often used as a figure of sexual comedy. (Likewise, the mature spinster is often described as liable to enthusiasms defined as spiritual or artistic, but really understood by the reader as relating to sexual latency.) Anthony Trollope offers an excellent comic example of a misunderstanding in flirtation, which suggests both that the mechanisms of extramarital flirtation were well understood and that even the limits of infidelity might be transgressed without major consequences under the right circumstances. A group of English travelers in Italy includes a middle-aged married woman, Mrs. Talboys, traveling without her husband. She serially takes up the company of various married men, and speaks often of her advanced views on the topic of free love. Although she is in fact completely conventional in her own monogamy, a young man, O'Brien, mistakes these statements for not only an invitation, but a kind of mandate to take the relationship further. He already has a broken marriage in England, and another illegitimate family in Italy, suggesting that he has difficulty navigating the limits of acceptable play. (Although he is welcomed by the other English couples to their social circle, they would not think of countenancing his second family.) One of the older men, Mackinnon, sees trouble coming:

> 'We shall have a row in the house if we don't take care. O'Brien will be making love to Mrs. Talboys.'

---

[42] See also Andrew Mangham, *Violent Women and Sensation Fiction: Crime, Medicine and Victorian Popular Fiction* (Basingstoke: Palgrave Macmillan, 2007).
[43] Ellis, *Studies*, vol. 3, 243–4.   [44] Ibid., vol. 6, 494–5.

> 'Nonsense,' said Mrs. Mackinnon. 'You are always thinking that somebody is going to make love to some one.'
> 'Somebody always is,' said he.[45]

When they go off together walking in the ruins,

> We watched them [...] quizzing the little foibles of our dear friend, and hoping that O'Brien would be quick in what he was doing. That he would undoubtedly get a slap in the face – metaphorically – we all felt certain, for none of us doubted the rigid propriety of the lady's intentions. (72–3)

This is indeed what happens, and Mrs. Talboys declares to all that, 'The man has insulted me [...]. You men grovel so in your ideas, that you cannot understand the feelings of a true-hearted woman' (74).

Though everyone judges O'Brien foolish for mistaking an innocent flirtation for a more serious one, they blame her more for publicizing it, thus making it impossible to discreetly ignore. One young lady suggests that she should have accepted and run off to Naples in the night: 'nobody would have known anything about it then, and in a few weeks they would have gradually become tired of each other in the ordinary way' (75). The men, much amused, point out there is 'no very great harm done' (79). O'Brien wonders what else he could have done under the circumstances, 'She told me [...] that matrimonial bonds were made for fools and slaves. What was I to suppose [...]?' and pleads, 'I give you my honour that I did it all to oblige her' (78–9). Trollope's story, originally slated for publication in *The Cornhill* was refused, likely for its salaciousness. Still, it was published in the unexceptionable *London Review* (2 February 1861) before its appearance in *Tales of All Countries* (1861), under the well-respected imprint of Chapman and Hall.

This, of course, is less a tale of successful flirtation than of the comedy to be derived from two people who do not understand each other or their own relation to unspoken but well-known rules of engagement. Many non-comic fictions dwell on the same theme: Mary Elizabeth Braddon's *The Doctor's Wife* (1864) uses a Madame-Bovary-like figure whose reading of novels has prepared her to be in love with a man not her husband, but not to consummate the flirtation. She is shocked when he attempts to take her away with him (also to Naples): 'Something like a cry of despair broke from Isabel's lips. [...] "You ask me to leave George, and be your –

---

[45] Anthony Trollope, 'Mrs General Talboys', in *Tales of All Countries*, 2nd series (London: Chapman and Hall, 1863), 46–82, 62. Subsequent references to this edition will appear in the text.

mistress!'" (273).⁴⁶ Her amazed suitor responds that she must have known where their conversations had been going:

> 'Oh, no, no, no!' cried Mrs Gilbert, despairingly, '[...] I never thought that it was wicked to come here and meet you. I have read of people, who by some fatality could never marry, loving each other, and being true to others for years and years [...] and never, never believed that you would think me like those wicked women who run away from their husbands.'⁴⁷

And indeed the Victorian novel is full of such couples – often known socially *as* a kind of couple, with the decorous assumption that the relationship has not crossed a certain line. The line seems broadly, but perhaps not universally, to be understood either as genital intercourse, or as provable genital intercourse, or as elopement from the lady's 'friends' – in other words, as public acknowledgment of a relation beyond flirting, or flirtage. A full range of other practices might variously be included in the dangerous, but not socially irreparable, practice of flirtation. Pleasure is to be had by prolonging contact and innovating around the point of no return, but not crossing it.

I suspect the attraction of the ephebe for the early mid-century reader is based in part on the same pleasures of a flirtatious non-fulfillment vertiginously tipping into the dangerous ground of what was coming to be recognized as a distinct transgression. Early forms of the novel explored long, playful narratives with small intermittent crises and only loose overarching forms – think Fielding or Sterne. The *Mysteries of London* are loosely organized around a good-and-bad-brother morality tale: the good brother, despite all woes, ends well, and the bad brother ends badly. The courtships in the novel are multiple over time and do not much affect the fortunes of the variously 'good' and 'bad' woman who ends up with the good brother at the end, if we were to select her and call her the 'heroine' of the courtship narrative, which is the least interesting plot element in the entire series. If the rise of the British novel is related to the rise of the modern individual (and that individual is, first and foremost, a woman, as Nancy Armstrong has argued⁴⁸), it is also a story of and for youth, of a particular kind of middle-class sexual innocence and experience defined in terms of reproductive marriage, and thus of a particular kind of courtship

---

[46] Mary Elizabeth Braddon, *The Doctor's Wife*, ed. Lyn Pykett (Oxford: Oxford University Press, 2008), 273.
[47] Ibid.
[48] Nancy Armstrong, *Desire and Domestic Fiction: A Political History of the Novel* (New York and Oxford: Oxford University Press, 1987).

narrative. But that does not mean that other stories did not continue to be told; in the total play of the mid-Victorian literary field, we may well find a more complex and subtle sexuality than we are prepared to see. And our choice not to have seen it would then be, as Foucault would say, all about us, still, and again, the 'other Victorians'.

CHAPTER 12

Physical 'Wholeness' and 'Incompleteness' in Victorian Prosthesis Narratives

Ryan Sweet

> I think you had better not go to look at him. He's a dreadful object – the worst I've seen. They cut off his legs close to the trunk, his arms at the shoulders, the nose and ears. He was such a handsome fellow, too! But I tell you, sir, now he's nothing better than a human bundle – a lump of breathing, useless flesh.
> Ernest G. Henham, 'A Human Bundle' (1897)[1]

Published in the metropolitan middle-class family magazine *Temple Bar* in 1897, Canadian–British author Ernest G. Henham's short story 'A Human Bundle' is a text that, in hyperbolic terms, perpetuates fears about physical 'loss' – anxieties central to nineteenth-century Western bodily discourse.[2] The quotation above, from a horrified medical student who has witnessed the shocking amputation of an unfortunate young man's legs, arms, nose, and ears, suggests what the 'loss' of body parts meant in the nineteenth century. For the medical student, the patient is neither human nor useful but rather 'nothing better than a human bundle'.[3] The student's harsh assessment is partly justified by the egregious nature of the medical procedures undertaken, but such a response raises a series of questions about what constituted physical 'normalcy' and difference in this period, which historical factors underpinned negative attitudes to 'non-normative' bodies, and to what extent was the apparent hegemony of physical 'wholeness' complicated by literary representations.

This chapter will explore how, as the concept of physical 'normalcy' became increasingly reinforced as culturally dominant, those who were perceived to be 'missing' body parts were marginalised. Buttressed by a

---

[1] Ernest G. Henham, 'A Human Bundle', *Temple Bar* 111 (1897), 42–58.
[2] For more on *Temple Bar*, see Peter Blake, 'The Paradox of a Periodical: *Temple Bar* Magazine under the Editorship of George Augustus Sala (1860–1863)', *The London Journal* 35 (2010), 185–209. For more on Henham's short story, see Ryan Sweet, '"A Human Bundle": The Disaggregated Other at the *Fin de Siècle*', *Victorian Review* 40 (2014), 14–18.
[3] Henham, 'A Human Bundle', 58.

post-Enlightenment belief that medicine and the emerging sciences could 'fix' the issue of bodily 'loss' – what disability-studies scholars call the 'medical model' of disability – prostheses came to the fore as devices that could supposedly standardise aberrant bodies, making them aesthetically acceptable and 'useful'. However, because prostheses were and remain devices that undermine binaries of self/other, organic/artificial, real/fake, and disabled/nondisabled, they also complicated the hegemony of organic 'wholeness'. Their very production was mandated by preferences for physical 'completeness', but their implementation shifted definitions of what it meant to be 'whole'. The conceptual complexity of the prosthetic provided material to fiction writers who responded to the growing dominance of physical 'wholeness'. Using two fictional case studies that represent artificial-hand users, English poet, novelist, and playwright Robert Williams Buchanan's 'Lady Letitia's Lilliput Hand' (1862) and the lesser-known short-story writer T. Lockhart's 'Prince Rupert's Emerald Ring' (1895), I argue that literary representations of prostheses often simultaneously reinforced and complicated the hegemony of physical 'completeness'.[4] Such stories perpetuated fears of physical disaggregation while also bringing into question the efficacy of prostheticising. Though for reasons of concision I primarily investigate upper-limb 'loss' in relation to ableist discourses, it should be noted that related social attitudes also permeated, and at times were problematised in, literary representations of other prosthesis users, including consumers of artificial legs, eyes, teeth, and hair.

This chapter differs from much historical work on prosthesis in terms of attitude. Whether wittingly or not, some histories of prostheses fall into a trap of endorsing a 'medical model' of disability by over-optimistically celebrating the success of prostheses without paying attention to either the 'normative' forces that helped to popularise them or the transgressive sources that challenged 'normalcy's' social dominance. Studies by scholars such as Erin O'Connor, Edward Steven Slavishak, and Guy Hasegawa, for instance, are extremely useful for the wealth of historical detail that they provide, but at times they express somewhat idealistic views about artificial limbs, especially legs, without fully unpacking the problematic social mandate that, in part, brought about their proliferation in the nineteenth

---

[4] Robert Williams Buchanan, 'Lady Letitia's Lilliput Hand', *Temple Bar* 4:5 (1862), 551–69, 114–31; T. Lockhart, 'Prince Rupert's Emerald Ring', *Chambers's Journal of Popular Literature, Science and Arts* 12 (1895), 300–4. I would like to thank Pamela K. Gilbert for bringing Buchanan's short story to my attention. The author attribution for 'Prince Rupert's Emerald Ring' comes from Sue Thomas, 'Chambers's Journal: Indexes to Fiction', *Victorian Fiction Research Guides* 17, accessed 13 November 2018, http://victorianfictionresearchguides.org/chambers-journal/author-index/.

century.[5] Failing to challenge the medical model in a manner that disability studies has shown is so important, these studies present prosthetic technologies as philanthropic, utilitarian, widely accepted and, at times, techno-utopian solutions to the perceived crisis of bodily 'loss' without considering, first, the social and environmental factors that made life difficult for those deemed to be 'missing' body parts; second, the extent to which prosthetists exploited and contributed to social demands for 'normalcy'; and, third, instances in which the efficacy of prostheticising was challenged in literary and cultural sources. This chapter thus adds complexity to our understanding of historical attitudes to prostheses by considering them in relation to the social mandate for physical 'wholeness', which encouraged the use of prostheses that could supposedly enable users to appear 'normal', and by highlighting how prostheses were not always fully endorsed by literary representations. As I show, transgressive sensation-fiction narratives, such as Buchanan's and Lockhart's short stories, though not entirely devoid of ableist inclinations, critiqued prostheses for not enabling haptic sensation and imaginatively explored the potential benefits of owning rather than hiding physical difference. With its focus on artificial hands, this chapter also adds to what is a relatively small body of work concerning the technological, cultural, and literary history of this form of prosthesis.[6]

To demonstrate how and why physical 'wholeness' became culturally dominant in the nineteenth century, and how literary representations of prosthetics coextensively endorsed and critiqued this model, this chapter is split into two. Part 1 surveys the historical factors underpinning the rise of physical 'normalcy'; Part 2 then turns to the transgressive representations of prostheses. Here I explore the motif of the uncanny artificial hand.

---

[5] Erin O'Connor, *Raw Material: Producing Pathology in Victorian Culture* (Durham: Duke University Press, 2000); Edward Steven Slavishak, 'Artificial Limbs and Industrial Workers' Bodies in Turn-of-the-Century Pittsburgh', *Journal of Social History* 37 (2003), 365–88; Guy R. Hasegawa, *Mending Broken Soldiers: The Union and Confederate Programs to Supply Artificial Limbs* (Carbondale: Southern Illinois University Press, 2012).

[6] This chapter therefore builds on the following recent studies: Sue Zemka, '1822, 1845, 1869, 1893, and 1917: Artificial Hands', *BRANCH: Britain, Representation and Nineteenth-Century History*, Extension of Romanticism and Victorianism on the Net (2015), accessed 13 November 2018, www.branchcollective.org/?ps_articles=sue-zemka-1822-1845-1869-1893-and-1917-artificial-hands; Clare Stainthorp, 'Activity and Passivity: Class and Gender in the Case of the Artificial Hand', *Victorian Literature and Culture* 45 (2017), 1–16; and Laurel Daen, '"A Hand for the One-Handed": User-Inventors and the Market for Assistive Technologies in Early Nineteenth-Century Britain', in *Rethinking Modern Prostheses in Anglo-American Commodity Cultures, 1820–1939*, ed. Claire L. Jones (Manchester: Manchester University Press, 2017), 93–113.

Part 1: Cultivating 'Completeness'

On a practical level, the perceived 'need' for prostheses in the nineteenth century can be partially attributed not only to an increased risk to bodily 'integrity' effected by industrialism but also to developments in surgical practice, hygiene, and pain relief. Innovations, such as the implementation of soft-tissue- and transfixion-flap modifications to amputation techniques, the introduction of anaesthetics in the 1840s, and the gradual adoption of Listerian principles of prophylactic antisepsis from the 1870s onwards, meant that more patients survived amputations and more survived with serviceable stumps suitable for being fitted with prosthetics.[7] These developments coincided with and, to an extent responded to, a rise in injuries to limbs stemming from the growing use of industrial machinery in the workplace (which was often poorly regulated) and the increasing efficacy of firearms used on the battlefield.[8] Part of the story of why prostheses became increasingly desirable commodities can thus be explained by the enlarged number of amputees effected by modernity in nineteenth-century Britain. But such a narrative only paints part of the picture. Also circulating in this period was an increasingly codified set of conventions that positioned physical 'normalcy' as positive and 'difference' as negative. To use David Bolt's terminology from his 'tripartite model of disability', we see the rise of 'normative positivism' (the privileging of 'normalcy', that is, ableism) and 'non-normative negativism' (the denigration of physical difference, that is, disablism).[9] A range of social, medical, and legal factors enmeshed, placing considerable pressure on amputees to use prostheses to not only help perform certain bodily acts but also attempt to 'pass' as 'normal' so as to avoid discrimination and social marginalisation.[10]

Theories of the Body and Mind

Though there has been considerable debate as to when a concept of physical 'normalcy' emerged, what disability-studies scholars tend to agree on is that the dominance of the 'normal' body is historically contingent,

---

[7] John Kirkup, *A History of Amputations* (London: Springer-Verlag, 2007), 68–95.
[8] See Jamie L. Bronstein, *Caught in the Machinery: Workplace Accidents and Injured Workers in Nineteenth-Century Britain* (Stanford: Stanford University Press, 2008), 8–9; and Kirkup, *A History of Amputations*, 49.
[9] David Bolt, 'Not Forgetting Happiness: The Tripartite Model of Disability and Its Application in Literary Criticism', *Disability and Society* 30 (2015), 1103–17.
[10] For more on disability and 'passing', see Jeffrey A. Brune and Daniel J. Wilson, eds., *Disability and Passing: Blurring the Lines of Identity* (Philadelphia: Temple University Press, 2013).

socially constructed, and, in societies where it is present, a pervasive marginalising force that works to the detriment of people whose bodies are perceived as 'non-normative'.[11] Aligning with the work of Lennard J. Davis, Rosemarie Garland-Thomson, and Lillian Craton, this chapter sees the nineteenth century as a seminal period in terms of the Western development of 'normalcy' as hegemonic.[12]

Among the most important and well-covered factors contributing to the rise of 'normalcy' in the nineteenth century was the development of bodily statistics. Belgian mathematician, statistician, astronomer, and sociologist Lambert Adolphe Quetelet's concept of *l'homme moyen*, or 'the average man', became popular in England in the 1830s.[13] Quetelet's *A Treatise on Man and the Development of His Faculties* (1835) 'calculated the mathematical norms for a range of physical and social categories[,] everything from head circumference to age of marriage to criminal tendency in order to draw a detailed portrait of the human norm'.[14] For Quetelet, his average man constituted a kind of paradoxical ideal:

> If the average man were completely determined, we might [...] consider him as the type of perfection; and every thing differing from his proportions or condition, would constitute deformity and disease; everything found dissimilar, not only as regarded proportion and form, but as exceeding the observed limits, would constitute a monstrosity.[15]

Quetelet's influential claims, which aligned 'normalcy' with health and difference with illness, evidence Bruce Haley's observations that Victorian understandings of health centred on the concept of 'wholeness'.[16]

---

[11] Lennard J. Davis and Katherine J. Kudlick argue that 'normalcy' is a post-Enlightenment construction. See Lennard J. Davis, *Enforcing Normalcy: Disability, Deafness, and the Body* (London: Verso, 1995); Lennard J. Davis, *Bending over Backwards: Disability, Dismodernism, and Other Difficult Positions* (New York: New York University Press, 2002); and Katherine J. Kudlick, 'Disability History, Power, and Rethinking the Idea of "The Other"', *PMLA* 120 (2005), 557–61. Elsewhere, Ruth Bienstock Anolik and Ato Quayson separately argue that equivocal concepts to 'normalcy' have existed for much longer. See Ruth Bienstock Anolik, ed., *Demons of the Body and Mind: Essays on Disability in Gothic Literature* (Jefferson: McFarland, 2010), 4; Ato Quayson, *Aesthetic Nervousness: Disability and the Crisis of Representation* (New York: Columbia University Press, 2007), 20.

[12] Davis, *Enforcing Normalcy* and *Bending over Backwards*; Rosemarie Garland-Thomson, *Extraordinary Bodies: Figuring Physical Disability in American Culture and Literature* (New York: Columbia University Press, 1997); Lillian Craton, *The Victorian Freak Show: The Significance of Disability and Physical Differences in Nineteenth-Century Fiction* (New York: Cambria Press, 2009).

[13] Adolphe Quetelet, *A Treatise on Man and the Development of His Faculties*, ed. Thomas Simbert, trans. R. Knox (Edinburgh: William and Robert Chambers, 1842).

[14] Craton, *Victorian Freak Show*, 32.   [15] Quetelet, *Treatise on Man*, 99.

[16] Bruce Haley, *The Healthy Body and Victorian Culture* (Cambridge, MA: Harvard University Press, 1978), 3–20.

The implications of Quetelet's work on 'non-normative' bodies are concisely noted by Davis: 'When we think of bodies, in a society when the concept of the norm is operative, then people with disabilities will be thought of as deviants.'[17]

Another significant context that contributed to the stigmatisation of physical 'loss' was the developing – though markedly controversial – scientific and philosophic interest in breaking down Cartesian boundaries between mind and body. This movement intersected with Quetelet's taxonomical work and built upon the principles germane to physiognomy and phrenology (popular sciences of assessing character by facial appearance and cranium shape, respectively). The impact of such work further solidified the premium on physical 'completeness'. For instance, pre-eminent psychiatrist Henry Maudsley, a key figure in the drive to develop a physiological approach towards phenomena of mind (labelled by some as the psycho–physiology movement), bolstered links between body and mind in his 1874 work *Responsibility in Mental Disease*. For Maudsley, the brain was not the only physiological matter that could influence the mind; for him, other parts of the body could affect the temperament of a subject in various ways. Associating physical deviances with specific moods and behaviours, Maudsley implied that those who displayed physical difference were also mentally aberrant, therefore legitimising the work of Quetelet. Endorsing a theory that suggested physical and mental degeneration are passed on to several generations, Maudsley and his associates supported a deterministic understanding of the human condition that stigmatised physical difference.[18]

This growing scientific interest in forging links between mind and body compounded with Quetelet's popularisation of social statistics, culminating in the publication of Cesare Lombroso's *Criminal Man* (1876), a work that famously attempted to demonstrate empirically a correlation between 'monstrousness' and criminality. Curiously, though Lombroso's text was never translated fully into English, its impact in Britain was profound.[19] The deviant body thus became an increasingly centralised topic as anxieties

---

[17] Davis, *Enforcing Normalcy*, 29.
[18] For more on Maudsley and the implications of his work on heredity with regard to disability, see Martha Stoddard Holmes, *Fictions of Affliction: Physical Disability in Victorian Culture* (Ann Arbor: University of Michigan Press, 2004), 66, 68.
[19] See Neil Davie, 'The Impact of Criminal Anthropology in Britain (1880–1918)', *Criminocorpus: Revue d'Histoire de La Justice, Des Crimes et Des Peines* 4 (2010), accessed 14 November 2018, https://journals.openedition.org/criminocorpus/319.

about physical aberrancy and 'degeneration' grew. Such a process of marginalisation reinforced the dominance of physical 'wholeness'.

In addition to the feared criminal traits of those who displayed physical difference, the premium on physical 'integrity' was also bolstered by medical and lingering folkloric views of the aberrant body as a direct physical threat to 'normative' society. For instance, anxieties surrounding 'maternal impression' – the theory that if a pregnant woman witnessed a person with a deformity, the 'shock' caused by such an encounter could result in her unborn child bearing a similar 'affliction' – thrived in Victorian Britain. Linked to such fears, Martha Stoddard Holmes explains that for many Victorians, 'any physical impairment had the potential to be perceived as transmissible by contact; by miasmic air; by a combination of contact, environment, and individual constitution; or perhaps simply by the social class into which one was born'.[20] The sheer variety of explanations listed by Holmes reveals the heightened level of anxiety that surrounded disability in terms of heritable and contagious risk.

Legal and Social Factors

In addition to the various scientific and medical developments that buttressed 'normative positivism' and 'non-normative negativism', several important legal and social changes also contributed. Linked to Quetelet's drive for standardisation, another event of the 1830s that further stimulated anxieties surrounding physical difference was the 1834 Poor Law Amendment Act. The new system sent able-bodied men seeking relief to the workhouse while providing limited out-relief to those deemed 'deserving' – that is, those perceived 'unable' to work, including the young, the elderly, and the disabled. Much discussion about the extent to which the unwaged disabled were 'deserving' of relief perpetuated as a result. The act thus brought public attention to the ability of aberrant bodies, the classifying of such bodies, and an association of physical difference with mendicancy.[21]

Related to this legal and social discourse, changing meanings of work further exacerbated links between physical difference and a perceived 'lack' of productivity, a factor that had particular implications for men – the primary breadwinners in this period. Texts such as Thomas Carlyle's *Past and Present* (1843) and Samuel Smiles's *Self-Help* (1859) were influential as they propounded the importance of industriousness and renounced

[20] Holmes, *Fictions of Affliction*, 63–6. [21] Ibid., 109–22.

idleness.[22] John Tosh plots the rise of this ideology between the Reform Acts of 1832 and 1884, when suspicions surrounding privilege gained momentum and faith in the idea of individual autonomy took its place.[23] Such ableist emphases on autonomy and industry meant that those exhibiting physical difference were seen as 'lacking' the necessary attributes to succeed in life. As Erin O'Connor explains,

> Victorian ideals of health, particularly of male health, centered on the concept of physical wholeness: a strong, vigorous body was a primary signifier of manliness, at once testifying to the existence of a correspondingly strong spirit and providing that spirit with a vital means of material expression.[24]

As we learn from Henham's 'A Human Bundle', where the maimed man is branded 'a lump of breathing useless flesh', for men in particular, physical difference — especially when obvious and extreme — was seen as an indicator of a subject's 'lack' of productive potential.

While physically 'incomplete' men were often believed to be unable to work, a point evidenced in autobiographical memoirs by disabled factory workers, such as William Dodd,[25] women 'missing' body parts were regularly represented as unmarriageable and thus not 'useful' in terms of procreation or social obligations — they were seen as part of the 'superfluous women' problem. Exceptions to this trend were imagined in literary texts, such as Wilkie Collins's *Poor Miss Finch* (1872).[26] But in reality barriers existed that made it difficult for physically and cognitively different women to enter the marriage market. For instance, the same contemporary medical science that warned of the transmissibility of disability placed disproportionate stress on women, raising proto-eugenicist concerns about 'non-normative' mothers extending their supposedly 'contaminated' bloodlines.[27]

---

[22] Thomas Carlyle, *Past and Present* (1843; Berkeley: University of California Press, 2005), and Samuel Smiles, *Self-Help: With Illustrations of Conduct and Perseverance* (1859; London: John Murray, 1958).
[23] John Tosh, *Manliness and Masculinities in Nineteenth-Century Britain: Essays on Gender, Family, and Empire, Women and Men in History* (Harlow: Pearson Longman, 2005), 96.
[24] O'Connor, *Raw Material*, 104.
[25] William Dodd, A Narrative of the Experience and Sufferings of William Dodd (1841), in *Factory Lives: Four Nineteenth-Century Working-Class Autobiographies*, ed. James R. Simmons Jr. (London: Broadview, 2007), 181–222.
[26] Wilkie Collins, *Poor Miss Finch*, ed. Catherine Peters (1872; Oxford: Oxford University Press, 2008).
[27] Holmes, *Fictions of Affliction*, 34–93.

Persuasive Prosthetists

Before turning to the fictional representations of prostheses, which, I argue, complicated the growing dominance of physical 'wholeness', it is worth considering the position that the emerging prosthesis market assumed amidst the culture described so far. Aligning with the trends in patent medicine described by historians such as James Harvey Young, Anne Digby, and Claire L. Jones, prosthetists of all types – including makers of limbs, eyes, teeth, and hair – capitalised on and contributed to the perpetuation of growing anxieties about maintaining or attaining physical 'integrity'.[28] As O'Connor has shown us, the notion of 'rebuilding' amputees to a condition of 'wholeness' was commonly evoked in nineteenth-century prosthesis discourses, especially regarding male amputees.[29] The American prosthesis firm A. A. Marks, one of the most famous and internationally successful makers of its time, for instance, included the following testimony from the Atlanta *Christian Index and Southwestern Baptist* in its 1888 catalogue:

> Mr. Marks has the most skilled mechanics in his manufactory, turning out frequently a dozen or more limbs a week. It is interesting to see his patrons leave their crutches in his office, and walk off apparently *whole* – men, too, who had lost both legs and who were brought in by attendants.[30]

After purchasing one of Marks's patented artificial legs with a rubber foot, John McKenzie, a Civil War amputee, similarly testified, 'I felt like a whole man again.'[31] Limb makers such as Marks were keen to assert to potential users the abilities of their devices to 'recomplete' 'disaggregated' bodies.

The popular consensus among historians of prostheses is that the artificial legs produced by high-end makers such as A. A. Marks, though prohibitively expensive and thus available to a limited group in Britain, were in many cases effective functionally for lower-limb amputees. Top-of-the-range artificial legs were, it seems, helpful in terms of enabling physical

---

[28] James Harvey Young, *The Toadstool Millionaires: A Social History of Patent Medicines in America before Federal Regulation* (Princeton: Princeton University Press, 1961); Anne Digby, *Making a Medical Living: Doctors and Patients in the English Market for Medicine, 1720–1911* (Cambridge: Cambridge University Press, 2002); and Claire L. Jones, *The Medical Trade Catalogue, 1870–1914* (London: Pickering and Chatto, 2014).

[29] O'Connor, *Raw Material*, 102–47.

[30] Quoted in George E. Marks, *Marks' Patent Artificial Limbs with Rubber Hands and Feet* (New York: A. A. Marks, 1888), 154.

[31] Quoted in Ibid., 232.

locomotion and, if disguised correctly by clothing, assisting a user to 'pass' as 'normal'. Artificial arms, by contrast, were not so effective. Sue Zemka explains that due to difficulties replicating the complex biomechanics of the human hand, artificial arms 'languished on an impasse between functionality and a natural appearance'.[32] Rudimentary hooks, available many years before the Victorian period, remained the most effective artificial hands up until and far beyond the turn of the twentieth century. Though, as Zemka states, one must be careful regarding the application of labels of 'progress' and 'improvement' to the nineteenth-century history of artificial arms, there certainly was enumeration in terms of new designs, manufacture, and marketing. Improvements in artificial arms were ultimately insubstantial, but the transatlantic attention paid to developing technologies to replace lost arms was unprecedented. In the 1820s, there were three artificial limb firms in London; by the 1880s, there were eighteen.[33] Furthermore, though we can certainly question the functionality of nineteenth-century artificial hands and arms, contemporary manufacturers were not shy in promoting their devices as great successes. Carefully constructed testimonials hinted at the somewhat ornamental nature of their artificial arms without making their limited functionality manifest. For instance, a commendation by Eli J. Wing for American maker John S. Drake's artificial arm read, 'It improves my form, so that a stranger would not notice that I had ever lost my shoulder, and it more than meets my expectation as to keeping my coat in place.'[34] Here we can see how prosthesis advertisements sought to balance honesty with endorsement while perpetuating the apparent need for amputees to use prostheses to 'pass'.

Part 2: Uncanny Hands

The relationship between literature and the contemporary prosthesis market was a complex one. On the one hand, literary texts often endorsed the physical preferences for 'wholeness' that made the production of artificial body parts such a growing industry in the nineteenth century. For instance, in Charles Dickens's *Our Mutual Friend* (1864–1865) – a text by an author for whom prostheses permeate his very conception of

---

[32] Zemka, '1822, 1845, 1869, 1893, and 1917', 2.
[33] Gordon Phillips, *Best Foot Forward: Chas. A. Blatchford & Sons Ltd. (Artificial Limb Specialists) 1890–1990* (Cambridge: Granta, 1990), 34–5.
[34] Quoted in John S. Drake, *Drake's Patent Artificial Legs, Hands, Arms, &c* (Boston: J. Drake, 1859), 33.

narrative and his sense of the organic structure of the novel – the amputee Silas Wegg is depicted as physically inferior to the able-bodied characters that he competes with (most notably Noddy Boffin and John Harmon Jr./John Rokesmith) in his battle for social mobility.[35] Other depictions, on the other hand, tended to mock attempts at replicating the natural form of the human body – for instance, Anthony Trollope's representation of Miss Ruff's aptly stern-looking artificial eye in *The Bertrams* (1859) – thereby problematising the social investment in occluding physical difference from public view.[36] A trope of prosthesis representation, which this chapter explores, used the uncanny verisimilitude of the high-end prosthesis as a narrative device to invite reader intrigue. While this chapter could explore better-remembered texts that used this representational model, for example Edgar Allan Poe's 'The Man That Was Used Up' (1839) or 'The Spectacles' (1844) – texts by yet another author who is seemingly fixated with the artificial body – in what follows I bring two neglected texts, which both focus on artificial arms, to the fore: namely, Buchanan's 'Lady Letitia's Lilliput Hand' and Lockhart's 'Prince Rupert's Emerald Ring'.[37] These texts, I argue, not only used prostheses as plot devices, but can also be read as having exposed the fragility of physical 'wholeness's' dominance. The use of highly finished prostheses reveals the complex and contradictory attitudes that encompassed responses to the use of such devices. If we consider prosthesis consumption as inspired by a 'medical-model' understanding of physical difference, an approach that sees the disabled body as 'defective' and in need of 'curing', the following

---

[35] Charles Dickens, *Our Mutual Friend* (1864–1865; London: Everyman, 2000). For more on Dickens's engagement with prosthesis, see V. R. 'The Wooden Legs in Dickens', *Notes and Queries* 171 (1936), 74–7; Michael Cotsell, *The Companion to Our Mutual Friend* (London: Allen and Unwin, 1986), 50–1; Michael Allen, *Charles Dickens's Childhood* (Basingstoke: MacMillan, 1988), 16, 77; Adrienne E. Gavin, 'Dickens, Wegg, and Wooden Legs', *Our Mutual Friend: The Scholarly Pages* (1998), accessed 13 November 2018, http://omf.ucsc.edu/london-1865/victorian-city/wooden-legs.html; Jay Clayton, 'Hacking the Nineteenth Century', in *Victorian Afterlife: Postmodern Culture Rewrites the Nineteenth Century*, ed. John Kucich and Dianne F. Sadoff (London: University of Minnesota Press, 2000), 186–210, 189; Herbert Sussman and Gerhard Joseph, 'Prefiguring the Posthuman: Dickens and Prosthesis', *Victorian Literature and Culture* 32 (2004), 617–28; Goldie Morgentaler, 'Dickens and the Scattered Identity of Silas Wegg', *Dickens Quarterly* 22 (2005), 92–101; Ryan Sweet, 'Legs of Wegg and Others', *Dickens Our Mutual Friend Reading Project* (5 August 2015), accessed 13 November 2018, https://dickensourmutualfriend.wordpress.com/2015/08/05/month-16-august-1865-legs-of-wegg-and-others/.

[36] Anthony Trollope, *The Bertrams* (1859; London: Trollope Society, 1993).

[37] Edgar Allan Poe, 'The Man That Was Used up: A Tale of the Late Bugaboo and Kickapoo Campaign', in *The Works of the Late Edgar Allan Poe*, 4 vols. (New York: Blakeman and Mason, 1859), vol. 4, 315–25; Edgar Allan Poe, 'The Spectacles', in *Prose Tales (Second Series)* (Boston: Dana Estes, 1884), 161–98.

analyses provide examples of Paul K. Longmore and Lauri Umansky's claim that '[the] "medical model", powerful though it has been in shaping the life experiences of people with disabilities, has never gone uncontested'.[38]

Reflecting their limited real-life success and uptake, unlike prosthetic lower limbs (in particular, peg legs), which were depicted frequently in literary stories – think, for example, of Captain Ahab, Arthur Conan Doyle's villain Jonathan Small, and a host of Dickensian figures, including not only Silas Wegg but also Simon Tappertit and Mr Tungay – prosthetic hands and arms appeared less often in nineteenth-century literature.[39] While hook-hand users, including, most famously, Captain Cuttle and Captain Hook, were occasionally represented, artificial hands – by which I mean more sophisticated prostheses that attempted to stand in aesthetically and functionally for absent limbs – were few and far between.[40] The few texts that included artificial-hand-using characters, such as Buchanan's 'Lady Letitia's Lilliput Hand' and Lockhart's 'Prince Rupert's Emerald Ring', brought to the fore the haptic differences between organic and artificial hands. As I later suggest, by focusing on the inability of artificial hands to replicate how organic hands feel to others, as well as how they enable sensory touch, these stories brought to the fore the inadequacies of a medical-model approach to hand 'loss', which sought to render invisible amputated stumps. On the one hand, then, these stories were buttressed by an ableism that saw the 'whole' organic body as sacrosanct, but, on the other, they also suggest how such ableist impulses might lead to absurd results regarding the use of prostheses for 'passing'.

Buchanan's 'Lady Letitia's Lilliput Hand' was written in the style of sensation fiction and published when that literary mode was at its height in 1862. It therefore appeared almost a decade before the author's career-defining public spat with Algernon Charles Swinburne and Dante Gabriel Rossetti, in which he famously labelled the latter as a member of 'the fleshly school of poetry' – a charge that seems somewhat rich after learning

---

[38] Paul K. Longmore and Lauri Umansky, *The New Disability History: American Perspectives* (New York: New York University Press, 2001), 259.

[39] Herman Melville, *Moby-Dick* (1851; London: Penguin, 2012); Arthur Conan Doyle, *The Sign of Four*, ed. Ed Glinert (1890; London: Penguin, 2001); Dickens, *Our Mutual Friend*; Charles Dickens, *Barnaby Rudge*, ed. Clive Hurst (1841; Oxford: Oxford University Press, 2008); Charles Dickens, *David Copperfield*, ed. Jeremy Tambling (1849–1850; London: Penguin, 2004).

[40] Charles Dickens, *Dombey and Son*, ed. Andrew Sanders (1846–1848; London: Penguin, 2002); J. M. Barrie, *Peter Pan: A Fantasy in Five Acts* (1904; London: Samuel French, 1977).

more about Buchanan's earlier short story.[41] 'Lady Letitia's Lilliput Hand' explores the history of an alluring yet highly mysterious woman whose most attractive features are her conspicuously dainty, perfectly formed hands. As the author, remarks, 'it was by her beautiful hands that the Lady Letitia achieved her choicest triumphs. Hands so tinily, delicately lovely were never imitated by sculptor; and when she waved them before her slaves, the heart was hushed with admiration.'[42] Helena Michie has identified how common it was for women's hands to function as sexual symbols in the Victorian novel.[43] As Clare Stainthorp puts it, 'Nineteenth-century norms of female dress pushed the localisation of the erotic to the peripheries of the body, the hand being one such site.'[44] But in the case of Lady Letitia, the narrator's 'normative positivism' is complicated as we learn more about one of her hands in particular.

We first meet Lady Letitia amidst a scramble of suitors attempting to take her hand in marriage. The frontrunner for her affections, the wealthy artist Edward Vansittart, is kept at arm's length by the protagonist after a second mysterious character, Mr Montague Vernon, appears on the scene. As we move forward, we learn that this new arrival is a disguised figure from Lady Letitia's past. Vernon is, in fact, Louis Carr, the once fraudulent associate of her late husband, the financially ruined gambling addict Lord Augustus Marlowe. The narrator reveals that Vernon/Carr had previously attempted to win Letitia's affections by manipulative and duplicitous means and intends to do so again by blackmailing her with misleading evidence that portrays her as Lord Augustus's murderer. The visual motif that Buchanan centres the unravelling mystery on is Lady Letitia's wonderfully formed left hand, which we learn is prosthetic. The narrator reveals that her hand was amputated after it was crushed by a heavy window during a deathbed struggle with her late husband, who had poisoned himself to frame Lady Letitia as his murderer, a desperate attempt at revenge after discovering that Carr's attempts to woo his wife had made some progress. All ends well, however. Lady Letitia manages to counter Vernon/Carr's blackmail by threatening to claim him as an accomplice and reveal his identity to the authorities – a move that would be disastrous for the blackmailer since he is wanted for gambling fraud.

---

[41] 'Thomas Maitland' [Robert Williams Buchanan], 'The Fleshly School of Poetry,' *Contemporary Review* 18 (1871), 334–50.
[42] Buchanan, 'Lady Letitia's Lilliput Hand', 552.
[43] Helena Michie, *The Flesh Made Word: Female Figures and Women's Bodies* (Oxford: Oxford University Press, 1987), 98.
[44] Stainthorp, 'Activity and Passivity', 9.

Carr flees, but is unluckily arrested and later hanged for his crimes, while Lady Letitia and Vansittart are happily reunited. Running counter to contemporary marital norms, Vansittart marries Lady Letitia even after she reveals all, including the fact that her most prized asset, her hand, is artificial. As a kind of postscript for the narrative, the narrator includes a note from Vansittart commenting on his marriage with Lady Letitia. We learn that she was a good wife and that she died after giving birth to his eldest daughter. Highlighting the narrative and symbolic work that the prosthetic body part does in this story, it ends with a Gothic yet sentimentalised image: Vansittart reveals that he keeps 'the Lilliput Hand' as 'a memento'.[45]

One of the ways that this short story exploits prosthesis use for narrative purposes, while also interrogating the use of such devices as solutions for physical 'loss', is through the way it draws attention to the sensory difference of Lady Letitia's prosthesis. The bodily variation that her hand presents is indeed a source of mystery, intrigue, and grotesqueness. Her hand is cold to touch, providing a grotesque morbidity as well as a sense of foreboding and uncanniness to her literary depiction. The coldness of her hand provides a hint of her 'non-normativity', echoing the concern of the British prosthesis maker Henry Heather Bigg, who in 1855 lamented the fact that 'touch instantly decides between the real hand and its counterfeit'.[46] Adding to the grotesqueness of Buchanan's depiction, there is a shocking scene in which her hand is stabbed right through without causing so much as a drop of blood or cry of pain. Her hand is thus depicted as conspicuously different to an organic one in that it both feels 'non-normative' and is unable to feel itself. As Pamela K. Gilbert and Stainthorp would point out, the fact that her hand is prosthetic exacerbates the tension between her passive, touched, aristocratic, feminine hand and the active, touching, middle-class, masculine hands of her suitors.[47] In aesthetic terms, the hand acts as a Gothic motif, a kind of uncanny vestige of the past that works as a sensational plot device. We could also label the stabbing scene an instance of 'bodily shock', a trademark of the sensation-fiction genre. In fact, the centrality of Lady Letitia's prosthetic hand provides evidence for Holmes and Mark Mossman's argument that

---

[45] Buchanan, 'Lady Letitia's Lilliput Hand', 131.
[46] Henry Heather Bigg, *On Artificial Limbs, Their Construction and Application* (London: John Churchill, 1855), 62. Quoted in Stainthorp, 'Activity and Passivity', 4.
[47] Pamela K. Gilbert, 'The Will to Touch: David Copperfield's Hand', *19: Interdisciplinary Studies in the Long Nineteenth Century* 19 (2014), accessed 13 November 2018, www.19.bbk.ac.uk/articles/10.16995/ntn.695/. Stainthorp, 'Activity and Passivity'.

'Disability can be seen as central to the very poetics of sensation fiction.'[48] However, chiming with Holmes and Mossman's elaboration that disability is in no way a stable signifier in sensation fiction, there is clearly embedded in Buchanan's narrative a comment on the pressures of 'normativity'.[49] Though clearly underpinned by a way of thinking about the body that privileges organic physical 'completeness', the haptic critique of the prosthetic that this story brings to the fore questions the efficacy and potential implications of using a hand that looks real but feels fake. 'Lady Letitia's Lilliput Hand' suggests that using such a device will always eventually invite suspicion, a feeling that no prosthesis user from this period wished to evoke since doing so would undermine her/his ability to 'pass'.

The greatest resistance to 'normative positivism' and 'non-normative negativism' that Buchanan's short story provides comes in the form of the 'non-normative' marital success that Lady Letitia eventually achieves. Ultimately, she is able to recapture Vansittart's affection and secure his hand in marriage, not by concealing her use of a prosthesis, but by revealing an artificiality and scandalous back story that its use conceals. Alison Kafer's concept of 'crip time' provides a helpful model for understanding Buchanan's representation as not merely conforming to, but rather disrupting, ableist traditions.[50] Kafer's 2013 book *Feminist, Queer, Crip* conceptualises crip time in opposition to common curative trends in imagining disabled futurity, which see disability as something that should be avoided or 'cured' at all costs. According to ableist thinking, the only conceivable alternative to being 'cured' is a life of 'unending tragedy'. Kafer instead seeks to imagine 'more accessible futures, [...] a yearning for an elsewhere – and, perhaps, an "elsewhen" – in which disability is understood otherwise: as political, as valuable, as integral'.[51] In other words, Kafer's project is to challenge the ableist thinking in our present that affects the real and imagined futures of people living with disabilities. It would be remiss to say that 'Lady Letitia's Lilliput Hand' participates in this kind of disruptive and progressive crip project, but what can be argued is that the disabled future that it imagines for the amputee Lady Letitia is one that resists the hegemonic 'normative' ways of thinking about disabled women in relation to marital futures. Lady Letitia can thus be read in relation to the transgressive, bold, and sexually active disabled female

---

[48] Martha Stoddard Holmes and Mark Mossman, 'Disability in Sensation Fiction', in Pamela K. Gilbert, ed., *A Companion to Sensation Fiction* (London: Blackwell, 2011), 493–506, 493.
[49] Ibid., 494.
[50] Alison Kafer, *Feminist, Queer, Crip* (Bloomington: Indiana University Press, 2013). [51] Ibid., 3.

characters of Wilkie Collins's sensation fiction – Madonna Blyth of *Hide and Seek* (1854) and Lucilla Finch of *Poor Miss Finch* most notably.[52] Unlike these novels, or indeed the 'familiar' disabled marriage narratives described by Talia Schaffer – which presented disabled characters as integral parts of domestic marital family networks – Buchanan's text provides a direct affront to the 'normative positivism' engendered by the curative concept of the concealing prosthesis, highlighting the success and attraction of disavowing 'passing' as the primary prerogative for a prosthesis user.[53] Vansittart's decision to keep hold of the Lilliput Hand after his wife's death is at once fetishistic and also revealing of a transgressive fondness for physical difference.

The insensitivity of an artificial hand is, however, also a focal point of Lockhart's similarly sensational, though decidedly less serious, 'Prince Rupert's Emerald Ring'. Very much a story 'with a secret', but not as socially transgressive as many sensation-fiction texts, the plot of Lockhart's short story centres on a valuable ring that goes missing following a wedding reception. After following several false leads, we learn that the ring in question was all along worn on the broken wooden hand of the jewel's inheritor, a wealthy war veteran called General Wylkyns. Ironically and unusually for a fictional representation of such a device, early in the story the functionality of Wylkyns's prosthetic is lauded. Slipping the emerald ring on his false hand, the General boasts, 'I can fish, shoot, hunt, carve, box – do anything with it, in fact.'[54] The asyndetic nature of this list highlights the enumerable ways in which his prosthesis is practicable. The artificial hand is even shown to possess some advantages over his organic one: first, his artificial fingers are slenderer than those of his original hand, which are too gouty for the ring to fit; second, when he slips over after drinking too much wine, his wooden hand takes the brunt of the force, meaning that he remains unharmed. Only after the mystery is revealed and the unfeeling nature of the false hand is brought to the fore are the inadequacies of prostheses shown.

The timing of this story, at the end of the nineteenth century, is particularly interesting since at this time prostheses were often heralded as lifelike. A testimonial in A. A. Marks's 1888 treatise on prosthetics, for example, stated, 'the arm I ordered of you last April gives perfect

---

[52] Wilkie Collins, *Hide and Seek*, ed. Catherine Peters (Oxford: Oxford University Press, 2009).
[53] Talia Schaffer, *Romance's Rival: Familiar Marriage in Victorian Fiction* (New York and Oxford: Oxford University Press, 2016), 160–98.
[54] Lockhart, 'Prince Rupert's Emerald Ring', 301.

satisfaction. The rubber hand is immense. I do not think there could be any thing gotten up to equal it. It looks perfectly natural; in fact, some of my friends did not know that I had lost my arm.'[55] Because of the supposed mimetic capacities of contemporary artificial limbs, we might consider Lockhart's story a critique of prostheses. The suggestion in this story is that each part that constitutes a body should be a feeling entity. The hand serves as a case study to make the point that, while prostheses may look and even function like real body parts, they remain an accessory rather than a truly integrated aspect of the structural 'whole' since they cannot harmonise with the body's nervous system. The ableist premium on physical 'wholeness' is thus again brought to the fore, while the logic of prostheticisation is ironically challenged. Here, however, it is not necessarily the prosthesis that is faulty but rather people's expectations of them. Clearly Wylkyns's hand is an effective functional aid for many physical activities, but it falls short when used in a manner in which it is intended to 'pass' as a 'normal' hand suitable for ring-wearing.

Analysing 'Lady Letitia's Lilliput Hand' and 'Prince Rupert's Emerald Ring' complicates our understanding of Victorian attitudes to prostheses, showing that, though ableist sentiments were often present, some texts did not fully accord to the status quo. Indeed, texts such as Buchanan's and Lockhart's challenged aspects central to the social dominance of physical 'wholeness'. Buchanan's short story used the burgeoning, socially disruptive sensation genre to present an ironically 'non-normative', two-way marital solution for the issue of physical 'loss': honesty and acceptance of physical difference. Lockhart, on the other hand, presents an otherwise useful prosthesis whose insensate limitations make us question whether the potential to 'pass' should really be a priority for prosthetic body parts. Though written for slightly different kinds of readers – 'Lady Letitia's Lilliput Hand' for *Temple Bar*'s metropolitan middle-class family readership and 'Prince Rupert's Emerald Ring' for *Chambers*'s popular readership with emergent middle-class sentimentalities – both texts bring into question the dominance of physical 'wholeness' by scrutinising the mandate to 'pass' as 'normal'.[56] Reading texts like these helps us to appreciate how physical 'wholeness' was being anatomised as it was being constructed.

---

[55] Quoted in Marks, *Marks' Patent Artificial Limbs*, 377.
[56] For more on the readerships of these journals, see Thomas, 'Chambers's Journal', and Peter Blake, 'The Paradox of a Periodical', 185–209.

Index

1848 Chartist petition, 186

A. A. Marks (company), 238
Abernethy, John, 77, 79
Abrams, M. H., 30
Acton, William, 224–5
Adorno, Theodor, 30
adventure fiction, 146
agoraphobia, 161
Ainsworth, William Harrison
   Jack Sheppard, 215–16
Alberti, Samuel, 57, 59, 64
Aldini, Giovani, 79
Alfassa, Mirra, 209
Alfred, Lord Tennyson. *See* Tennyson, Alfred
   (1st Baron Tennyson)
Allbutt, Thomas Clifford, 140, 162, 165
   'Nervous Diseases and Modern Life', 165
Allen, Grant, 39, 53
   Recalled to Life, 39–52
Almeida, Hermione de, 107
Alter, Joseph, 201
Anatomical Venus, the, 57, 59, **61–3**, 64–7, 71, 73
anatomy
   culture of, **74–93**
   displays of. *See* museums, of anatomy
   emergence as discipline, 75
   legislation of, 75–7
Anatomy Act 1832, 75, 77–8, 86, 88
Anderson, Amanda, 4
anesthesia, 5, 27, 30, 233
   advent of for surgery, 44
   discovery of agents for, 139
Animated Skeleton, The, 93
Apothecaries Act 1815, 12
Aries, Phillipe, 215
Armstrong, Nancy, 228
Aruvumadan, Srinivas, 209–10
Athenaeum, The, 47

Auerbach, Erich, 29
Austen, William
   Anatomist Overtaken by the Watch ..., The, 74

Baba, Shivapuri (Swami Govindananda Bharati), 193–4
Bacon, Francis, 6, 8
Bailey, J. B., 85
Baillie, Matthew, 105
Bain, Alexander, 41
Balzac, Honoré de, 46, 225
Baron, John
   Life of Jenner, The, 104
Barraclough, George, 125
Barrie, J. M.
   Peter Pan, 241
Barthes, Roland, 26
Bates, A. W., 60
Beatrice, Princess of the United Kingdom, 194
Beddoes, Thomas, 100
Beer, Gillian
   Darwin's Plots, 43
Benjamin, Walter, 30
Bennett, John Hughes, 21, 24, 28, 37, 193
Benson, Edward Frederic
   Dodo: A Detail of the Day, 170
Bernard, Claude, 7–8, 11
   as vivisectionist, 45
   Introduction to the Study of Experimental Medicine, An, 7, 45
Besant, Annie, 15, 205–9
   Introduction to Yoga, An, 205–7
   'Occult Chemistry', 206
Bhattacharya, Sumangala, 206
Bichat, Xavier, 7, 9
   General Anatomy Applied to Physiology and Medicine, 7
Bigg, Henry Heather, 243
biology, 54, 102, 104, 151, 169–70

Bishop, John, 76, 86
Blackwell, Elizabeth, 225
Blackwood's Edinburgh Magazine, 33, 80, 93
Blake, Sophia Jex, 113
Blavatsky, Helena, 209
body snatching, **74–93**
  as gothic motif, 86
Bolt, David, 233
Boston Medical and Surgical Journal, The, 26
Bostridge, Mark, 121
Braddon, Mary Elizabeth, 145
  Doctor's Wife, The, 227–8
Brain, 43, 51
British Medical Journal, The, 4
Broca, Paul, 41
Brodie, Benjamin, 162
Brontë, Charlotte
  Jane Eyre, 197
Browne, James Crichton, 51, 162
Browne, William A. F., 108–9
  'Mad Artists', 108
  'Mad Poets', 108–9
Buchanan, Robert Williams
  'Fleshy School of Poetry, The', 108
  'Lady Letitia's Lilliput Hand', 16, 231, 240–6
Bull, Sara Chapman, 194
Burke and Hare (William Burke and William Hare), 76–7, 92
Burnett, Frances Hodgson
  Secret Garden, The, 197
Burney, Fanny, 44
Burton, Richard, 225
Butler, Judith, 213
Byron, Anne Isabella Noel (11th Baroness Wentworth and Baroness Byron), 105
Byron, George Gordon (6th Baron Byron)
  Don Juan, 105

Cabot, Arthur Tracy, 27–8
  'Oration to the Massachusetts Medical Society', 27
Cairnes, J. E.
  Some Leading Principles of Political Economy, 159
Caldwell, Janis McLaren, 19, 32
Canguilhem, Georges, 22, 104
Cantor, Geoffrey, 188
Carlisle, Anthony, 8–9
  Means of Preserving Health and Prolonging Life, The, 8
Carlyle, Thomas
  Past and Present, 236
Carpenter, William, 41
Carver, Mrs.
  Horrors of Oakendale Abbey, The, 78

case history, 5, 21, 23–5, 33–4
Casper, Stephen T., 40
Cassell's Household Guide ..., 200
Certeau, Michel de, 147
Chadwick, Edwin, 175, 177, 184, 186
  Report on the Sanitary Condition of the Labour Population ..., 178, 185
Chamberlin, J. Edward, 167
Chambers's Journal, 246
Charcot, Jean Martin, 42
Charles IV, King of Spain and the Spanish Empire, 103
Charon, Rita
  Narrative Medicine: Honoring the Stories of Illness, 1–2
Childers, Joseph W., 175–6
cholera, 11, 44, 177
  1826–37 pandemic of, 184
  1854 London epidemic of, 44
  epidemics in Manchester, 179
Class, Monika, 153
Claybaugh, Amanda, 24
Cleere, Eileen, 177
cocaine, 140–1
Cohen, William A., 212
Coleridge, Samuel Taylor, 29, 100–1, 104
  and opium abuse, 104
  'Eolian Harp, The', 101
  Hints towards the Formation of a more Comprehensive Theory of Life, 101
  Omniana, 100
Collins, Wilkie, 25, 38, **64–5**, 145
  Armadale, 64
  Guilty River, The, 65
  Heart and Science, 42, 65
  Hide and Seek, 245
  Law and the Lady, The, 57–8, 63, 65–73, 215, 217–18, 220–1
  Memoirs of the Life of William Collins, 64
  No Name, 65
  Poor Miss Finch, 237, 245
  The Law and the Lady, 11
  Woman in White, The, 65, 220
colonial medicine, 14–15, **193–210**
Conan Doyle, Arthur, 39, 51, **137–8**, **143–7**, 145, **147–52**, 152–3
  'Adventure of the Crooked Man, The', 137
  Round the Red Lamp, 13, 136, 138–9, 142–3, 148
  'Curse of Eve, The', 147, 149
  'Doctors of Hoyland, The', 150–1
  'Los Amigos Fiasco, The', 146–7
  'Medical Document, A', 135
  'Physiologist's Wife, A', 138
  'Third Generation, The', 150

'Scandal in Bohemia, A', 51
Sherlock Holmes (character), 52
Study in Scarlet, A, 52, 146
The Sign of Four, 241
consumption, 106–8
Corbett, Mary Jean, 214
Family Likeness, 213
Corelli, Marie
Romance of Two Worlds, A, 170
Cornhill Magazine, The, 38, 92, 227
Coulson, William, 200
Coyer, Megan, 80–1, 85, 184
Crabbe, George, 180–1
The Borough
'Physic', 100
Craton, Lillian, 234
Cruikshank, Isaac
Resurection Men Disturbed, or, a Guilty Conscience ..., 74

Dames, Nicholas
Physiology of the Novel, The, 41
Darwin, Charles, 43
Descent of Man, The, 43
On the Origin of Species, 43, 167
Darwinism, 116, 173. *See also* Darwin, Charles
in fiction, 32
Daston, Lorraine, 4, 29
Davidoff, Leonore
Family Fortunes, 213
Davis, Lennard J., 234–5
Davy, Humphrey, 102–3
'Spinoist, The', 102
'Written after Recovery from a Dangerous Illness', 102
Dawson, Gowan, 184, 188
De Quincey, Thomas
Confessions of an English Opium-Eater, 83
Decker, Clarence, 49
degeneration, 40, 116, 137, 167–8, 172–3, 210. *See also* Nordau, Max, *Degeneration*
detective fiction, 11, 39–40, 51, 66, 72
medical, 137
Devi, Indra (Eugenie Peterson), 209
Devries, Blanche, 194
Dickens, Charles, 25, 38, 64, 86, 215, 240
Barnaby Rudge, 89, 241
'Black Veil, The', 89
Bleak House, 89
David Copperfield, 241
Dombey and Son, 241
'Great Day for Doctors, A', 89
Great Expectations, 89
Hard Times, 180
Little Dorrit, 164

Martin Chuzzlewit
Sairey Gamp (character), 119, 121, 126, 131, 134
Old Curiosity Shop, The, 216
Oliver Twist, 174
Our Mutual Friend, 89, 239–41
Pickwick Papers, The, 89
Tale of Two Cities, A, 89–92
'Use and Abuse of the Dead', 89
Digby, Anne, 149, 238
disability, 15, 235, 240
'medical model' of, 231, 241
and futurity, 244–5
and sensation fiction, 244
transmissibility of, 237
diseases
infectious, 44–5, 103
Dixon, Ella Hepworth
Story of a Modern Woman, The, 34
Dodd, William, 237
Dowse, Thomas Stretch, 165
Du Maurier, George
Trilby, 171–2

Eastern Hospital, the, 130–2
Ebenstein, Joanna, 62
Edinburgh Magazine, The, 80
Ehrlich, Paul, 139
Eliot, George, 7, 23–4, 28, 38
Adam Bede, 33
Daniel Deronda, 14, 157, **157–63**, 163–4, 173
Felix Holt, 158
'Lifted Veil, The', 34, 152
Middlemarch, 22, 92, 157
Mill on the Floss, The, 222
Ellis, Havelock, 214, 222–6
Elliston, Robert William, 9
empiricism, 5, 9, **25–9**, 26, 77, 148
and scepticism, 7
Engels, Friedrich
Condition of the Working Class in England, The, 186
experimentalism, 11, **38–54**, 137

Farmer, Sarah, 194
Farr, Samuel, 177
Faubert, Michelle, 4
Ferrier, David, 11, 42, 54, 92, 160, 162
1881 trial for animal cruelty, 42, 92
Functions of the Brain, The, 42
Fessenden, Thomas Green
Terrible Tractations!!: A Poetical Petition against Galvanising Trumpery ..., 97–100
Feuerston, Georg, 193

Fiedler, Leslie, 119–20, 134
Fielding, Henry, 228
fin de siècle, the, 36, 210
  and sexual subcultures, 215
  anxieties of, 116
  fiction of, 197
  gothic fiction of, 54
  medicine and fiction of, **135–53**
  New Woman fiction of, 170
Flaubert, Gustave, 46
Forde, Kate, 57
Fordyce, George, 28
Forster, Thomas, 79
Foucault, Michel, 32, 215, 229
Frank, Arthur W.
  Wounded Storyteller, The, 1
Freud, Sigmund, 14, 116, 173, 214
Fritsch, Gustav, 42
Fry, Elizabeth, 122
Fuller, Sophie, 170
Furneaux, Holly, 213, 215

Gabbard, Chris, 15
Galison, Peter, 4, 29
Gallagher, Catherine, 26, 33, 35
Galt, John, 82
  'Buried Alive, The', 80
Galton, Francis, 166–7
  English Men of Science, 166
Gardner, Edward, 104
Garland-Thomson, Rosemarie, 234
Garrett, Elizabeth, 5
Gaskell, Elizabeth, **180–2**, 183
  'Libbie Marsh's Three Eras', 184
  Mary Barton, 177, 180–1
  North and South, 177, 180
  'Sketches among the Poor, No. 1', 181–2
Gaskell, William, 14, 177–9, **180–2**, 188
  Cottonopolis, **190–2**
  'Sketches among the Poor, No. 1', 181–2
  'Temperance Rhyme, A', 189
  Temperance Rhymes, **182–3**, 190–1
genre fiction, 11, 15, 39, **51–4**
  and depictions of sexuality, 212
germ theory, 11, 45, 115–16
Gibson, John, 111
  'Verses Composed upon that Sublime Subject . . .', 97
Gilbert, Pamela K., 243
Gillett, Paul, 170
Gilman, Sander L., 167
Gissing, George, 39, 49–50
  'At High Pressure', 165
  New Grub Street, 50

Odd Women, The, 50
Whirlpool, The, 14, 50, 157, **163–73**
Gladstone, William Ewart, 49
Glover, David, 166
Gordon, Lucie Duff
  Letters from Egypt, 198
gothic fiction, 11–12, 40, 54, 136, 144, 148
  early versus late-Victorian, 93
gothic, the, 152, 243
  anatomical, 78
  fiction of. *See* gothic fiction
  language of, 30
  of displayed bodies, 65
  paintings, 66
Greenhalgh, Trisha, 16
Greiner, Rae, 24
Guy's Hospital, 82, 105, 124, 126

Haggard, H. Rider, 40
  She, 34
Haley, Bruce, 195, 234
Halkin, Diane, 132
Hall, Catherine
  Family Fortunes, 213
Hamlin, Christopher, 185–6
Hardy, Thomas, 39, 49–51
  Jude the Obscure, 50, 169, 171
  Tess of the D'Urbervilles, 50, 171
Hare, William. *See* Burke and Hare (William Burke and William Hare)
Harley, John
  'Pathology of Scarlatina . . ., The', 23
Hasegawa, Guy, 231
Hawthorne, Nathaniel, 98
Haygarth, John, 100–1
Hazlitt, William, 219
Henham, Ernest G.
  'Human Bundle, A', 230, 237
heredity, 43, 166–9, 172
Hill, Kate, 56
Hinton, Charles Howard, 52
Hippocrates, 6
Hitchcock, Tim, 224
Hitzig, Eduard, 42
Hoffmann, Felix, 5
Holland, Henry, 41
Holmes, Martha Stoddard, 236, 243
Holmes, Oliver Wendell
  'Stethoscope Song, The', 107
Homburg, 158–9, 163
Hopkins, Gerard Manley, 112–13
  'Felix Randal', 111–12
  'Loss of the Eurydice, The', 112
Howitt, Mary, 183

Howitt, William, 183
Howitt's Journal, **183–8**
  temperance in, **188–9**
Hughlings Jackson, John, 42, 160, 162
Hunter, John, 5–8, 65, 75. *See also* Hunterian Museum, the
Hunter, Kathryn Montgomery
  Doctors' Stories: The Narrative Structure of Medical Knowledge, 2
Hunter, William, 74, 76
Hunterian Museum, the, 56, 61, 65, 75
Hurley, Kelly, 40–54
Hurwitz, Brian, 16
Hutcheon, Linda, 54
Huxley, T. H., 53
hysteria, 30, 116, 142, 161, 165

Idler, The, 138
Illustrated Handbook to Dr Kahn's Museum and Gallery of Science, 59, 61–3, 66, 71, 73
Ishizuka, Hisao, 14

Jacob's Island, 174, 176, 181
Jakobson, Roman, 26
James, Henry, 2
Jarvis, Claire, 223
Jenner, Edward, 5, 97, 103–4
Jerome, Jerome K., 138
Jones, Claire L., 238

Kafer, Alison, 244
Kahn, Joseph, 57, 60. *See also* Kahn's Anatomical and Pathological Museum (Kahn's Museum)
Kahn's Anatomical and Pathological Museum (Kahn's Museum), 57–8, **59–61**, 65. *See also* Kahn, Joseph
  sexual specimens of, **61–3**
Kaye, Richard, 213–14, 219, 223
Keats, John, 105, 107
  'Ode to a Nightingale', 104–7
Keen, Suzanne, 50–1
Kennedy, Meegan, 3–4, 81, 153
Kerner, Karen, 143
Kerr, Norman, 144
Kincaid, Jim, 216
  Child Loving, 215
Knox, Robert, 76, 92
Koch, Robert, 11, 44, 107, 115
Korg, Jacob, 49

La Specola (Museum of Zoology and Natural History), 57, 62, 64
Laennec, R. T. H., 113
Lamb, Charles, 8

Lancet, The, 4, 60, 124, 137–8, 142, 144
Langdon-Brown, Walter, 140
Laycock, Thomas, 41
Lear, Edward
  'Growling Eclogue, composed at Cannes, December 9th, 1867', 114–15
Lecercle, Jean-Jacques, 89
Lefebvre, Henri, 147
Leigh, John, 178
  'On Some Circumstances Affecting the Sanitary Condition of the Town of Manchester', 178
Levine, George
  Darwin and the Novelists, 43
Levinstein, Edward
  Morbid Cravings for Morphia, The, 145
Lewes, G. H., 24–5, 36, 41, 158, 162
  Problems of Life and Mind, 160
Lister, Joseph, 5, 44
literary realism, 4, 10–11, **19–37**
  and medical practice, 150, 152
  French school of, 27
Lockhart, John Gibson, 105–7
  'Cockney School of Poetry, The', 105
Lockhart, T.
  'Prince Rupert's Emerald Ring', 16, 231, 240, 245–6
Logan, Peter, 19, 195
Lombroso, Cesare
  Criminal Man, 235
London Review, The, 227
Longfellow, Henry Wadsworth
  'Santa Filomena', 120
Longmore, Paul K., 241
Lott, Emmeline, 198
Lukács, György, 31

MacGregor, George, 78
Madame Brennar's Gymnastics for Ladies, 200
madness, 31, 72, 217
  artistic, 105
Main, Alexander, 157
malaria, 13, 97, 116–17
Manchester, 14, **177–80**, 182, 185, 190–2
Marcus, Sharon, 212–13, 219
Marcus, Stephen, 211
Marks, A. A., *See* A. A. Marks (company)
Marks, George E.
  Marks' Patent Artificial Limbs, 245
Marsh, Howard
  Diseases of the Joints, 30
Martineau, Harriet
  'Deerbrook', 92
  Eastern Life Present and Past, 198
Mason, Michael, 219, 224–5

Maudsley, Henry, 170, 235
  Responsibility in Mental Disease, 235
Mayhew, Henry, 174–7, 181, 186, 191
McKeon, Michael, 33
Meade, L. T., **136–8**, **143–7**, **147–52**, 152–3
  Hooded Death, The, 139
  Medicine Lady, The, 137
  Stories from the Diary of a Doctor, 13, 136–7, 139, 142–3, 148–9
  'Creating a Mind', 149–50
  'Little Sir Noel', 149
  'My First Patient', 137
  'Silent Tongue, The', 151–2
  'Strange Case of Captain Gascoigne', 139
  'Wrong Prescription, The', 143–6
Medical Act 1876, 113
medical history. *See* case history
medical professionalism, 12–13, 57
  and poetry, **97–118**
  and women, 12–13
  in language, 23
  in nursing, 13, **119–34**
medical realism, **19–37**
  in sensation fiction, 64
  in the United States, 26
  of Charles Dickens, 92
Mendel, Gregor, 43
mental illness
  and poets, 108
  distinct from neuromimesis, 31
Meredith, George
  Ordeal of Richard Feverel, The, 218–19
  Sandra Belloni, 170
Meville, Herman
  Moby-Dick, 241
miasma theory, 21, 116
Michie, Helena, 242
microscopy, 28, 39
Mighall, Robert, 93
Mill, John Stuart, 101
mimesis, **29–31**, 33
  neurological (neuromimesis), 30–1
Mind, 43
Minerva Press, 78, 93
Modernism (literary movement), 35, 38
monomania, 90
  and anatomical culture, 90
Moore, George, 39, 48–9
  Confessions of a Young Man, 48
  Esther Waters, 48–9
  Modern Lover, A, 48
  Mummer's Wife, The, 48
morphine, 5, 140–1, 143–6, 164, 172
Morris, William
  'Earthly Paradise, The', 158

Mossman, Mark, 243
Mudie's Lending Library (Mudie's), 33, 48, 219–20
Murder Act 1752, 76
Murphet, Howard, 193
museums, **56–73**
  of anatomy, 56–7
Myers, F. W. H., 51

Naples, Joshua, 76
narrative medicine, 1–3
naturalism, 39, **45–51**. *See also* Zola, Émile
  as distinct from realism, 46
Neurological Society of London (later Neurological Society for the United Kingdom), the, 43
neurology, 159–61
  British developments in, 42–3
  Continental developments in, 41–2
  critiques of by gothic fiction, 54
  emergence as discipline, 41–2
  origins of, 40
neuroscience, 40
New Criticism, 2–3
New Poor Law, the, 16, 175, 182, 184
New Woman, the, 170–1, 218
  fiction of, 51, 170, 211, 215
Newcombe, Suzanne, 201
Nightingale Training School (later Nightingale School of Nursing), the, 123
Nightingale, Florence, 119–21, 123, 126, 134, 178
  Notes on Nursing, 120
Noakes, Richard, 184, 188
Noble, Margaret (Sister Ninevita), 200, 205, 207–9
  Studies from an Eastern Home, 207
Nordau, Max, 116, 172
  Degeneration, 166
North, Marianne, 198
Nurse Elisia, 129–30

O'Connor, Erin, 231, 237–8
Obscene Publications Act 1857, 60
'On the Pleasures of Body-Snatching', 81–2
Orwell, George, 25
Osler, William, 107
Otis, Laura, 38

Pacini, Fillipo, 44
Page, Herbert W.
  Injuries of the Spine and Spinal Cord . . ., 31
Paget, James, 29–31
Pall Mall, The, 92
Parssinen, Terry M., 143

Index

Pasteur, Louis, 5, 115
Patmore, Coventry
  'Angel in the House, The', 120
Pattison, Dorothy, 134
Petchey, Edith, 198
pharmacology, 13, **135–53**
picaresque novel, 33, 221
Pick, Daniel, 168
Pickstone, John, 178
Poe, Edgar Allan
  'Man That Was Used Up, The', 240
  'Spectacles, The', 240
Poor Law Amendment Act 1834, 236
popular fiction. *See* genre fiction
Practitioner, The, 144
Prakash, Gyan, 197
Pre-Raphaelite Brotherhood, the, 108
Procter, Richard
  'Dual Consciousness', 38
prosthesis, 15–16
  narratives of, **230–46**
pseudoscience, 41, 59
psychology, 159, 215
  as philosophical model (psychologism), **29–31**

quackery, 26, 57, 59–60, 63, 65, 100
Quetelet, Lambert Adolphe, 235
  Treatise on Man and the Development of His Faculties, A, 234–5

Rachman, Stephen, 1
railway trauma, 31
Reade, Charles, 25
  Drink, 48
  It is Never Too Late to Mend, 25
'Recent Confession of an Opium-Eater, A', 82–4
Reimers, J. W., 57
Revolutions of 1848, the, 186
Reynolds, G. W. M., 86–9
  Mysteries of London, The, 86–9, 212, 228
  Mysteries of the Courts of London, The, 86
Ribot, Théodule, 168
  L'Hérédité Psychologique, 167–8
Richardson, Benjamin Ward, 163–4
  Discourses on Practical Physic, 164
  Diseases of Modern Life, 163
Richardson, Ruth, 76–7
Rolleston, George, 162
Romanticism, 38
Ross, Ronald, 13, **97**, 117–18
  'Vision of Nescience', 116–17
Rossetti, Dante Gabriel, 108, 241

Rothfield, Lawrence, 12, 19–20, 46
  Vital Signs: Medical Realism in Nineteenth-Century Fiction, 10
Rousseau, George S., 19
Rowlandson, Thomas
  Resurrection Men, 74–5
Royal College of Surgeons, the, 56, 65, 75, 77, 79
Royal Society, the, 23, 166
Rudy, Jason
  Electric Meters, 41
Ruston, Sharon, 79
Rylance, Rick, 38

sanitary reform, **174–92**
science of (sanitary science), 14, 192
Sansome, Arthur, 28
Sappol, Michael, 78
Sarti, Signor, 57
satire, 27, 33, 35, 74, 98, 146
  of the medical profession, 81
Saturday Review, The, 47
Savile Clarke, Henry
  'Lines by a Lunatic M.D.', 115
Saxe, John Godfrey
  Guneopathy, 114
scarlet fever, 23, 135
Schaffer, Talia, 213–14, 245
Scharlieb, Mary, 198
Schnitzler, Arthur
  Reigen, 116
Schofield, A. T., 142
scientific romance, 39–40, 52–4
Sedgwick, Eve Kosofsky, 213
sensation fiction, 11–12, 58, 65–6, 70, 92, 143–4, 148, 211, 241, 243, 245–6
  and disability, 244
  and factual basis, 25
  medical realism of, 65
sentimental fiction, 27
sexology, 40, 54, 215, 224
sexuality, 15, 126, **211–29**
Sharkey, Seymour, 143
Sharp, Gordon, 141
Shelley, Mary
  Frankenstein, 78–80, 87–9
Shelley, Percy Bysshe
  To a Skylark, 104
Sheppard, Elizabeth Sara
  Charles Auchester, 170
  Counterparts, 170
Shiel, M. P., 53
Shuttleworth, Sally, 188
Singleton, Mark, 194, 201
Slavishak, Edward Steven, 231

smallpox, 5, 46
  vaccination against, 97
Smiles, Samuel
  Self-Help, 236
Smith, Robert Angus, 179–80
Smith, Sheila M., 174
  Other Nation: The Poor in English Novels of the 1840s and 1850s, The, 175
Snow, C. P., 19
Snow, John, 44
social problem novel, 174, 176, 180, 182, 192
South, John F.
  Household Surgery, or Hints on Emergencies, 189
Southey, Robert
  Omniana, 100
  'Surgeon's Warning, A', 74
Southwood Smith, Thomas, 14, 77, 177, **183–8**, 191–2
  'Address to the Working Classes of the United Kingdom . . .', 185–6
  Philosophy of Health, The, 187
  'Report on the Physical Causes of Sickness and Mortality . . .', 184–5, 188
  Treatise on Fever, 186
Spencer, Herbert, 41
St. Bartholomew's Hospital, 30
St. John's House, 122–3
Stack, Mollie Bagot, 200
Stainthorp, Clare, 242–3
Staples, Franklin, 27
Stebbins, Genevieve, 15, 209
  Dynamic Breathing and Harmonic Gymnastics . . ., 201–5
  Genevieve Stebbins System of Physical Training, The, 204–5
Steel, Flora Annie
  Voices in the Night, 197
Sterne, Laurence, 228
Stevenson, Robert Louis, 38, 40
  'Body Snatcher, The', 92–3
  Strange Case of Dr Jekyll and Mr Hyde, 38, 54, 93
Stiles, Anne, 4, 195
Stoker, Bram, 40
  Dracula, 42, 54, 93, 197
'Story of a Nurse, The', 13, 126–9
Strand, The, 137
Summers, Anne, 123
Swinburne, Algernon Charles, 241
Sydenham, Thomas, 6, 8
  method of, 6–7
    against experimentation, 8
Syman, Stefanie, 194
syphilis, 108, 116, 150

Talairach-Vielmas, Laurence, 57, 68, 70
Temple Bar, 230, 246
Tennyson, Alfred (1st Baron Tennyson), 109–12
  'In the Children's Hospital', 12, 113
  'Locksley Hall Sixty Years After', 109–10
Terrific Register, The, 58
Thackeray, William Makepeace
  Vanity Fair, 33
Thomas, Ronald, 51
Thomson, James
  City of Dreadful Night, The, 159
Tilt, Edward
  Health in India for British Women . . ., 197–8
Tod, Jan, 195
Topham, Jonathan R., 184, 188
Tosh, John, 237
Towne, Joseph, 82
Townsend, Camille, 212
travel narrative, 195, 197–8
Trelawney, George
  In a Cottage Hospital, 131–4
Trollope, Anthony, 23
  Bertrams, The, 240
  Chronicles of Barsetshire (series), The, 34
  Doctor Thorne, 35
  Last Chronicle of Barset, The, 164
  'Mrs General Talboys', 226–7
  Prime Minister, The, 164
  Way We Live Now, The, 33, 159, 164
Trotter, David, 161
tuberculosis (TB), 11, 45, 137
  pulmonary, 107, 111

Umansky, Lauri, 241

vaccination, 5, 97, 103, 120, 139
  against smallpox, 97
  and Edward Jenner, 103
  expedition by Charles IV, King of Spain and the Spanish Empire, 103–4
verisimilitude, 25–9, 33–4, 150. *See also* literary realism
uncanny, 240
Verne, Jules, 53
Vesalius, Andreas, 75
Victoria, Queen of the United Kingdom of Great Britain and Ireland, 193–4, 210
Violetta, Verdi
  Traviata, La, 108
Vivekenanda, Swami, 194, 207
  Raja Yoga, 194
vivisection, 39, 41, 53
  British sentiments against, 39, 51, 110

Vizetelly, Henry, 47
Vrettos, Athena, 20, 30

Waddington, Keir, 81
Wakley, Thomas, 4
Walker, Donald
  Exercises for Ladies, 199–200
Walker, Sarah, 219
Warren, Samuel
  Passages from the Diary of a Late Physician, 35, 84–5
  'Grave Doings', 84–5
Weissman, August, 44
Wells, H. G., 39, 53–4
  First Men in the Moon, The, 54
  Invisible Man, The, 53
  Island of Doctor Moreau, The, 42, 53
  Time Machine, The, 54
West, Samuel, 141–2
Westphal, Carl, 161–2
Whitman, Walt, 112–13
  Leaves of Grass
  'Wound-dresser, The', 112–13
Wilde, Oscar, 13, 98, 116
  Ballad of Reading Gaol, The, 98–9, 109
  'Harlot's House, The', 116
Williams, Thomas, 76, 86
Williams, William, 138
Willis, Martin, 81
Willis, Thomas
  Cerebri anatome, 40

Wilson, Erasmus
  Healthy Skin, or the Management of the Skin, 189
Wood, Ellen
  East Lynne, 212
Wood, Jane, 170
Wooldridge, Charles, 98
Wordsworth, William, 101–2, 109, 181–2
  'Lines Suggested by a Portrait from the Pencil of F. Stone', 101–2
  'Tintern Abbey', 102
Worgan, John Dawes, 103
  'Address to the Royal Jennerian Society', 103–4

yoga, 194, 200–1
  Raja, 207. *See also* Vivekananda, Swami, Raja Yoga
  scientific cultures of, **205–10**
Yonge, Charlotte Mary, 213
Young, James Harvey, 238
Young, Thomas, 3, 188
  Introduction to Medical Literature, 187
Youngston, A. J., 6

Zemka, Sue, 239
Zola, Émile, 27, 39, 45–51
  British reception of, 47–8
  'Experimental Novel, The', 46, 48
  L'Assommoir, 45, 47–8
    British reception of, 47–8
  Nana, 46–7
  Rougon Macquart (series), 46

CPSIA information can be obtained
at www.ICGtesting.com
Printed in the USA
LVHW080920030821
694401LV00004B/296